Linux for Windows® Addicts:

A 12-Step Program for Habitual Windows Users

MICHAEL JOSEPH **MILLER**

D0573237

Osborne/**McGraw-Hill**

Berkeley   New York   St. Louis   San Francisco
Auckland   Bogotá   Hamburg   London   Madrid
Mexico City   Milan   Montreal   New Delhi   Panama City
Paris   São Paulo   Singapore   Sydney
Tokyo   Toronto

i

Osborne/**McGraw-Hill**
2600 Tenth Street
Berkeley, California 94710
U.S.A.

For information on translations or book distributors outside the U.S.A., or to arrange bulk purchase discounts for sales promotions, premiums, or fund-raisers, please contact Osborne/**McGraw-Hill** at the above address.

Linux for Windows® Addicts: A 12-Step Program for Habitual Windows Users

1234567890 DOC DOC 01987654321

ISBN 0-07-213081-4

Publisher
    Brandon A. Nordin
Vice President and
Associate Publisher
    Scott Rogers
Executive Editor
    John Read
Project Editor
    LeeAnn Pickrell
Acquisitions Coordinator
    Ross Doll
Proofreaders
    LeeAnn Pickrell
    Jennifer Malnick
    Susie Elkind

Indexer
    Valerie Robbins
Computer Designers
    Black Hole Publishing
Illustrator
    Lyssa Sieben-Wald
Cover Design
    Greg Scott
Series Design
    Peter F. Hancik

This book was composed with Corel VENTURA™ Publisher.

To Mickey Miller, whose recognition of his Microsoft addiction, enthusiasm for learning about other computing options, and fervor for eschewing Microsoft products, put me to shame. I gratefully acknowledge his extensive feedback and faithfully pledge to reimburse him for the red pens (and to help keep his new Linux system in top form).

About the Author

Michael Joseph Miller is the author of *Migrating from NetWare to Windows NT* (Sybex), but finds that most people don't hold that against him. His other published work includes *Managing an Inherited NetWare Network* (Sybex) and some poetry. He has managed NetWare, NT, Solaris, and Linux networks, including the primarily Linux-based development environment at PROLIFIC, Inc., the electronic design automation (EDA) software firm where he works.

CONTENTS

PART II

Beyond Addiction: 12 Steps to Recovery

ACKNOWLEDGMENTS

Had Dr. Paul de Dood confined himself to talking about automating standard-cell library layout, rather than suggesting this topic, this book would not be. And had he not made up for it with the patient tolerance of a sleep-deprived friend and employee, I'd hold it against him.

Had Jim Sumser been anything but thoroughly—even excessively—excited by the subject matter and approach, this book would not be, or worse, it would be painfully boring. Had Kevin Shafer listened to Laura Lewin and her associates, this book would have been published elsewhere. Had John Read not become its vocal and energetic champion, it would have never made it to Osborne.

Had I not felt graciously prodded for the manuscript by Ross Doll, LeeAnn Pickrell, and Jan Benes, this book would not be in existence today.

Had Daniel Albers not introduced Paul to the glory of Linux, this book would not be, or worse, it would be the dramatically less compelling, *Solaris for Microsoft Addicts: An 86-Step Program.*

Had a whole host of developers, especially those writing GNU and Linux code, practiced lawn darts instead, there'd be nowhere for us to turn, and this book would not be here. Of course, they'd make history's most awe-inspiring lawn darts team.

Had a host of friends and family, including Peter and Deb Kilner, Daniel Wilburn, David Dwyer, and Rick Langeloh been less encouraging and inspiring, I would have abandoned this task early on. Rick's application of the subject matter in his homily at our wedding was particularly apt.

Had my wife Karen complained about the time sunk into this project, rather than supporting me in word, deed, and prayer, this book would not be. Her love, joy, peace, patience, kindness, goodness, faithfulness, gentleness, and self-control continue to inspire me. Against such things there is no law, indeed.

INTRODUCTION

t has been in vogue for a while now to hate Microsoft. For everyone you know who thinks Bill Gates is a genius and a shining example of American ingenuity at its productive best, there seems to be another who vilifies him as a competition-stifling, dirty-deal-making, coercive shyster, void of original ideas.

This book isn't about that.

Some see *open source* or *free software* as a revolutionary way of providing maximum benefit to computing users. Some feel that "open source" will change the way computing businesses operate throughout the world, for better and worse.

This book isn't about that, either.

This book isn't about resolving questions of morality, ethics, or value to the social order. It's about investigating your options for retiring your Microsoft products and using a cooperatively developed, freely distributed operating system called Linux.

If you're reading this book because you loathe everything you think Microsoft stands for, welcome. If you're reading this book because you work in Microsoft's marketing department, welcome. And especially if you're reading this book because you want help moving from Windows to Linux…welcome.

I don't think everyone can—or should—migrate from Microsoft to Linux. And I don't feel that this is life's most important decision by any stretch of the imagination. But I know how much time I spend in front of my own computer and helping others with theirs. And I also know how much satisfaction I've gotten from using Linux and how nice it is not to be locked into a single company's operating systems. This book is intended to help readers see their need to change and gives constructive steps to facilitate that change.

WHO SHOULD READ THIS BOOK

This book is intended for users of Microsoft operating systems, whether they're happy about it or not. You should read this book if

▼   You run a Microsoft operating system on your personal computer.
   This book is meant to serve as the bridge from your experience as a Microsoft user to your new life as a recovering Microsoft user. While large amounts of documentation exist already, much of it is created by people who don't use Microsoft products. I do use Microsoft products on a daily basis. I also use Linux on a daily basis, and I think you'll like using Linux once someone shows you how.

■   You administer a Microsoft network.
   If you are a Microsoft system administrator thinking about experimenting with the Linux operating system, this book will give you a good start.

■   You're curious about the hubbub over Linux.
   Computer book companies don't normally publish books like this one, and to be honest, computer book authors don't normally write books like this one. You want commentary on the whole Microsoft versus Linux confrontation? It's here. You want general information on Linux? It's here. And I think you'll have fun reading it.

■   You hate Microsoft.
   While I'm not sure this is the healthiest way to express yourself, I'm meeting more and more people who feel this way. The ones I know have enjoyed reading this book and have been encouraged by the ease with which they've been able to end their reliance upon a company they dislike so much.

▲   You love Microsoft.
   I'm even less sure that this is a healthy feeling; you have to know that a company can't love you back, but that's your choice. If you read this book and decide you still love Microsoft and its products, good for you. I've got to warn you, though, that it's possible that considering Linux will awaken you to a need you didn't even know you had. So read on, but read carefully.

HOW THIS BOOK IS ORGANIZED

This book is divided into two parts. The first part is a set of essays on computing, which is a nice way of describing what Dennis Miller might call a "rant." There's quite a lot of confusion out there, so Part I attempts to explain what Linux is, give some background on the conflict between Microsoft and the Linux camp, and discuss some differences in terminology and perspective between the Linux and Microsoft operating systems.

The second part of the book focuses on specific steps you can take to install, configure, and use Linux systems in conjunction with or instead of Microsoft systems. There are 12 of these steps, and each one is given a chapter of its own:

▼　Step 1: Install Linux

■　Step 2: Configure X

■　Step 3: Compile a Kernel

■　Step 4: Connect to a Network

■　Step 5: Manage Users and Groups

■　Step 6: Mingle with Microsoft, Network with Novell

■　Step 7: Enable Printing

■　Step 8: Establish a Web Server

■　Step 9: Manipulate Email

■　Step 10: "Make" More Software

■　Step 11: Share and Schedule

▲　Step 12: Free Your Office

GETTING MORE INFORMATION

If you're looking for more information about using Linux or for answers to particular questions that aren't answered in this book, there's help available. In addition to references to documentation and web sites found in context, there is an appendix containing web addresses for a variety of Linux-related resources I've found useful.

But because everything in the computing world is dynamic, and because Linux in particular is being enhanced at a rapid pace, more information is available at a central location on the Web. Check **http://www.msaddicts.com** for the latest lists, news, updates, and experiences. And if you still don't find what you're looking for, drop me a line at **mjm@msaddicts.com**.

PART I

Facing Addiction: Three Essays on Windows and Linux

xperts on addiction tell us that a person must recognize the need to change and want to change, before change can take place. Before running headlong into the process of recovery from use of Microsoft products, we should stop, take stock of our circumstances, and consider the available recourse.

Part I synthesizes some of the primary reasons people find for undertaking a change from Microsoft operating systems to Linux.

Thousands of people have already taken steps to overcome the Microsoft habit. Naturally, only you can decide to make a change to Linux, and only you can determine to start your treatment, as only the most overzealous fanatics can force an operating system down the throats of unwilling users. We hope you'll decide to join us by stepping back from the Dark Side.

CHAPTER 1

Confessions of a Former MS Junkie

Hi. My name is Mike, and I'm a Microsoft user. I'm not ashamed to say it. I've come to grips with it. I'm probably not much different from you. I like using PCs, I like the power, appearance, and ease of use of a graphical user interface. I like finding and using software that helps me be more productive, enables me to learn and solve problems, and amuses me. I like using powerful, inexpensive hardware that's readily available.

But I'm not a slave to Microsoft anymore. I'm free from the endless upgrading, the compatibility problems, and the ongoing expense of doing things the Redmond way. "How so?" you ask, as though you hadn't read the title of this book.

Linux.

If you haven't heard much about Linux, it's not for lack of publicity. Stock-market speculators, Information Systems flunkies, business managers, and computer hobbyists are discussing, debating, and deploying Linux around the world. The press coverage of Linux continues with everything from basic facts to bald-faced lies to unabashed plugs seeing print. To make sure we're all on the same page, this chapter describes the background of this operating system by and for the people.

WHAT IS LINUX?

Linux is a free, open-source, collaboratively developed Unix-like operating system available for most hardware platforms. It offers extensive networking support, numerous features for interoperability with other systems, and vast numbers of native and ported applications.

If all those terms make sense to you, feel free to move on. If you're fuzzy on some or all of them, allow me to explain further. That is, after all, my job here.

NOTE: Most English speakers pronounce Linux as "Lih-nucks." Its creator, Linus Torvalds, calls it "Lee-nucks," but he's from Finland and pronounces his own name "Lee-nus." So some people have anglicized the operating system's name the same way they would his first name: "Lie-nucks." Confused yet? Wait, there's more. GNU, which is mentioned later in this chapter, is pronounced "Guh-new," not "new." The GNOME desktop environment is known as "Guh-nome," not "nome."

Free

This term is almost self-explanatory. Linux allows you the freedom to use and distribute it without paying for it. If you're accustomed to using Microsoft's operating systems, and you're a little skeptical about not having to pay $100 or so every two or three years to see a new set of features and some new bugs, I understand. But Linux is freely available from a variety of sources on the Internet, and it can be purchased on CD for next to nothing (I've purchased many distributions for $1.95 per CD-ROM).

Linux is often distributed with manuals, additional software, and other value-added items…and you'll usually pay more for these distributions. But the reality is that if you just want to experiment with Linux, you can get it without paying for it (and without the Software Publisher's Association asking the local sheriffs to raid your home or office). Don't do this with Microsoft operating systems; it's not only risky, it's wrong.

I should point out one more thing here. Some people will argue about what "free" means in this context. In particular, the folks at GNU, which created the licensing terms under which Linux is distributed, are fussy about the use of terms like "free" and "open source." If you're willing to trade some time for further semantic precision, I recommend reading up on the controversial issues at the GNU web site (**http://www.gnu.org**).

Open Source

Open Source might be a more unfamiliar concept. Although the Open Source Initiative has codified a specific definition it uses to certify open source software, you'll find that lots of people use the phrase to mean subtly different things. The most important aspect of open source software is that you have the right to see the source code for the software, and you cannot deny anyone else that same right. This aspect is also the one that people argue about the least.

The folks at the Open Source Initiative (**http://www.opensource.org**) assert that open source "promotes software reliability and quality by supporting independent peer review and rapid evolution of source code." At the very least, using open source software means that you can tinker with the program (or pay someone else to) to make it work the way you want it to. For many businesses and individual users, this is a major advantage.

When Free Software Ain't

If Linux is supposedly free, why do you see it packaged for $20–$80? And how's anybody supposed to make money on the proposition? The Free Software Foundation's take on this is that the "free" in "free software" refers to freedom, not price. Specifically, it refers to "users' freedom to run, copy, distribute, study, change and improve the software." So the producers of "free software" can sell that software for as much as they want, so long as the freedom of use remains intact.

Whether this is a viable way of running the software industry or not remains uncertain. It's also irrelevant, because lots of companies will never stop producing proprietary software. But one thing to note is that software created to run on Linux systems does not have to be "free software," either in price or in freedom. My company, for example, does most of its software development on Linux systems. Our product may be purchased for the Linux platform. But for the foreseeable future, our software and the algorithms it contains will remain proprietary.

For additional information on the nuances of software freedom, see the Free Software Foundation's web site (**htttp://www.gnu.org/fsf**).

How Now GNU/Linux?

Some people refer to Linux as GNU/Linux. This doesn't have much to do with bearded antelopes, but instead with the GNU Project, a longstanding effort to create a Unix-compatible operating system that can be freely run, studied, redistributed, and improved. In this way of thinking, Linux is the *kernel* (the core of the operating system that handles things like reading files, managing memory, and sending instructions to the CPU) for an operating system that's mostly GNU software.

It's true that the GNU Project has generated many of the vital pieces of the puzzle that makes up Linux as we know it. It's also true that many of the puzzle pieces outside the Linux kernel are not GNU software. I'll continue to use the term Linux to refer to the organism as it exists now, influenced as it has been by GNU. If you want to call it GNU/Linux, that's okay with me—not that I expect you to seek my approval anyway! For more GNU news, see the GNU Project's web site (**http://www.gnu.org**).

Collaboratively Developed

This is a respectable way of saying, "Volunteer geeks around the world, as well as some who have been paid, created and maintain Linux." To some people, this is a scary concept. Your next door neighbor might be a Linux kernel hacker. Your kids' Sunday School teacher might write documentation for Linux. Your Aunt Genette might write device drivers for new network cards.

Others consider this a major benefit of Linux. People who have the time, talent, and inclination work on what they want to work on. If somebody purchases a piece of hardware not yet supported by Linux, they can theoretically write the necessary supporting software. Others can use this new software and improve it. Thus the community writes and updates software.

There's no monolithic corporate structure involved. There are politics, but because there's not a marketing plan or a sales force involved in the development of the core Linux software, all disagreements can be debated and resolved using the best technical solution. At this point, final decisions are the responsibility of Linus Torvalds, the creator of Linux, which creates a potential single point of failure but also provides some consistency.

Unix-Like

Being a Unix-compatible operating system is considered advantageous and disadvantageous by different groups of people. It might seem like a disadvantage to you if you're like I was before using Linux—unfamiliar with Unix commands, uncomfortable with command-line tools, and unsure that such an ancient operating system could compete with the familiar Windows and Mac OS interfaces I was accustomed to. For the record, I was wrong.

It's true that Linux is primarily a command-line-based operating system. I've come to see this as a good thing: The command line a powerful tool when I want to use it; I have a choice of windowing systems to run on top of Linux; and I don't have to waste system power keeping a graphical user interface (GUI) running on systems that are used as servers.

It's also true that most Windows users aren't familiar with Unix commands. Their names are often weird, and the underlying concepts aren't always clear. I don't see this as a big problem, either. Most of the commands you'll need to use can be issued from a graphical tool in Linux, so you don't usually have to resort to the command line except by choice. And the commands you have available are much more powerful than what you can get in a DOS command box in Windows. We'll talk about this further in later chapters, but honestly—you don't have to worry about this.

As far as Unix being old … this is also true. If you're trying to infer that its age makes it obsolete, though, think again. The graphical interfaces available for Linux incorporate most of the interface features that make using Windows or the Mac OS relatively easy. And speaking of old and interfaces … can you believe these guys at Microsoft want you to use a mouse with your new PC? For crying out loud, the mouse is 36 years old! And the keyboard is even older! The age argument is dumb when I make it, and it's a dumb argument when Microsoft makes it.

Worried about networking? Don't bother; Unix does it naturally and has been doing it for a good long time. Another cool feature common to Unix-like operating systems is that they support multiple users at one time. In other words, you can have multiple people logged in at once—including people running different graphical user interfaces, or logged in from other machines on the Internet, text-only terminals, point-of-sale systems, you name it. Whether you're running Linux on a workstation or server, you can have multiple user accounts with multiple configurations, so everyone in the family can tweak things just the way they like them!

Multiple Hardware Platforms

Back in the olden days, when I wrote *Migrating from NetWare to Windows NT*, NT was supported on a variety of hardware platforms. Not a huge variety, mind you, but I played with NT on a dual-CPU MIPS box, and I talked to NT users on Digital's Alpha platform. But NT hasn't supported MIPS for years, and it's no longer being supported on Alpha, either.

This isn't the worst thing going on in the world, and it's not a problem if you own Intel stock. If you'd like another choice, though, you're going to have to look elsewhere, and Linux is an excellent answer. Linux runs not only on Intel-based machines (and compatibles like AMD), but on Sun workstations, PowerPC-based computers, and even Amigas. There are other supported platforms, but you get the idea.

Even within the Intel product line, Linux supports a wider range of processors than does Windows; most distributions can be run on 386-based machines (try running Windows 2000 on one of those!) all the way up to the latest Pentium III processors. If you're already using Windows, your system is probably Pentium-class or higher—but isn't it nice to know that old hardware you have sitting in the closet may also work just fine?

What D'Ya Mean, Easy?

People seem to think that whatever operating system they're used to is easy. I spent a couple of hours talking to a guy who was getting a DSL line for his iMac. He told me how much easier it was to set up Mac networking than Windows networking. He told the phone company DSL installers how much easier it was. Then he proceeded to take about as long to set up networking as I would have needed for a Windows system. (It didn't matter much, as the DSL line hadn't been properly configured on the back end and we couldn't get to the Internet.)

I don't mean to slam the Mac or to praise Windows for its ease of use. The point is that people usually mean "familiarity" when they talk about ease of use. Another case in point: My wife laughingly talks about quitting her job at Sun Microsystems, where she used a Sun workstation, and starting work as a teacher, where she was provided with a Macintosh computer. It took her a long time to figure out that the Mac's power was turned on from the keyboard.

Is the keyboard a better place to put a power switch than somewhere on the computer's case? I don't think so, though I don't think it's any worse, either. But as you consider whether to try Linux, and whether to move to Linux, think about this: Anything that seems alien to you now will seem familiar later. So the question is: Which operating system offers you the most compelling functionality? I'll discuss that in Chapter 2.

Extensive Network Support

Windows has come to support a variety of networking functions, as well as a wide range of protocols used by different networking systems. But it's topped in most areas by Linux, which has been shaped by a community dedicated to standards and open communications and is based on Unix, which was networked long before you could issue a "net start" command in Windows for Workgroups.

Mail systems, web servers and browsers, network management tools, server clustering tools, enterprise databases, and most of the other types of network functionality you might want are all available for Linux systems, and more are becoming available all the time.

Interoperability

Linux does a good job of following the standards in use in computing today. So if you want to connect Linux systems on your network and access files and printers between Windows and Linux machines—you can do it. If you want to connect to Macintosh computers, SNA hosts, NFS partitions, and a host of other ... well, hosts—you can do it.

Heck, Linux has long allowed you to hook up your amateur (ham) radio to your computer. You want interoperability? Beat that. And of course, there are DOS and Windows emulators available, so you can run many of the old programs you may have—even some that won't run on the current versions of Windows.

Applications

But there's more to Linux than some washed-up old programs gathering dust on your shelves. You want word processors, electronic mail, presentation graphics tools, spreadsheets? You've got several to choose from. You want a web browser? No problemo. You want drawing and image editing programs, MP3 sound tools, databases, and programming tools? Done.

There are thousands of applications available for Linux—and hundreds of them are even useful. There's lots of overlap in some areas, where you'll find 10 solutions to the same problem. And there are some areas in which there aren't really any options yet viable. This isn't unlike the Windows world. Many Linux programs are polished, well documented, and powerful, and many of them could use some improvement.

Business suites are particularly noteworthy with respect to the presence of applications for Linux. Microsoft has all but sewn up this market in the Windows environment with its Office products, which aren't available on Linux. Unless Microsoft decides to port Office to Linux, you'll have to use another product if you use Linux. Although most of the major suites include Microsoft file format compatibility, it's standard operating procedure for Microsoft to change these formats with every software release, forcing their own users to upgrade and causing users of other products to curse vehemently.

(Personally, I think Microsoft's interests would best be served by offering their own Linux distribution and porting their major applications to it. If they can win the office suite war on Linux the way they did on the Mac OS, Microsoft could balkanize applications on Linux, at least among business buyers.)

The point is that since memos, sales presentations, letters, financial information, and other documents are often sent in Microsoft formats, you'll have to take this into account when you consider migration to Linux. Windows has interoperability features and supplemental tools, but in the end, Microsoft has a reason to maintain proprietary file formats, networking protocols, and anything else that could be shared between machines. As I write, that reason is at $89^{31}/_{32}$. If Microsoft wants to continue to sell to its existing customers, it has to make sure its existing customers can't move to something else.

WHERE DID LINUX COME FROM?

Linux was created by Linux Benedict Torvalds, commonly known to people in the Linux community (including those who've never spoken to him, traded email with him, or even heard him speak) as "Linus." He began developing Linux as an alternative to Minix, a small Unix-like operating system used mostly in academic settings. At the time, Linus was a student in Helsinki, Finland. Even from the beginning, although he was clearly the chief architect and developer, he solicited the input of interested parties around the world.

Linus released Linux version 0.02 in 1991, when it supported the 386 processor, had no floppy drive support, and had major bugs. Linus anticipated some doubt about the need for his project in a newsgroup posting from October 1991:

> I can (well, almost) hear you asking yourselves "why?" Hurd will be out in a year (or two, or next month, who knows), and I've already got Minix. This is a program for hackers by a hacker. I've enjoyed doing it, and somebody might enjoy looking at it and even modifying it for their own needs. It is still small enough to understand, use and modify, and I'm looking forward to any comments you might have.

Just for background purposes: Hurd is the name of the kernel the GNU Project folks have been developing for the GNU operating system. Hurd uses a different type of architecture and was under development before Linux…but Linux caught on. Minix, as I mentioned, is another Unix-like operating system, but it's not free, and…well, had you heard of it before you heard of Linux? Don't worry, that's true for most everyone. The "for hackers by a hacker" comment is particularly interesting, as some people would have you think Linux hasn't progressed much since then. Hey, hackers still like it, but it has come a long way in the intervening nine years.

WHO KEEPS LINUX GOING?

A network of programmers around the world keeps Linux going. It's a factious, loosely knit bunch at best, with a few individuals making key contributions and playing key roles. Linus is still the project manager, though others are important as well. But the bottom line is that there are people of all types of backgrounds working on Linux. Many are hobbyists who are programming for the love of programming and for the glory they feel when their contributions are useful and used. Some work for companies funding Linux development, including some who make distributions.

Others contribute to Linux because they want to support hardware or features they need themselves; after all, if it doesn't exist, but you need to create it, there's no point in not sharing it. Hardware vendors are also beginning to work on drivers themselves, rather than refusing to cooperate at all (as some have done in the past) or merely making technical information available to others (which has also happened with some frequency).

There are also the software vendors themselves. Oracle, for example, isn't excited about working with Microsoft, and the acrimony between those companies is fairly well known. It has made its database offerings available on Linux (as have many of its competitors). Some of the Oracle database administrators (DBAs) I know are now making contributions to the Linux community because once they used Linux, they didn't want to go back to Windows. There are a number of software companies that make both commercial and open-source products, funding development of the latter by selling the former.

What's with the Penguin?

The Linux logo (some firmly contend he's a mascot, not a logo, but that's not important right now) is a penguin. The penguin design you see on web sites, Linux distributions and promotional material, and as stuffed animals, was drawn by Larry Ewing in response to Linus Torvalds' request for the artistically talented to bring his vision to life:

> Now, when you think about penguins, first take a deep calming breath, and then think "cuddly". Take another breath, and think "cute". Go back to "cuddly" for a while (and go on breathing), then think "contented".

> With me so far? Good.
>
> …

> So when you think "penguin", you should be imagining a slightly overweight penguin (*), sitting down after having gorged itself, and having just burped. It's sitting there with a beatific smile - the world is a good place to be when you have just eaten a few gallons of raw fish and you can feel another "burp" coming.

> (*) Not FAT, but you should be able to see that it's sitting down because it's really too stuffed to stand up. Think "bean bag" here.

> Now, if you have problems associating yourself with something that gets off by eating raw fish, think "chocolate" or something, but you get the idea.

The penguin is just a full and contented waterfowl. (In his original message, Linus speculated about another reason the penguin might be looking so satisfied, but we've skipped that musing to avoid undue jocularity in our juvenile readership.) That's the obvious embodiment of this lean, extensible, cooperatively produced operating system, huh? No? Well, Linus heard enough comments along these lines that he responded to them:

> Some people have told me they don't think a fat penguin really embodies the grace of Linux, which just tells me they have never seen a angry penguin charging at them in excess of 100mph. They'd be a lot more careful about what they say if they had.

> And upon further review, I'd be a little testy if I'd consumed a few pounds of raw herring, too.

(And, I have to point out, hoping to glean some goodwill from users in the process. You decide whether I'm being more cynical than they are.)

Finally, many people contribute to the Linux community without writing a line of code. The Linux Documentation Project, for example, allows people with good communication skills to help others. There are many who work to advocate the use of Linux, and others who actively work to clear up the fear, uncertainty, and doubt (FUD) created when companies trash Linux with erroneous claims. And there are some who provide links to Linux-related stories on the Web, information on security issues, and the latest developments on kernels, window managers, and the like. Just because one isn't a hacker doesn't mean one can't contribute.

WHAT'S A DISTRIBUTION?

A *distribution* is simply a set of software that includes the Linux kernel and other important operating system components, plus a selection of tools and applications that the designers think are useful for themselves or for a target market.

These days, there are literally dozens of different "distributions" of Linux, including names you may have heard of: Red Hat, OpenLinux, Linux-Mandrake, Slackware, SuSE, and TurboLinux. There are others you may not be familiar with: Yellow Dog Linux, Bastille Linux, Bad Penguin Linux.

Because of the straightforward distribution permissions in the licensing agreement that comes with Linux, distributions are easy to make, and many are targeted at particular types of users. WinLinux 2000, for example, is supposed to be easy to install. Now, I think one reason many people believe Windows is easily installed is that they haven't installed it themselves—it came with the computer. But if you're afraid of the installation process, perhaps that distribution has something to offer.

Other distributions are also easy to install: OpenLinux, for example, has a very automated installation process (it allows you to play Tetris while you wait for files to be copied from the CD during the installation process). Red Hat and SuSE have different types of installation tools intended to make things easy during installation.

Many people like the Slackware distribution, which has been around for years, because it eschews most of these installation tools; it tends to be a distribution used by people who want to get their hands dirty. Its installation process isn't difficult, it just provides less hand-holding than some of the other distributions.

The bottom line is that no distribution has a lock on every good idea in the Linux world. Most distributions include slightly different sets of included applications (some, like SuSE, include just about everything out there!) and have a somewhat different look and feel. When you get past that, though, they're all pretty similar. It's a little bit like versions of Windows you get with a new computer. They're all Windows, after all, but most hardware vendors customize the setup, the desktop, the set of included applications, and the drivers and utilities. Sometimes these are more difficult to install than others, but if you're having trouble, just ask a 12-year-old, and you should be okay. That's a joke, people…chill out a little, okay? Sheesh!

12 Questions to Decide: Is Linux for You?

It's widely understood that the preliminary step to overcoming an addiction is realizing that you have an addiction. In this vein, I'd like to ask 12 questions to help you determine your addiction status:

1. Have you ever gotten your Windows PC running smoothly, but it still only stayed up for a couple of days?

    Many of us who use Linux used to make promises to keep our Windows systems running, but could not keep them. Then we turned to Linux, realizing: If you do not run Windows today, Windows cannot crash today.

2. Do you wish people would mind their own business about your operating system and stop telling you which one to use?

    We who use Linux do not *tell* anyone to use Linux. Well, many of us do, actually. But we also talk about our own use of Windows, the trouble we got into, and what we switched to. If you're interested, we can tell you more.

3. Have you ever switched from one version of Windows to another, hoping this would keep you from experiencing problems?

    Many who use Linux have tried *every* version of Windows. We used the version 1.0 runtime. We used Windows 3.0, Windows for Workgroups, Windows NT, Windows 95, Windows CE, Windows 98, and Windows 2000. But if we used any computer with Windows on it, we usually crashed eventually.

4. Have you had to restore data or recreate it because of a system crash during the past year?

    Do you save your documents every thirty seconds or restart your machine on a regular basis? This is a pretty sure sign that your Windows use is problematic.

5. Do you envy people who can use Windows without having problems?

    At one time or another, most of us who use Linux wondered why most people tolerate the expense and lack of innovation of the Windows OS.

6. Have you had problems connected with Windows applications during the past year?

    Many analysts say that problems with Windows will only get worse—never better. Eventually, it will collapse under its own weight, or be dismantled by the courts. The only hope is to use another operating system.

7. Has Windows caused trouble at home or work?

   Before we used a stable, extensible, open-source operating system, most of us said inherent computer instability made us waste time. We could not see that Windows made everything worse. It solved remarkably few of our problems.

8. Do you ever try to get "extra" performance out of your system with expensive upgrades because it's not powerful enough?

   Most of us used to update our hardware with every revision of the processor, video board, and disk, hoping to compensate for the bloat in our operating system. Now even older systems function usefully.

9. Do you tell yourself you can stop using Windows any time you want to, even though you keep buying expensive applications and upgrades when you don't want to?

   Many of us kidded ourselves into thinking that we upgraded our Windows software because we wanted to. After we started using Linux, we found out that once we started to buy Windows-based products, it's difficult to stop.

10. Have you missed days of work or school because of Windows?

    Many of us now admit that when we claimed our dogs or spouses had eaten our work, the truth was that a system crash had trashed our data.

11. Do you have "Blue Screens of Death"? Or black ones?

    These are signs that your operating system isn't adequately protected from its own operation and the behavior of its applications. When we started to use Linux, we found out that this is not inherent to all operating systems, and we didn't want to be black and blue anymore.

12. Have you ever felt that your life would be better if you did not use Windows?

    Many of us started to use Windows because it seemed to make us more efficient and because it seemed easy, at least for a while. Until we started using Linux, though, we felt trapped by expensive applications, frequent upgrades, incompatibility, proprietary protocols and interfaces, and lack of customization.

What's Your Score?

If you answered "yes" more than four times, you may have a serious Windows use problem. But only *you* can decide whether you think Linux will work for you. Try to keep an open mind as you read this book and I will try to show you the techniques I used to kick the Windows habit myself.

Linux may not currently solve all your computing problems. But many people out there are using it each day to accomplish tasks they used to rely upon Windows to perform. They're finding that by doing so, they're saving time, money, and frustration, and making their computing lives much more manageable.

WHY SHOULD I CARE ABOUT LINUX?

There are several good reasons people should care about Linux. You can see which ones apply to you:

▼   Linux offers an alternative

■   Linux offers freedom

■   Linux works well

■   Linux continues to improve

▲   Linux is fun

Linux Offers an Alternative

There's lots of resentment toward Microsoft these days for the way they seem to try to stifle competition. Whether they've done so legally or not is still being decided in the court system, but there are many people who would be happy to find an alternative—almost any alternative.

A Macintosh is not an alternative that will satisfy everyone who falls into this category. It's restrictive in its own way, with more proprietary, more expensive hardware, limited native applications, limited interoperation with other systems, and (pardon me in advance) a retarded user interface.

Linux is an option for people who (for whatever reason) don't want to give any more money to Bill Gates, but who aren't willing to trade in their existing Windows-compatible hardware. My father, for example, was excited to hear that I was writing this book, because he would like to be able to do all the things he needs to do without involving Microsoft. If you feel the way he does, give Linux a try.

Linux Offers Freedom

So you may not care that Linux runs on almost any hardware available, but that's one way it offers freedom. Maybe you care instead about not having to pay about $100 every time Microsoft comes out with a new operating system. You don't have to buy a new copy of Linux; you can download it, copy it from a friend, or get a cheap CD. Or you can purchase a shiny, new boxed copy with a complete manual and several CDs worth of the latest applications. You're free to choose.

Maybe you don't like the way the interface looks on your PC. Maybe, unlike me, you *like* the look of the Mac OS. Great! There are multiple window managers available for Linux, and you can make your desktop look like Windows, a Mac, a Sun workstation, or whatever else floats your boat. You're free to choose.

Maybe you need to link to other computers, even some weird ones. Perhaps you've got an OS/2 disk, or a Mac disk with all your data on it, and you'd like to keep reading from it for a couple of years. Once again, feel free. Want to make a copy of your software to run on your new computer? You're free to do so—legally and ethically.

Get the idea? If you've got the ability to write your own programs, you've got even more freedom, as there are many development tools, libraries, and extensions you're free to use. And there are countless projects you're free to contribute to (or to start yourself).

Linux Works Well

I'll talk about this more in the next chapter, but Linux works well right now. In my office, I have two systems. The older Pentium Pro system runs Linux, and it stays up. The newer Pentium II system runs the flavor du jour of Windows, and it stays up between crashes. If one program crashes on my Linux box, I kill it and no other programs are harmed. If one program crashes on my Windows box, I try to kill it, wait for a while, try to kill it again, and hope that someday control will return to my keyboard and mouse.

My Windows box talks to my Linux box very well. This is because my Linux box speaks Windows very fluently. I save my files to the Linux box (as I mentioned, it doesn't go down, and I've never had a problem with file corruption on my Linux box, while I've had many cases of ScanDisk finding the lifeless remains of a file I was working on before the Windows box crashed).

My company's software is used in designing integrated circuits. It is very sophisticated and process-intensive. Our compute farm consists of multiprocessor machines running Linux, and when we have to perform a benchmark or do some work for a client, all those CPUs are running as fast as they can. This is an excellent way to crash a Windows system, but it doesn't faze Linux. I manage more servers for this company than I have for previous firms, but I've got a much smaller staff (me, myself, and I). This works because the Linux boxes work hard, they work continuously, and they work well.

Linux Continues to Improve

Because it is developed by a community of motivated people, because it's an alternative to a company that spends a fair amount of time and resources defending itself against charges of being a monopoly, because it offers freedom to developers and users alike, and because it works so well, Linux will continue to improve.

Do I think it will be the operating system in use forever? Of course not. But it's already better than the others I've used in important ways, and it is improving at a tremendous rate. More sophistication, broader support, and more functionality are continually being injected into the mix. If I sound like a cheerleader, it's because I'm excited about the advances that are being made right now. And they don't even need to license a Rolling Stones song to start me up.

Linux Is Fun

It's fun to be able to choose from a wide range of applications, most of which are free. It's fun being able to completely control your computer, and it's fun not having to do so. It's fun to see how fast leading-edge functionality is being incorporated into the operating system. It's fun to have software being developed to solve problems rather than to make a focus group be willing to spend some money.

It's fun to share knowledge and information with people around the world. It's fun to find better ways of doing things. Does Linux have a lock on these things? Certainly not, not even in the computing world. But it fosters these things, and these things foster it, and that is also fun.

Final Question: Is Linus a Sex Symbol?

I don't see him that way, but thanks for asking. As he commented in an interview with the *San Jose Metro*: "During normal life, small girls do not come up to me and throw their underwear at me or anything like that. I think my wife would be slightly unhappy if that started to happen." On the other hand, he does appear to be able to match his pants and his shirt, a skill that has frequently eluded the figurehead of the Microsoft empire.

CHAPTER
2

Why Would You
Want to Kick
the Habit?

The usefulness of the 12 steps described in Part II of this book hinges upon your desire to stop letting Microsoft dictate what you can do in your computing life. In Chapter 1, I explained a little about the Linux alternative, and maybe you're interested. Unless you're convinced a change needs to occur, however, the change won't happen.

So what makes a person decide to overcome a Microsoft addiction? This chapter describes many reasons, ranging from superior technical aspects of Linux to a purely amusing analogy used to prophesy Microsoft's impending extinction. Weaving their way through most of these reasons are Microsoft's strained credibility and outrageous claims.

After Microsoft posted a document describing "Linux Myths" from its perspective (some portions of this document are quoted in this chapter for your amusement and edification), a flurry of debunking articles were posted various places on the Web by various Linux supporters. I can't tell if the Myths document influenced many people, but it certainly stirred up partisans from each side of the Microsoft/Linux conflict. Perhaps the best description of the document's impact was posted to the Slashdot web site:

> The Microsoft faithful will wave this around as proof of their belief and the Linux zealots will point to it as more proof that Microsoft is nothing more than a hive of marketing droids who can lie better than they can write code.[1]

Like scientists debating the relative merits of their as yet unproven hypotheses, the rabid in each group tend to see their point in any available evidence. If Microsoft finds a hardware configuration with which its products provide superior performance, the Linux camp points out that the configuration is unrealistic and the tests are biased. If the Linux community seems to be winning mindshare by emphasizing stability, Microsoft poo-poos anecdotal evidence—and offers its own anecdotal evidence supporting Windows' stability.

And here's the point of including this chapter: If you haven't already heard Microsoft dismiss Linux, you will. And if they present their case effectively, they'll "put some truth in every lie to tickle itching ears,"[2] to quote Keith Green out of context. So I'm going to show you some things Microsoft and others have said about Linux and discuss ways in which their criticisms are true or otherwise. And by the time we're done, you should have an idea how the marketing machine works, and you may see how Linux could be better suited to meet your needs than you'd have suspected.

WHO SHOULD USE LINUX?

The subject of who should use Linux, and what it should be used for, is a popular one in the press and in marketing efforts. Many people will agree that Linux has largely been in the domain of the technically savvy user, but that situation (and popular perception) is

---

[1]   Jack William Bell, "All FUD?" slashdot.org, October 5, 1999.
[2]   Keith Green, "No One Believes In Me Anymore," *For Him Who Has Ears To Hear*, 1977.

beginning to change. Linux is no longer used only by hackers, IS dweebs, and Twinkie-munching weirdoes. Ordinary folks use Linux and like it.

Nonetheless, don't be surprised to see an occasional statement like this one, from Microsoft's Linux Myths document: "The Linux operating system is not suitable for mainstream usage by business or home users."[3] This is particularly amusing, given that Microsoft and its attorneys worked long and hard in the DOJ trial to push Linux as a viable alternative to Windows. For example, Microsoft executive Paul Maritz was quick to point out that Linux was becoming easier to use, as "Linux developers are currently working on 'Windows-like' user interfaces—'Gnome' and 'KDE'—to simplify its operation."[4]

Truth be told, GNOME and KDE both promise more power and flexibility than the Windows user interface, but my point is that Microsoft wants to play the game both ways by saying Linux isn't a competitor, and yet it is. The same situation exists when Microsoft refers to Linux used on servers. Microsoft manager Ed Muth noted

> Linux is a competitor on the client and the server. My analysis is that Linux is a material competitor in the lower-performance end of the general purpose server industry and the small to medium-sized ISP industry.[5]

For a time, Ed Muth provided most of the public comments for Microsoft's anti-Linux campaign. See the sidebar about him later in this chapter for more information, and keep your eyes peeled for more of his commentary.

Muth was willing to consider Linux a competitor to Windows NT for "lower-performance"[6] servers. Thus it's interesting that when Microsoft set up performance tests comparing Windows NT with Linux, it didn't specify lower-performance configurations. Instead, they set up monster servers with multiple processors and four Fast Ethernet network cards each, noting that, "This class of system is what enterprise customers typically use for their enterprise servers."[7] When they compared systems, they didn't do it where Muth claimed Linux was a competitor.

A sad aspect of this whole performance-testing situation is that a third party test performed by Bloor Research "found neither product suitable for use as an Enterprise Level Server."[8] In other words, even if you believe the performance numbers Microsoft produced, you shouldn't really be considering Windows for your configuration anyway.

---

3   Microsoft Corp., "Linux Myths," www.microsoft.com, October 4, 1999.
4   Paul Maritz, "Direct Testimony of Paul Maritz,"
     <http://www.microsoft.com/PressPass/trial/mswitness/maritz/maritz_full.htm#4>.
5   Ed Muth, "Microsoft Responds to the Open Source Memo Regarding the Open Source Model
     and Linux," www.microsoft.com, November 5, 1998.
6   Ibid.
7   Microsoft Corp., "Windows NT Server 4.0 faster, more scalable than Linux as a file and Web
     server, tests show," www.microsoft.com, April 21, 1999.
8   Bloor Research, "Linux versus NT: The Verdict," www.bloor-research.com, October 20, 1999.

So let's come back to users of desktop computers. For you, Muth has more useful advice: "The more I study Linux, the weaker I think the value proposition is to consumers."[9] I almost blew out my pancreas laughing about that comment when I read it in *PC Week Online*. I just pictured a Microsoft manager carefully evaluating the value of a Microsoft product, and then carefully evaluating the value of Linux. He's got a spreadsheet open, and he's giving each product a grade for documentation, performance, stability, price, and features, and … what a surprise! The Microsoft manager comes to the conclusion that his product is better than its competition.

As thankful as we all are to Microsoft for its careful and fair evaluation of its products versus competitors, we might consider that other parties may come up with other results. For example, Bloor Research, the company that evaluated Linux against NT, issued a press release summarizing their study:

> We compared the products according to the following nine criteria: Cost/Value for Money, User Satisfaction, Application Support, OS Interoperability, OS Scalability, OS Availability, OS Support, Operational Features and OS Functionality. We have rated Linux as superior in seven of the nine categories.[10]

So who should use Linux? Almost anybody can. There are reasons you might like it more than Windows, and there are reasons you might like it less, but there's no longer a cut-and-dried division between who will and who won't. So we'll look at some of the other areas of dispute to make some sense of them.

BUILT-IN FUNCTIONALITY

However unintentionally, Microsoft's Linux Myths document contained a number of impressive untruths. For example, the document claims that "Linux does not support important ease-of-use technologies such as Plug and Play, USB, and Power Management."[11]

This is untrue for all three technologies, which are supported to varying degrees in Linux. But it's true that Linux took some time to gain USB support, and that relatively few devices were supported when Microsoft claimed that none were supported. Plug and Play functionality is included with Linux, while it was not at all comprehensive at the time of the "Myths" document. Power management has been supported reasonably well for some time (applications engineers from my company use Linux-based laptops regularly for demos and work at customer sites), so Microsoft just whiffed on that one.

But an interesting point is made by Andy Patrizio in *Wired News*:

> In its zeal to debunk Linux, Microsoft occasionally stretches things. For example, it points out that Linux lacks universal serial bus, plug and play, and power

---

9   Scott Berinato, "Microsoft exec dissects Linux's 'weak value proposition,'" www.zdnet.com/pcweek, March 4, 1999.

10   Bloor Research, "Linux versus NT: The Verdict," newsalert.com, October 19, 1999.

11   Microsoft Corp., "Linux Myths."

management. But it neglects to mention that those features are not native to Windows NT, either.[12]

Now, nobody expects Microsoft to go highlighting its products' deficiencies, or pumping up its competitors' products (except, of course, during anti-monopoly hearings). But according to Patrizio, this is a particularly galling case of pointing out a speck in someone else's eye while a log sticks out of your own.

So what's the truth about Linux functionality versus Windows functionality? For now, it's still harder to get drivers—the software that allows you to use a computer device—for Linux than for Windows. More hardware vendors write their own drivers for Windows than write their own drivers for Linux. Microsoft supports more peripherals—computer add-ons like scanners and printers—than does Linux. This is particularly so if you like to use very new devices (for which the Linux community has not produced drivers) or if you own devices intended to work with Windows (such as "winmodems" and other devices that offload processing to the computer).

On the other hand, hardware manufacturers of all sizes are becoming more familiar with Linux and its user community and are writing drivers or are providing hardware or specifications to make sure their products are supported under Linux. This trend should continue, making it easier to ensure Linux compatibility with whatever hardware you own. The version 2.4 kernel, in particular, offers many improvements in how Linux manages devices, making its Plug and Play and USB support more useful in the real world, and making support for FireWire (also known as IEEE 1394 and i.LINK) possible from the operating system kernel.

The Muth Of Sauron?

Microsoft manager Ed Muth, for a time, was frequently being quoted in articles, interviews, and press releases. Muth's job, at least in public, appeared to primarily involve badmouthing Linux. Unfortunately, he didn't seem well-prepared for this task and said a number of things untrue enough to be silly. He's well represented (or at least frequently represented) among the quotations you'll find in this chapter.

In the absence of another explanation, I'll assume he was just doing a distasteful job he'd been given. While I understand the need to do the occasional unpleasant task in the course of one's job, however, I started to wonder about the frequency of Muth's drive-by babblings.

And that's when Muth began to remind me of a character from Tolkien's *Lord of the Rings* trilogy: The Mouth of Sauron. This was a minion and spokesman of

---

12   Andy Patrizio, "Microsoft Lambastes Linux," wired.com, October 8, 1999.

Sauron, the being who was attempting to take over Middle Earth. In the last book of the trilogy, the Mouth confronts the forces arrayed in a last desperate attack against Sauron's dominion.

Just as the Mouth is having a little fun taunting those allied against his master, however, they attack. And although Sauron has created a trap to defeat them, at the last moment, Sauron's source of power is destroyed and he and the Mouth are defeated by their enemies.

Naturally, nobody who is thinking straight believes Bill Gates and his employees to be anything like Sauron and his forces. But if you'll indulge some facetiousness, there are some parallels to consider:

Mouth	Muth
Works for powerful Sauron	Works for Bill Gates
Black sorcerer	Microsoft Group Product Manager
Produced "evidence" that Frodo was dead	Produced "evidence" that Linux was dead
Didn't really know where Frodo was	Didn't really know what Linux was
Sternly countered by wizard Gandalf	Sternly countered by Open Source Initiative President Eric Raymond
Disappeared from the book	Disappeared from the press

HARDWARE PLATFORM SUPPORT

Despite the remarkable progress being made by the Linux developers, especially in the 2.4 kernel, I'd still say Windows has an advantage in its support for computer peripherals. Hardware platforms themselves—the processor type and supporting architecture—are another story.

Out of the mouth of Ed Muth we have another astounding claim, this time that Linux "lacks a port for the great majority of hardware platforms in the marketplace."[13] If he means it doesn't yet run on most refrigerators and doorbells, he's probably right. But look at the hardware platforms it has supported for years, according to the Linux kernel release notes for version 2.0:

> Linux was first developed for 386/486-based PCs. These days it also runs on ARMs, DEC Alphas, SUN Sparcs, M68000 machines (like Atari and Amiga), MIPS and PowerPC, and others.[14]

---

13   Ed Muth, "Linux 'Lacks an Extraordinary Number of Features' of Windows," businessweek.com, April 27, 1999.

14   "README," Linux Kernel 2.0, < http://www.kernel.org/pub/linux/kernel/README>.

Microsoft once supported four of these platforms: Intel, Alpha, MIPS, and PowerPC. It now supports one such platform: Intel. And Intel announced Linux support for its next-generation Itanium chip long before Windows 2000 was even available. In the intervening time, other improvements have been made, of course. IBM now supports Linux on its S/390 mainframe computers. You can even use the version 2.4 kernel on systems intended to run Windows CE.

So what's Muth talking about? I haven't the slightest idea. If you want to run an operating system on anything other than an Intel-compatible computer, don't even consider Windows. Of course, if you're suffering from a Windows addiction, you probably already use an Intel-compatible computer. So let's talk about something else.

APPLICATIONS SUPPORT

One great thing about the Windows environment is the wide variety of software available. From genealogy software to groupware to integrated circuit design software, you've got options. And wouldn't you know it, Ed Muth points out that "there are fewer applications available for Linux, there's no long-term development road map, and there's a higher technical risk in using it."[15]

We'll talk about the development road map shortly, but the "fewer applications" comment deserves consideration. I agree with Muth that there are fewer applications available for Linux than for Windows 9x. On the other hand, one reason Microsoft's Windows 2000 has experienced "slow" sales in 2000 is because "a lack of applications is still holding back many users from upgrading."[16]

1999 was a breakout year for Linux in part because many large commercial software packages were made available on the platform for the first time. This is partly because many large companies are delighted to support a platform that competes with Microsoft, which hasn't engendered much love for itself in some quarters. But a more important reason is that these companies realized that people actually want to use Linux as more than just web servers and hobby machines.

2000 has been another good year for Linux applications support, as more commercial software products have become available for Linux users, and especially, as large companies such as IBM and Sun have made significant products available under the GNU General Public License (GPL).

I expect 2001 to be another step forward for Linux as more companies release software on the platform. But in the meantime, a vast amount of software development has happened outside the corridors of IBM, Corel, Lotus, Oracle, and SAP. Developers of open source software have created mail systems, databases, web tools, desktop environments, office suites, utilities, MP3 sound file utilities, and a dizzying array of other applications.

---

15   Berinato, "Microsoft exec dissects Linux's 'weak value proposition'."
16   Dominique Deckmyn, "Microsoft under the Win 2k gun," *Computerworld*, August 7, 2000.

The best sources of information on such software are **sourceforge.net** and **freshmeat.net**, which keep tabs on the latest versions of many Linux-compatible programs. On both these sites, you can search their databases for something specific, list packages by category, or browse the latest releases of everything. Another place to get this kind of information is in the Linux Weekly News (**lwn.net**), which has an "Announcements" page summarizing each week's releases.

USER SUPPORT SERVICES

Some folks are confused about how one gets support for Linux. Because the kernel and its components have been collaboratively developed and deployed worldwide, there is an imposingly large amount of documentation available. If you pay full price for a distribution, for example, you generally get a relatively complete manual (some distributions are markedly better than others, and depending on what language you speak and what distribution you're using, you may find some inelegant grammar).

Most distributions also include a set of "how-to" documents and guides maintained by the Linux community and the Linux Documentation Project (**www.linuxdoc.org**). There are web sites, Usenet groups, and magazines devoted to Linux and largely focused on support issues.

So the issue is not really whether support is available, it's whether you'll have the time, patience, and inclination to sort through what's available to find what you need. If you're not a "do-it-yourselfer," you have two more options. One is to find a Linux geek who can help you out. Pizza and a frosty beverage are often adequate enticement for these helpful elves, especially if your attitude and personal grooming don't make dealing with you a pain.

The other option is to pay for support. If you think this is something you'll want to do, I suggest that you stick with one of the major distributions: Red Hat and Caldera, for example, offer an array of support options. Installation support via email is often included for the first 30 to 90 days if you purchase the full distribution.

All of these support options are similar to what's in the Windows world. Microsoft is no longer offering "free 90-day phone support for people who buy the company's Windows and Office software products,"[17] opting to allow two no-charge phone calls before charging $35 per call. Microsoft maintains documents containing "how-to" information, and if you're inclined to, you can sort through them at Microsoft's web site. As with Linux, the best Windows support will probably come from a knowledgeable coworker, friend, or family member. But you can also purchase support from Microsoft or third parties.

Microsoft doesn't want to let it go at that. For example, the Linux Myths document notes that "commercial support services for Linux will be fee-based and will likely be priced at a premium."[18] Well, since one would expect "commercial" support services to

---

17   Charles Cooper, "MS kisses free software support goodbye," *ZDNet News*, August 11, 2000.
18   Microsoft Corp., "Linux Myths."

cost something, that part's no shocker. And the "premium" pricing part is just silly—are they guessing? Support plans are available from the Linux distributors, from hardware vendors, and from third parties. Find one that fits your budget.

INNOVATION

Much of the software that goes into a Linux distribution isn't particularly innovative, at least in terms of functionality. Most of the time, what's available with Linux is available under other operating systems as well. This isn't to say that Linux isn't innovative. In its development and distribution models, it breaks from the norm. And some of the software it runs is superior to what can be found on other platforms.

That's not the way Microsoft sees it, of course. For example, Ed Muth sets a peculiar standard for high-quality software in this statement from *BusinessWeek*:

> High-quality software comes from having adequate capital and consistency of purpose in order to deliver great software to the marketplace on a regular basis with features that move the state-of-the-art ahead rather than copy things that people have historically done.[19]

In other words, unless you've got lots of money and are focused on world domination, you can't innovate? Please. Innovation isn't exactly Microsoft's strong suit anyway, unless you count enhancing and marketing the pants off someone else's idea, as shown in Table 2-1.

Microsoft Technology/Product	Predecessor
Active Directory	NDS
Active Server Pages	CGI
Excel	1-2-3
Exchange	Lotus Notes
Internet Explorer	Netscape Navigator
SQL Server	Sybase SQL Server
PowerPoint	Harvard Graphics
Windows	Mac OS
Word	WordPerfect

Table 2-1. Microsoft Innovations: a Short List

---

19   Muth, "Linux 'Lacks an Extraordinary Number of Features' of Windows."

Let me hasten to point out that some of Microsoft's successful technologies were purchased or licensed from their original creators. And some of the products or technologies in the list of predecessors in Table 2-1 were enhancements of someone else's idea to begin with (take Netscape Navigator, for example, which added features to the framework begun by the NCSA Mosaic web browser). But the fact that Microsoft successfully markets products derived from derived products doesn't make it more innovative. Eric Raymond gets even more down and dirty, speaking in his "Halloween III" paper of

> ...Microsoft's own long record of buying or outright stealing key technologies rather than innovating. MS-DOS: bought (from Tim Paterson). PC1 BIOS code: stolen (almost bit-for-bit from Gary Kildall's CP/M BIOS). On-the-fly disk compression: stolen (from Stac Electronics). Internet Explorer: bought or stolen, depending on who you believe (from Spyglass). And the list only *starts* with these.[20]

Ouch. Making the issue muddier is the Microsoft tendency to disparage anyone else's design model. So, for example, Ed Muth contributed this insight:

> In order to move the ball ahead for the industry and for the consumer, you need to have consistency of purpose, which of course the Linux movement does not have. It has no long-term road map, and it can't have one because it's an atomistic, developer-driven movement rather than a commercially and customer-based movement.[21]

Microsoft's sole consistency of purpose is its desire for more money. There's nothing wrong with this; I think public companies should be profit motivated. But let's not pretend that Microsoft's real purpose is to provide the best solution for computer users.

If that's so, please explain to me why if you want to *view* special characters like tabs and carriage returns while composing a document in Microsoft Word, you don't go to the View menu but to the View tab on the Options entry of the Tools menu. Tell me why you don't Insert or Format headers and footers, you View them in order to insert or format them. I can't tell you how many users I've had to assist with problems like these. None of those users were particularly helped by having a paper clip winking at them like in some Fantasia-induced hallucination.

In all fairness, there are weird menu choices in most applications I've seen, including many for Linux. All the same, the alleged advantage of Microsoft's consistency of purpose doesn't seem to make its applications superior. And if Microsoft claims it is customer-based, I must respond that non-commercial Linux software is user-based. The reason it exists is that someone wanted to use it. That seems like a better motive to me than wanting to pick the customer's pocket one more time.

---

20   Eric Raymond, "Halloween III—1.4," www.opensource.org, November 16, 1998.
21   Ed Muth, "Linux 'Lacks an Extraordinary Number of Features' of Windows."

STANDARDS

Another area in which Linux appears to have a strong advantage relates to compliance with standards. To the extent possible, it is important to the Linux development effort to keep and maintain compliance with recognized standards. This is a reasonable expectation of all software, but it's not necessarily something software vendors feel obliged to follow. Consider Ed Muth's statement:

> To better serve customers, Microsoft needs to innovate above standard protocols. By innovating above the base protocol, we are able to deliver advanced functionality to users…. This would be a value-add and would in no way break the standard or undermine the concept of standards, of which Microsoft is a significant supporter. Yet it would allow us to solve a class of problems in value chain integration for our Web-based customers that are not solved by any public standard today. Microsoft realizes that customers are not served by implementations that are different without adding value; we therefore support standards as the foundation on which further innovation can be based.[22]

For one thing, Ed sounds a bit like he's addressing issues of the DOJ trial here. But what's particularly odious is the idea that if Microsoft adds value, the standard is irrelevant, and that's what's left, sticking grotesquely to the pan, when you boil his argument down. For example, the reason your web browser works better with some web sites than others is that Netscape, Microsoft, and others decided to "innovate" beyond the adopted standards—generally in incompatible ways.

As a competitive advantage for Microsoft, this type of innovation is wonderful. It gives you a reason to push your products over your competitors'. But for the user who wants to be able to use any current browser and retrieve any arbitrary content, there's no value added. This situation isn't limited to browsers; for example, Microsoft has "innovated" its Java implementations far enough away from the standard to be sued by Sun. Between Sun's recalcitrant attitude toward letting a standard exist, and Microsoft's insistence on ignoring a standard, Java is probably less important in your computing life than it could be.

In the Halloween documents—leaked Microsoft memos in which a Microsoft engineer warned about the viability of open source software (OSS) such as Linux as a competitor to Windows—some ominous suggestions are made, including this one from "Halloween I:"

> OSS projects have been able to gain a foothold in many server applications because of the wide utility of highly commoditized, simple protocols. By extending these

---

22   Muth, "Microsoft Responds to the Open Source Memo Regarding the Open Source Model and Linux."

protocols and developing new protocols, we can deny OSS projects entry into the market.[23]

In other words, by "innovating" beyond the standards—the rules everyone else has agreed to play by—Microsoft could prevent competitors like Linux from making inroads. At this time, only Microsoft has the user base to pull this off and have a chance of getting away with it. The good news is that there are enough people aware of these tactics, and enough people tired of being jerked around, that it's getting harder for Microsoft to pull stunts like this.

STABILITY

Stability is one of an operating system's most difficult characteristics to evaluate. Different hardware, software, drivers, and loads all influence system stability, and accounting for each of them in a test environment doesn't help much for real-world users. But there are some interesting trends you may see reflected in computer press articles. One is a presumption of instability of Windows systems. Another is increasing evidence of instability of Windows systems. A third involves more stories about people moving away from Windows to other platforms. And finally, more vendors are starting to offer products and services for both Windows and Linux.

Windows: Presumption of Instability

If you run Windows on your PC, how often do you need to reboot the system? Do you consider this a normal part of computer life? Would it surprise you to know that system crashes used to be an unacceptable sign that there was a problem with the system hardware or software?

It's amazing to me how much rebooting takes place on a daily basis in Windows-based environments. Mind you, I've worked in Windows-based environments most of my life. But try this, for example: If your company has an Information Systems help desk, call them up and tell them your cursor won't move and your keyboard isn't responding. See how long it takes before they suggest that you reboot. Then buy lunch for the harried help desk attendant whose time you just wasted.

This presumption extends well beyond common users and overworked help desk employees, though. Consider this suggestion from the Aberdeen Group in an *InfoWorld* article:

> Dual-processor Pentium III Xeon systems should also help IT managers trying to overcome Windows NT's tendency to spike to 100 percent usage when subjected to numerous simultaneous interrupts, which in turn leads to system crashes, said

---

23   Vinod Valloppillil, Microsoft Corp., "Open Source Software: A (New?) Development Methodology," August 11, 1998, <http://www.opensource.org/halloween/halloween1.html>.

analysts at the Aberdeen Group, in Boston. Deploying a second processor should help alleviate some of those crashes, they said.[24]

Did you catch that? Windows tends to get overloaded when there's lots of device activity, and that causes it to crash. So one solution is to add a second microprocessor to the system to prevent it from crashing! That, my friends, is a presumption of instability.

Windows: Evidence of Instability

The second way in which I'm seeing more commentary on Windows instability is in press accounts of problems with Windows-based systems. For example, take the failure of systems on the U.S. Navy warship Yorktown. A civilian engineer, Anthony DiGiorgio, was quoted this way in Government Computer News:

> But according to DiGiorgio, who in an interview said he has serviced automated control systems on Navy ships for the past 26 years, the NT operating system is the source of the Yorktown's computer problems. NT applications aboard the Yorktown provide damage control, run the ship's control center on the bridge, monitor the engines and navigate the ship when under way. 'Using Windows NT, which is known to have failure modes, on a warship is similar to hoping that luck will be in our favor,' DiGiorgio said.[25]

Is it the fault of Windows NT that the application crashed? Not likely. But the operating system is certainly culpable for locking up when a single application crashed. Even more interesting is that the original decision to use NT was a political rather than technical decision, according to Ron Redman, deputy technical director of the Fleet Introduction Division of the Aegis Program Executive Office.

> 'Because of politics, some things are being forced on us that without political pressure we might not do, like Windows NT,' Redman said. 'If it were up to me I probably would not have used Windows NT in this particular application. If we used Unix, we would have a system that has less of a tendency to go down.'[26]

And while I've heard people try to dismiss DiGiorgio as a big mouth, and write off Redman as trying to cover his own behind, the story stands. I saw the same trend back in the mid-90s when I wrote about moving from Novell NetWare to Windows NT: System instability, once recognized, will kill an operating system. Back then NetWare had memory management and processor protection issues, and now Windows is being shown to have its own problems.

---

24   Michael Vizard and Ed Scannell, "Pentium III Xeon gets thumb's up from app vendors," *InfoWorld Electronic*, www.infoworld.com, March 17, 1999.

25   Gregory Slabodkin, "Windows NT Cripples US Navy Cruiser," *Government Computer News*, July 13, 1998.

26   Ibid.

My experience with Windows 2000 is that it is more stable—though perhaps slower—than its predecessors are. Faster hardware is inexpensive enough that I'm happy for the tradeoff. But even the new and improved OS has problems, including an example identified by Tolly Research, in which "engineers discovered that modest traffic loads (three or more simultaneous file uploads) brought the server to its knees. When configured with Intel PRO/100 Server Adapters and running Intel's Adaptive Load Balancing software, we observed blue screens galore."[27]

Linux Success Stories

If people generally believe Windows is unstable and are reading articles about how it's behaving badly in important places, it's reasonable to think that some will move to alternatives. This type of story is appearing more regularly in computer magazines, and Linux is increasingly being described as the chosen alternative.

Rather than regale you with several of these stories, allow me to compare another comment made by the illustrious Ed Muth with the experiences of one Microsoft customer. Muth was quoted in the Microsoft Daily News on the subject of third-party support for Windows:

> With the amount of industry support behind Windows NT Server, Microsoft is always expanding the capabilities and usefulness of the platform to the industry and our customers," said Muth. "We work closely with hundreds of third parties to ensure companies deploying the Windows NT platform have the software they need to run and enhance both small and large enterprises. [28]

By comparison, consider the remarks of Alex Heffer, of New Zealand company's Excellent Systems:

> At times, problems with Windows, Novell and NT networking have been close to destroying our business and yet during this same period Retail-Plus has performed very reliably under Unix at our five largest sites. … Heffer said customers wanted Windows systems because of the Microsoft marketing machine, but third-party developers got the blame when the operating system did not work as promised.[29]

Those "hundreds of third parties" Microsoft works with are certainly important. They're convenient for finger-pointing when the customer isn't happy. Heffer says Excellent Systems turned to Linux because unlike other Unix implementations they'd employed before, it was affordable. Affordable and reliable are particularly desirable in combination, if you ask me.

---

27   Kevin Flood, "Win 2000 Forecast: Blue Skies or Blue Screens?" *Network World*, August 21, 2000.
28   Microsoft Corp., "Windows NT Server 4.0 faster, more scalable than Linux as a file and Web server, tests show."
29   Adam Gifford, "Software firm puts store in Linux system," *The New Zealand Herald*, October 12, 1999.

Proliferation of Options

The last sign that Linux can be considered a stable option is that ever-larger numbers of hardware and software vendors are cooperating with the Linux community. This is good news for many reasons, not the least of which is that we now have options when it comes to spending our money and expecting a return.

Ed Muth brings up the example of Hewlett-Packard. HP isn't known as a bleeding-edge business; the company's products tend to feature solid engineering backed by capable (if somewhat expensive) support. Muth points out that HP has been heavily involved in selling products that run or run on Windows NT:

> Take HP…. They have long supported multiple OSes on X86. They are fundamentally in the hardware business. You would expect them to support Linux. But the deep investment is in NT.[30]

If "deep investment" means they realize they've thrown money down a hole, I agree. But Muth is correct in his assessment that HP has made a commitment to the NT platform. I don't think you'll see NT options disappearing from HP's plans any time soon.

However, HP has also invested in Linux and open source software in general. The Aberdeen Group's profile on the Open Source Solutions Operation, an HP group formed to drive the company's open source strategy, includes the following statement (italics from the original):

> HP is making the right moves with its evolving Linux strategy. OSSO is coordinating the efforts of HP systems, services, and software divisions worldwide. It is making a concerted, ongoing effort to ensure that its customers understand that *Linux is a viable alternative for powering e-services*. The open source model for software development means that the pace of enhancements to services for customers can proceed at Web speed rather than be tied to a *software provider release date*.[31]

See "Doesn't Microsoft Produce Better Software" later in this chapter for a further discussion of Microsoft's problems with the Windows 2000 "software provider release date." HP clearly recognizes that Linux is an example of how software can be produced and improved better and faster over the Web. Do you suppose HP is pumping Linux as an e-service platform because they believe it's unstable?

PERFORMANCE

This section is as much about the uselessness of benchmarking as it is about performance. Linux is designed to be able to run on less powerful hardware than Windows requires.

---

30   Berinato, "Microsoft exec dissects Linux's 'weak value proposition'."
31   Aberdeen Group, "HP Embraces Open Source and Linux for E-Services," www.aberdeen.com.

Whither the Press Bias?

All the excitement about Linux has prompted a peculiar, whiney response from Microsoft regarding press coverage. The folks in Redmond don't seem to be used to seeing someone else get press, so Ed Muth and others have made comments decrying the "hype" regarding Linux.

LinuxWorld's Nicholas Petreley has an explanation for why the computer press isn't covering stories like the Linux Myths release as fact anymore, contending that

> …the press hasn't suddenly developed a conscience. What the press has developed is a sense that Microsoft isn't always going to be paying its bills. And it has developed a suspicion that Linux may pay more of them in the future…. As a result, although Microsoft has always used underhanded marketing tactics, you're now reading more about them. You're reading more about Microsoft PR blunders. You're reading more stories about how institutions are ripping out Windows NT and replacing it with more secure and stable alternatives. And you're reading fewer stories that are obviously manufactured by Microsoft's commissioned data. So fans of the truth, as well as fans of Linux, have cause to celebrate. Microsoft may still have a good portion of the trade press in its pocket. But it now has to fight a little bit harder to get its propaganda on the front page.[32]

> If it's true, that's good news for Linux enthusiasts and anyone else who would like to see more even-handed coverage in the press.

Unlike Windows, Linux is modular, allowing you to reduce system overhead as much as you can by eliminating modules you're not using. Graphical user interfaces run on top of Linux, their bulk isn't built into the core system software. The Linux kernel code is scrutinized by many more programmers than is the Windows code. All these are reasons Linux is known to perform well.

That's just what the experience of users tells us, though. For a more scientific-looking evaluation of performance, we turn to the efforts of a company named Mindcraft, which performed some benchmarks comparing systems running Windows NT to systems running Linux. When the results were released, the Linux community got bent out of shape because the testing methodology was a mite suspect, as described by Eric Raymond in his Halloween VI document:

> The Mindcraft fiasco in March set a pattern continued by its sequels; Microsoft got the benchmark results it wanted—only to be embarrassed when it came out that Mindcraft had apparently run them on Microsoft-supplied machines, at a Microsoft

---

32   Nicholas Petreley, "Celebrating 'Linux Myths,'" www.linuxworld.com, October 8, 1999.

site, with the benevolent assistance of Microsoft technicians tuning both Windows and (even more helpfully) Linux—and then neglected to mention in its press release that Microsoft had paid for and hosted the whole exercise. Mindcraft's credibility was, of course, utterly destroyed.[33]

Raymond's comment doesn't address the peculiar configuration of the test systems, which were supposedly set up in a typical fashion for enterprise users. Testing done by c't magazine in Germany indicates that multiple processors and multiple Fast Ethernet network cards tend to worsen Linux' performance relative to Windows NT, and goes on to say that:

> …additional CPUs for plain web server operation with static HTML pages are a waste…. It seems that CPU performance is not the decisive factor with these tasks…In the web server areas most relevant for practical use, Linux and Apache are already ahead by at least one nose.[34]

So unless you're looking to configure a computer with as many processors and network cards as possible, the Mindcraft results aren't very relevant. Perhaps realizing this, Microsoft appears to have commissioned the Gartner Group to do several reports slamming Linux and predicting dominance of Windows 2000.

Microsoft and the Gartner Group both claim the study was independent, but there was some confusion about a Microsoft copyright that appeared on the original reports, disappeared from later versions, and vanished completely when the reports were removed from the Gartner Group's web site. Eric Raymond's post-mortem on the fiasco was typically sarcastic:

> Whatever occurred, I'm sure the large amounts of money that Gartner admits to having received from Microsoft before and after this incident have done much to soothe their upset at looking like patsies.[35]

The moral of the story is to do your own investigating. It doesn't matter what Microsoft-funded studies show (nor should you blindly jump on the results of a Red Hat–funded performance study). Try Linux yourself and see how it works for you. If you're getting anxious, skip ahead to Chapter 4.

FEATURES

Talking exhaustively about an operating system's features could fill a book, and comparing two or more OSes, feature by feature, would take even longer. Fortunately, Microsoft has done us all the favor of describing, via the "Linux Myths" document it produced, the

---

33   Eric Raymond, "Halloween VI: The Fatal Anniversary," www.opensource.org, October 31, 1999.

34   Jürgen Schmidt, trans. Eva Wolfram, "Mixed Double: Linux and NT as Web Server on the Test Bed," c't, < http://www.heise.de/ct/english/99/13/186-1/>.

35   Raymond, "Halloween VI: The Fatal Anniversary."

features in which, it contended, Linux was more limited than certain flavors of Windows. I'll examine Microsoft's claims versus reality for the following features:

- ▼ File system integrity
- ■ File system journaling
- ■ Clustering/high availability
- ■ Large memory support
- ■ Huge file support
- ■ Swap space support
- ▲ Security

File System Integrity

A file system refers to the way a computer stores files to disk. For example, DOS used a file system called the File Allocation Table (FAT). Windows 98 uses an enhanced version known as FAT32. And Windows NT can use FAT or a file system known as NTFS. Linux can use all these filesystems and more, but its native filesystem is currently one called ext2.

For most purposes, ext2 is effective; it resists fragmentation (so you don't get to watch a disk defragmenter move all those colored blocks around like you do in Windows), it's fairly flexible, and it handles large disks well. When a Linux system doesn't shut down properly (if you turn it off without telling it to shut down first, for example), the system knows to check the filesystem because it wasn't properly closed.

Even if the filesystem was properly closed, however, ext2 periodically forces a file integrity check on startup. It is possible to tweak the system to make this less frequent, but it's a good thing to maintain file system integrity so you don't lose files, so that's not recommended.

The Linux Myths document points out that the filesystem check can take a long time if you've got large partitions involved, noting that

> …the system must check the integrity of the file system during system restart, a process that will likely consume an extended amount of time, especially on large volumes and may require manual intervention to reconstruct the file system.[36]

This is a reasonable criticism, and something you should consider if you're thinking of moving a particularly large data set to Linux. On the other hand, an "extended amount of time" may really amount to minutes. Curious about the current recovery times, I shut off power to two of my Linux systems to crash them hard and then powered them up. Neither system took more than three minutes to check its file systems (on 36GB of disk partitions for each server). While this result is anecdotal and unscientific, it is still a real-world example of what you might expect.

---

36   Microsoft Corp., "Linux Myths."

If you've ever experienced an NTFS volume check after an NT system crashes, you know that this process can be very time-consuming if the volumes are large. The filesystem is more likely to need checking if the system has been powered down improperly, so power outages, clumsy handling of the computer cables or power switches, or—dare I say it—an operating system known to be unstable (see the section on "Stability" earlier in this chapter) may all induce a filesystem check.

With respect to filesystem integrity and checking, my experience is that Linux filesystems and Microsoft NTFS filesystems are similar. As a user, you'll be happiest if your system doesn't go down unexpectedly, and Linux is good at staying up for a long, long time. Heaven help you if you're using FAT32 partitions on your Windows systems; the combination of the instability of the Windows 9*x* platform, the fault-intolerance of FAT32, and the relative uselessness of the Scandisk utility conspire to make this a far less stable choice than either Linux or Windows NT or Windows 2000.

Filesystem Journaling

One solution to the filesystem integrity problem is what's known as a "journaling" file system. These highly fault-tolerant filesystems are used on high-end systems to prevent loss of data. Andy Patrizio noted in Wired News that

> …while Microsoft points out that Linux lacks a world-class journaling (error tracking) file system of its own, it fails to mention that SGI is porting its XFS file system to Linux.[37]

There are a number of new filesystems under development for Linux. One of the nice things about the Open Source community comes into play here: If you want to know how some of these projects are progressing, you can actually look at the code. You probably don't want to do that. Heck, most people reading this book probably don't need a journaling filesystem in the first place.

But isn't it nice to think that if you want to try out something under development, you can do it? And that you can see for yourself whether a product or tool is real or simply "vaporware?" I've dealt with too many third-party software companies, let alone vapor-spitting OS vendors, who've told me that the next release will be ready "next week," "next month," or even "next year." I like being able to tell (by how much code has been written and how well it works) whether the development staff is on vacation or is working like hummingbirds charged on a feeder full of Mountain Dew.

Clustering/High Availability

Another high-end feature used to prevent loss of data and to maintain system accessibility is known as high availability. This feature is commonly implemented in a failover system or a cluster.

---

37   Patrizio, "Microsoft Lambastes Linux."

A failover system is one that shares the same data as the server you want to make available at all times. If the first server crashes, the second server steps in as seamlessly as possible so that your users can keep working or buying or whatever your users do. One problem with failover systems is that the additional servers don't do much while they're waiting for the first server to fail. So you buy two really expensive systems and use only one at a time.

A clustering approach makes available the processing power of a whole group of computers. This way, all the systems are available for use at all times. Some clusters are designed to provide high-availability computing to users. The Linux Myths page points out that there are no "commercially proven clustering technologies to provide High Availability for Linux."[38]

Another use of clustering is to provide parallel computing capabilities. In other words, you run 2, or 10, or 100 computers as one massive computer. This can be significantly more cost-effective than buying a supercomputer, and you can do it using off-the-shelf Linux software and your existing hardware. Nicholas Petreley pointed out that you will not

> ...find a Microsoft clustering solution competitive with Beowulf clustering for Linux.... The Linux portion of the above solution weighs in at $49. You can't even use Windows NT to create the same solution today.[39]

Most readers of this book won't need either functionality, but this is a difference between the two systems.

Large Memory Support

How much memory is in your Windows PC? If you've got more than two gigabytes of RAM in your system, you've got an impressive system. And you won't be able to access the whole amount with plain vanilla Linux. As pointed out on Microsoft's Linux Myths page, "Linux only supports 2 gigabytes (GB) of RAM on the x86 architecture, compared to 4 GB for Windows NT 4.0."[40]

This is a problem I wouldn't mind having on my desktop systems (none of which, by the way, will even accommodate more than 2GB), but if you find yourself in this conundrum, use the version 2.4 kernel, which supports 64GB on Intel hardware.

Huge File Support

While we're on the subject of big, what size is your largest file? The Linux Myths page notes that "The largest file size Linux supports is 2 GB versus 16 terabytes (TB) for Windows NT 4.0."[41] And this claim is true when Linux runs on the 32-bit systems Windows

---

38   Microsoft Corp., "Linux Myths."

39   Nicholas Petreley, "Removing the plank," www.linuxworld.com, March 1999.

40   Microsoft Corp., "Linux Myths."

41   Microsoft Corp., "Linux Myths."

supports. One could argue that a 2GB file is plenty large for most users, but perhaps that's a matter of design sense. Furthermore, this is no longer a limitation if you're using the Linux 2.4 kernel.

Swap Space Support

One last claim made in Microsoft's Linux Myths document regarding Linux functionality is that "The Linux SWAP file is limited to 128 MB RAM."[42] The truth of the matter is that Linux doesn't use swap files by default; it uses partitions (again, it's another design choice that doesn't mean much, but it gives you an idea of how carefully Microsoft does its marketing research). And while older versions of Linux limited any one swap partition to 128MB or less, you could make multiple swap files to accommodate large swap spaces. And starting with Linux kernel version 2.2, the 128MB limit for a single swap partition was eliminated.

Security

From the way the Redmondites go on about security, you'd think they've got security figured out. If you stay up to date on computing news, you'll know that's not true, and that there is periodically a new revelation of another security loophole in a Microsoft product.

I am in no way claiming that Linux comes out of the box secure as a fortress; it's good practice to check for security updates on an ongoing basis, especially if your computer is connected to the Internet.

Configuration Effort

Hand-configuring Linux security can be time-consuming, especially if you want to close every possible door into the system. As usual, Microsoft blows the effort required out of proportion in its Linux Myths document:

> Configuring Linux security requires an administrator to be an expert in the intricacies of the operating system and how components interact. Misconfigure any part of the operating system and the system could be vulnerable to attack. Windows NT security is easy to set up and administer with tools such as the Security Configuration Editor.[43]

It doesn't matter how easily configured the security module is if it doesn't work. Andy Patrizio of *Wired News* responds to the Microsoft document this way:

> Microsoft criticizes Linux for a lack of security. It fails to disclose that the US Army recently switched from an NT server to a Mac server because NT wasn't secure enough.[44]

---

42   Microsoft Corp., "Linux Myths."
43   Microsoft Corp., "Linux Myths."
44   Patrizio, "Microsoft Lambastes Linux."

In case you missed that story, here's part of the recap, courtesy of *ArmyLINK* News:

> Christopher Unger, web site administrator for the Army Home Page, didn't want to talk about specifics of what the hacker did to the web page or what the Army is doing to protect its sites from future hackers. However, he said the Army has moved its web sites to a more secure platform. The Army had been using Windows NT and is currently using Mac OS servers running WebSTAR web server software for its home page web site.[45]

Microsoft's Linux Myths document adds some additional rhetoric in an attempt to make Linux security updates sound difficult to find, understand, and implement:

> Linux system administrators must spend huge amounts of time understanding the latest Linux bugs and determining what to do about them. This is made complex due to the fact that there isn't a central location for security issues to be reported and fixed. In contrast Microsoft provides a single security repository for notification and fixes of security related issues.[46]

Jonathan Corbett of the Linux Weekly News has a pretty straightforward response:

> They must sign up for their distribution's security announcement list, and apply the updated packages when they are released. The time gets significant when there are large numbers of systems to update, but that is true of NT 'service packs' as well. Microsoft makes no mention of the difference in turnaround times—Linux bugs are fixed much more quickly. We also humbly suggest the LWN security page as a central place to look to keep up on security issues.[47]

I'd add that in my years administering Microsoft systems on file and application servers, the application of service packs was always an occasion for some trepidation. Some large companies have a "wait to implement" policy for Microsoft's service packs, because it's often found that while one problem is fixed, another is introduced. The reality is that operating systems are complex, and keeping any of them running optimally takes a non-trivial amount of effort.

Security is a vital issue, especially for business users. With the proliferation of "always connected" or shared Internet access methods (for example, DSL and cable modems), security is becoming an issue for home users as well. Whether you use Windows, Linux, or anything else, proper security configuration is a must. There is extensive information on how to secure both operating systems as much as possible. All I can do is encourage you to use it.

---

45   Connie E. Dickey, " Web page hacker arrested, government sites becoming more secure," ArmyLINK News, September 1, 1999.
      <http://www.dtic.mil/armylink/news/Sep1999/a19990901hacker.html>.
46   Microsoft Corp., "Linux Myths."
47   Corbett, "A look at Microsoft's Linux Myths."

Security Evaluations

Another longstanding item in Microsoft's bag of confusing tricks is the security certification ruse, as trotted out again by the Linux Myths gang:

> Every member of the Windows NT family since Windows NT 3.5 has been evaluated at either a C2 level under the U.S. Government's evaluation process or at a C2-equivalent level under the British Government's ITSEC process. In contrast, no Linux products are listed on the U.S. Government's evaluated product list.[48]

For years after Microsoft began touting its C2 evaluation, it failed to mention that the C2 security level only applied to NT systems that were not connected to a network. Furthermore, the evaluation applies to a particular hardware/software configuration; if you use different hardware, you're out of luck. Microsoft has been trying to milk this misleading information for years, much to the chagrin of Novell, which had actually been evaluated as C2 in a network-connected configuration long before NT 4.0 finally passed in 1999. Congratulations to Microsoft for passing the evaluation at long last, but since they represented NT as secure before its evaluation, it doesn't seem to be the most important measure of security, does it?

Secure Design

One last salvo from the Linux Myths document aims at the basic design of Linux. As the document points out:

> Linux was not designed from the ground-up to support symmetrical multiprocessing (SMP), graphical user interfaces (GUI), asynchronous I/O, fine-grained security model, and many other important characteristics of a modern operating system.[49]

Once again, *Linux Weekly News* Executive Editor Jonathan Corbett had as good a response as any, noting that the pot is as black as the kettle:

> One could also argue that Windows—even NT—was not designed for multi-user environments and the need to protect users—and programs—from each other.[50]

A more realistic criticism of Linux security is also mentioned in the Linux Myths document, however.

> Linux security is all-or-nothing. Administrators cannot delegate administrative privileges: a user who needs any administrative capability must be made a full

---

48   Microsoft Corp., "Linux Myths."
49   Microsoft Corp., "Linux Myths."
50   Corbett, "A look at Microsoft's Linux Myths."

administrator, which compromises best security practices. In contrast, Windows NT allows an administrator to delegate privileges at an exceptionally fine-grained level.[51]

This security isn't handled in the same way in Linux and NT, but the same task can be accomplished. If I'm the superuser of a Linux system (call me "root," and smile when you say it), and I want to give you the ability to administer some files or folders, I make you part of the group that has ownership of those files.

While this is a little different than what NT people are used to (and more like what Novell bindery-based administrators are used to, by the way), it's simple and it's consistent. Using the Windows products, I have to change access control and file permissions in different tools. In Linux, the two tasks are strikingly similar, and there are non-command-line utilities available to perform these security operations. They're not as colorful as the Windows tools, but they work.

The Myths document is now naked and bleeding, and with its dying gasp, it makes this allegation about Linux security:

> Linux only provides access controls for files and directories. In contrast, every object in Windows NT, from files to operating system data structures, has an access control list and its use can be regulated as appropriate.[52]

While it's true that access control under Linux is not as elaborate as under some other operating systems, this statement isn't really accurate.

For example, under Linux, devices are represented by files. So my floppy drive is known as /dev/fd0. That's not the sexiest name you'll find, but it allows me to set different access levels to allow different access levels, depending on who is trying to use it. My company's Chief Technical Officer, for example, can read from or write to my floppy drive if he wants to. The sales staff, on the other hand, can't access it at all, allowing me to scoff at and mock them.

IMPENDING EXTINCTION

I have disparaged others for making silly claims, and it would be inappropriate for me to do so without hypocritically making a silly claim of my own. So allow me to finish out this chapter by pointing out Microsoft's problems with respect to evolution. Some people are worried about Microsoft's well-being because of the initial antitrust case ruling and the pending class-action suits. Other theorists, however, anticipate a more chilling turn of events.

Microsoft Demise Theorized by Evolutionists

The following extended quotation is a tongue-in-cheek warning memo created by Robert G. Brown, in an article on *LinuxToday*, following the release of the Halloween documents.

---

51   Microsoft Corp., "Linux Myths."
52   Microsoft Corp., "Linux Myths."

Linux Beats Windows from the Shelf

Microsoft doesn't have its story straight on whether Linux is doing well or not. This is understandable, given the desire on one hand to destroy the competition, and the desire on the other hand to claim that there *is* competition. So we see apparent contradictions in Microsoft's portrayal of the success or failure of Linux.

Ed Muth told *PC Week* in March 1999 that "2 to 20 percent of Linux shipments turn out to be 'shelfware'.... From what we can tell, real-world deployments of Linux are very thin."[53] His premise is that despite huge numbers of Linux distributions being downloaded and purchased, the actual use of these systems is more limited.

What's amusing about this allegation is that two months later, according to Microsoft evidence entered in the DOJ trial, a Microsoft company email was sent, "dated May 25, 1999, from David Cole to Jim Allchin and others entitled 'Linux is beating Windows.'"[54]

I don't doubt Muth's shelfware numbers, by the way. I'd be stunned if less than 2 percent of Linux shipments remained on the shelf, but I'd be surprised if Windows "shelfware" numbers aren't similar. At my company, for example, many of the computers we purchase come with Windows preinstalled. The first thing I do to most of these computers is blow away the Windows partitions in preparation for installing Linux. So we have many Windows licenses sitting on the shelf.

This is another example of Microsoft spinning facts for its own purposes. There is a movement, by the way, which encourages people to seek refunds if they don't use the Microsoft software preinstalled on their computer. See **www.linuxmall.com/misc/refund** for more information about this process. Another option is purchasing computers with Linux preinstalled; some vendors will even configure your system to dual-boot between Windows and Linux (in case you don't feel quite ready to jump completely on the wagon).

The documents struck him as funny, and after I read his posting, they struck me as funny, too. In Robert's defense, he acknowledges that his analogy isn't completely scientifically accurate, but I hasten to point out that this isn't rocket science…it's evolution.

All large, cumbersome reptiles with immense calorie requirements and primitive or nonexistent homeothermic mechanisms take note: small mammals seem to be successfully competing with us in certain ecological niches. This could be serious.
It is reasonable that these mammals are successful. They have fur and regulate

53   Berinato, "Microsoft exec dissects Linux's 'weak value proposition'."
54   "Transcript of Trial Before the Honorable Thomas P. Jackson United States District Judge," <http://www.microsoft.com/PressPass/trial/transcripts/jun99/06-03-pm.htm>.

their body temperature and hence can move around when it is dark and cold. They bear their young live and hence are not as vulnerable during the gestation stage. They reproduce relatively rapidly, and as they care for their young a larger fraction survive to adulthood. Their calorie requirements are relatively modest, at least on an individual basis. They are a real threat.

Since the large, bright flash occurred last month somewhere over the horizon (followed by the earthquake), it seems to be snowing and the plants we rely on for food are dying. Very soon we could be cold and hungry.

We need to adopt a strategy of growing fur and homeothermic regulation, but in order to compete we must grow *better* fur. Our fur will be so good we can patent the very idea of fur and force the little rats to wear the scales instead! Also, we'll be so temperature regulated that we will fairly glow with heat wherever we go, even in the subzero arctic. Wooly snakes, hairy tyrannosaurs—we can do it. While we're at it, developing the ability to catch, kill, and eat small furry animals is definitely called for, at least until the plants come back.

While we work to evolve these improvements, we need to start a public relations campaign promoting the idea that scales are beautiful, that cold masks a warm heart, and that you can't be a *really* great lover unless you weigh at least a ton. Overcome by our message, the rodents will languish and fail to reproduce while we exterminate them.

Right.[55]

The Extinction Story Explained

If that description was too oblique for your tastes, let me help you:

```
Dinosaur = Microsoft
Mammal = Linux
```

I trust you know how the competition turned out last time.

LINUX QUESTIONS AND ANSWERS

I have tried to use technical issues as the framework for my arguments in this chapter. However, not all the pertinent questions about issues involved in upgrading from Microsoft to Linux are technical. Here then, are my answers to questions I've seen asked or inferred by users, marketers, and the press.

---

55   Robert G. Brown, "Robert G. Brown's thoughts on Microsoft's memo," linuxtoday.com, <http://linuxtoday.com/stories/616.html> November 4, 1998.

Is Linux a "Dirty Communist Plot?"

Given the growing number of public companies focused on Linux or selling products that run on Linux, this question may not seem particularly astute. See the Linux Weekly News Stock Page at **lwn.net/stocks/** for a current list.

On the other hand, Microsoft President Steve Ballmer's comment that Linux has "the characteristics of communism that people love,"[56] was widely reported. And if you read the Free Software Foundation's comments on unauthorized copying of software (which the Software Publishers Association refers to as "piracy"), you might wonder whether illegally duplicating software should really be referred to as "sharing information with your neighbor."

So to what extent are Linux, its supporters, and the supporters of free software in general anti-capitalistic? Let me answer with a question: To what extent are Microsoft and its supporters anti-capitalistic? After all, Microsoft is currently dealing with the ramifications of being judged monopolistic.

That's simply the smart-alecky answer; it begs the question. My answer to the question is that beliefs and motives vary. The opinions of Free Software Foundation President Richard Stallman aren't the same, for example, as the ones held by Linus Torvalds. Linus seems to have a very laissez-faire attitude about software, while Stallman holds fairly radical views on how inappropriate property and copyright laws are for software.

In a Microsoft Internet Developer article, writer Douglas Boling addressed this point:

> Or is it the money that's the problem? Some folks are just plain anticapitalist. I'm not saying that Stallman is anticapitalist, I'm saying the whole free software movement is. But understand my distinction. Giving away software is a great marketing tool. It's hard to compete if your competition is free.[57]

Boling is basically saying that the company that created the software has the right to distribute it for free or for cost, but that right should not be granted to other parties. Stallman describes free software as having more in common with free speech than free beer, but Boling disagreed in another article, pointing out that "if you can freely distribute copies of a program you didn't produce, it's pretty much free in the beer sense as well as the speech sense."[58]

That's another smart-alecky response because beer and software are not alike. (And profound statements like that one really make you glad you purchased this book, don't they?) If you buy a beer and I drink it, I deprive you of the beer. If you buy some software, you can use it even if I use it, too. The beer analogy is inappropriate.

Should the company that paid someone to write software have exclusive rights over its distribution? Should the author of a program have those rights? Should software be freely distributed by its users? There is no single answer to those questions in the Linux community, and that's why Linux isn't a Red plot.

---

56   Graham Lea, "MS' Ballmer: Linux is communism," *The Register*, July 31, 2000.
57   Douglas Boling, "Free Software. Is it Worth the Cost?" *Microsoft Internet Developer*, May 1999.
58   Douglas Boling, "Free Software 2.0," *Microsoft Internet Developer*, June 1999.

Linux? In China?

Speaking of communism, Bill Gates had an odd exchange with an interviewer regarding the acceptance of Linux and Windows in China. In "Bill Gates Unplugged," an interview run in the September 2000 *Red Herring* magazine, Gates claimed that reports of the Chinese government's support for Linux over Windows was the result of poor journalism.

It's understandable that Microsoft is excited about the prospect of selling products in China, but there must be a very impressive conspiracy to misrepresent the opinion of the Chinese government, given how easy it was to find a quotation from the Ministry of Information Industry saying it would "give its full support to the development of Red Flag Linux, as well as all the other Linux systems."[59]

Will Linux Put Software Developers out of Work?

Relieved as we all are to find that Linux is *not* a communist plot, we can turn our attention to the plight of the software developer—the poor, misunderstood purveyor of vaporware, bloatware, or just-right-ware.

Software development can be a very profitable business, and it can certainly produce high salaries and the potential for riches. As a Silicon Valley native, I have seen plenty of programmers join the ranks of the nouveaux riche. While I appreciate them pushing up my home value, I confess that I'm not terribly concerned about whether they'll be able to afford a second Humvee (though it's fine with me if they can).

On the other hand, I want people to write programs and write them well, and money is recognized as a motivator. I would be unhappy if the availability of free software reduced the number of competent programmers. Douglas Boling describes the situation this way:

> To quote the [GNU] manifesto, "The real reason programmers will not starve is that it will still be possible for them to get paid for programming; just not paid as much as now." That's a bright future for a high school counselor to put in front of a kid.[60]

I'm sure our hearts are all bleeding for the kid who won't be paid as much for his programming. Sorry, kiddo, just a Ford Expedition for you! Look, this is just a flawed line of thinking. People write open source software for several basic reasons.

▼ Someone pays for the software

■ Programmers have a need for the software

---

59   Graham Lea, "High prices, false steps help Windows lose to Linux in China," *The Register*, August 8, 2000.

60   Boling, "Free Software 2.0."

- Programmers need collaborative help
- Programmers want to share their efforts
▲ Programmers want to be recognized for their work

These reasons often cluster together. For example, if someone is paid to write some software and enjoys sharing the software, they might release the software as open source so others can use it. Another person may desire certain functionality but can't complete the project alone.

And don't underestimate the incentive of recognition, of figuring something out, of being the one who figured it out and made it better. For all the programmers happy to be cogs compensated with stock options, there are many others to whom craft is paramount. These craftsmen enjoy refining each other, stimulating new ideas and enhancing old solutions to deal with current problems. There are other motives, of course, but these will do.

Someone Else Paid

The first motive arises when someone else needs software and is willing to pay for it. In this case, the programmer is compensated for the work, is able to pay the rent and purchase adequate quantities of CDs, DVDs, Doritos, and Mountain Dew. There are three options available to this programmer: Ignore the program once the client's check clears; keep the program in hopes of selling it to someone else; or distribute the program for further use, testing, and enhancement. He or she is welcome to choose the most desirable path, but if the program isn't easily marketable, or if it will lie fallow, or if it could be better if more people helped, why not make it available for use and embellishment?

They Need the Software

The second motive stems from a personal need for particular software functionality. Eric Raymond's research paper "The Cathedral and the Bazaar" describes his experiences developing a program called fetchmail. He began development because he wanted a better mail tool than the one he had available, and he collaborated with others to speed development and debugging.

A person in this situation isn't likely to pay someone else to write something they can create themselves. So by doing some work and then sharing it, the programmer is not taking any food off the plates of others. And if the tool becomes useful to other people—let alone popular—they now have the potential of selling improvements and customizations to others. (And if it's wildly successful there's always speaking engagement money and a high-profile job from a company hoping to gain some press.)

They Need Help

Sometimes a project is too large for a single programmer to tackle. Actually, in any case where people who didn't write the program want to use the program, it's best to have some collaboration. It's better to have people who didn't write the program test the program, and the user documentation is usually better when written by someone who didn't write the program.

If you've ever worked with a programmer who didn't want input, you'll particularly appreciate this motive. The developer who doesn't acknowledge that feedback is useful isn't likely to produce programs that are useful (at least to anyone else). I'll talk about the usefulness of the Internet in software development later in this chapter. Suffice it to say that the availability of skilled and interested collaborators around the world is an inducement for many programmers to share their source code.

They Enjoy Sharing

I have spent many mornings trying to encourage sharing among the kindergartners in Sunday School classes. It would make me happy if someday one of those hyperactive tykes will let me use a program they wrote. And I'd be sorely disappointed to find that financial gain is the only motivator they recognize. One reason Linux has developed so quickly and so well is that Linus has delegated things so effectively that many people have participated.

Consider these four motives for making "free" or "open source" software. The only way the software gets written in any case is if the author desires to do it. Contrast that with the development model of a large company where someone else tells you what kind of program to write, what features it will have, which bugs you should fix, and who can use it. Which programmer do you think will be more satisfied? Which product do you think will work better in the end?

How Can a Bunch of Geeks Compete with Those Super-Geniuses at Microsoft?

I'm confident that Microsoft employs many smart people. I've even known a few myself. Like other large companies, however, it employs its share of dim bulbs. And despite his popular perception as an übermensch, Bill Gates doesn't have the market cornered on perception or smarts. One example: For a guy who insists that his web browser is part of his operating system, he was pretty late to the Internet bandwagon.

Even if you have a balanced view of Microsoft as a software producer, though, it is legitimate to wonder whether an informal, worldwide band of programmers is any match for a highly centralized, ambitious company. As I consider this matchup, several questions come to mind.

▼ Why would anyone make good software free?

■ Doesn't Microsoft produce free software?

▲ Doesn't Microsoft produce better software?

Why Would Anyone Make Good Software Free?

In the last section, I discussed reasons someone might create free software. However, conceding that there are reasons for free software to exist isn't the same as believing free software can be high quality. To quote Douglas Boling again:

> While free distribution is a great marketing tool (think about all those samples you get in the mail), what does it say about the product itself? Frankly, it says that the product (or the effort that went into making the product) has no value. Is that what you software engineers out there want?[61]

I don't mean to pick on Boling; on the contrary, I think he brought up some very good issues because he's asking questions I'm still hearing people ask, more than a year later. That's not to say I find his conclusions convincing, and of course, I'll tell you why.

To me, the value of a product is in its usefulness to me, not in its price. In fact, the price of a program can only lessen its value in my eyes (if it costs more than the functionality I get from it). For example, I recently downloaded Bluefish, an HTML editor distributed under the GNU Public License (GPL). It has nearly all the functionality I desire, and I paid nothing for it. I sent a postcard to its author, as he requested, but that's the extent of my financial investment. If I were to purchase a tool with a similar feature set (nearly all the functionality I desire), I'd have to spend about $100. Would spending the money give me warm fuzzies that told me the commercial tool was better? Not a chance.

What gives me warm fuzzies is that I can share the GPL software with my friends without qualms of conscience, let alone fear of reprisal. I can try to coax a hacker friend to add the remaining functionality I desire, or I can ask the author or pay the author to make those additions. In my view, this software is better in every way—not only despite being free, but because it's free.

Doesn't Microsoft Produce Free Software?

Boling's comment regarding free software distribution brings up another interesting point: Microsoft tries hard to portray itself as a magnanimous benefactor of the user. Sure, they don't think that free software is very useful, but since it's getting lots of press, they wouldn't mind getting a little coattail publicity. For example, in a *BusinessWeek* article, Ed Muth mentioned:

> Microsoft does distribute a great deal of free software. There is a great deal of free software in terms of tools and utilities that are part of a resource kit.[62]

This is a little bit like suggesting that "Osborne distributes a large number of free pages. There is a great deal of free pages in terms of pages that are part of this book." No matter how many of the pages are free, though, you paid dearly enough for some of them to cover the book's costs.

---

61   Boling, "Free Software. Is it Worth the Cost?"
62   Muth, "Linux 'Lacks an Extraordinary Number of Features' of Windows."

Here's a little more perspective on Microsoft's contributions to the free software world. The prices in Table 2-2 were gathered from shop.microsoft.com as I wrote this chapter.

Doesn't Microsoft Produce Better Software?

Perhaps you'll believe that free software can be good, and that Microsoft doesn't really produce free software. But perhaps you're thinking about how Microsoft dominates many of the PC software markets, and you're thinking that I'm not giving Microsoft's products enough credit. Perhaps they're dominant because they're better!

And I'll agree that they should be. Given the manpower available to Microsoft, the amount of time they've had to build their applications and their operating systems into a cohesive bundle, and the amount of money they've extracted from users like you and me, I believe Microsoft should have the best PC applications available in the markets they choose to enter.

But I'm not ready to consider the unstable operating systems Microsoft offers me the best available. I'm unwilling to consider a lifetime of system reboots acceptable. I don't want to commit to having to purchase new applications every few years, at a dear price, just to maintain compatibility with those using newer versions of the same tool. And I am not optimistic about the future of the Microsoft-powered PC platform because Microsoft is more interested in expanding its list of features than it is in making its OS and application offerings solid.

Resource Kit	Price
Microsoft Windows 95 Resource Kit	$49.95
Microsoft Windows 98 Resource Kit	$69.99
Microsoft Windows NT Server 4.0 Resource Kit	$149.95
Microsoft Windows NT Server 4.0 Resource Kit Supplement 4	$49.99
Microsoft Windows NT Workstation 4.0 Resource Kit	$69.95
Microsoft Window 2000 Server Resource Kit	$299.99
Microsoft BackOffice 4.5 Resource Kit	$249.99
Microsoft Office 2000 Resource Kit	$59.99
Microsoft Internet Explorer 5 Resource Kit	$59.99

Table 2-2.   Price of Free Resource Kit Software

Consider Windows 2000 (the operating system formerly known as NT 5.0). *PC Magazine* columnist John Dvorak suggested back in 1998 that

> …the unprecedented delays to Windows NT 5.0 indicate to me that something is terribly wrong with the base code, and that all the corporations out there who intend to subscribe to this system better have some insurance.[63]

Why have there been problems with the Windows 2000 code? Nicholas Petreley suggested reasons in March 1999:

> Given the obvious road hazards in the NT roadmap, and Microsoft's history of missing target dates and changing product directions on a moment's notice, this fact—that the marketplace will decide—is exactly what Microsoft should be worried about.[64]

In short, an over ambitious feature set, an inability to ship on time, and a lack of ongoing focus delayed Windows 2000 for *years*. Petreley warned that Microsoft's trouble releasing its new OS might give the market time to pick another OS. In April 1999, Ed Muth said, "We're making good progress to complete the product with the expectation of shipping it this year."[65] You know that shipment date wasn't met, and in the intervening time, Linux became a viable alternative.

It's true that Windows 2000 is a huge, complicated piece of software. In April 1999, ZDNet quoted Microsoft's Jim Allchin as pegging the "Windows 2000 Professional Client and all its components at 29 million lines of code, and the server as 'within a few million of that.'"[66] Allchin provided sizes of other Microsoft OS products for comparison:

> Windows NT 3.1 was 6.5 million lines; NT 3.5, 10 million; NT 4.0 16.5 million; and the most recent service pack of NT 4.0 is a 'good jump up from that,' Allchin said. He added that the size has little to do with the platforms' reliability. 'When we ship the system, it will have higher reliability than any system currently has with Microsoft,' Allchin said. 'But it's a large beta. It still has lots of bugs, and that's why it's still a beta.'[67]

Now, I'll confess that I was no ace in Computer Science, but I didn't fail the software engineering class where we covered this basic concept: Dramatically more code yields dramatically more opportunity for unexpected errors. Allchin's "see no evil" approach doesn't warm the cockles of my heart. When John Dvorak heard the anticipated size of the finished product, he freaked out.

---

63   John C. Dvorak, "The Windows 2000 Jinx," *PC Magazine Online*, November 16, 1998.
64   Petreley, "Removing the plank."
65   Muth, "Linux 'Lacks an Extraordinary Number of Features' of Windows."
66   Scott Berinato, "With end in sight, Windows 2000 team gets quantitative," *PC Week Online*, April 16, 1999.
67   Ibid.

> 35 million lines of code? What exactly does this thing do? … This has disaster
> written all over it. Microsoft had over 3,000 bugs in Windows 95, which was under
> five million lines of code for sure. … Good luck to all you optimists out there who
> think Microsoft can deliver 35 million lines of quality code on which you can
> operate your business.[68]

Perhaps things are even worse than Dvorak speculated. Consider the words of a Windows development leader named Marc Lucovsky in an internal Microsoft memo.

> Our customers do not want us to sell them products with over 63,000 potential
> known defects. They want these defects corrected. How many of you would spend
> $500 on a piece of software with over 63,000 potential known defects?[69]

Microsoft's operating system strategy is based on many of us doing exactly that. To be fair, not all those bugs are real problems with the existing product, but some are. Microsoft indicates it's guessing "28,000 of these are likely to be 'real problems.'"[70] It's a sad and disconcerting state of affairs, given that Windows 2000 is touted as—and may well be—the most stable Windows operating system yet.

Despite the flames rising from his own house, though, our good friend Ed Muth thought he saw some smoke coming from the direction of Linux:

> Without a long-term technical road map, without multimillion-dollar test labs,
> someone wants me to believe these visionary programmers and developers will
> want to do the best work of their lives and then give it away. I do not believe in that
> vision of the future.[71]

I guess that's one thing separating visionary programmers and Microsoft group product managers. Muth displays more problems with "the vision thing" in this statement, quoted in *P&L Communications News*:

> Complex future projects to add such functions as automatic translation of e-mail
> require big teams and big capital. These are things that Robin Hood and his merry
> band in Sherwood Forest aren't well attuned to do.[72]

Are you laughing about this? Okay, if you don't work from Microsoft, are you laughing about this? Can you believe that someone voluntarily identified himself and his com-

68   Dvorak, "The Windows 2000 Jinx."
69   Mary Jo Foley, "Bugfest! Win2000 has 63,000 'defects,'" zdnet.com,
      <http://www.zdnet.com/zdhubs/stories/special2000/0,9968,2436920-1,00.html>.
70   Ibid.
71   Berinato, "Microsoft exec dissects Linux's 'weak value proposition'."
72   Leslie Helm, "Microsoft facing a new opponent in the open-source movement: 'Wave of the
      future': Free software will be the high-tech story to watch in 1999," *P&L Communications News*,
      <http://www.plcom.on.ca/news/top_stories/linux/articles/981230.php3> December 30, 1998.

pany with Prince John and the Sheriff of Nottingham, and the open source community as Robin Hood? This is why Eric Raymond refers to Muth as "Sheriff Ed."[73]

But to return to the issue at hand, I'd like to suggest that a better question might be, not *doesn't*, but *shouldn't* Microsoft produce better software? The answer, of course, is "yes." But as long as Microsoft insists on denying the promise of open source software, and the competence and collective power of a world of creative, motivated programmers, it's destined to keep bloating feature count into software that crashes too often and doesn't follow any standards. Eric Raymond eloquently described the status quo in "Halloween V":

> What Sheriff Ed doesn't get is that this is a vision of the *present*. Linux is where it is today because thousands of 'visionary programmers and developers' have *already* made this choice, and are reaffirming it every day. Even scarier (from Microsoft's point of view), capitalism and the hacker gift culture are learning how to complement and support each other.[74]

I mentioned in the introduction to this book that I'm not religious about Linux, nor am I dogmatic about Microsoft or Windows. The contents of the last two chapters may have you doubting my veracity on those points, but it's true: I use Microsoft software, and unlike some of the luminaries I've quoted or mentioned in these chapters, I believe the company has had a positive overall impact on the state of personal computing.

However, unless Microsoft starts to understand what and whom it is facing, it won't stand a chance of continuing to thrive. I believe it's too large a company to continue growing at its previous rates (at least through legal means), and that means it can make fewer paper millionaires and will attract fewer young programmers who are hungry for stock options. It is too widely disdained by those who excel in the crafts that sustain it. So if it's going to survive over the long term, let alone thrive, Microsoft will have to recognize corporately what one of its executives, Paul Maritz, testified to in the DOJ hearings:

> It is unlikely in any other established industry that a single person, aided only by independent volunteers, could create a product that would emerge to challenge the industry leader. Yet this is the story of Linux, and the nature of the software business.[75]

Doesn't Linux Lack Direction and Focus?

Even without the "multimillion-dollar test labs" and "long-term technical road map" that Ed Muth believes are necessary for high-quality software design, Linux exists. Without those advantages, its development continues and its adoption into homes, schools, small businesses, and Fortune 500 companies is accelerating. How is that possible?

---

73   Eric Raymond, " Halloween IV: When Software Things Were Rotten,"
       <http://www.opensource.org/halloween/halloween4.html>.
74   Raymond, "Halloween V."
75   Maritz, "Direct Testimony of Paul Maritz."

If you've read the Dilbert comic strip for any length of time, you might speculate that the absence of pointy-haired managers may be one reason. Microsoft's Paul Maritz mentioned another in the DOJ trial, saying, "Today, the number of developers working on improving Linux vastly exceeds the number of Microsoft developers working on Windows NT. "[76]

This statement reflects Vinod Valloppillil's analysis of open source software (OSS) in the leaked Halloween document. Valloppillil observed, "The ability of the OSS process to collect and harness the collective IQ of thousands of individuals across the Internet is simply amazing."[77]

These individuals are working on code they need, or on problems that intrigue them, or in areas they see they are suited to help with. Do all open source projects succeed? Of course not. But because they tend not to be as marketing- or sales-driven, these projects can be addressed as technical problems with technical solutions. And for you and me as users, that's what they should be, shouldn't they?

What's Good About Open Source Software?

I've talked about the advantages of the open source process, but how about the final result? What's in it for you?

The best thing about the end result of open source projects is that programs become like any other product. If you purchase a car, you are free to tinker with it. You can put neon lights on the running boards, hang fuzzy dice from the mirror, load it up with amplifiers and subwoofers, and put a chromed exhaust pipe extension out the back. (I'm making up an example. Please don't consider this a suggestion.)

If you prefer, you can replace the wheels and tires with different ones, put in racing seats, add a sunroof and air conditioning, and drop in a larger engine. Most people don't go to that extreme, but it's possible to do all these things. After all, it's your car, and as long as your state doesn't think you're over your emissions limit, and your motor vehicles department doesn't think you've made the vehicle a deathtrap, the law won't care.

So why can't you expect to do the same kinds of things with your computer software? And if I may take the analogy further, if you don't want to go back to the dealer to have your car serviced, and you don't feel up to doing so yourself, wouldn't you go to an independent repair shop? If one shop didn't do a good job, wouldn't you go somewhere else?

These options are available because automobiles are commodities. They all work similarly, but they differentiate themselves enough to find eager purchasers and lifelong devotees. But unless you lease your car, the manufacturer doesn't still lay claim to your vehicle.

The software world is very different. You usually don't own the software you paid for; you've licensed it from the company that owns it. And as I write this, many commercial software companies have succeeded in pushing UCITA, the Uniform Computer In-

---

76   Ibid.
77   Valloppillil, "Open Source Software: A (New?) Development Methodology."

formation Transactions Act, through the National Conference of Commissioners for Uniform State Laws (UCCUSL).

This act, if made law in your state, makes even the most ridiculous software licensing terms binding upon you. It allows your software providers to put a backdoor in their programs that allows them to "pull the plug" on the software you're using if they feel you've breached the license agreement.

What kind of world is that for software users? For all the hot air coming out of Redmond about their customer-driven approach, do you suppose anyone thinks Microsoft really cares about their needs? As one of my college professors said, "Nobody cares what you think except your mother and your wife (before marriage)." And as Linux kernel savant Alan Cox wrote in a piece for osopinion.com:

> Many people talk about the Open Source advantages of price and of reliability. They actually miss the biggest advantage of all by doing so. Open Source is about commodity product in a grown up market. It is about competition, choice, and putting power in the hands of the consumer.[78]

---

78   Alan Cox, "The Risks of Closed Source Computing," osopinion.com,
     <http://www.osopinion.com/Opinions/AlanCox/AlanCox1.html> October 22, 1999.

CHAPTER
3

New OS, New Freedoms, New Concepts

In the previous chapters, we looked at differences between Linux and Windows by focusing on how they are developed and distributed. In this chapter, we begin addressing the nitty-gritty details that distinguish the two operating systems.

If you're used to using Windows products, especially if you didn't use DOS very much, some of the underlying concepts behind Linux may be confusing. Perseverance will pay off, though, because many of the conceptual and implementation differences from Windows give Linux its power.

STRANGE CONCEPTS

Unix and its imitators, including Linux, use some concepts that are foreign to most Windows and Macintosh users. As I mentioned in Chapter 1, if some of these ideas seem weird and incomprehensible now, they'll seem straightforward later, when you're more familiar with them.

Kernel

I've mentioned the kernel before, but this is a good a time to mention it again, because it's talked about frequently in the Linux world, and it's not something most Windows users think about. The kernel is the part of the operating system that handles the most basic functions and controls interactions with the computer hardware. A kernel is just a program built to allow you to control your computer without knowing every detail about its inner workings.

The Linux kernel is modular—that is, when the kernel program is created (and we'll do that ourselves in Chapter 6), it can be created and customized to include some features and to exclude others. For example, if you don't have a SCSI interface in your computer, you don't have to include the SCSI modules in the kernel. By excluding unnecessary components, you can create a smaller, more efficient kernel, which will use fewer resources and can improve performance.

Shells

If the kernel is the low-level program insulating you from the details of the computer hardware, the *shell* provides another layer of insulation. The shell provides the text-based user interface; it is the program that tries to figure out what you mean when you type something on the command line. For a new user, selecting a shell is somewhat arbitrary, as many features are the same between the various shells.

What do you do with a shell? For starters, all the commands you'll read about in this chapter are typed into the shell. The shell looks something like a DOS prompt (select the MS-DOS Prompt or Command Prompt on your Windows system if you've forgotten), but it's far more powerful than the DOS prompt. For example, most shells allow you to type part of a filename or command and then press the TAB key to automatically finish the name (or get a listing of the options, if more than one exists). Most shells can also be used for script programming, which is described in the "Shell Scripts" section below.

The three most common shell options are listed here; you'll find all three of them in most Linux distributions.

▼   bash

■   tcsh

▲   zsh

How do you select among the three? I recommend that you use the GNU Bourne Again Shell, called "bash." Bash does not offer some of the more esoteric features of the other shells, such as command-line spell-checking and tracking of logins and logouts. But it's widely used, it runs the most common types of shell scripts, and it's what the root user is set up to run.

The Z shell (zsh) is the most feature-laden of the three, so if you have to have every available shell function, it can be useful. However, I use the TC shell (tcsh), which is based on an earlier shell, csh. Don't use csh, which often isn't even an option due to some unpredictable behavior and functional limitations. Tcsh uses syntax similar to the C programming language, which makes it popular with C-literate users.

Shell Scripts

A *shell script* is a program written using a shell. These scripts are very similar to the batch files used under DOS or Windows, but they offer far more power and control. Shell scripts handle everything from automating routine tasks to performing product installations or working as full-fledged applications. Running a shell script isn't difficult; if you're using the same shell as the script is, you can just type the script name. If you're not using the same shell as the script is, you simply type the shell name before the script name:

```
millerm@romans:~> zsh atone.zsh
```

You can tell which shell a script uses by its first line. Shell scripts are text files, and their first lines should always have a pound sign and an exclamation point, followed by the full path to the shell program, like this:

```
#!/bin/bash
```

Environment Variables

Have you ever played with a CONFIG.SYS file on a DOS machine? Maybe you have and you never want to do anything like that again. While you may not have to tinker with *environment variables* in Linux, either, they can be used to make it easy for programs (including shell scripts and commands you run from a prompt) to find files or know your preferences.

An environment variable simply holds information that's available to the whole environment (that is, the whole shell). Information that could be widely useful, such as the name of the shell you're using, your account name, groupnames you belong to, and other options, are stored in environment variables and are accessible to programs that want to make use of them. The path, which is a list of directories Linux will search through to find a file when you try to run a program from the shell, is also set as an environment variable.

Users and Groups

Another difference between Windows systems and Unix-like systems is the way users and groups are handled. If you've ever shared a Windows NT system with other people using different accounts, perhaps you've seen how NT can handle multiple users. Each user can have a separate desktop setup defined, for example. However, most home users of Windows use a single login name to get onto the computer, in part because Windows 95 and Windows 98 didn't handle multiple accounts very well, and in part because most people don't think it's necessary for Mom, Dad, and the twins to have separate accounts.

In the Linux world, we definitely want everyone to have a separate account. And there are a number of special accounts that we don't want anybody to use. Not to mention a superuser account that should only be used for special, powerful functions. How does this all fit together? Let's talk about it.

Superuser/Root

The superuser of a Linux system is named "root." The superuser is a person (or a group of people, if more than one has this level of access) who has ultimate control over the

Overly Sensitive Software?

Unlike DOS and Windows, Unix is very case-sensitive. That is, the cAsE yOU uSe tO tYpe coMaNDs mAtTeRs. Some commands and applications that run under Linux help you out by allowing you to be case-insensitive, but it's generally very important to type a command or file name exactly as you see it. You can have many similar files in one directory: "README," "ReadMe," "readme," and "Readme." All four of these would be different files; each could have different contents, and you would enter each name exactly as it appears in the directory listing. Although you can create filenames that include a space (for example, "read me"), this can cause problems in Linux, so it's better to avoid doing so (by using underscore characters instead of spaces, for example).

This isn't necessarily a bad thing, but it takes getting used to. Compared to some of the Windows products, which have a tendency to convert the filename from whatever you entered to initial-capped format, it gives you a little more control. On the other hand, it requires more attention, and that's not always fun.

system. All files, all devices, and all processes running on the system must comply with the superuser's commands. Root has control over the creation of new users and can set permissions on directories and files as necessary.

Root performs software installations, identifies and tidies up after system problems, and maintains security. The person (or persons) who have access to the root account should not normally log in as root, however. Those who have superuser access should have their own user accounts; the root account is only used to perform root functions such as software installation or user creation.

The superuser account should be used only when needed because it is capable of deleting files needed by the operating system. It can trash other users' files. It can kill vital processes. And all of these things can happen by mistake if you're careless, tired, or confused enough. For day-to-day use, Linux also provides ordinary user accounts.

User Accounts

Each user of a Linux system should have a unique user account. Account names consist of short strings of characters: a user's name or nickname can be the best account names. Users on a Linux system can be logged into the same machine at the same time (either remotely, on separate "virtual consoles," or in different windows).

Each user gets a home directory in which files and programs may be placed. These home directories are ordinarily placed in /home, so the full path to my home directory is

```
/home/millerm
```

By default, all users who are part of the same group (see the "Groups" section below) can view the files in other group members' home directories, but cannot modify them. Unless you change their access, ordinary users cannot change **any** files on a Linux system outside their home directories.

Groups

Linux, like other network operating systems, uses groups primarily to provide access privileges for different sets of people. For example, if users "mom" and "dad" want to share a directory containing financial information without giving access to their children, users "erin" and "matt," they can use "root" to create a group, put "mom" and "dad" in that group, and give the group exclusive access to the financial data.

Attributes

File and directory attributes are part of the DOS and Windows environments, so they're not an entirely foreign concept. However, the way they are used in Linux may be a little hard to decipher at first. In the directory listing below, look at the leftmost column to see the attributes of each file and directory:

```
-rw-r--r--   1 millerm  users       190 Nov 24 11:48 README
drwxr-xr-x   2 millerm  users      1024 May 24  1999 jdk
```

```
drwxr-xr-x   2 millerm   users        1024 Mar 29  1999 msword
-rwxr--r--   1 millerm   users        2829 Mar 16  1999 spam.zip
-rwxr--r--   1 millerm   users       51200 Mar 16  1999 survey.tar
drwxr-xr-x   3 millerm   users        1024 Jul 17 10:53 webmin
drwxr-xr-x   3 millerm   users        1024 Aug 26  1998 x11
```

As you can see, there are 10 attributes possible for each item in the directory. The first attribute indicates whether the item is a directory or not. If the first character in the attribute list is a "d," it's a directory. If the first character is "-," the item isn't a directory. That's pretty straightforward, right? Well, that's one down and nine to go.

The next three characters indicate what the owner is allowed to do with the item. For example, the first item in the directory listing is a file named "README" (we can tell it's a file because there's no "d" in the first attribute position).

As we can tell from where his username is located, "millerm" owns this file. The second, third, and fourth attribute characters indicate whether the owner user can read ("r"), write ("w"), and execute ("x") the file. Notice that the owner of README can only read and write the file; because it's not marked executable, he can't "run" this file.

As we can tell from where its groupname is located, "users" has access to the file. The next set of three permission characters indicates what the members of the group "users" can do with this file. The permissions set for README restrict the members of the group to reading the file, because only the "read" attribute is set.

The final set of three characters indicates what kind of access is allowed to the rest of the world. In the case of the README file, it's the same as the access allowed to the "users" group: read only; no write; no execute.

Together, these attributes allow a rich set of privileges to be maintained, with file owners, groups of users, and the rest of the world receiving different access based on the type of file. In the Linux world, this can sometimes come into play when you're attempting to install new software. When the software needs to be installed outside your home directory (in which, by default, you enjoy full access privileges), you will sometimes be instructed to perform part of the installation as root. This is because ordinary users don't have the right to add or change files in most of the core Linux directories. That's good, because it helps keep people from accidentally deleting or changing vital files. If you're going to do that on a Linux system, you'll have to work at it.

Virtual Consoles

Linux allows you to access a computer in several different ways. When you start Linux without a graphical user interface (GUI), you see a command prompt that takes up the entire screen. Even without a GUI and without being connected to a network, it's possible to have multiple shells running and multiple users logged in, using *virtual consoles*.

A virtual console is just another command prompt on the same computer. You can select different virtual consoles by pressing the ALT key and one of the function keys. Most distributions put the default console on ALT+F1, so to switch to another virtual terminal, you could press ALT while pressing F2. This will bring up a screen with a logon prompt, so you can be logged in with your user account and as root without even having the X Windows GUI loaded.

This feature can be useful if you need to kill a job that has frozen your first virtual console—simply switch to a different virtual console and you can do everything you need to. Many Linux distributions post installation progress messages to virtual consoles, so you can use the console-switching trick to check for errors or watch the installation progress.

Mount

While Windows is moving away from strictly using them, as a general rule, drives have letters associated with them. Every Windows user knows that A: and B: almost always refer to floppy drives, and that C: is likely to be a hard disk, and that D: is sometimes a CD-ROM drive. These ideas are leftover from the DOS era and have been retained in Windows alongside references to machines, shares, and folders.

Linux uses a different naming mechanism. In the Linux world, drives can be addressed by their device names or their *mount points*. Don't panic if that sounds meaningless. First, it means is that under Linux, all devices are represented by a particular filename (the device name). For example, my floppy drive is known as /dev/fd0. Secondly, drives can be accessed using another filename, and that filename is the mount point. For example, my floppy drive is mounted as /fd0. Other people might mount it to /floppy or /mnt/floppy (which is probably the best choice), but whichever they choose would be their mount point.

Linux manipulates the drive using its device name, but in most cases, users must access the drive using its mount point. This means the floppy "drive" is known to the operating system as /dev/fd0, but when a user wants to see the contents of a particular floppy "diskette," the device must be mounted, and the contents are viewed and manipulated from that mount point.

Another example would be a hard disk. The device name of the first SCSI hard drive on a system is /dev/sda. That hard disk is often divided into several logical partitions to separate different types of files. The first partition on the first SCSI hard drive is known as /dev/sda1. But if you decide to put home directories on that partition, it's mount point would be /home. All three locations will exist: /dev/sda, /dev/sda1, and /home. But the users would access the data on that partition using the mount point /home.

Using a common filesystem structure to name devices and their contents is subtly powerful. It gives Linux administrators a consistent way of accessing devices on the system without having to use clumsy front ends. The distinction between devices and content will become particularly important during the installation process when you're trying to figure out what mount points to use and what disk partitions to access from each one. If you're not clear on the subject now, dealing with the specific examples in Chapter 4 should help you understand better how to partition and mount a drive.

X

All major Linux distributions come with a copy of XFree86, which is a windowing GUI. If you have used Windows since version 3.11 or earlier, this shouldn't be an alien concept; back in those days, you ran DOS, then when you needed to get into the Windows GUI, you typed **win**. Perhaps you felt like a loser as you typed **win** over and over, but soon you can say you're an X Windows user and an ex-Windows user. Ahem.

But let me get back to the concept at hand. One reason this model (running the GUI on top of the operating system, rather than integrating it into the operating system) works well is that it allows you to forego the GUI when it's unnecessary. If your computer spends most of its time acting as a web server, for example, why would you want to waste system resources on a GUI that's not being used?

Separating the GUI from the operating system doesn't simply allow you not to run a GUI, it gives you a choice of the GUI you want to run. In the Windows world, you can customize your desktop with colors, patterns, and even themes. In the Linux world, you can run an amazing variety of window manager programs, including Window Maker, Enlightenment, IceWM, olvwm, and fvwm (not to mention fvwm95...guess what it looks like).

There are also comprehensive desktop environments like KDE (which includes its own window manager, kwm) and GNOME (which can be integrated with several window managers). While a window manager is in charge of the look and feel of your desktop, it does not do anything to ensure that the applications you run are in any way consistent in look and feel. Because people all over the world create applications you may use, and because some of them have different ideas about how an interface should look, you may not have the comforting homogeneity of a Windows desktop.

A desktop environment attempts to alleviate this problem by providing a set of tools that use the same look and feel, provide similar help functions, and allow application in-

Did Your GUI Crash Your PC?

The modular design of Linux and XFree86 is a very different approach than the one Microsoft has taken. And while it may be comforting to have the GUI loaded at all times, having that GUI loaded not only uses computer resources, it may also make your computer unstable. Windows NT 4.0, for example, was criticized for being less stable than earlier versions because Microsoft moved the Win32 subsystem (which handles user input and video output) into the kernel mode.

The advantage of packing more functions into the kernel area is that these functions can run faster. The disadvantage is that these particular functions are among the most likely to crash, and putting them in the kernel mode allows them to take the rest of the computer with them. Linux and XFree86 are designed to avoid this eventuality because their designers consider system crashes unforgivable. Isn't *that* good news!

tegration functions (such as dragging a file from a file manager and dropping it into another program). A desktop environment can still run applications that aren't part of its standard tool set, but as long as you use the applications that are designed for the environment, you'll get the benefits of similar interfaces.

STRANGE PLACES

The way directories are named on a Linux system is fairly cryptic. This hearkens back to when computer hardware was less powerful and more expensive, and wasting processing power on descriptive directory names was unheard of. This means the standard directory structure seems a little awkwardly named. Like everything else, though, this just takes some getting used to. I'll try to help by describing the scenery of a Linux file system.

root directory: /

The highest point on the directory structure is called the root directory. Yes, it uses the same name as the superuser. Think of them both as being top level, and both may be easier to remember. A single character, the forward slash ("/"), represents the root directory. To change to the root directory, for example, you can use the following command:

```
millerm@romans:/home> cd /
```

In this example, I move from the /home directory to the / directory. So the next prompt I see looks like this:

```
millerm@romans:/>
```

NOTE: The / directory is not the same thing as the root user's home directory, which is /root. Rather, the /root directory is a subdirectory of /.

Every other directory on a Linux system is contained somewhere in the hierarchy beneath that root directory. This is not analogous to a Windows system, where each drive is given its own letter and its own directory structure. Under Linux, all the disks on your system are mounted to directories somewhere beneath the root, either directly off the root directory, or further down.

home directory: ~

While I'm talking about unusual directory names, let's consider the home directory. Now, if you and I have different user accounts and different home directories (and I say we should), which one is the home directory? The answer is different for each user. My home directory, for example, is called /home/millerm. If I want to access that directory, I can type the tilde (~) and my system knows I want my home directory. If you try to change directories using the tilde, though, you won't reach my home directory; you'll reach yours.

This is a convenient way of helping you find your way home. It also makes it faster to access your home directory. For example, I downloaded a small program that displays the periodic table of the elements. Since it resides under my home directory, I can run it from someplace else (the forward slash in the prompt indicates that I'm in the / directory) with the command:

```
millerm@romans:/> /home/millerm/downloads/gperiodic
```

Since I'm a lazy slob, however, I want to save myself some keystrokes, and I can do so by running the same command using the tilde shortcut:

```
millerm@romans:/> ~/downloads/gperiodic
```

"dot" Files

Another strange Linux place is the "dot" file. These are files whose names start with a period. Ordinarily, these files are hidden from view. For example, if I list the files in a directory named secret:

```
millerm@romans:~> ls secret
millerm@romans:~>
```

There aren't any files here, according to the directory listing command. But if I tell the command to look for directory contents that start with a period, I get results:

```
millerm@romans:~> ls -a secret
.      ..      .secret
```

Now I see that there are entries named "." and ".." as well as a file named ".secret." The "." entry is a shortcut that refers to the directory I'm currently working in, and the ".." entry refers to its parent directory. The ".secret" file was present all along, but it's shielded from view unless a person is looking for "dot" files. This is a nice way of tucking configuration files away so they don't clutter up your home directory. Making something a "dot" file doesn't provide any real security, so it's purely a tidiness device. The same trick can be used to hide directory names.

Standard Linux Subdirectories

Although there are variations in some distributions, most packaged versions of Linux have very similar directory structures. The commonality comes from adherence to the Linux File System Standard (FSSTND) or the more recent Filesystem Hierarchy Standard (FHS), which has a web site at **http://www.pathname.com/fhs**. The names of the standards aren't as important as your expectation that you'll get a Linux filesystem without many surprises.

It's also not that important that you remember what each standard directory contains. In the interests of giving you an idea of what to expect, though, I'd like to show you the contents of a Linux system's root directory, and describe the most important contents and functions in the directory tree.

III 3-1

This directory contains commands that are used by the superuser and regular users alike. These commands are generally vital to the system and include operations such as copying, moving, and deleting files, logging in, creating and opening archives, identifying the system name, and viewing text files. You would rarely want to alter the contents of the /bin directory (and if you did so, you'd have to do it as root).

/boot

This directory contains most of the files required for booting the system. Other files needed when the computer starts up are stored in the /etc and /sbin directories. Don't expect to make changes to the /boot directory by hand.

/dev

The /dev directory contains device files and other special files. Examples of the kinds of devices you might find in /dev are shown in Table 3-1.

Device Name	Device Type
/dev/ide	Entire IDE master hard drive
/dev/hdb1	Partition 1 on the IDE slave hard drive
/dev/fd0	First floppy drive, type autodetected
/dev/lp0	First parallel printer
/dev/midi00	First MIDI port
/dev/null	Nowhere (to get rid of something forever, send it here)
/dev/psaux	PS2 keyboard port
/dev/ramdisk	RAM disk
/dev/scd0	First SCSI CD-ROM drive
/dev/sda	Entire first SCSI hard drive
/dev/st0	First SCSI tape drive
/dev/tty1	First virtual console

Table 3-1. Examples of Devices in /dev

This is by no means an exhaustive list, but it's probably more than you'll need to know anyway. This is another directory in which you won't do much fiddling, if any.

/etc

This directory contains the configuration files your Linux system needs to start up and run properly. Many of these files can and should be edited—automatically, using a configuration utility or a text editor. Most Linux distributions provide quite a bit of assistance configuring the files in the /etc directory to make life easier; some of the questions you answer during an installation process will automatically populate the needed /etc directory files.

/home

This directory typically has a child directory for each user on the system. For example, if Mom, Dad, Erin, and Matt are the only users on the system, the /home directory might contain four user directories:

```
/home
    /dad
    /erin
    /matt
    /mom
```

There are other ways to arrange things; for example, if you have a large number of users, they might be grouped into departmental subdirectories. Some systems don't use a /home directory at all and place the home directories elsewhere, but this is less common.

/lib

This directory contains the library files required for the programs contained in the /bin and /sbin directories. A library is a program file that contains code that could be used by several different programs; by putting that shared code in a library, programmers can make the sharing applications smaller. Unless you're Microsoft, this is generally considered good practice. You may occasionally need to update a library in this directory, but for the most part, you can move on, for there's nothing to see here.

/mnt

This directory is used for temporarily mounting filesystems. For example, although I tend to mount my floppy drive /dev/fd0 to a separate directory I've created off the root directory (/fd0), I could just as easily mount /dev/fd0 to /mnt/floppy. (In fact, many Linux distributions help you by creating this mount point by default.) Using /mnt/floppy would make my root directory less cluttered, but it would also require a few more keystrokes, and as anyone who has seen my office can attest, I'm more lazy than tidy. If you're not, the /mnt directory may be your friend.

/opt

This directory may or may not be used in your Linux distribution. It is provided as a place for third-party applications, but in practice, most of these applications either install to the /usr/local directory or are managed as packages and install themselves elsewhere. Still, you may find that an application you want to run will create or populate the /opt directory and its subdirectories.

/proc

This directory is used to transmit data to and from the Linux kernel. There are some text files in this directory that can be viewed for system information such as the kernel version, system uptime, and information about the processor and memory on the system.

/root

The /root directory is typically used as the superuser's home directory. Root is not like the lesser users—the root account should only be used for system administration—so there shouldn't be much junk accumulating in this directory. And if you're wondering, the answer is yes, I've got some junk accumulated in some of my systems' root directories. But as soon as I'm done with this chapter, I'll go clean /root out. Are you happy now?

/sbin

Vital system administration commands usable only by root reside in this directory. If a command is needed to start up the system, and only the superuser uses it, it belongs here.

This includes filesystem checking commands, shutdown commands, and some networking commands.

/tmp

This directory provides a place for the system to store temporary files. Don't plan to store your own temporary files here—programs will do that themselves.

/usr

The /usr directory contains files and programs used by everyone on the system. Located here are most programs and utilities that are installed with the Linux distribution and that are available for use by regular accounts (not just the superuser). The filesystem hierarchy specifies that this directory have read-only access; in other words, you shouldn't be changing the contents of the /usr directory.

/usr/local

The /usr/local tree is one exception to the rule that you don't make changes to the /usr directory. Remember that under Linux, a filesystem may be mounted under any directory name. In fact, some people point /usr/local to a separate partition from the one /usr uses. This is because in many Linux installations, /usr/local is where most third-party applications are installed.

This means your /usr/local directory might start out empty—or nearly so—and you might fill it up with the programs you pull off the web, purchase, or share with neighbors. It also means that if you want to back up the unique files on a system, you'll want to backup the /usr/local directory as well as /etc, /home, and /opt.

Note that Red Hat and other distributions that use the Red Hat Package Manager (RPM), which helps install applications and system updates, tend not to use the /usr/local directory as much as distributions that don't rely on RPM.

/usr/src

The /usr/src tree contains the Linux source code. This is important because you may someday wish to compile a kernel for yourself (and in fact, we'll be doing just that in Chapter 6). When you install a distribution onto your PC, it should populate the /usr/src tree with the kernel source files and headers. If you want to recompile this kernel, you can do so from the files contained here. If you want to download and compile a newer kernel, on the other hand, it's recommended that you do so in a directory you control, such as a specific place in your home directory. This will avoid confusion by any programs expecting the original header files hanging off the /usr/src directory.

/var

The /var directory is the Linux system's repository for *variable data*. Variable data includes lock files, log files, mailbox, spool data, and cached data. There may be interesting data in this directory tree, but most of it gets there because programs put it there.

PROCESSES AND REDIRECTION

Whether you use Windows or Linux, your operating system is capable of handling more than one "process" at a time. For example, if you open the Task Manager in Windows, you can see the applications you have open. Underlying these applications are often many different processes performing different tasks: Fetching input from your keyboard; performing calculations; placing images on your screen.

When you use Linux, you have far more control over each of these processes (whether you want to use that control or not is entirely up to you and your computer). You can create, reprioritize, and remove processes on your system, and you can redirect output from a usual process to another process.

Processes

Let's talk about process control first. If you're using Linux with X Windows and a window manager, there are several processes running even before you start an application. There's the shell you logged into, X Windows, the window manager, any applets that run on the window manager's desktop, plus any other programs you're running in the background, such as web servers, mail programs, and scheduled jobs.

Foreground

I mentioned processes running in the background, but before I explain more about them, I should mention programs running in the foreground. A program running in the foreground is ready to accept user input or update the display on the screen, so interactive programs like word processors run best in the foreground. The bash, tcsh, and zsh shells all provide a command, fg, to bring a process from the background to the foreground.

Background

A background process is one that is not waiting for something else to happen. For example, when users want to use my company's software to automate complicated IC layout, they can issue a command to tell the computer to produce the layout, and while that job runs in the background, they can check mail, browse the web, or even play a game. Doing any of those three foreground tasks while the background job is running will make the layout automation slower, but it will continue until it is finished.

kill

If you can create a process by running a program, how do you remove that process? Naturally, you kill it. If you decide that a program has locked up, or if you need to free up more computer power and want to weed out some unnecessary processes, you can use the **kill** command to kill some or all of them. Ordinary users can use the **kill** command to weed out their own processes, while root can kill anybody's processes. So use this power with extreme caution, for crying out loud.

Cron

Processes are not created only when you invoke a program; they can be scheduled to occur on an ongoing basis. One mechanism used to do this is the crontab, which is a file that contains instructions for what jobs to run and when to run them. Each user has a crontab that can be edited to perform ongoing tasks like deleting temporary files, performing backups, or sending status reports. Another, similar mechanism for scheduling jobs is the **at** command.

Daemon

Both the crontab and the **at** command work because there is a cron daemon determining what jobs need executing and making sure they run when they're supposed to. So what's a daemon? Simply a process lurking in the background, tirelessly executing the commands it has been given. I'm not personally very excited about the name; I don't want a familiar spirit in my computer doing my bidding. But it's just a name, so I promise not to get agitated if you don't.

top

So how do you find out which processors are the top users of system resources? You betcha, it's the **top** command. Top is great for identifying processes that may be dragging your system performance down, and it provides additional information such as overall CPU utilization, number of active user sessions, system uptime, memory usage, and swap usage.

ps

To determine the status of all processes on the system, you can use the **ps** command, which stands for "process status." This command can list all or some processes, and has a variety of options controlling the information it shows you. This command is particularly useful when you're interested in both active and inactive processes.

Redirection

Most command-line programs act on input that you enter on the keyboard, right? And most command-line programs produce output to the screen, right? That's right. But that's not the only way those programs can be used. Linux allows you to redirect a program's input and output in clever ways to produce the information you're looking for.

stdin

The usual source for command input is known as the standard input file, which is commonly referred to as stdin. What file is this? It's the keyboard "file." That is to say, in normal operation, the standard input for a command is what you type on the keyboard. This isn't rocket science at all, is it?

stdout

I doubt it will surprise you to find that there's a standard output file. And hopefully you won't be surprised to find that it's known as stdout and it's ordinarily your monitor. So commands generally expect input from the keyboard and intend to output to the screen.

>

This type of redirection takes the output intended for stdout and sends it to a file. For example, if I want to keep a list of the files in my home directory, I can redirect the directory listing information from the screen to a file using the following command:

```
millerm@romans:~> ls > jan_31.txt
```

Instead of displaying the file listing on the screen, this syntax creates (or overwrites) a file named jan_31.txt, which contains the output of the **ls** command.

>>

This type of redirection appends to another file the output intended for stdout. For instance, if I want to keep a single file containing my home directory's contents for several dates, I could do this:

```
millerm@romans:~> date > home_ls.txt
millerm@romans:~> ls >> home_ls.txt
```

These commands create a file named home_ls.txt, put the current date in the file, and then append the directory listing to the file.

<

This type of redirection gives a program input from a file rather than keystrokes. For example, if I want to mail that list of my home directory's contents to Bill Gates, I can use sendmail with a file redirection:

```
millerm@romans:~> sendmail billg@microsoft.com <home_ls.txt
```

I doubt that Bill Gates is remotely interested in my home directory's contents, but on the other hand, Microsoft has been accused several times of secretly acquiring data from users of its software, so who knows? If I get to choose the data he sees, though, I'd rather send him my Linux server uptime reports:

```
millerm@romans:~> sendmail billg@microsoft.com </proc/uptime
```

|

The other redirection symbols use files for program input and output. Redirection using a "pipe" can redirect one program's output directly to another program's input. For example, if there are many processes running on my Linux box, I can redirect output from the **ps** command to the **more** command. This allows me to see one screen at a time.

```
millerm@romans:~> ps -aux | more
```

Ignore the **-aux** portion of the command for now; they are just options that indicate what kind of output I want from the **ps** command. Another example would be redirecting the output from the **ls** command to the printer, which I could accomplish this way:

```
millerm@romans:~> ls | lpr
```

I could have redirected the **ls** output to a file, and then printed the file, but why bother? Redirection allowed me to pipe the output straight to the printer without the extra step of creating the file.

ODD COMMANDS

In the last section I gave several examples of different commands, some of which you may not have seen before. There are many Linux commands that seem strange, especially at first glance. While many of them are very powerful, most are easy to use for the basic purposes. And don't be downhearted that I'm spending time on these commands. For the most part, you can use graphical tools to perform these tasks, but it doesn't hurt to be exposed to the underlying power of Linux, right?

File Commands

The first set of commands deals primarily with files. Some can be used with directories as well, but we'll deal with directory-specific commands in the next set.

ls

The **ls** command shows information about files or the contents of a directory. It is equivalent to the "dir" command in DOS, but it can be configured much more extensively. By default, the **ls** command lists the contents of the current directory, sorted alphabetically, excluding filenames that begin with a dot. Note that the sorting mechanism sorts capital letters before lower-case letters, so filenames in all caps or initial caps will appear at the beginning of the list.

ln

The **ln** command creates a link between files or directories. This is an important feature of Linux, so if you've been snoozing, perk up for a minute. Using the **ln** command, you can make a file that points to another file. I mentioned earlier that the Linux kernel you're using should be stored in /usr/src/linux. If you want to keep track of which version you're using, you can store each version in its own directory in /usr/src, and then create a link from /usr/src/linux to the version you want to use. When you get a new version, you don't have to rename any directories, you just change the link.

This kind of link is known as a "symbolic" link. The closest concept in the Windows world is a shortcut, which just points to another file or directory. In Windows, a shortcut can be identified by the .lnk extension. When you look at a Linux directory that includes a symbolic link, **ls** can tell you what the link points to:

```
millerm@romans:/usr/src> ls -l
total 4
lrwxrwxrwx   1 root     root           11 Dec 29 07:53 linux -> linux-2.2.13/
drwxr-xr-x  15 root     root         1024 Dec  2 15:52 linux-2.2.13/
drwxr-xr-x   3 postgres postgres     1024 Jul 12 10:24 pgsql/
drwxr-xr-x   3 root     root         1024 May 22  1998 sendmail/
```

The arrow pointing from linux to linux-2.2.13 shows that it's a symbolic link. A hard link, on the other hand, makes two (or more) files indistinguishable. It essentially points the filenames to the same data on the drive—like having a file with two names.

cp

The **cp** command is straightforward; you can use it to copy a file to another name or location, or to copy multiple files to a directory. It's analogous to the DOS copy command. You must have read permissions on a file to copy it, and you must have write permission in the destination directory to create the copy.

mv

The **mv** command is also easy to learn. It simply renames or moves a file or files. While the **cp** command leaves copies in the old location, the **mv** command eliminates the original files. You must have write permissions on a file to move it out of its original location, and you must have write permissions in the destination directory to move it into its new home.

rm

This command allows you to delete files and directories. You must have write permissions for the files and directories you want to delete, and by default, the command will not remove directories. To do that, you must specify the **-r** option to "recurse" through the directory structure. But please be careful recursing, or you'll be cursing for sure.

cat

The **cat** command is similar to the type command in DOS. It is simply a way of showing the contents of a file on the screen. As odd as it may seem, it has another function: It can be used to join (concatenate) multiple files. I have not yet figured out how to punch holes or bait hooks with it, but who knows what other mighty powers it may possess?

more

If you've got more than one screen of information in one file, the **cat** command will frustrate you by scrolling the beginning of the file off the screen before you can read it. Enter the **more** command, which also displays the contents of a file, but it displays the contents one screen at a time. You press the SPACEBAR when you're ready to continue with the next screen of information. This can continue until you've finished reading the file or until you press the **q** key to quit early.

less

Okay, let's say you've happily been scrolling through a README file using the **more** command, but that you hit the SPACEBAR one time too many. Or let's say your memory is as bad as mine, and you immediately forgot what you read on the last screen. Just when you think you can't take any "more," you get to use "less."

    Less works the same way **more** does, but it allows you to scroll forward or backward through the file and offers more controls. For example, while **more** limits you to using the spacebar to page one screen ahead, **less** allows you to page using the SPACEBAR or scroll up and down using the arrow keys and PAGE UP/PAGE DOWN keys. You can quit **less** by pressing the **q** key, just as you can with **more**.

head

But perhaps you don't want to see the whole file at all. Maybe you just want to glance at the beginning of a file to see what it contains. The **head** command accomplishes this task. When you run **head** on a file, it displays the first part of the file on the screen.

tail

Not to leave out those who only want to see the end of a file, Linux includes the **tail** command, which displays only the last few lines. This can be useful with log files, which often store the most recent information at the end.

lpr

The **lpr** command is used to send the contents of a file to a printer. Depending on how the printer is configured in Linux, it may be able to tell the difference between a text file and a formatted file (Postscript, for example). We'll visit printing in significantly more detail in Chapter 8.

grep

Given the ease of use of search tools available with desktop managers such as GNOME and KDE, you may never need to use the command line to search for text within a file. But if you do, you'll use **grep**. **grep** can find all instance of any given string of characters within the files or directories you specify.

diff

The **diff** command compares the contents of two files. It then displays the lines where the files differ. This is useful if you lose track of changes you've made to a file. There is a particularly handy option for the **diff** command (**-y**) that places the differing lines side by side in the output to make comparison easier.

Directory Commands

Many of the previous commands can be used on either files or directories. The following commands only make sense when applied to real directories (or links to real directories).

pwd

This command displays the full name of the current directory (the "working" directory). It will resolve all symbolic links in the path, so you know exactly where you are in the directory structure.

cd

This command, like its counterpart in DOS, changes the directory. You can change to a directory using an absolute address (/home/millerm/systems, for example) or using shortcut characters (~/systems).

mkdir

This command allows you to create a directory. You must be the superuser or have write permission in the parent directory if you want to successfully execute this command.

rmdir

This command allows you to remove an empty directory. If you want to eliminate a poor, defenseless, unarmed directory that happens not to be empty, you'll have to use the **rm** command with the **-r** option. You brute.

Multiuser Commands

If you're not using a Linux system with multiple users logged in, these commands may not be particularly useful. If you want to know who is using the system, though, there are some command-line options for doing so, and I want to tell you about some of them.

users

This command simply lists the users who are currently logged into the Linux system. For example

```
millerm@romans:~> users
david dedood dedood dedood dedood karen millerm
```

Wow, it looks like user dedood has gone berserk, doesn't it? While that may be true, it's more likely that dedood has several terminal sessions open within X Windows. Each time he opens one, it counts as another login session as far as the **users** command is concerned.

who

The **who** command reports similar information, but for each user currently logged in, it indicates the login name in use, the terminal being accessed, the login date and time, and the X Windows display information. If I run who on the same system, I find

```
dedood    tty1     Jan  4 05:42
dedood    ttyp4    Jan  4 05:48 (:0.0)
dedood    ttyp0    Jan  4 05:48 (:0.0)
dedood    ttyp1    Jan  4 05:48 (:0.0)
karen     ttyp3    Jan 30 18:02 (genesis.nodomain.)
millerm   ttyp5    Feb  6 23:37 (exodus.nodomain.)
david     ttyp6    Feb 12 08:19 (numbers.nodomain.)
```

So it looks like dedood logged onto the system on January 4 at 5:42 in the morning, then started X Windows. The rest of the users logged on later from three other machines.

finger

Even more information about a user can be obtained using **finger**. There are some variations in which bits of information are displayed, and some data may not be available for **finger** to tell you, but **finger** can return the following bits of information about the user you specify:

▼ Account name

■ Real name

■ Terminal name

■ Idle time

■ Login time

■ Office location

■ Office phone

■ Contents of .plan file

■ Contents of .forward file

▲ Contents of .project file

Each user on a system may populate the listed dot files to provide personal information to be viewed by other users (less sociable people may prefer not to, and that's okay, too). If you don't specify a user to finger, a very abbreviated list of data is shown for each user currently logged onto the system.

Security Commands

As we continue our whirlwind tour of Linux commands, I'd like to point out just three security-related commands. Many security functions can be performed from within X Windows, so that's often where people choose to go, but it's only wise to know the basic commands just in case.

passwd

The **passwd** command sets a user account password. When you run **passwd** as a normal user, you can change the password for the account you're currently using. When you run **passwd** as root, you can change the root password or the password for any other user account. Be careful not to forget the root password, because it can be a hassle to recover.

chmod

The **chmod** command is used to change the permission attributes of a file or directory. If you have write permissions to the file or directory you wish to change (either as a user or a group), you should be able to use **chmod**.

chown

The **chown** command changes the owner and/or group attributes of a file or directory. If you want to change ownership of a file or directory, you must be root or be the current owner.

Networking Commands

Although there are many network-related commands available on a Linux system, I've selected a few that are particularly noteworthy. Others, such as **ping**, may also be useful, but we'll cover them all in more detail in Chapter 9.

ftp

Guess how the file transfer protocol is used. That's right, it's used to transfer files! The widespread appeal and availability of the Internet has made ftp a familiar concept to many users, even those who haven't used the version included in Windows. And although you can use many web browsers to access ftp sites, you can also use a command-line tool. The **ftp** tool allows you to specify whether the files you're transferring are text files or binary files; it allows you to transfer multiple files at one time; and it even allows you to delete files on the remote system (if you have the rights to do so).

rlogin

The **rlogin** program allows you to log in to a remote system as though it were local. It establishes a terminal session on another network-connected system so you can access files and programs on that system. This means you can make use of the processing power on other systems without having to sit in front of them. Of course, the owners of the other systems can prevent you from using **rlogin** to get onto their systems, but I assume they'll play nice if you play nice.

rsh

This program allows you to execute a command on a remote host. While the **rlogin** command established an interactive terminal session by logging you onto the remote computer, **rsh** simply passes another command to the remote host. As useful as **rlogin** and **rsh** are, they allow possible routes of access to outsiders who can get to your computers across a network. The functionality of these programs is incorporated into a more secure utility called **ssh**.

telnet

The **telnet** command is another way to access a remote computer; it is more restrictive than the **rlogin** and **rsh** programs, but it is widely supported. For example, if you have a web site hosted at an outside ISP, you may be able to telnet to the ISP's computer to manipulate files and directories. While ftp works well for transferring files from one host to another, telnet is more appropriate for accessing the files once they've reached the remote host.

WEIRD AND WONDERFUL TOOLS

There are a few more programs and utilities that don't quite fit into the previous categories. Because you're likely to run into some of these as you install Linux or programs that run on Linux, I want to mention them here.

make

I'll discuss using **make** in greater detail in Chapter 13, but you should know about it now so that it doesn't confuse you before then. There is a GNU program called "make" that allows you to re-create a large program to run on your system. I say re-create because you're not writing code yourself, you're simply running **make** to compile and link a program so it will run on your computer.

Because programmers don't know the details of every user's configuration, and because most of them want their programs to work on several different hardware platforms and operating systems, you'll find that many programs available for Linux are distributed as source code.

This is nothing to be alarmed about, as most programmers have obligingly created installation scripts that do most of the work for you. But part of the process of creating the program to run on your Linux machine is running **make**, sometimes with some command-line options. You'll usually find information on what those options are in the installation instructions that come with the program; they're usually found in a file named README or INSTALL or something similar.

man

The **man** command shows you the manual pages for a given Linux command. Simply type **man** followed by the name of the command you want to learn about. For example, if you forget how to use the **man** command, you can type **man man**. The manual pages are usually formatted into the following sections:

▼   Name of the command

■   A synopsis of its use

■   A description of its functions

■   Details of its options

■   Environment variables it uses

■   Names of related commands

■   Descriptions of any known bugs

▲   Tips for use

info

The **info** command is similar to the **man** command, but it uses a hypertext system that allows you to follow links from within the manual pages themselves. Many of the programs contained in a Linux distribution no longer have current information in the man pages; if this is the case, the man page will tell you to use the **info** command to get the latest information. Once you're in an info file, you can tab from hyperlink to hyperlink and press ENTER to follow the one you want.

lilo

The lilo program is responsible for loading Linux (its name comes from "Linux loader"). Lilo loads the Linux kernel when your system boots up, and it can also be configured to boot into another operating system. For example, if you have a computer with Windows already installed, you can set your computer up to run either Linux or Windows. Lilo can be configured to let you choose on startup, or it can automatically boot into one operating system or the other.

Because lilo boots your system, it needs to know if the kernel ever changes. If you recompile a kernel by hand, for example, you *must* run **/sbin/lilo** to update the boot information. It doesn't matter if the new kernel has the same name; every time you update the kernel manually, you should rerun lilo.

Some pundits have criticized Linux for this configurability, claiming that the ability to tweak the operating system is not desirable in most corporate computing environments. So keep in mind that unless you intentionally and badly misconfigure your Linux system, only the root user is capable of installing a reconfigured kernel. So don't give root access to anyone you don't trust to make configuration decisions that are suitable for your computing environment.

Text Editors

Because Unix is largely based on text files, and because it has long been used by programmers, there are a variety of text editors available for Linux users. Later, we'll take a quick look at the graphical editors available in XFree86, but for now, here's a short list of some commonly used text editors.

I run the risk of agitating some who prefer editors I've left off the list, including the joe and jed editors, but if you're not already familiar with them, I'm not going to push you to use them. The three I'll mention are pico, vi, and Emacs.

pico

The pico editor seems to be particularly appealing to new Linux users, while the other two editors tend to be favorites of those who started using them some time ago. One of the Internet Service Providers (ISPs) I use, for example, recommends pico for users who are unfamiliar with their Unix-based systems.

The name "pico" is short for "Pine composer," which refers to the pine mail tool. Its behavior is based on what's found in pine, so if you think you'll be doing much text-based mailing and editing, you can save yourself some time by picking pine and pico—then you'll only have to learn one set of editing commands.

When you edit a file in pico, a list of commands appears at the bottom of the screen or window. Pico commands use combinations of the control key and a letter; for example, to exit pico, you hold the control (CTRL) key down while pressing the **x** key. Context-sensitive help is available.

vi

The vi editor and its ilk are, in my opinion, the least likely text editors for new users. The vi commands are difficult to remember, the editor is devoid of any assisting menus, and the help functions may not help much due to differences in terminology between the Windows world and the Unix world.

That said, I should add that vi is the editor I use most frequently. The original reason this happened was that I'd forgotten enough of Emacs (which I used in college and will describe shortly) that I wasn't very efficient with it, and I was working with a vi bigot. He was insulting enough about Emacs that I quickly switched to vi to shut him up. I'd recommend this approach anytime you need to need to arbitrarily choose among several tools that could do the job.

As a Linux user, you won't be running the "vi" editor, but rather expanded clones such as nvi, vim, or elvis. The feature sets of these different copies may not be the same, but the look and feel is identical. The clone programs are used because they add functionality you won't find in the "vi" editor itself, such as multiple level undo and multiple windows.

Vi is a quick and dirty editor that works well once you're familiar with it. Instead of using control commands as pico does, vi uses typed commands preceded by a colon (":"). For example, to quit vi without saving the document I've been working on, I type **:q!**, which means "quit and don't worry that I haven't saved the document, even though I've changed it."

If that doesn't seem awkward enough, you've got to be careful which mode you're in; unless you're in edit mode, most of the keys on the keyboard have some other function (because then you're in "command" mode). You may find yourself moving around a document instead of adding to it. Vi is fine, but unless you're motivated by experience or an external reason, I'd use something else.

Emacs

Emacs is another old favorite for many Unix users. It offers a menu system, context-sensitive help, and complete extensibility (provided you or someone useful to you knows Lisp). Emacs uses the CTRL, SHIFT, and ALT keys, the F10 key.... If there's a key combination available, it's likely Emacs makes use of it in some way.

Most popular text editors have several to many non-text-editing features, but Emacs really takes the cake for extended functionality. If you're looking for a text editor that isn't similar to a mailer—it *is* a mailer, Emacs might be for you. If you're looking for a text editor that can run in text mode but takes advantage of X Windows features, Emacs might be for you (though many editors go "both ways"). If you're looking for a text editor with calendar and diary features, not to mention web-browsing capabilities, Emacs might be for you. And certainly, if you've got the time and inclination to bend its power toward your purposes, it's a mighty ally.

PART II

Beyond
Addiction:
12 Steps to
Recovery

The structure of Part II is based upon the following 12-step program, which I advocate for those who, like so many of us, have decided they want to be free from a daily reliance upon Microsoft. These 12 steps are

Step1. Admit we are powerless over Microsoft—unless we install Linux.

Step 2. Believe that X Windows is highly configurable, won't crash our systems, and could restore us to sanity.

Step 3. Decide to turn our systems over to the power and flexibility of customized kernels.

Step 4. Connect fearlessly to a local or wide area network.

Step 5. Manage users and groups.

Step 6. Make a list of Microsoft and Novell systems and establish contact with them all.

Step 7. Admit that printing and print services are easy to configure.

Step 8. Establish a reliable web server.

Step 9. Contact others via email.

Step 10. Continue to look for new software and promptly make it.

Step 11. Share files to improve conscious contact and schedule our jobs to carry them out.

Step 12. Having become Linux users as a result of these Steps, we continue by employing Linux-based office applications.

CHAPTER
4

Step 1:
Install Linux

We are now ready to take the first step toward freedom from our Microsoft addiction. We do so by admitting that we are powerless over Microsoft unless we install Linux.

Now we're down to brass tacks, as people used to say back in the days when you could find brass tacks. We'll be installing two different distributions of Linux in two different situations. In both cases, we'll perform the installation on a computer that's already running Windows. In both examples, I'll assume we want to keep Windows loaded (I wouldn't want my investment in Microsoft products reduced to shelfware, and maybe you aren't ready to make a clean break yet).

In the first case, we'll do an installation of Linux to the existing Windows partition. While this will be convenient, it makes Linux run noticeably slower than it should. In the second case, we'll perform the installation using a partition-adjusting program that comes bundled with some versions of Linux.

The method that is right for you depends a little on the hardware you have available, as well as how much you'll want to use Windows and Linux on your system. In my opinion, if you're willing to install an additional hard disk in your system to accommodate Linux, you'll have the easiest installation experience. The software installation will be very similar to what we do here, but you'll be able to skip some of the steps required to squeeze Linux onto a disk already full of Windows.

But before we begin loading the software itself, let's get our bearings, shall we? It's a good idea to collect a few pieces of information from our systems before we start mucking around too much. And naturally, we want to be sure we're as ready as possible in case something goes wrong.

PRE-INSTALLATION COUNTDOWN

I'd like you to do three things before you continue experimenting with Linux. Consider this the countdown to installation, and I promise we'll start putting in Linux disks as soon as we're done here. But as George C. Scott's character in *Dr. Strangelove* might have said, "Don't blast off without me." The three pre-installation tasks are

▼ Back up your data

■ Identify your hardware

▲ Check hardware compatibility

Back Up Any Data You Want to Keep

Imagining things that could go wrong isn't just part of my genetic makeup, it's part of my daily work life. And if you, dear reader, are anything like many of the delightful people I've supported from various Information Systems departments, you're not that concerned about what could go wrong.

Maybe you open files you receive from people you don't know. You might shut down your computer from time to time without using the Shut Down command. Perhaps you wait quite a long time before saving a document you're working on. And it's possible that you occasionally delete files without knowing what they are. For these reasons and more, Linux attempts to protect you from yourself by separating the "root" account from ordinary user accounts—so that on a daily basis, using your normal account, you won't be able to accidentally wreak havoc upon your system. Speaking of wreaking havoc, see the sidebar below.

Regardless of how bold and reckless you are, you need to take a quiet moment to seriously consider what your important data are. Then you have to back it up before proceeding, because we're about to do some major, invasive, elective surgery. Are your Quicken data files vital? Are your product design meeting minutes important? Is your address book file necessary? Then don't make any changes to your system without backing those files up. If it helps, think of it this way: The rule is to back up only the files you want to keep. Don't need your in-process thesis? If you didn't back it up, I guess you didn't.

Now that you know what's important to you, copy those files somewhere safe. If you've got a tape drive, dump the vital data there (even better, back up your whole system to tape). If you have a CD recorder, write the files out to a CD. If you're limited to a Zip disk, or worse, a floppy diskette, I still implore you to save anything important to you. Installing Linux isn't difficult, but any major change to your system could cause you to lose data, and if you send me email complaining about lost data, I'm going to say I told you so.

Identify Your Hardware

This may sound like a pain in the nether parts, too, but identifying your hardware may save you some frustration later. Although you can get this information from paperwork that came with your computer and its peripherals, it's sometimes easier to let the com-

---

Dangerous Communiqués

I'd like to mention one other, marginally related activity: Passing along junk email. The two biggest offenders seem to be "good luck" messages that ask to be sent to all your friends, and hoax virus warnings. Let me explain two things that may help you: There's no such thing as good luck; and there are several places to check for virus hoaxes on the Web, including **http://www.antivirus.com/vinfo/hoaxes/hoax.asp**. If you're not motivated enough to make sure it's not a hoax, then don't go the extra mile to bother people with a warning. I know that passing these messages along doesn't inherently harm your computer, but if one of your irritated correspondents finally snaps and sends you a real virus, or punches you in the nose, don't say I didn't warn you.

puter tell you. Table 4-1 shows information you should know to get through the Corel Linux, Caldera OpenLinux, or Red Hat installation process.

Device	What To Know	How To Know	Corel	OpenLinux	Red Hat
Mouse	Brand, Port	Windows Device Manager		Yes	Yes
Keyboard	Type	Windows Device Manager		Yes	Yes
Video Card	Manufacturer	Display Control Panel			Yes
	Model	Display Control Panel			Yes
	Video RAM	Display Control Panel or Box			Yes
Monitor	Manufacturer	Display Control Panel or Monitor		Yes	Yes
	Model	Display Control Panel or Monitor		Yes	Yes
	Frequency (horizontal and vertical)	Documentation		Yes	Yes
	Current Resolution	Display Control Panel		Yes	Yes
	Current Color Depth	Display Control Panel		Yes	Yes
Network	DHCP	Network Control Panel	Yes	Yes	Yes
	IP Address	Network Control Panel	Yes	Yes	Yes
	Gateway	Network Control Panel	Yes	Yes	Yes
	Name Server	Network Control Panel	Yes	Yes	Yes
	Netmask	Network Control Panel	Yes	Yes	Yes

Table 4-1. Hardware Information to Know

Some of this information won't initially be needed. For example, Corel Linux will not ask you about your network configuration during the installation process itself. But if you want networking to work, you'll have to know this information. There is additional information you should know about your hardware for later, including your CPU type and the amount of memory in your system, but we'll deal with issues like those in later chapters.

Finding Hardware from System Properties Panel

The System Properties control panel in Windows is an excellent resource for identifying your existing hardware. To open this control panel in Windows 9x, you can

1. Right-click the My Computer icon on your Windows desktop.
2. Select the Properties menu option.

The System Properties window should open with the General tab selected. This page should tell you what type of CPU you have and how much RAM Windows recognizes. The Device Manager tab can provide additional information. If you click that tab, it should open a window like the one shown in Figure 4-1.

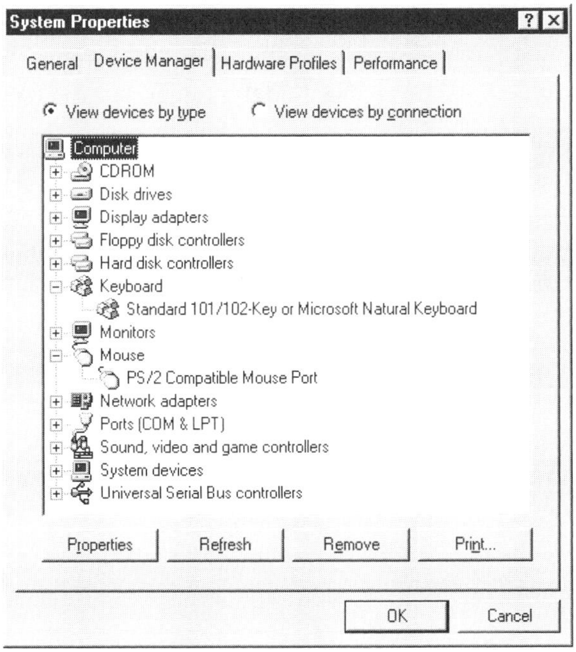

Figure 4-1. Use the System Properties control panel to identify hardware

The icons on the Device Manager tab represent categories of devices. If you double-click on the icons next to plusses, you will see the installed devices from that category. This screen can be used to determine whether you have a SCSI controller, a network card, a modem, and a sound card. It can tell you what kind of mouse is installed, how many disk drives it thinks you have, and what type of CD-ROM it recognizes.

In Figure 4-1, the Mouse entry in the Device Manager list is expanded to show a generic PS/2 mouse. The Keyboard entry in this list will provide information about the type of keyboard attached to your computer.

Finding Video Information from Display Panel

Information about your video display is best collected from the Display control panel. To open this control panel:

1. Right-click on your Windows desktop (somewhere there isn't an icon).

2. Select the Properties menu option.

This opens the Display control panel, and it defaults to the Background tab. We're not interested in the background, so click the Settings tab to see a screen like the one shown in Figure 4-2.

Don't be alarmed if there's only one monitor shown on your Settings tab; the system pictured in Figure 4-2 has two graphics cards. Notice that there is a description of the display; it should mention the monitor and graphics card. Sometimes the information contained in the Display line is not adequate. For example, in Figure 4-2 the Hitachi, Ltd CM800 is the monitor manufacturer and model number, but the Rage Pro Turbo PCI is just the model of the video adapter.

For more information, click the Advanced button on the Settings page. This will bring up the display properties page, which defaults to the General tab. Click on the Adapter tab for more information about the video adapter. In Figure 4-3, you can see that the adapter is manufactured by ATI Technologies and uses a Mach64 chipset. These pieces of information may be useful later. Back in Figure 4-1, notice that the Screen Area section shows the current resolution Windows is using, and Colors shows the current color depth. While you can experiment with different settings in Linux, if you're happy with your Windows screen configuration, you might want to record it to duplicate it.

Finding Network Information from Network Control Panel

If the Windows system is connected to a network, you'll want to collect some information about the network configuration. This is easily accomplished from the Network Control Panel:

1. Right-click on the Network Neighborhood icon and select Properties.

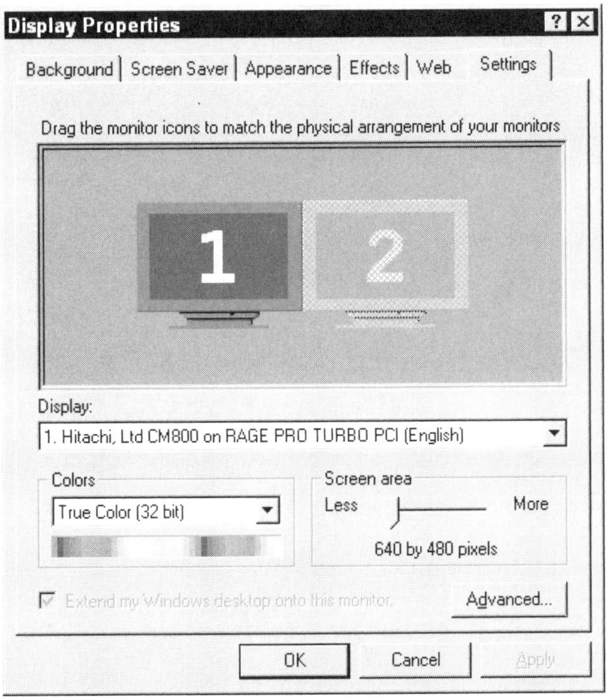

Figure 4-2.   Use the Display control panel to identify hardware

2. When the panel comes up, be sure the Configuration tab is selected and click TCP/IP, and then click Properties.

3. The TCP/IP Properties window opens; click the IP Address tab if it isn't already selected. You should see a window similar to the one shown in Figure 4-4.

4. If the Obtain An IP Address Automatically option is selected, make a note that your computer uses the Dynamic Host Configuration Protocol (DHCP). Linux can be configured with the same option.

5. If the Specify An IP Address option is selected, copy down the IP address and subnet mask. You'll want to duplicate these settings in Linux.

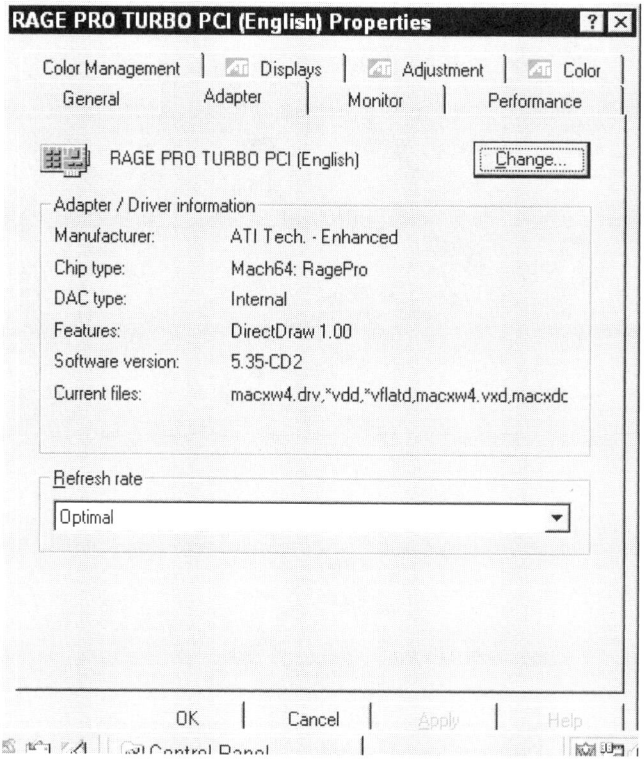

RAGE PRO TURBO PCI (English) Properties   [?] [X]

| Color Management | Displays | Adjustment | Color |
| General | Adapter | Monitor | Performance |

RAGE PRO TURBO PCI (English)   [Change...]

Adapter / Driver information

Manufacturer:	ATI Tech. - Enhanced
Chip type:	Mach64: RagePro
DAC type:	Internal
Features:	DirectDraw 1.00
Software version:	5.35-CD2
Current files:	macxw4.drv,*vdd,*vflatd,macxw4.vxd,macxdc

Refresh rate

[Optimal ▼]

| OK | Cancel | Apply | Help |

Control Panel

Figure 4-3.   The Adapter tab shows detailed information about the video card

NOTE: If your networked Windows PC automatically obtains its IP address (as noted in Step 4), you may not have any information on the Gateway or DNS Configuration tabs. If this is the case, your Windows machine is getting this information from the DHCP server that provides its IP address. Linux should be able to make use of the same service, so you shouldn't have to worry.

6. Click the Gateway tab to bring up the information Windows knows about your network router. Copy down the addresses of any gateways you see. These will be used when configuring IP networking in Linux.

7. Click the DNS Configuration tab to show the DNS configuration, and copy down the hostname, domain name, and DNS search order as you see them listed on this tab.

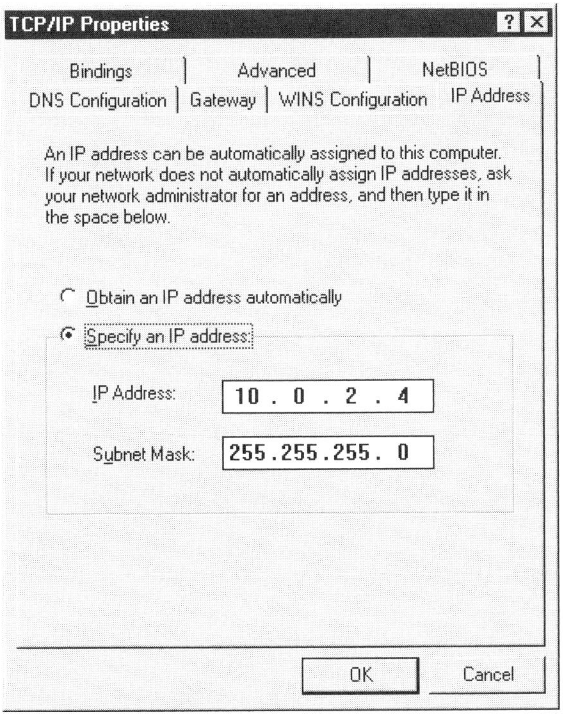

Figure 4-4. Obtain IP address information from the Network Control Panel

Finding Hardware from the System Information Tool

Not all systems running Windows have Microsoft's System Information utility loaded, but if you have the utility, it is another resource for finding hardware information. To start the System Information tool (if you have it), perform the following steps:

1. Click the Start button.
2. Select the Programs menu option.
3. Select the Accessories group.
4. Select the System Tools entry.
5. Select the System Information icon.

This opens the System Information tool, which is a little overblown for our modest purposes, but can be used to identify hardware configuration information. For example, Figure 4-5 shows the tool open to the multimedia components section, where the settings

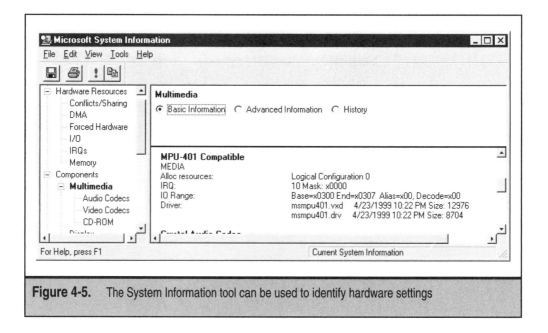

Figure 4-5.   The System Information tool can be used to identify hardware settings

for the MPU-401 Compatible sound system are available. The audio system is set to IRQ 10 and I/O address x0300 to x0307. If Linux doesn't automatically detect this hardware, having this information means you can tell the system how to configure itself.

Checking Hardware Compatibility

I can't stress enough the importance of making sure your hardware is compatible with the Linux distribution you're using. While the list of compatible devices is long, and the frequency of updates is increasing, your installation experience will be unpleasant if your vital hardware is unsupported.

The good news is that the Linux distributions will almost always tell you which devices they support. For lists of supported hardware for the distributions I'll demonstrate in this chapter, consult the following URLs:

Corel Linux   http://linux.corel.com/products/linux_os/hardware.htm
Caldera OpenLinux   http://www.calderasystems.com/support/hardware/
Red Hat Linux   http://www.redhat.com/support/hardware/

In particular, you should note that support for "WinModems" and "WinPrinters" is nearly nonexistent as I write this. Modems and printers that rely upon their Windows-based software to perform certain tasks just won't work with Linux yet, though Lucent has released some drivers for its software-based modems and open-source developers are working on the problem. If you have a very low-cost modem or printer, you might want to scrutinize its compatibility in particular.

Now that you've gone through all that rigmarole, it's time to commence with the Linux installation. The first Linux installation process I'll illustrate uses Corel Linux 1.0

NOTE: Booting Linux from an installation diskette or CD-ROM may set off the antivirus program in your computer's BIOS. If this happens, you'll get a warning message while the system starts up. In most cases, you'll be able to continue installation, but you might consider disabling the virus check—after you check the diskette for viruses.

INSTALLING COREL LINUX FROM WINDOWS

One of the easiest ways to install Linux is by using Corel Linux. This is one of several distributions that allow you to try out the operating system without even creating a Linux partition on your computer. If you just want to explore Linux, it's one of the least intrusive ways of getting started, because it doesn't require any changes to your hard disk layout: If you have enough free disk space in Windows, you should be able to install Corel Linux.

On the other hand, if you opt to install Linux on top of an existing Windows partition, which is how Corel accomplishes this handy little feat, you can expect some seriously sluggish performance. The only point to doing things this way is to see what the installation process is like and to play with Linux without buying another disk or partitioning things yourself.

Still, I'm going to illustrate the Corel Linux installation process because it's incredibly easy. If your hardware is on the compatibility list, your chances of installation success are high and the demands the process will place on you will be minimal. And you certainly don't have to install Corel Linux to a Windows partition; if you're willing to add a disk drive or have some unallocated space on your existing disk drive, it's still worth a try. The installation process is even easier in those cases because you don't have to configure Windows to be aware of Linux at all.

One tradeoff you make by installing Corel Linux rather than another distribution is that others tend to offer more application options than Corel does. But if your goal is to try Linux without worrying about repartitioning your hard disk or installing a new disk, I recommend Corel. If you're willing to repartition the system yourself, or to add a new hard disk (or let your existing disk be wiped clean), while you can install Corel Linux, you might consider OpenLinux or Red Hat, which are discussed later in this chapter.

What If My Computer Won't Boot from the CD-ROM Drive?

If you're using older hardware to install Linux, and if you don't purchase a retail version of Linux (one that comes with a boot floppy), you may run into trouble if your computer won't boot from a CD-ROM. If this is the case, first check your computer's BIOS setup program to see if you can set the system to boot from CD-ROM. If that's not an option, you'll have to make a boot floppy. Most distributions include the tools to do this from Windows. In Corel Linux, the process goes like this:

1. Insert a floppy disk—one that doesn't contain any vital data—in your computer's floppy drive.

2. Double-click on the My Computer icon on your Windows desktop, and then right-click on the floppy drive icon when it appears. Select the Format option from the menu.

3. In most cases a Quick format will work fine, so click Start to commence the format. When the format finishes, click Close to close the summary window and then click Close again to close the Format window.

4. Back in the My Computer window, right-click on your CD-ROM's icon and select the Explore option. Double-click on the Tools folder to open it.

5. Double-click Bootflop.bat to start the program, which will open in a DOS box. Be sure you've got the right disk in the drive (well, you've formatted it, so it's pretty much too late now anyway), and press any key to create the boot floppy.

6. The program will let you know which track and head is being accessed and will tell you when it's done. Close the window, and you've got your boot disk!

Installing Corel Linux

To begin installing Linux, close the Windows programs you have open, and then insert the Corel Linux CD-ROM in your CD-ROM drive. If your computer automatically detects CD-ROMs, you should automatically be presented with the Corel Linux Autorun screen. If you don't see this splash screen after a few moments, you may not have CD-ROM autoplay enabled in Windows. To commence with the installation, simply double-click on the My Computer icon, and then double-click on your CD-ROM drive's icon.

Installing Corel Linux is very easy:

1. To move along from the startup screen, click the Next button. You should see a screen similar to the one shown in Figure 4-6.

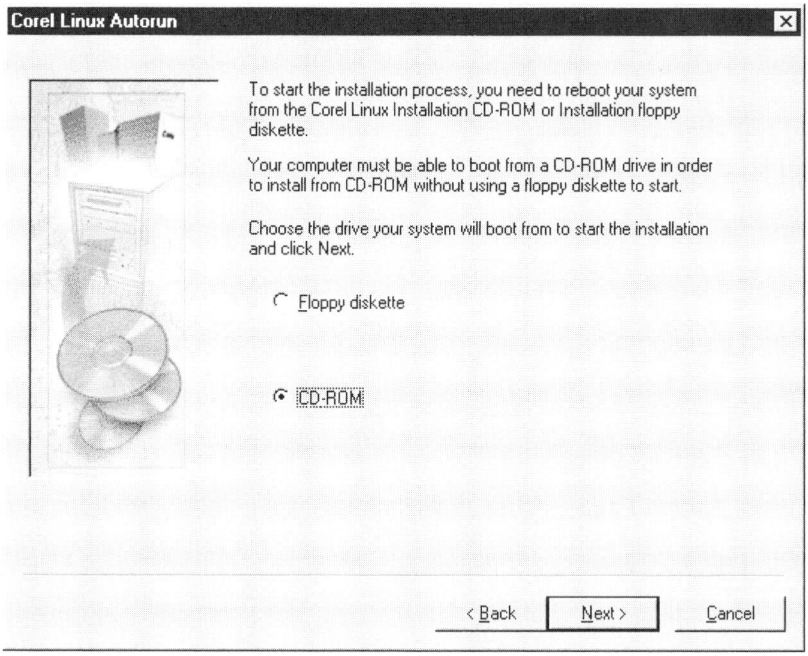

Figure 4-6. Choose the type of device to use to boot the Corel Linux installation

2. Select the CD-ROM option if your computer will boot from a CD-ROM. If it won't, select the Floppy option. If you don't know which is right, insert the diskette and use the Floppy option. The CD-ROM option has been selected in Figure 4-6. Click Next to continue.

3. Corel Linux will warn you to save your work. Make sure you've closed any open applications, and then click the Restart button.

4. Your computer should shut down and restart. If the computer doesn't boot from the Corel Linux CD-ROM, and you asked it to in Step 2, insert the installation floppy disk and reboot.

5. When the computer starts up again, it will display a startup screen. As the boot process proceeds, the screen will tell you the system is "Loading Corel Linux." Then it will add a message indicating it is "Starting Corel Linux." Finally, it will begin "Detecting Hardware."

6. Once that process is complete, the screen will blank out for a moment. You should see a message telling you the system is "Starting graphical install," and

then the license agreement screen appears. Read through the agreement, and if you can live with its terms, click Accept.

7. On the next screen, as shown in Figure 4-7, you'll be prompted for a user name. Enter a user account name—one word, in all lowercase letters—then click Next.

8. Next you'll be given the option of installing the standard desktop or seeing advanced installation options. Select the standard desktop installation.

9. Now you will see your choices for where to install the Linux operating system.

   ■ Take over disk (by wiping out the existing contents)

   ■ Use free disk space (by squeezing in some Linux partitions)

   ■ Edit partition table (manually adjusting the partition sizes)

   ■ Install in DOS/Windows partition (create virtual partitions in free space within the existing Windows partition)

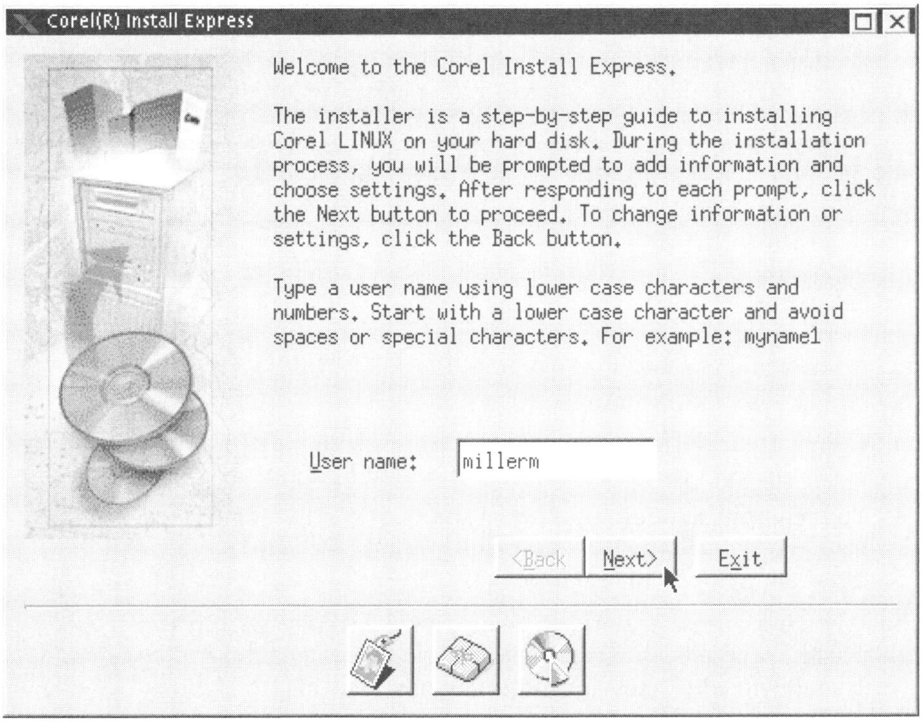

Figure 4-7.   Corel Linux prompts you for a user name (but not for a password)

Installing Linux to a Windows partition is slow, so if you've got free disk space, select that option, as shown in Figure 4-8. If Windows is taking up your full disk drive, though, select the last option and click Next.

10. If you have given it the go-ahead to create a partition, Corel Linux reports back with the partition size that it was able to fit onto your disk drive. You may want to adjust the size to leave more space for Windows, or you can just accept the default. Click Next when you're satisfied with the partition size.

11. When the next screen appears, it will summarize the installation options you selected. If they look like the options you selected, simply click the Install button to commence installation. The installation progress will be shown, but the progress bar tends to stall a few times during the installation. Be especially wary of a slowdown at 98% completion, where things slow down for a long time, even on fast machines. Don't simply assume the system has crashed; give it plenty of time to finish.

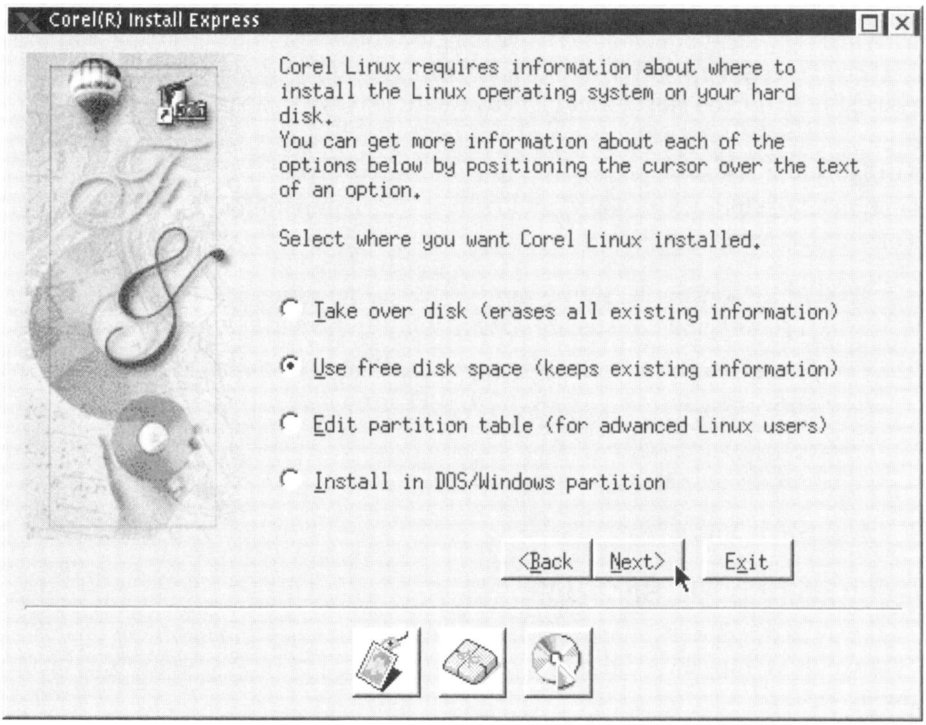

Figure 4-8.   Install Corel Linux to free disk space if you have space available

12. When the installation process has completed, it will let you know. Remove the floppy disk and CD-ROM, and then click OK to restart the computer. (Your CD-ROM drive should open automatically when the system goes down; take the Corel CD out at that time.)

13. Unless you opted to install on a Windows partition, the boot screen gives you several choices; select Corel Linux and press ENTER to boot into Linux. The system will then perform further configuration, which can take several minutes. If you installed Linux to a Windows partition, see the following section on "Getting into Linux from Windows" for more information on how to start Linux.

14. Once the configuration has been completed, you will see the GUI's login screen. There's no default password to get in as either root or as the user you added in Step 7. Press ENTER to log in as root, and you've installed Linux. We'll talk about configuring the X Windows environment in the next chapter.

Getting into Linux from Windows

If you were able to place Corel Linux on its own partition, it will automatically overwrite the hard disk's master boot record (MBR) and give you the option of starting Windows or Linux when you start up. But if you installed Linux on a Windows partition, this doesn't happen. So how do you start Linux? There are three ways to do it.

Starting in DOS Mode

This option tells Windows 9*x* you want to run in DOS compatibility mode and then starts Linux from that mode:

1. To start in DOS mode, simply press F8 while Windows is starting. This should bring up the Windows startup options. One of them is DOS Safe Mode—select it.

2. Doing so takes you to a DOS prompt; you'll need to change directories to the CDL directory, and run STARTCDL.BAT from there:

```
C:\WINDOWS> cd \cdl
C:\CDL> startcdl.bat
```

This will launch Linux.

Creating Startup File Boot Options

Another way of doing things is somewhat more elegant: you edit your CONFIG.SYS and AUTOEXEC.BAT files in Windows to provide startup options for Windows or Linux. Follow these steps:

1. From your Windows desktop, click the Start button, select Run, and enter sysedit.

2. The sysedit program allows you to edit your startup files, including CONFIG.SYS and AUTOEXEC.BAT. Select CONFIG.SYS first. It may be empty, or it may have entries in it already. If there are entries, add the following lines before them:

```
SWITCHES=/F

[MENU]
menuitem=WIN, Windows
menuitem=LINUX, Corel Linux
menudefault=LINUX, 5

[WIN]
```

This establishes a startup menu, defaulting to run Linux after providing a choice for five seconds. If you wish to change the default startup option to Windows, change the menudefault line by removing LINUX and adding WIN. If you wish to change the decision time, simply change 5 to the number of seconds you want the system to wait before booting the default option.

3. If there were already entries in your CONFIG.SYS file, add the following line after them. (If there weren't existing entries, just add this after the lines you inserted in Step 2.)

```
[LINUX]
```

4. Select File | Save to save the new CONFIG.SYS contents, and then select the AUTOEXEC.BAT file.

5. Enter the following lines before any entries that already appeared in your AUTOEXEC.BAT file:

```
@ECHO OFF
GOTO %CONFIG%
:WIN
```

6. Any existing entries would follow the :WIN tag. After them (or immediately after WIN, if there are no existing entries) enter these lines:

```
GOTO END

:LINUX
C:
CD CDL
STARTCDL.BAT
GOTO END

:END
```

7. Naturally, if Corel Linux is installed on a drive other than C:, you'll need to change the first line after the :LINUX label to reflect the correct drive letter. Save the AUTOEXEC.BAT file, and reboot your system.

Now when you boot up, you'll be given two choices:

▼ Windows

▲ Corel Linux

Twiddling the Startcdl.bat File

This option may or may not work for you, but if you're like me and get too distracted during startup to reliably press F8, or if you're loathe to change your Windows startup files, here's an option that works for me: Alter the MS-DOS properties of the Corel Linux startup file. Here's how:

1. Double-click the My Computer icon on your Windows desktop, then double-click on your hard disk's icon.

2. Double-click on the CDL directory Corel Linux installed, and then right-click on STARTCDL.BAT and select the Properties menu option.

3. Click the Program tab, and then click the Advanced button

4. Check the MS-DOS Mode box, which will shut other programs down when STARTCDL.BAT runs. Click OK.

Now when you want to run Linux, you can just boot into Windows and double-click the STARTCDL.BAT icon. This works best if you add a shortcut to your desktop by dragging the STARTCDL.BAT file from Windows Explorer to the desktop.

INSTALLING OPENLINUX FROM WINDOWS

Installing Corel Linux is incredibly easy—far easier, in my experience, than installing any version of Windows. But as I mentioned before, it's a little limited in scope, and it shows its version 1.0 nature in a few ways. A more established version of Linux is Caldera Systems' OpenLinux. Although it will ask for more input when you begin, it comes with more software and has a longer track record.

In the course of this second installation, I'll describe the installation of OpenLinux 2.3 on a system running Windows 98. This Windows system has a 8GB hard disk drive that is wholly used by the Windows partition (the C: drive). This partition is not full; the C: drive has well over 6GB of free space, so there's plenty of room for a Linux installation. OpenLinux comes bundled with a limited edition of PowerQuest's PartitionMagic, which allows you to shrink your Windows partition to add the necessary Linux partitions.

Preparing the Drive

Our first move is to ready the disk for installation. OpenLinux will automate this process, but we can help it out by tidying up the Windows partition first. We'll first remove any files we know aren't necessary, and then defragment the hard disk, check to see that there's enough space available, install the partitioning software, and create the Linux partitions. Those tasks are easily accomplished one by one.

Removing Unnecessary Files

If you're pretty sure you've got plenty of available disk space, you don't have to go through this step. If you're like most of us, however, and fill all available space with junk, it's a good idea to go through this procedure, even if it isn't strictly necessary.

Using Disk Cleanup   If you're using a version of Windows that includes it, the Disk Cleanup tool is an excellent option for removing unnecessary files.

1. Click the Start button.
2. Select the Programs menu option.
3. Select the Accessories group.
4. Select the System Tools entry.
5. Select the Disk Cleanup icon.

This will bring up a window asking you to select the disk drive you want to clean. Select the hard disk on which you'll be installing Linux, and click OK. The tool will then load with a screen similar to the one in Figure 4-9.

The list of file types Disk Cleanup can delete on your system may be slightly different, depending on the applications you use. To rid yourself of the detritus left behind by web browsers, applications that don't fully delete their temporary files, and files that are sitting in the Recycle Bin, check all the boxes and click OK. Disk Cleanup will check to make sure you want to do what you just told it to do, so click OK again. After the files are deleted, the tool closes automatically.

Cleaning Up Manually   If you don't have the Disk Cleanup tool on your system, you can do the same kind of cleanup manually. People usually have many recycled files and temporary web files, so I'll just mention these two.

To remove files from the Recycle Bin, follow these quick steps:

1. From the desktop, right-click on the Recycle Bin icon.
2. Select the Empty Recycle Bin menu option.

To remove temporary files from Internet Explorer, follow these steps:

1. Open Internet Explorer.

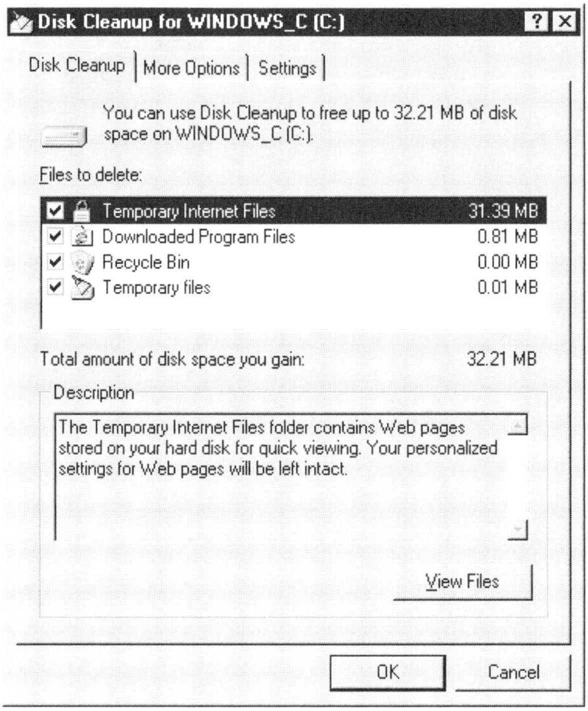

Figure 4-9. Removing unnecessary files with Disk Cleanup

2. Go to the Tools menu.

3. Select the Internet Options entry.

4. Make sure you're on the General tab.

5. Click the Remove Files button.

Neither task is particularly difficult, so lacking the Disk Cleanup tool isn't a terrible problem. Now that we have eliminated the useless files, we can tell Windows to organize the rest more efficiently on the disk.

Defragmenting the Hard Disk

The next step in the process of readying the hard disk for OpenLinux is defragmenting the hard disk. This procedure reorganizes the data on the drive so it's in an efficient order, packed at the beginning of the disk. Defragmenting the drive allows us to repartition the drive more confidently.

To defragment the hard disk, close any applications you have open, and then follow these steps:

1. Click the Start button.

2. Select the Programs menu option.

3. Select the Accessories group.

4. Select the System Tools entry.

5. Select the Disk Defragmenter icon to start the utility.

6. Make sure the correct hard disk is selected and click OK.

This will initiate the disk defragmentation process on your computer. Windows will rearrange the programs and data while you wait. If you wish, you can click the Show Details button to watch little squares, representing blocks of data, being rearranged on your disk. This slows the process down noticeably, but it's more entertaining.

Once the defragmentation is finished (which could easily take half an hour or more if you've got a sizeable disk drive and fragmented data), it will ask if you want to quit Disk Defragmenter. Click Yes and you're ready to move on!

Checking for Free Disk Space

In this next step, you just make sure there's adequate room on your hard disk to fit Linux in along with Windows. The minimum recommended available space is 800MB, and as always, the more space, the merrier.

1. Right-click on the My Computer icon on your Windows desktop, and select the Explore option.

2. When Windows Explorer opens, right-click on the hard disk icon and select the Properties option.

3. Look at the amount of free space on the target disk. If it's greater than 800MB, you should have enough space. If it's much less than that, consider adding a hard disk or removing some applications. But hopefully your disk will have ample space.

Running PartitionMagic

The OpenLinux eDesktop 2.4 package includes a CD-ROM labeled "Installation from Windows and Commercial Packages." This disk contains the "Caldera Edition" of PowerQuest's PartitionMagic software. The retail PartitionMagic product is used to create, delete, resize, and move many different kinds of disk partitions, but the version that comes with OpenLinux is focused on one task: Creating space for Linux on your Windows system. And although it's not as useful as the full product, it is easy to use and will work fine for the task at hand.

Installing PartitionMagic   Insert the "Installation from Windows and Commercial Packages" CD-ROM, and after the system detects the CD, you should automatically be presented with an OpenLinux 2.4 installation menu. (If this doesn't happen after a few moments, double-click on the My Computer icon, and then double-click on your CD-ROM drive's icon. This should bring up the installation menu.) Follow the steps described here to start the installation:

1. Click the 1. Prepare Hard Disk For Linux option on the first menu, then click the PartitionMagic option on the next menu.

2. The installation process will start; click Next to continue and display the Read Me file; when you've seen all you need, click the Next button

3. The installation program now allows you to change the directory where PartitionMagic will be installed. The default option will be fine, but you can change it if you want. Either way, click Next when you're ready to move on.

4. The installation program will allow you to add the PartitionMagic icons to the folder of your choice. Accept the default or change it as you see fit, then click Next.

5. Once the software has been installed, the program will want to restart the computer to create the Linux partition. Click Finish to let it restart the computer.

6. You will be prompted to remove the CD-ROM from the drive; do so, and then click OK.

The system will reboot and start the PartitionMagic program. When the system reboots, it tells you it is starting an MS-DOS-based program.

Creating a Linux Partition   When the PartitionMagic program starts, it displays a window like the one shown in Figure 4-10.

There are three main areas in the window:

▼   Selected partition identification information

■   Linux partition size

▲   Selected partition size information

Make sure that the drive letter that appears in the Drive Info For Selected Partition window is the one you want to resize. If it is not, click the Select Partition button to select the correct partition.

Once you've selected the partition to resize, decide how large you wish to make the new Linux partition. The options are 300MB, 800MB, 1640MB, or the Maximum Free Space. Because 300MB is really too small to play with, if you've got the option to allocate more space, do so. For now, even if you've got loads of space, I don't think you need to set aside the "maximum free space," which leaves you with merely 100MB of growing room on your

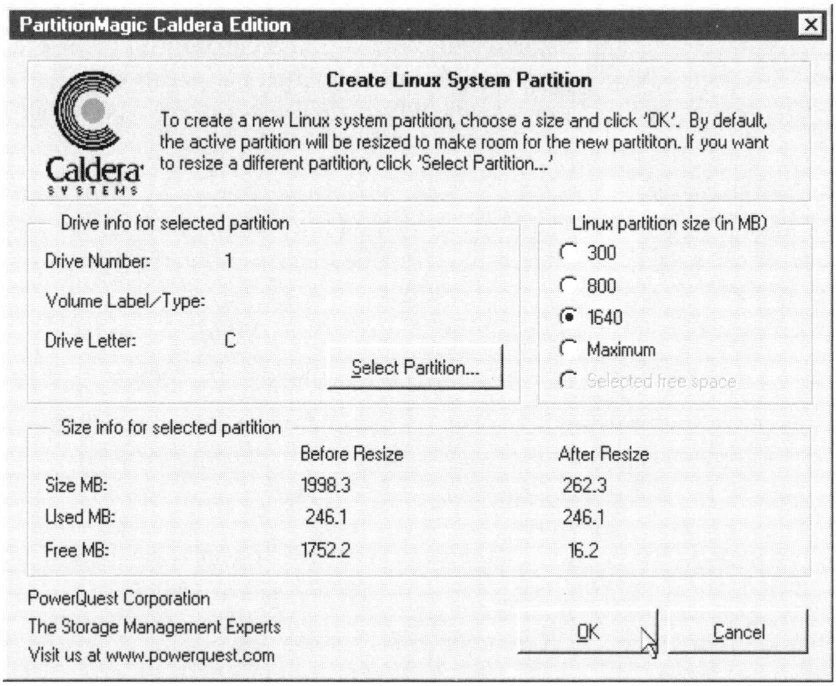

Figure 4-10.   Create the partition for OpenLinux using PartitionMagic Caldera Edition

Windows partition. That's not enough if you're going to be actively using Windows. I'd opt for 1640MB unless you don't have enough space, in which case 800MB is fine.

The Size Info For Selected Partition area of the window shown in Figure 4-10 shows the current breakdown of total, used, and free space in the Before Resize column and the hypothetical breakdown in the After Resize column. You can select different Linux partition sizes and see what the net effect will be on the size of your Windows partition.

Notice that in Figure 4-10, the 1640MB partition selected leaves only 16.2MB free on the Windows partition. This would seriously cramp your style if you ever wanted to actively use Windows again, so I'd only recommend it if you've already realized you never want to use Windows again. Later in the book, we'll look at ways you can access data from the Windows partition, while using Linux. But for now, decide how big you want to make the Linux partition, and follow these steps:

1. Click the "radio button" next to the desired Linux partition size.
2. Click OK.

3. PartitionMagic will ask you to confirm the resize; click Yes.

The partition resizing and creation will take place, and the progress of the process will be tracked onscreen. The program will inform you when the partitioning has finished, and it will have some instructions for you, which we'll cover in the next section.

Installing OpenLinux

So far we have used PartitionMagic to create the Linux partition on our Windows system's hard disk. The process should have finished and presented a Partition Creation Complete window.

Follow these steps to start the OpenLinux installation process:

1. Insert the OpenLinux 2.4 "Binaries and Installation" CD-ROM.

2. If your computer won't boot from a CD-ROM drive, insert the OpenLinux 2.4 Boot Floppy. (This is unnecessary if your system can boot from a CD.)

3. Click OK to reboot your computer.

The system will reboot, and a graphical screen will appear while OpenLinux boots from the installation disk. You will see several options, as shown here:

▼ Standard install mode (recommended)

■ VESA install mode

■ Cautious install mode

■ Expert install mode

■ Non-graphic install mode

■ Unattended install mode

■ Demo install mode

▲ Collect hardware data

Select the default, Standard Install Mode, and press ENTER or wait until the installation process begins automatically. You will see messages indicating that the kernel is loading and booting, and then automatic hardware and installation source detection begin, and the Lizard installation tool starts by opening an interactive installation screen.

From this first screen, select the language you wish to use, and click Next. If your mouse isn't working, it probably wasn't properly detected; you'll have to use the arrow keys to select the language, then use the TAB key to highlight the Next button. Pressing ENTER or the SPACEBAR will allow you to continue to the Set Up Mouse screen, shown in Figure 4-11.

The next screen allows you to set up your mouse. Because mice are usually automatically detected, this screen is used chiefly for fine-tuning. You may select the type of

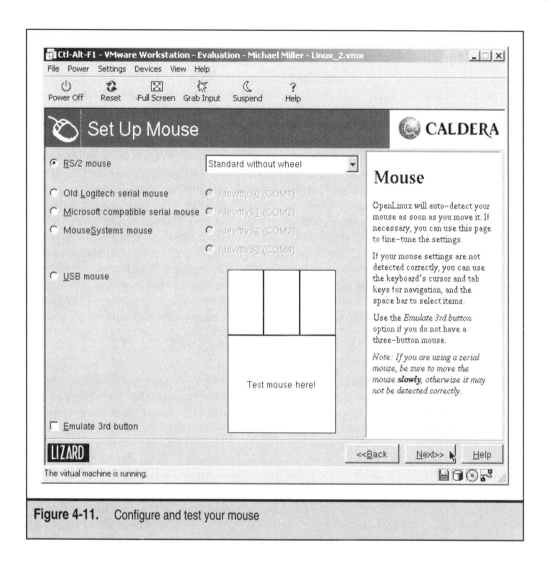

Figure 4-11.   Configure and test your mouse

mouse you're using, then test it if you wish by moving the cursor over the Test Mouse Here! area. Click the mouse buttons to make sure they work. If you're using a two-button mouse and you want to emulate third-button behavior, check the Emulate 3rd Button box. Then click Next.

The Select Keyboard Type screen allows you to select the keyboard you're using, as shown in Figure 4-12. There are several options for keyboard models. If your keyboard model isn't listed by name, just select the generic version with the right number of keys. (This may help: Most keyboards with the special "Windows" keys are 104-key keyboards.)

One Key, Two Key, Red Key, Blue Key

Many Windows users are accustomed to having two buttons on their mice. For mice in right-handed configuration, the left key is usually for selecting items via click or double-click, and the right button is for context-sensitive menus. And just as some Windows users have sneered at one-buttoned Macintosh mice, some Unix users sneer at two-buttoned Windows mice.

In Linux, the middle button is typically used to paste selected information into the current window. In other words, you select some text using the left button, then you point the cursor to the place you want that text duplicated, and click the middle button. This system works well, and it's particularly useful because drag-and-drop functionality is not very comprehensive in the X Windows world. (So sneer right back, Mac users!)

If your mouse only has two buttons, you can make it act like a three-button mouse by enabling third-button emulation. This just entails telling Linux that when you press the right and left keys together, you want that combination to act like the third button would. Note that most mice with scrolling wheels allow the wheel to be clicked like a button, so they work as three-button mice without emulation.

Then select the country mapping for your keyboard. A space is provided for you to type in to test the keyboard if you so desire. When you're done typing, "The quick brown fox jumped over the lazy dog," or perhaps a more profound message like the one in Figure 4-12, click Next to continue to the Select Monitor screen.

The Select Monitor screen provides three ways of specifying your monitor information. The simplest method is finding your monitor manufacturer in the list, clicking the plus sign next to the manufacturer name to show the available model numbers, and then selecting the correct model.

This isn't always possible, because as large as the monitor database is, there are many monitors not listed. In this case, there are two options. The better approach is to dig up your monitor's manual and find the horizontal and vertical sync ranges. This is standard information included in every monitor manual (and if you're lucky, it may be printed on the back of the monitor). Enter the horizontal and vertical sync rates in their respective boxes, and type a monitor name in the box to remind you why you set the rates as you did.

Not everybody has this information available, but there's still a recourse if you find yourself in this situation. Simply select a monitor description from the Typical Monitors entry at the top of the monitor manufacturer list. You should be able to use the same screen resolution you had in Windows.

When you've got a monitor description one way or another, click the Next button to continue to the Select Video Mode screen shown in Figure 4-13.

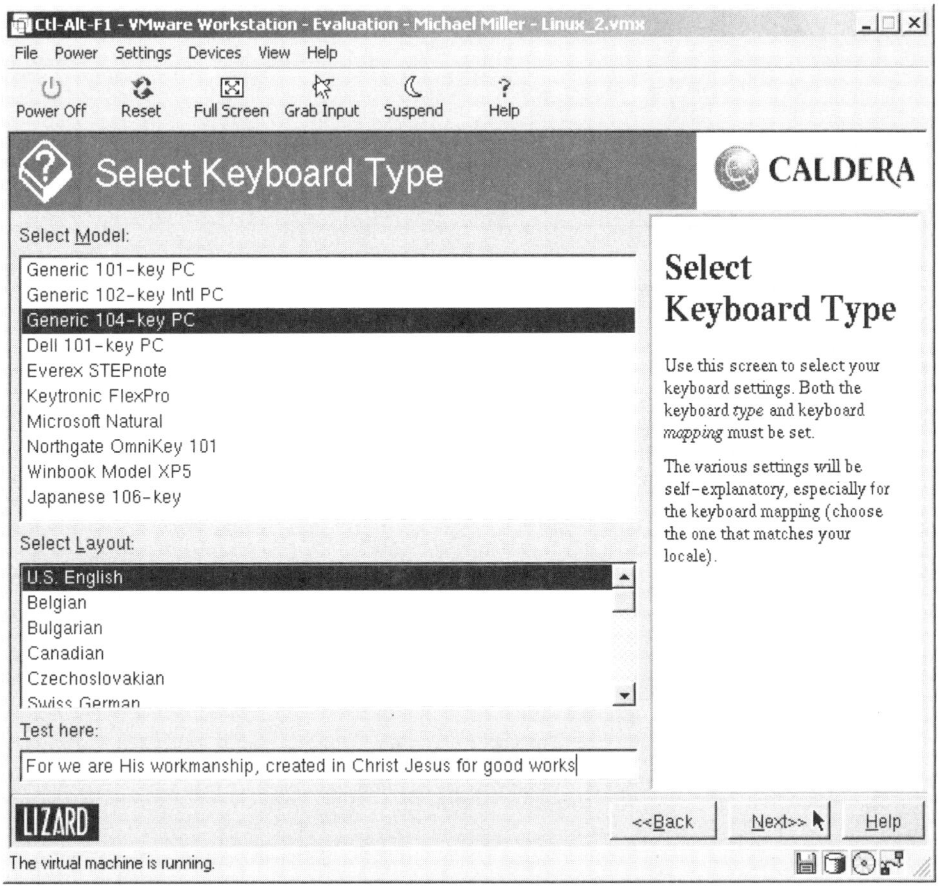

Figure 4-12. Select a keyboard layout

This screen displays the video modes compatible with your video board and monitor. Select the resolution and refresh rate you wish to use, and then choose the color depth you desire (I suggest that you select the highest color depth your chosen mode will support).

You can also select the size of the virtual desktop, if any. A virtual desktop is simply a desktop area that's larger than what your monitor is showing. In other words, if you select a video mode with a resolution of 1280 by 1024 pixels, and a virtual desktop of 1600 by 1200 pixels, you will have a larger desktop area than you can see at one time. If you move the mouse to one edge of the desktop, your view of the desktop will scroll until you reach the edge of the virtual desktop. Many people swear by this capability, but I find it a

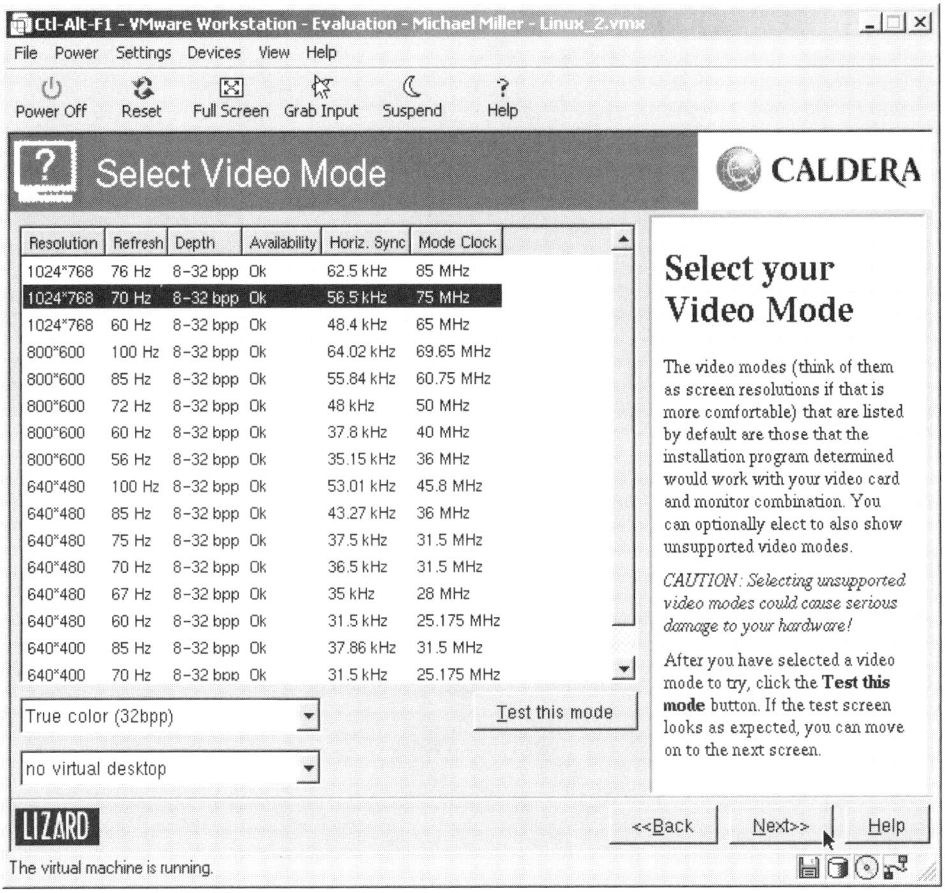

Figure 4-13. Select your preferred X Windows video mode

little disorienting; for me, it tends to induce motion sickness. I'm sure you'll have your own opinion on the subject.

Once you have the video mode nicely selected, click the Test This Mode button to make sure the mode you've selected actually works. OpenLinux will pop up a window telling you the test can be cancelled by clicking the left mouse button and that it will last ten seconds. Click OK to continue with the test.

You should see an X Windows desktop with a colorful Video Mode Test window displayed. Don't worry about the image being perfectly centered on your screen; if it is easily viewable, you're in good shape. Click Next to continue to the Installation Target window shown in Figure 4-14.

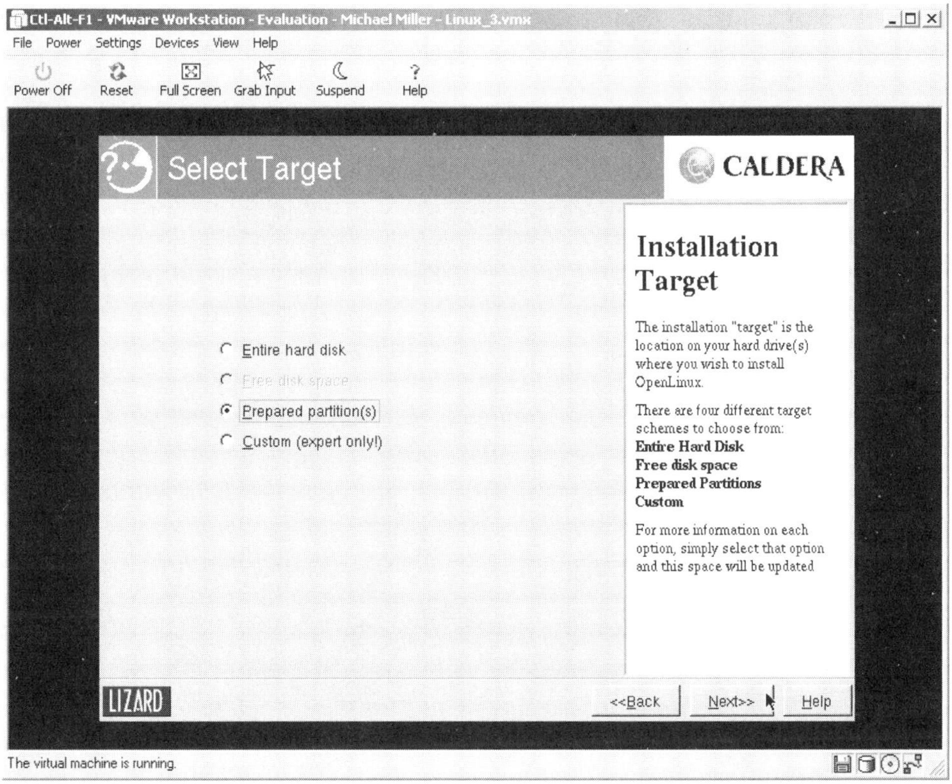

Figure 4-14.   Select the partition you prepared for OpenLinux

This window allows you to specify the desired destination of the Linux files. If you wanted to blow your Windows installation away, you could select the Entire Hard Disk option. If you're familiar with Linux partitioning, you can select the Custom option for more control over the process. But the installation process should have automatically detected the partition you created using PartitionMagic, and it should have selected the Prepared Partition(s) option. Be sure that option is selected, and then click Next to move on to the Select Root Partition window.

TIP: Before I go on, I should mention that if you select the Custom option here, you can set a mount point for your existing Windows partition, giving you immediate access to your Windows data when you start Linux. I'll show you how to do that later in the book, so we'll pass it up for now. If you decide to take this route during installation, please be careful not to format your Windows partition; just add the mount point (what you call it is up to you, but I'm fond of **/mnt/windoze**).

The Select Root Partition screen isn't much use if the Linux partition you created using PartitionMagic is the only one on the system. There won't be any choices for you; you should simply click the Next button to continue to the Format Partitions screen shown in Figure 4-15.

There should be two partitions: A root partition with mount point "/"; and a virtual memory partition. The virtual memory partition is more commonly known as a *swap partition*. When memory is scarce, the operating system uses the disk space in the swap partition to swap things in and out of RAM. Check to see that the partitions have the correct mount points, that the root partition is the size you specified, and that the swap file is as least as large as the amount of RAM in your system (preferably twice as large). Then click the Format Chosen Partitions button, but remember that once you do so, you can't undo what you've done.

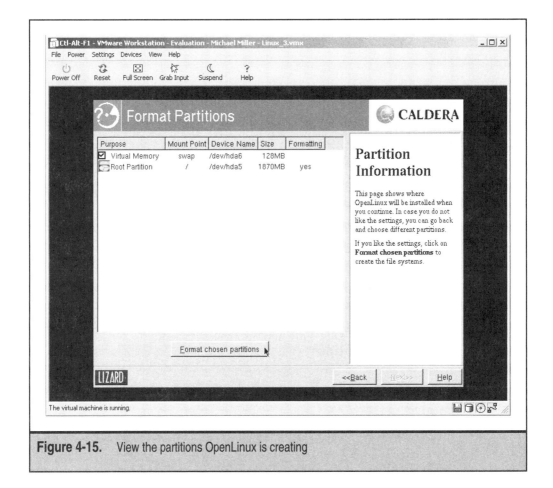

Figure 4-15. View the partitions OpenLinux is creating

If the root partition size is set to 0, click the Back button to return to the previous menu, and select the Custom option. Click Next to continue, and you'll see a partition list. You should see a root partition in the list; click on it and then click Edit. Set the root partition's mount point to "/" and make sure it's flagged as bootable, then click OK to continue. Don't alter the Windows partition. Click Next to continue to the Select Installation screen.

The Linux partitions created by PartitionMagic won't cause this problem, but if you do a custom installation, it's possible to get a warning that the root partition is not completely contained in the first 1024 cylinders. Unless the root partition is contained within the first part of the hard disk, LILO can't load the operating system, and that's bad. Spring for a second disk drive or for the full version of PartitionMagic, which will give you complete control over your disk partitions and help you avoid this problem. Another option is to ignore the error message, make a note of the root partition's device name, and plan to boot from the installation diskette. In this case, every time you start Linux, you'll stick the OpenLinux installation diskette in your floppy drive, wait for it to come up to the boot prompt, and then quickly enter:

```
boot root=/dev/hda1
```

If your root partition is on a different drive or partition, the last four digits of that line might be different. So make a note of the correct device name, then click the OK button to continue to the Select Installation screen.

This screen allows you to choose the packages you'll install on the Linux system by selecting your computer's primary function. Table 4-2 gives a list of all these options; if you opted for a small Linux partition, one or more of the options may be grayed out and unavailable due to size constraints.

Installation Option	Description
Minimum Installation	Ultrabasic Linux installation without applications
Recommended	Commonly used workstation and server packages
All Packages	The whole nine yards
Business Workstation	Common business applications, LAN, and security packages
Development Workstation	Programmer's tools
Home Computer	Dialup and LAN networking, Internet applications, games
Custom Selection	Reads a list of packages from a floppy

Table 4-2.   OpenLinux Installation Options

If you're experimenting at home, I'll cleverly suggest the Home Computer option, and if you're experimenting at work, I suggest the Business Workstation option. Don't fret too much about having to make this decision without knowing precisely what software is involved, as you can add additional applications later. When you've selected the configuration you want, click the Next button to start installation.

While the installation process is running, a graph at the bottom of each screen will keep you informed about its progress. In the meantime, several additional screens will appear, allowing you to enter information while the installation proceeds. It may be hard to navigate through some of the next screens because the installation process takes up much of the computer's processing power. If you get frustrated, you can just wait until Linux has finished copying files before you deal with the next few screens.

OpenLinux next asks you to set the root password. Remember that root is an administrative account with virtually unlimited powers. Set the root password to something private, retype it to confirm the spelling, and click Next to continue to the Set Login Name(s) screen, shown in Figure 4-16.

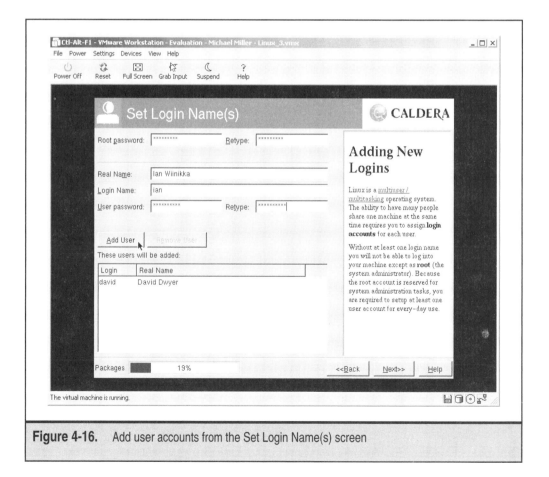

Figure 4-16.   Add user accounts from the Set Login Name(s) screen

Mere mortal users can be created from this screen. If you will be the only user on the system, you can just create your own account. If others will be able to log onto the computer, you can add them, too. The screen in Figure 4-16 has one user already entered and one more being created.

For each user you create, you will enter

▼ The user's full "real name" (so you know who they are)

■ The user's account name, or "login name"

▲ The user's initial password (twice to check spelling)

After you've entered this data, click Add User; rinse and repeat as necessary until the tingling sensation in your scalp goes away. When you've finished adding users, click Next to continue to the Set Up Networking screen, shown in Figure 4-17.

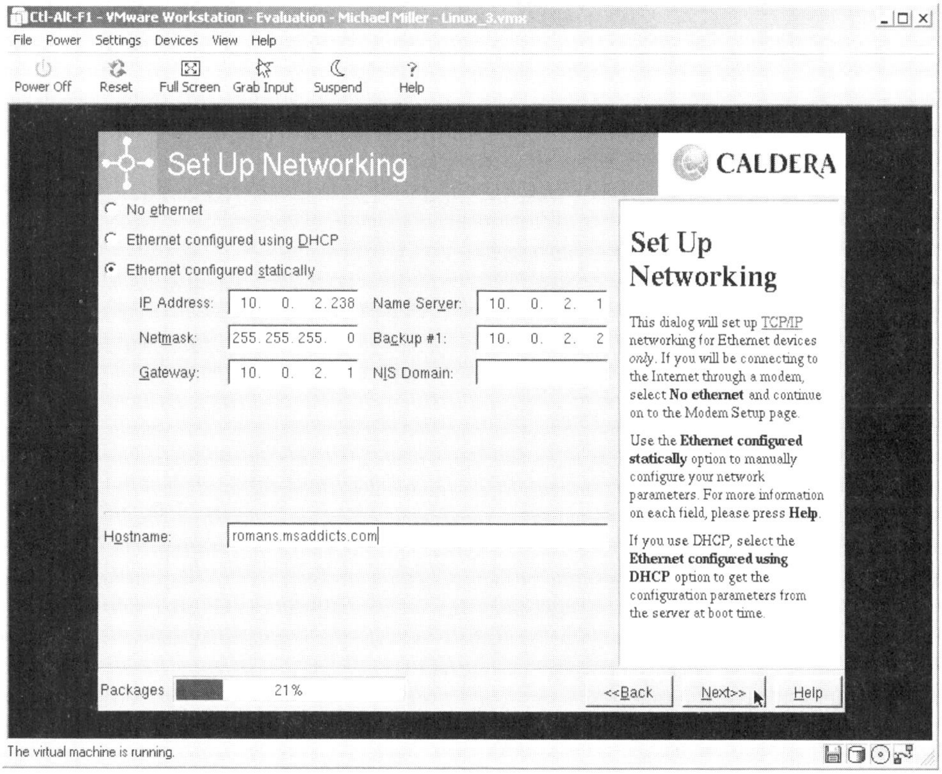

Figure 4-17. Configure your Ethernet networking as desired

If you don't have a network card in your computer, or if you don't plan to use it, you can select the No Ethernet option, and you're done with network configuration.

If your network automatically assigns TCP/IP addresses using DHCP, select the Ethernet Configured Using DHCP option. If your DHCP server is properly configured, it will provide the additional networking information without manual intervention from you, so you're done with the network configuration.

If your network uses static IP addresses, select the Ethernet Configured Statically option. Then enter the following information:

▼ An IP address for the system (and for heaven's sake, make sure it's unique on your network!)

■ The netmask used on your network in the Netmask field.

■ Your router's IP address in the Gateway field.

■ The IP address of your primary name server in the Name Server field.

■ The IP address of your secondary name server in the Backup #1 field.

■ If your network uses NIS, the appropriate domain name in the NIS Domain field. If it doesn't, or if you don't know what NIS is, ignore the NIS Domain field.

▲ Your host's "fully qualified" name in the Hostname field. Combine your hostname and domain name to enter the "fully qualified" name. In Figure 4-17, the hostname is **romans** and the domain name is **msaddicts.com**.

When you have configured networking as you want it, click Next to move onto the Set Up Modem screen (if OpenLinux couldn't completely configure the modem on its own). In this window, you'll be asked to specify the model of your modem; if your modem is in the list, configuration is a piece of cake. If it isn't, there are some generic modem settings at different speeds that you can try. In addition to the modem model, you can specify the serial port in the Device field. Linux serial ports are numbered differently from Windows serial ports; for example, Windows COM1 translates to Linux ttyS0, and Windows COM2 translates to Linux ttyS1. If you know the COM port of your modem in Windows, it's easy to designate its port in Linux. If you don't have a modem, you can indicate that in the Model field. When the modem is configured, click Next to continue to the Set Up Internet Provider screen.

The next screen allows you to configure a connection to an Internet Service Provider. While its database of ISP data is extremely minimal, OpenLinux allows you to easily add the details of your own service provider. If you have a dial-up connection to an ISP, follow these steps to configure it:

1. Check the Use Dial-Up Networking box.

2. Check your country and region to see whether your ISP is listed. Click the plus signs next to countries and localities to see what ISPs are available.

3. If your ISP is not listed, select the User Defined option and click the Details button. This will open a window in which you can enter:

   ■ Your ISP's name

   ■ Your ISP's dial-up phone number

   ■ The primary DNS server IP address

   ■ The secondary DNS server IP address

4. If your dial-up connection uses PPP (by far the most common type of modem connection), make sure the Speaks PPP Natively box is checked, and then click OK.

5. If you want to allow all users to dial out of the system, you can check the Save Authentication Information box and enter your login name and password for the ISP account.

When you've finished configuring the ISP information, click Next to continue to the Linux Loader screen shown in Figure 4-18.

You should see a list of bootable partitions, which should include the Linux partition you created earlier and the Windows partition you started with. Be sure to check the box next to each non-Linux partition with an operating system you wish to boot.

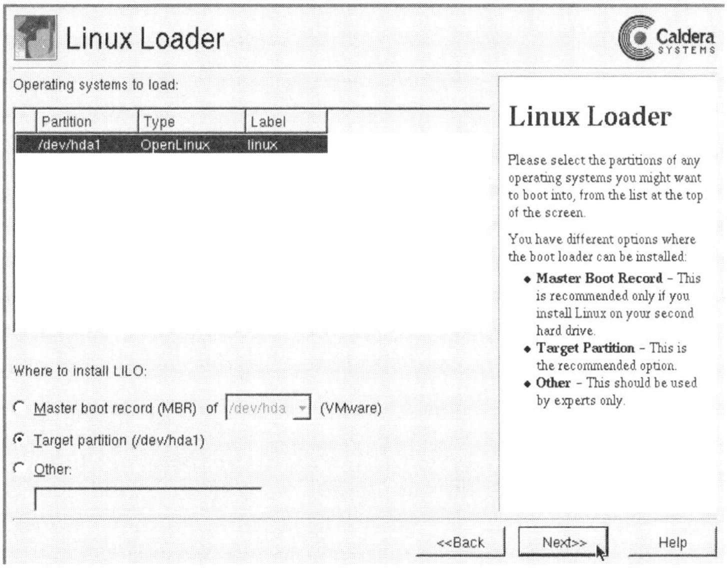

Figure 4-18. Use the Boot Loader to load Windows and Linux

The write master boot record area at the bottom of the screen allows you to select where the boot loader is installed: the Master Boot Record (MBR) of a drive or the Target Partition. For this installation, we don't need to touch the MBR. We'll be loading BootMagic later to make sure we can access Linux and Windows. Leave the box unchecked, and click the Next button to open the next screen.

If OpenLinux recognized your sound card, a Test Sound Card display will appear, allowing you to test digital sound and MIDI playback. You may also set the sound volume and balance between left and right speakers from this screen. Click the Next button to continue when you've finished amusing yourself.

The following screen, Set Up Printer, allows you to configure a printer attached to your computer or one attached to another Unix system on your local network. For a local printer, you first give the printer the name by which it will be known. Make it one word or an abbreviation; the default, **ps1**, is fine. Then select the model from the drop-down list of printers. If you don't see your printer in the list, you can check **http://www.linuxprinting.org** to see which printer it most closely resembles. Select the print-quality variant you like most, the port to which the printer is attached, and the paper size you use. Click the Add button to add this printer definition to the list of known devices, and click the Test button to make sure the printer works.

If you're on a network with other Unix or Linux systems already installed, you can set up an existing printer for use with your new Linux system. To do this, enter the name you'd like to call the printer, and then from the Model list, select Remote Printer. The only other information you'll have to know is the name of the print queue on the remote machine, and the IP address of the remote machine. Enter those in the Destination field with the queue name, followed by an ampersand, followed by the IP address, like this:

```
lj@10.0.2.15
```

When you've added all the printers you want to use, click Next to move to the Choose Time Zone window. This screen allows you to find a city in your time zone; when you click on that city, the time zone will be set to the city's time zone. For example, I live in the San Francisco Bay Area, which is in the Pacific time zone. San Francisco and San Jose are not on the map, but Los Angeles is, so I click on it to set my time zone. Alternately, you can scroll through a list of time zones and select one that way.

Since we'll be running Windows and Linux on the same system, and since you have probably set your clock to local time in Windows, select the Hardware Clock Runs In Local Time option. Then click Next to continue.

The next screen is the Entertainment screen, which rewards you for all the hard work you've done by letting you play PacMan. If you get to this screen before the installation process is done, you may find that the game is extra-challenging from time to time; when the system gets a little preoccupied copying files, you may have trouble controlling PacMan until it's too late. When the installation process is complete, and you have had your fill of dots, power pills, and ghosts, click the Next button to continue.

The next screen allows you to create a rescue diskette. It's not a bad idea to have one of these, just in case something went wrong. So insert a blank diskette into the specified drive, and click the Write Disk button. Once the rescue disk has been written, click the Finish button.

The system restarts Linux and loads X Windows and the KDE desktop environment. We'll talk more about X Windows in Chapter 5, but for now, we'll just log in to have a quick look before shutting down. Select the root user by clicking on its icon or typing **root** into the login field shown in Figure 4-19.

Type root's password in the password field and click the Go! button or press ENTER. This should open the KDE desktop with two windows open: The KDE file manager (kfm) and the KDE installation wizard. We'll deal with KDE installation in Chapter 5, so if you're in an all-fire hurry to get KDE configured, you can skip ahead and come back when you're finished.

When you've ready, reboot Linux by following these steps:

1. Remove the installation CD from your CD-ROM drive.

2. If you used the boot/install diskette, remove it from your floppy drive.

3. From the KDE desktop, click the K icon on the panel at the bottom-left end of the screen.

4. When the menu appears, select the Logout entry from the bottom.

5. A logout confirmation box appears; click Logout to confirm your intentions.

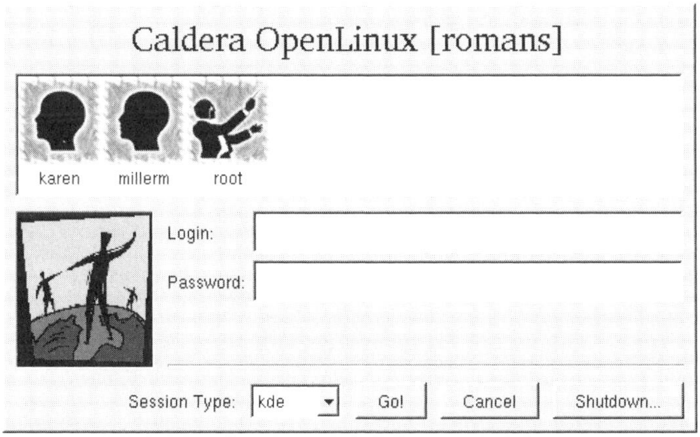

Figure 4-19.   Log into your OpenLinux machine as root before rebooting

This process takes you back to the login screen. To shut down

1. Click Shutdown.
2. Select Shutdown and restart.
3. Click OK.
4. When the system boots up, select Windows.

Installing BootMagic

Insert the "Installation from Windows and Commercial Packages" CD-ROM, and after the system detects the CD, you should automatically be presented with the OpenLinux 2.4 installation menu. (If this doesn't happen after a few moments, double-click the My Computer icon, then double-click your CD-ROM drive's icon. This should bring up the installation menu.) Follow the steps described next to start the installation:

1. Click the 1. Prepare Hard Disk For Linux option on this menu.
2. This time, click the BootMagic entry.
3. The installation process will start; click Next to continue.
4. The BootMagic software license will be displayed; read it, and click the Yes button if you agree to the license.
5. You will be presented with another description of the terms of the BootMagic license; type **YES** to agree to the license terms, and click Next to continue.
6. The installation will then notify you of the BootMagic installation directory, C:\BTMAGIC.PQ. Click OK to continue.
7. The installation program will allow you to add the BootMagic icons to the folder of your choice. Accept the default or change it as you see fit, then click Next.
8. The BootMagic installation program will ask you whether you wish to create a boot diskette. You should probably do this, just in case. Make sure the box labeled Yes, I Would Like To Create This Diskette is checked. Then insert a blank diskette in the floppy drive and click Next.
9. Be sure you've got the blank diskette in the floppy drive and click OK.
10. Be sure the next window contains the correct drive letter for your floppy drive and click OK.
11. Click Start to copy system files to the diskette. When the files have been copied, click the Close button to continue.
12. The BootMagic diskette contents will be copied. When prompted, remove the diskette, label the diskette **BootMagic Rescue Diskette**, and click the OK button to continue.

13. The installation program should now show you the BootMagic Configuration screen, where Windows and Linux should be listed, as shown in Figure 4-20. If you wish to make Linux the default operating system, select it in from the list and click Set As Default.

14. To set the startup delay, click one of the three options:

   ■ **None**   This option boots straight into the default operating system.

   ■ **Indefinite**   This option waits to boot until you select an option.

   ■ **Timed**   This option waits the specified number of seconds before booting the default OS.

15. When you're satisfied with the BootMagic configuration, be sure the BootMagic Enabled box is checked, and click Save/Exit.

The next time you reboot your system, you should see the BootMagic screen. Select the operating system you want to use, and you're off to the races!

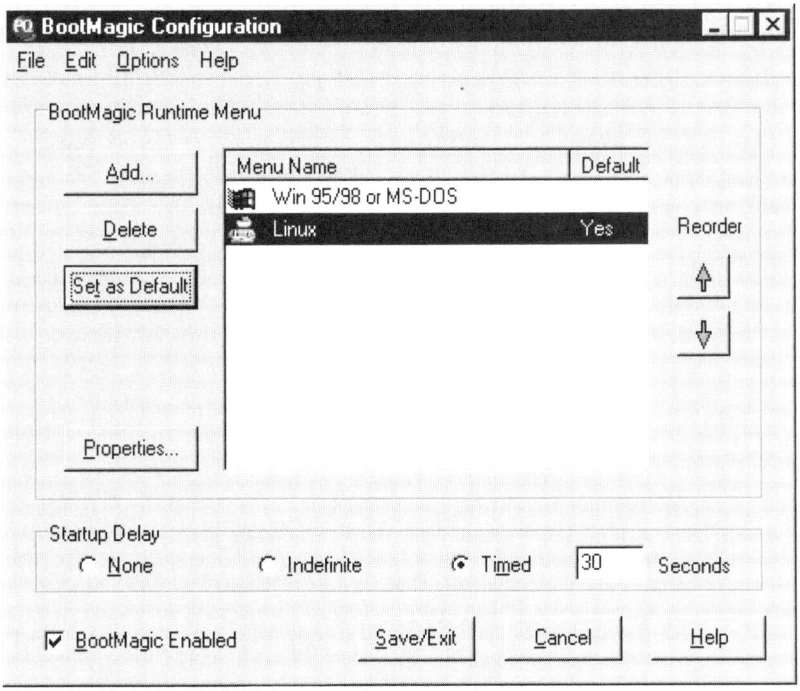

Figure 4-20.   The Linux partition should now be added to the list of bootable operating systems

INSTALLING RED HAT LINUX TO AN EMPTY DISK

In the Corel Linux installation I walked through earlier in this chapter, we installed Linux to an existing Windows partition, despite anticipating performance problems. In the OpenLinux installation, we used PartitionMagic to create space on a drive for Linux. But what if you already have available disk space? Perhaps you want to play it safe and avoid touching your Windows disk at all. Or maybe you just don't have enough space on the Windows disk. And there's always the chance you're so fed up with having your computing life run by Microsoft that you just want to wipe your disk clean and start fresh with Linux.

The type of installation I'll illustrate with Red Hat can be performed with every major distribution of Linux. And while I'll be using the graphical install because Windows users seem more comfortable with it, you should know that many Linux users prefer the text-based installation process Red Hat has used for years. That installation option, which is a prompted step-by-step process similar to the graphical process, is still available, and if you've got a spare hard disk to play with anyway, you might try that type of installation.

Initial Configuration Information

The first step is to boot your system with the Red Hat CD in your CD-ROM drive. If your system cannot boot from a CD, be sure to insert the Red Hat installation floppy disk. When the system boots up, it will present you with a text-based installation screen giving you your options: You can use the graphical setup, the text-based setup, or the expert-mode setup. We'll be using the graphical setup, so simply press ENTER to continue. If you wait long enough without selecting an installation option, the graphical process will begin by default.

A series of text messages will scroll across the screen as Linux boots up. Then a Red Hat splash screen appears, and the next thing you know, you can select your installation language. For me, this is English. When you've chosen the option you desire, click Next to continue.

Next comes the keyboard configuration screen, which is quite similar to the one used in the OpenLinux setup process. It allows you to select a keyboard model, a country layout, and a deadkey variant.

I have a keyboard that isn't listed among the options, so my best option is the Generic 104-key PC keyboard; choose the description that matches your keyboard model, or choose a generic description that applies. I trust you'll be able to decide which keyboard layout you use, but for some users in the U.S., the Deadkeys and ISO9995-3 options may be a little confusing. Unless you know you'll use deadkeys (where a character like ">" is typed before a letter to produce another language-specific character), or that your keyboard has the ISO9995-3 layout, don't worry about them and use the U.S. English keyboard.

The Deadkeys option is only needed if you'll be using deadkeys, so if you want, you can disable them if your language doesn't require them. Leaving them enabled should not cause you any difficulty. When you've selected the options you desire, click Next to continue.

The next step is selecting a mouse. Be sure to check the Emulate 3 Buttons box if you have a two-button mouse; this will enable you to select-and-paste by pressing the left and right mouse buttons simultaneously.

If you use a serial mouse, you may be a little disconcerted by the Port and Device names listed. Don't worry about them; as I mentioned in Chapter 3, Linux refers to everything as a file, so those are the filenames corresponding to mice. Select the one you want by looking at the list of COM ports—for example, if your mouse was on COM1 in Windows, it will be /dev/ttyS0 in Linux. If it seems clunky now, take heart that you won't have to deal with it very often, and you'll get used to it. Once you're at peace with your mouse, click Next to continue.

The next screen is a worthless welcome screen; the help text in the box on the left side of the screen tells you to read the manuals. Tell your computer, "Yes, Mom," and click Next to get to the next screen, which is shown in Figure 4-21.

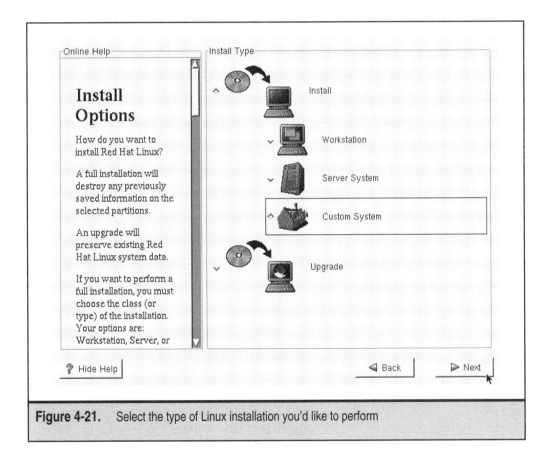

Figure 4-21.   Select the type of Linux installation you'd like to perform

We'll do a Custom System installation, not because I particularly recommend it, but because we selected pre-packaged configurations in the previous two examples. The complete list of options is described in Table 4-3.

> **CAUTION:** If you select one of the Workstation installation options, all Linux partitions on all your computer's hard disks will be deleted, and if you select the Server System option, all partitions, including your Windows partitions, will be removed from all your computer's hard disks. If this isn't what you had in mind, opt for the Custom System option instead.

If you do one type of installation and decide later that you would have liked some other packages, you can easily add the software you need without reinstalling. To select the Custom Systems option, simply click its checkbox and then click the Next button.

Configuring Partitions in Red Hat

The next screen allows you to choose to partition the hard disk using Disk Druid or fdisk. Either will work, but I think you'll find the Disk Druid approach a little more friendly, so select that option and click Next to continue.

The Disk Druid screen shows the existing disks and partitions available. If you have a hard disk that hasn't previously been used with Linux, you won't have any partitions available, and you'll have to add some. To add another partition, click the Add button, which brings up a window similar to the one in Figure 4-22. You can designate the mount point, the partition size, whether the partition can expand, the partition type (which you should set to Linux Native for everything except the swap space), and the drive the partition should be located on.

Installation Option	Description
Workstation	Installs commonly used workstation packages and X Windows into available disk space; allows you to select between the GNOME and KDE desktop environments.
Server System	Wipes the disk clean and installs server-related packages without configuring X Windows.
Custom System	Allows the user to determine how the disk is partitioned, which packages to install, and what GUI to use.
Upgrade	Upgrades from an earlier version of Red Hat Linux to the latest kernel and the latest versions of the installed packages.

Table 4-3. RedHat Installation Options

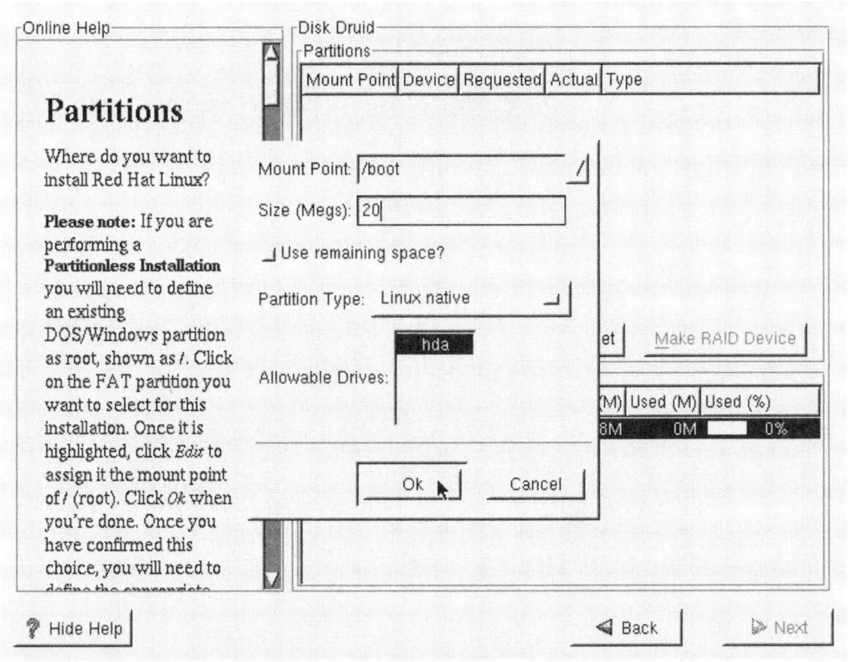

Figure 4-22.   Add a partition using Disk Druid

There are different approaches for allocating disk space on a Linux system, but at a minimum, you need a root partition and some swap space. A root partition smaller than about 1GB won't give you enough room to play with, and I suggest that you make the swap space equal to about double the amount of RAM installed on your system. Notice that in Figure 4-23 three partitions are listed: A 20MB partition on hda1, a 1200MB partition on hda5, a 400MB partition on hda6, and a 300MB partition on hda7.

At this point I should give you a quick refresher on what Linux calls different hard disks. Each disk drive on a Linux system is given a device name, depending on whether it's an IDE drive or a SCSI drive. If your system is properly configured (which is likely, but not certain) and has one IDE hard disk, that disk drive will be known to Linux as /dev/hda. Each partition on that disk drive gets a number. There can only be four primary partitions on a disk drive, which are numbered 1–4. One of these may be an "extended" partition that holds additional "logical" drives that are numbered starting with 5.

The partitions listed in Figure 4-23 are all on the first IDE hard disk; the 20MB partition is partition 1 (known as hda1), the 1200MB partition is partition 5 (known as hda5), the 400MB partition is partition 6 (known as hda6), and the 300MB partition is partition 7

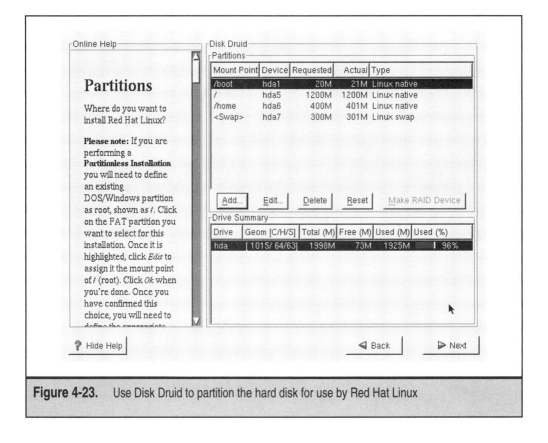

Figure 4-23.   Use Disk Druid to partition the hard disk for use by Red Hat Linux

(known as hda7). Notice also that the Type entry differs between the partitions. Each of the partitions is listed as *Linux native*, except hda7, which is listed as *Linux swap*. A Linux native partition refers to one that will use the standard Linux filesystem, ext2. The Linux swap partition is, not surprisingly, used as a swap partition (which, you may recall, can be larger than 128MB, even if Microsoft said it can't be).

What's missing in this configuration is a mount point for hda1, hda5, and hda6. Red Hat knows what to do with the hda7 swap space, but you'll need to tell it what mount points to use for the Linux native partitions you create. In this case, we'll make hda1 the /boot partition, hda5 the / partition, and hda6 the /home partition. To make this so, select the hda5 partition and click the Edit button to bring up the window shown in Figure 4-22.

Remember, the root partition is the top of the directory structure, and it's known as /. You set mount points using the box like the one shown in Figure 4-22, where the mount point has been set to /boot. This box could be used to set a number of different mount points or to alter the type of filesystem on a given partition. This allows you to segment different directories on the Linux system to different disk partitions, which makes disk management easier. Red Hat also allows you to designate a partition that can grow as needed until it fills the disk, which might be an approach if you really don't know how much space to allocate.

Click OK to return to the main Disk Druid screen, where you should now see the mount point for hda5 pointing to /.

If disk drive you use exceeds the 1024-cylinder limit (you can see this in the Drive summary section of Figure 4-23; in the second column it indicates the number of cylinders, heads, and sectors), you'll want to add one more partition to mount as /boot (like the one in Figure 4-22).

The /boot partition is a small partition (Red Hat recommends no larger than 16MB, but I like round numbers when I can use them) that contains the Linux kernel and other files needed while the computer boots. A /home partition is very useful for keeping user data separate from system files, and I strongly recommend that when you install Linux "for real," you include a /home partition. This will allow you to more easily upgrade your system, because you can leave the user data untouched and completely reinstall the operating system. That's a nice feature if you want to add a disk drive or try a new Linux distribution.

When you have at least a swap space, a root partition, and (if you need it) a /boot partition, click the Next key to continue. By the way, the installation program won't let you continue if you're missing the root partition, complete with mount point. Red Hat will let you continue without creating a swap partition, but you'll be sorry if you do, because your system's performance will be very poor. Try turning off the swap file in Windows sometime and then opening a couple of Word or Excel documents, and you'll get the picture. And yes, I've done stupid things like these before. I'm a curious person.

Red Hat may ask you whether it can turn on the swap space immediately to improve performance. By all means, tell it yes by clicking OK. The next screen asks you which partitions you want to format. The root partition (and the /boot partition, if you created one) should be selected. If you want to check for bad disk drive blocks while the formatting is performed, check the box. Click the Next button to continue.

The next screen, shown in Figure 4-24, allows you to configure LILO to boot Linux. If there were other operating systems on the machine, LILO could be configured to boot them, too. That's the Linux way: Do your best to play politely with everybody. Microsoft's operating systems, on the other hand, are the family of mean kids on the desktop operating system playground; you might sometimes feel lucky if you get them to cooperate amongst themselves, and you don't really expect them to do anything with the other operating systems but beat them for their lunch money.

The LILO Configuration screen provides several options. First, it asks if you'd like to create a boot diskette. This is a good idea in case something goes wrong with LILO, which happens occasionally. The box should be checked by default; make sure you've got a blank diskette handy, and leave it checked.

The second option allows you not to install LILO. You want to install LILO. Don't uncheck that box. Accidentally unchecking that box will make it necessary for you to use the boot disk you're creating.

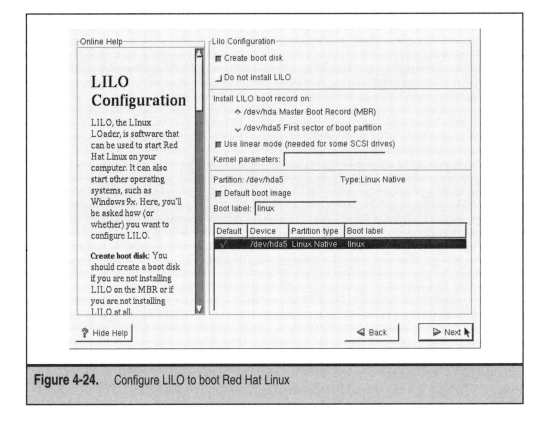

Figure 4-24.   Configure LILO to boot Red Hat Linux

The next option allows you to specify the LILO installation location. The Master Boot Record is a fine place to install LILO's boot record unless you're installing to a system with Windows NT or Windows 2000. Since this is a system with one blank disk, we'll keep the MBR option selected.

The Use Linear Mode option isn't needed for all drives, but it shouldn't hurt to enable it. Check the box to enable it. The box below it allows you to pass parameters to the kernel each time the system starts. That shouldn't be necessary, so leave that box blank.

In Figure 4-24, there is only one bootable partition listed. There may be more if you install Linux on a system with Windows already installed. To set the operating system you wish to load by default, just select the partition from the list, and mark the Default Boot Image checkbox. The boot label for your bootable Red Hat Linux partition will default to "linux," but you can change it to something else. Add a boot label for any other operating systems you plan to boot, and then click Next.

Additional Red Hat Configuration

If you have one or more network cards, you'll see the Network Configuration screen next, as shown in Figure 4-25. For each Ethernet card in your computer, there should be a corresponding tab labeled with the device name. In Figure 4-25, there's one network card with the device name eth0.

If your computer uses DHCP (you can determine that from the Network Control Panel in Windows, as you may recall), make sure the Configure Using DHCP box is checked. The Activate On Boot option tells Linux to start your network card when you boot the computer; most people want that to happen, so leave that box checked.

The remaining boxes specify settings for computers that don't use DHCP. You can simply add the information you copied from Windows; the installation program will attempt to fill in some of the blanks based on the information you add. In Figure 4-25, the host named **corinthians** is located at IP address **10.0.2.239**. When I typed this address, the installation program guessed that my netmask was 255.255.0.0. As you can see from Figure 4-25, I modified that mask to match the one used on my network, 255.255.255.0. Once

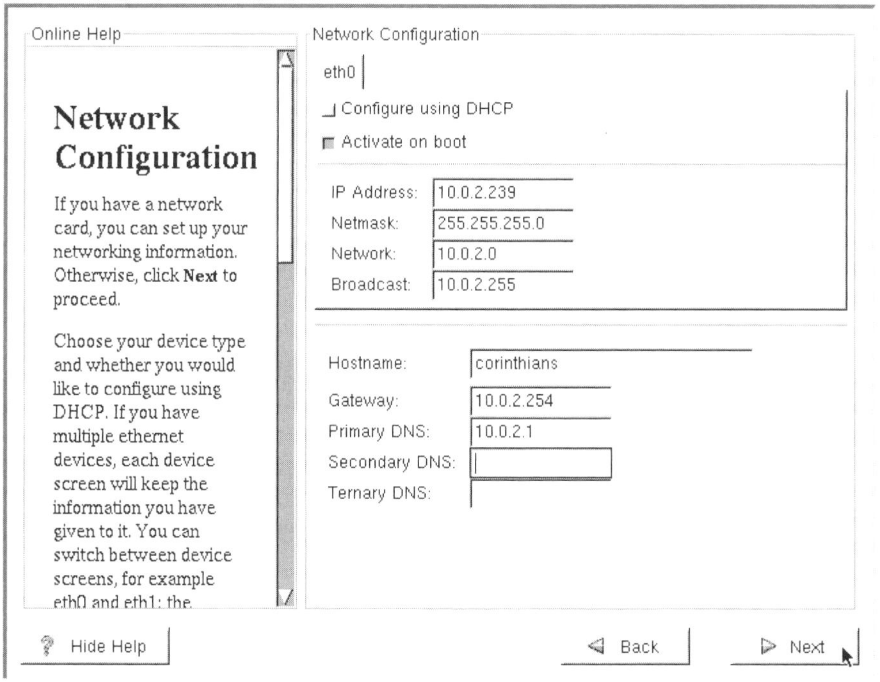

Figure 4-25.   Configure your Ethernet cards to communicate with the network

I did that, the program correctly filled in the Network and Broadcast entries. It also correctly guessed the Gateway and Primary DNS entries. I filled in the Hostname field, and the result is what you see in Figure 4-25. Set the IP address, netmask, and hostname, and ensure that the other settings are correct for each Ethernet card, and then click Next.

This brings you to the Time Zone Selection screen. This screen shows a map with many dots representing cities in various time zones. To correctly set the time zone settings for Linux, select a city in your time zone from the map provided or the list below it. If you have been running Windows on the system, it is doubtless set to local time, not Universal Coordinated Time, so make sure the System Clock Uses UTC box is unchecked. Click Next when your time zone is configured.

Next up is the Account Configuration screen, which is where you enter the root password and where you add the user accounts you plan to use. To set the root password, simply type the password you desire in the Root Password and Confirm fields. To add user accounts, type a user's account name in the Account Name field. Type this account's password in the Password and Password (Confirm) fields. And type the user's full name in the Full Name field for future identification. Then click the Add button. Repeat until you've added all the users you need, and then click Next. (If the Next button isn't enabled, it probably means you didn't type the same password in the Root Password and Confirm fields. Get it right, would you?)

The next screen shows the Authentication Configuration options. Most people can just leave the defaults. The Enable MD5 Passwords option allows long passwords, while the Enable Shadow Passwords stores the passwords more securely. Those are good things, so they should be checked.

The remaining three options are targeted less at home and power users, and more at network administrators. If you're on a network that uses the Network Information Service (NIS), you can enable it. If you're on a home network, you aren't using NIS. If you're not hooking into a bunch of Unix boxes on the same network, you aren't using NIS. If you're still unsure, find a network geek nearby and ask. Network geeks can often be identified by the short, brightly colored Category 5 patch cables they carry.

The Lightweight Directory Access Protocol (LDAP) is a standard for minimal directory services—that is, tools for managing information about users throughout an organization. If you are interested in using LDAP on your Linux system, review the Red Hat Linux Reference Guide for information on how to configure and use it. The Kerberos option is designed to authenticate users and data, and while it is a good way of securing a network from evil folk sniffing for passwords, it can be a very complicated solution to fully implement. So we'll ignore it for now. Once you've determined whether or not you're using NIS, LDAP, and Kerberos, click Next.

Red Hat Package Selection

The next step in the process is Package Group Selection. This is like shopping for the software you want to install on your system. There is a list of available package groups, some of which are already selected. You may add or remove them as you wish, but keep in mind that the whole shooting match will cost you nearly 2GB of disk space. Select from the packages shown in Table 4-4. The packages in the Recommended Packages column are ones I think will be interesting for you to run on a test system, but feel free to add or remove from the list as you desire, or as you're constrained by space—the recommended packages total just over 1GB of disk space.

You can actually select even more specifically by clicking the Select Individual Packages box, which shows you what individual packages are contained in each of the groups. You can read a description of each package and decide whether you want to include it or omit it. This is similar to the way a Windows installation allows you to select individual utilities to be included or omitted during an installation, and for most people, just taking the whole group is usually a fine choice in either operating system.

Recommended Packages	Other Packages
Printer Support	Laptop Support
X Window System	News Server
GNOME	NFS Server
KDE	IPX/NetWare Connectivity
Mail/WWW/News Tools	SQL Server
DOS/Windows Connectivity	DNS Name Server
Graphics Manipulation	Authoring/Publishing
Games	Kernel Development
Multimedia Support	Everything
Networked Workstation	
Dialup Workstation	
SMB Server	
Anonymous FTP Server	
Web Server	
Network Management Workstation	
Emacs	
Development	
Utilities	

Table 4-4. Select the Red Hat Package Groups You Want to Install

X Configuration and Installing Red Hat

Once you have separated the package groups into the sheep and the goats, you can click the Next button to continue to the X Configuration screen. The first screen shows you the monitor Red Hat has identified. If the hardware isn't correctly identified, you can select it from the list (by manufacturer and then model). Generic settings are also available if your monitor isn't in the database, and you can set your own monitor sync rates from your monitor's documentation (check the manufacturer's web site if you've misplaced the specifications). Then click Next to continue.

The next screen shows the video card configuration as probed by Red Hat. From this screen, you can change the video card driver (if Red Hat misidentified your card), correct the amount of video memory installed, select the default desktop environment (choose between GNOME and KDE if you're installing them both), and test the configuration to make sure everything works the way you configured it.

Checking the Customize X Configuration box on this screen will bring up another screen from which you can select the color depth and screen resolution you desire. Checking the Use Graphical Login box causes Linux to boot straight into the GUI you have installed. Use this if you don't expect to use the command line much. The Skip X Configuration checkbox is there in case you didn't select X Windows for installation on your system. You can also check it if you want to configure X Windows later. If that's the case, you can log in as root after Linux is installed and run Xconfigurator from the command line. Click Next to continue.

The next window just lets you know that the installation process is about to begin. Click Next to start the installation. You'll have to wait while the packages are installed, and unlike OpenLinux, Red Hat Linux doesn't allow you to play a game while you wait. So go walk the cat, take some cookies to a neighbor, or pop open a frosty root beer. Once the packages are installed, click Next.

If you requested a boot diskette, you will be prompted to insert a blank disk. Do so (or opt out by checking the Skip Boot Disk Creation box) and click Next. The boot

What About Sound?

Have you noticed that the Red Hat installation process hasn't mentioned your sound card? While other distributions (including OpenLinux, as we saw earlier) perform sound card setup during installation, Red Hat defers this step until after the system has been configured. I've had very good success with Red Hat's *sndconfig* tool, which is a command-line utility that generally auto-detects your sound card and plays a recording of Linus Torvalds pronouncing "Linux" to make sure it works. If you have a sound card, once your Linux system boots up, log in as root and run this utility.

disk will be prepared. Once it's done, eject the diskette and click Exit to reboot. If you installed LILO and chose to have Linux boot up by default, Red Hat should start when the system comes up.

Both Corel Linux and OpenLinux use the K desktop environment, KDE, as the GUI interface running on Linux. Red Hat has included another widely-used desktop environment, GNOME, with its past few versions, though it gives you the option of installing KDE instead or in addition. In the next chapter, I'll show you how to navigate and configure KDE, and I'll introduce GNOME as well.

CHAPTER
5

Step 2:
Configure X

The first step in freeing yourself from Microsoft's grasp was installing Linux. If you have succeeded in climbing that step, congratulations are in order. But before you get too proud of yourself, there is more self- and computer-improvement to undertake to continue your transformation. The second step is to believe that X Windows is highly configurable, won't crash your system, and could restore your sanity.

After you install Linux, many popular distributions automatically boot you straight into X Windows when you start your computer, thereby saving you the anguish of having to look at that frightening command line. But how do you control the appearance of the X Windows environment that has been created for you? And what do you do to reconfigure the GUI if your hardware changes? You look for answers here, that's what you do.

SETTING UP X

There are several options for setting up the X Windows software for your system. Not all distributions include all these tools, but most will contain at least one. Perhaps the most widely available tool is XF86Setup, which isn't sexy, but is fairly straightforward. The lizardx and Xconfigurator tools may be available on your distribution, but you'll have to check to make sure.

You should log on as the root user to run all three tools. If you aren't already logged in as the root user, you can become root by entering **su** at a console prompt and then entering the root password as prompted. And I'd recommend running all three tools from console mode rather than from within X, if only to avoid occasional unexpected results.

It's best to know six things before you start configuring X:

▼ Video board make and model

■ Amount of video memory

■ Monitor make and model

■ Monitor vertical and horizontal refresh rates

■ Mouse type and port

▲ Keyboard type

You should have this information already if you went through the installation procedure in the previous chapter. But if you're changing hardware, consult its documentation for specifications you don't know. It's always best, for example, not to guess at the refresh rates of your monitor. Guess too high, and bad things have been said to happen.

XF86Setup

The XF86Setup program generally accompanies the XFree86 files on a Linux system. Some distributions don't include the XF86Setup program (Red Hat, for example, wants you to use Xconfigurator instead), but most do. To run XF86Setup, log on as root, and from a console prompt, enter:

```
root@romans /root> XF86Setup
```

Use the capitalization exactly as shown. If the typesetter and I didn't misspell it, and X is already installed on your system, you will probably see the following message:

```
Would you like to use the existing XF86Config file for defaults?
```

As nice as this sounds, it doesn't always yield the results you want, so I'd recommend against using the existing file. Select No to continue. Next, you'll be told you're about to enter graphics mode. Press ENTER to start graphics mode.

> **NOTE:**   This handy X Windows survival tip may be useful even while you're configuring X: If something goes wrong, you can exit X Windows and return to the text console by pressing CTRL-ALT-BACK-SPACE together. This will shut down X Windows without saving work you may have done (or your X configuration information), so use it judiciously.

You'll see a gray screen with buttons at the top. Click the Mouse button and a screen of mouse configuration instructions will appear. They may or may not be helpful, so click Dismiss when you've read them or decided they're too confusing. Don't worry, the next screen's pretty simple, as shown in Figure 5-1.

This is the screen from which you can configure your mouse to run in X. Most recently built computers use the PS/2 port to connect a 2-button mouse, but you might still have a serial mouse, or one with 3 buttons. This screen gives you the opportunity to make sure X knows what it needs to about your mouse.

First, you want to make sure that X and your mouse are speaking the same language by checking the mouse protocol. You can do this by pressing the button at the top of the page that corresponds to your mouse. So, for example, if you're using a PS/2 mouse, you'll want the PS/2 button selected. (If your mouse isn't working yet, press the P button on your keyboard to change the selected protocol button.)

Next, look at the device the mouse is connected to. As I mentioned in Chapter 3, physical devices in Linux are referred to as files under the /dev directory. So, for example, if you have a PS/2 mouse, the corresponding device is /dev/psaux. If your mouse is attached to the first serial port (known as COM1 in DOS and Windows), the corresponding device is /dev/ttyS0. If your mouse is attached to the second serial port (the DOS/Windows COM2), select the device /dev/ttyS1.

If you have a serial mouse, you'll have to set the speed, or baud rate, that the mouse communicates over the serial port. The 1200 baud setting should work fine, and I wouldn't change it if I were you. If you have a PS/2 mouse, you won't have to worry about this setting; the option will be hazed out as shown in Figure 5-1. You can set the mouse sensitivity by using the Resolution setting, but I would resist the temptation to do so unless you

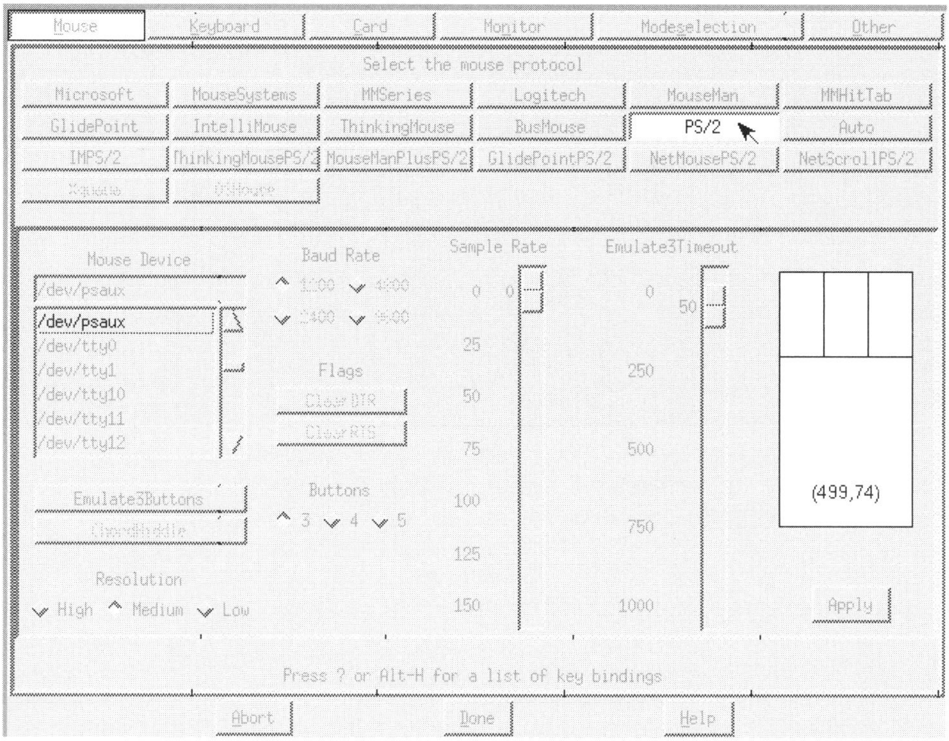

Figure 5-1. Configuring a mouse for X Windows

know what you're doing, as a case of "spastic cursor" may result, and that's never a pretty sight.

Finally, if your mouse has only two buttons, rather than the three that are generally expected in X Windows, you can fix things by clicking the Emulate3Buttons button. This allows you to "chord" the left and right buttons on your two-button mouse to emulate a third button. If you have the opposite problem and have more than three buttons, you can indicate a four or five button mouse by clicking the appropriate radio button under Buttons.

The rest of the options are primarily used to tune specific (older) mice. If you have a disability that makes chording the keys on your mouse difficult, you might set the Emulate3Timeout higher. This may give you the additional time you need to produce a mouse click from the phantom middle button.

Once you're finished with the mouse setup, press the A key on your keyboard or click the Apply button. Your mouse should be working; if it's not, you may need to do some more fiddling. If it is, you can continue on by clicking on the Keyboard button.

The basic information you supply on the Keyboard configuration page is the layout of the keyboard. One nice thing about XF86Setup is that as you select different keyboard types, it shows you an image of the selected keyboard layout. Most current U.S. keyboards correspond to the 104-key layout. If you change the settings on this page, press the A key on your keyboard or click the Apply button. Then click the Card button to configure the graphics board.

When you open the Card page, you'll see a list of the graphics boards known to your version of XFree86. Scroll through the list to find your specific card (they're listed by manufacturer, so to find a Viper 770 card, you'd scroll down to where Diamond, the Viper 770 manufacturer, appears in the list).

You can check X-related information for the card you've selected by clicking the Read README File button. In the event that you need to do further configuration with the card, you can click the Detailed Setup button. This allows you to see the X Server that has been selected, to specify additional settings for the X configuration files, and to specify details such as chip sets, clock chips, RAMDACs, and video RAM. Hopefully this won't be necessary; most of the hardware I have used has behaved well without specifying this information manually. Via con queso.

You don't have to "apply" the changes from the Card screen, so you can simply click the Monitor page to continue. If you have your monitor documentation (the Web can be useful for this purpose if you threw the manual away in a frenzied fit of cleaning), the horizontal and vertical sync rate values should be easy to find. If you can't find this information anywhere, give it the old college try by selecting a setting that seems reasonable. If you were running non-interlaced at 1024 by 768 under Windows, for example, you might try the same setting under Linux. If you have an old monitor, please be careful about

Uh, What Was That Card Called?

If for some reason you don't know what kind of video card you have (shame on you!), you may be able to gather this information from a console prompt. Outside XF86Setup, while logged in as root, enter

```
root@romans /root> SuperProbe
```

Use the capitalization just as you see it here. This utility probes your video card; if it recognizes the card, it will tell you what it found (though you may be on your own for identifying the amount of video RAM). If you don't want to exit XF86Setup, you can run SuperProbe from another virtual console by pressing CTRL-ALT and one of the function keys; I suggest trying CTRL-ALT-F2. This should give you a prompt where you can log in and run SuperProbe. When you're done, log out and return to your original console (since XF86Setup runs under X, try CTRL-ALT-F7, where the console running X is generally found).

exceeding the specifications. If you have a newer multifrequency monitor, this shouldn't be as critical.

Once you're done with the Monitor page, move on to the Modeselection page. Here you may specify the resolutions you want to support under X Windows. You can select multiple resolutions (once you start X Windows, you'll be able to cycle through these values using the CTRL-ALT-+ key combination). You may also select one color depth, which sets the number of colors displayed. The 8bpp mode uses 8-bits per pixel and provides 256 colors. The 16bpp mode provides 64K colors (a mode Windows often calls *High Color*), while the 24bpp and 32bpp modes generally correspond to what's called *True Color* under Windows. Using greater color depth, in general, allows you to view more colors under X but requires greater video resources (more video RAM, for example). Another factor you might consider is that some programs want to be viewed with more or fewer colors. For example, several of the Loki Entertainment Software games I use—for research purposes only, of course—like a 16bpp setting. So I give it to them.

You could now click the Other button to view the options on that page, but they're not ones people generally wish to change, so I'll pass by them. Once you've selected the modes you wish to use, you can click the Done button to try starting X Windows with your new configuration settings. After you click Done, XF86Setup tells you it will try to start X using the configuration information you just gave it. Click the Okay button and XFree86 should start in a few moments. It will be an ugly gray color, but don't worry about that.

When X starts, you will see a message indicating that your X Server is running. The screen allows you to tune the way the image displays on your screen, using a tool called xvidtune. Quite frankly, if you've got a recent monitor, it's much easier to use the resizing tools built into the monitor to adjust the size and positioning of the display. If you've configured the same resolution as you used in Windows, you probably won't need to do any image adjustment.

You can also abort the X configuration by clicking the Abort button or by pressing CTRL-ALT-BACKSPACE, but if things look right, click the Save The Configuration And Exit button instead. You'll be sent back to the console prompt. Since you're logged in as root, you should log out and log back in with your regular user account. Then continue to the section called "Starting X" later in this chapter.

Lizardx

As root, from a console prompt, you may start lizardx by entering **lizardx** with capitalization exactly as shown. OpenLinux will start X Windows for you, and everything should look very familiar. The Caldera folks smartly made the X configuration process look the same whether you're installing it for the first time or the tenth time. I'll describe each screen as I did in Chapter 4, but you'll have to go back to the Install OpenLinux section of that chapter if you want to see screen captures from the process.

The Set Up Mouse screen appears first, allowing you to configure your mouse if need be. You may select the type of mouse you're using, then test it by moving the cursor over the Test Mouse Here! area. Click the mouse buttons to make sure they work. If you're us-

Configuring XFree86 4

While running XF86Setup used to be mandatory unless your Linux distribution included another tool, that's no longer the case if you use XFree86 4.0.x. The latest versions of the X Window System incorporate a configuration mode that configures things far more automatically than that. However, many available distributions don't yet use XFree86 4, which is more powerful than its predecessor, but may not be as stable.

You can determine which version of XFree86 you're using by running the following command from a console prompt or xterm:

```
millerm@romans ~> XFree86 -version
```

This will tell you the version number and build date. If you're using a distribution that includes XFree86 4, it can be configured by the root user with the following command from the command line:

```
root@romans /root> XFree86 -configure
```

This will generate a configuration file, called XF86Config.new, in the current user's home directory. You can test this configuration by running the following command:

```
root@romans /root> XFree86 -xf86config /root/XF86Config.new
```

If this results in an X Windows session that looks good, the root user can replace the existing configuration file with the new one (saving the old one just in case):

```
root@romans /root> cd /etc/X11/
root@romans /etc/X11> mv XF86Config XF86Config.orig
root@romans /etc/X11> cp /root/XF86Config.new ./XF86Config
```

ing a two-button mouse and you want to emulate third-button behavior, check the Emulate 3rd Button box. Then click Next.

The Select Keyboard Type screen gives you the chance to select the keyboard layout and country mapping. A space is provided for you to type in to test the keyboard if you need to check on things. Click Next to continue.

The Select Video Card screen is really where we wanted to go, since it's where we can select a new video card. I had trouble finding video adapters that didn't work, but I tend to read the compatibility lists vendors provide. If the card has been correctly identified, whether by you or by OpenLinux, you should click the Probe button gather clock and memory information.

A screen pops up telling you the screen may go black for a moment before returning. Click the Probe button to continue. Once the probe is complete, you should see a message saying the probing occurred successfully. Click OK to clear that box and see what information has been probed. If you think the amount of video RAM is incorrectly detected, set the amount manually. Then click the Next button.

The Select Monitor screen that appears next allows you to select your monitor from a list by manufacturer and model. If your monitor isn't listed, find the horizontal and vertical sync ranges from your monitor's manual or the manufacturer's web site. Enter this information if you can get it, or select a monitor description from the Typical Monitors entry at the top of the monitor manufacturer list. Click the Next button to continue.

The Select Video Mode screen displays the video modes compatible with your video board and monitor. Select the desired resolution, refresh rate, and color depth. If you want to create a virtual desktop, you can enable it here. Click the Test This Mode button to make sure the selected mode works.

A pop-up window will indicate that test can be cancelled by clicking the left mouse button, and that it will last ten seconds. Click OK to continue with the test. You should see an X Windows desktop with a colorful Video Mode Test window displayed.

When you return to the Select Video Mode screen, click the Finish button if everything worked right. (If it didn't, use the Back buttons to reconfigure things so they work.) You'll see a message pop up telling you that you'll have to logout and restart the X Server to incorporate the new settings. Click OK to continue.

You'll be dropped back to the console prompt, from which you can restart the system or just start right into your window manager by running startx.

Xconfigurator

The Red Hat distribution of Linux, and many of the distributions that are derived from it, include another tool for configuring XFree86 semi-automatically. As root, from a console prompt, you may start Xconfigurator by entering the following command, with capitalization exactly as shown:

```
root@romans /root> Xconfigurator
```

The Xconfigurator opens with an information screen telling you about the underlying file that will be modified when you run the tool. Select OK and press ENTER to continue.

The next screen tells you which video card the system identified through probing. If the result doesn't look outrageous, select OK and press ENTER to continue.

On the next screen, you're given a chance to select your monitor from the list Xconfigurator knows. Scroll through the list to find your monitor's listing; if it's not in the list, choose the Custom option at the top of the list to be given the opportunity to add the vertical and horizontal sync frequencies for your monitor. Once you've got the right monitor selected, select OK and press ENTER to continue.

Next, you'll be notified that Xconfigurator will probe for PCI video boards. Don't be worried if you have an AGP video board; those will be identified, too. This screen also informs you that the system could lock up during probing, but this is unlikely if you have a reasonably recent video card. Select Probe and press ENTER to continue.

You'll get one more warning that the probing is about to begin. This one lets you know that the screen may blink several times as probing takes place. Press ENTER to continue.

Successful probing results in the Xconfigurator selecting a default resolution and color depth setting for you. Xconfigurator tends to select the highest resolution and color depth possible with your video card, and if the result is okay with you, select Use Default and press ENTER.

If you'd rather select different values than the default Xconfigurator chose for you, select Let Me Choose and press ENTER. This brings up a screen like the one shown in Figure 5-2. As Figure 5-2 indicates, you can choose multiple resolutions from multiple color depths if you wish. When you've selected the combinations you want, select OK and press ENTER.

The next screen informs you that X will be started so the configuration may be tested. When X comes up, it will bring up dialog box. If you can read the text in the box, click Yes. If you can't, Xconfigurator will time out in 10 seconds and you can try running it again.

Once you click the box to affirm that X came up successfully, Xconfigurator will ask if you want to have X start automatically when you start the computer. I don't like doing this because it adds time to the boot process when I'm doing maintenance on a system. You may not have any reason to hang out at the console prompt, though, and if you don't,

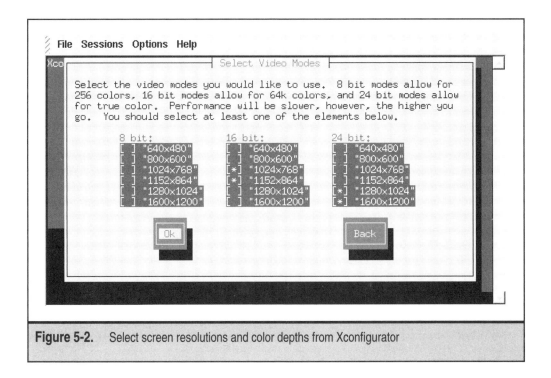

Figure 5-2. Select screen resolutions and color depths from Xconfigurator

there's no real reason not to have X start automatically. Click Yes to start X when you start the computer, and No to boot to a console prompt instead.

There's one more dialog box that appears after you've made that selection. This box tells you the name of the modified file, tells you how to change between resolutions (CTRL-ALT-+) and how to kill X heavy-handedly (CTRL-ALT-BACKSPACE). It also refers you to XFree86 documentation. Once you've read the notice, click OK to continue. Continue to the "Starting X" section below to start X.

STARTING X

This task isn't very difficult once you know what to do, but it isn't always mentioned in the documentation. Many distributions assume that you'll be starting the desktop manager automatically whenever you start Linux, and others assume you already know how to start X. Here's how you do it:

1. Log in with your ordinary user name at a console prompt.

2. At the prompt, enter the following command:

```
millerm@romans /home/millerm> startx
```

Configuration Files

X Windows should appear using the window manager you've specified. If you're interested in digging a little deeper, you can start by looking at the startx file itself, which is a shell script that starts X Windows based on certain startup files. It is usually found in a di-

---

Behind the Scenes

All three of these tools, and others like them, modify a configuration file known as XF86Config. This file is most often found in /etc/X11 or /usr/X11R6/lib/X11 (and sometimes there is a link from one location to the other). This file contains the information XFree86 uses to respond to your keyboard and mouse and to tell your graphics subsystem what to do. It's a text file, so you can browse it using a "pager" (a program used to read a page of text at a time), like this:

```
root@romans /root> less /etc/X11/XF86Config
```

If you're interested in tweaking your configuration, this file is the place to do it. Documentation for XFree86 is normally found in /usr/X11R6/lib/X11/doc, and there are some Linux-HOWTO documents available on the subject as well (see Appendix A for more information on the HOWTO documents and where to find them).

rectory called /usr/X11, but you can locate it by entering **which startx** from the console or from an xterm.

One common place for doing individualized X Windows configuration is the .xinitrc file found in each user's home directory. Because this filename starts with a period, it is normally hidden, so you'll have to use **ls -a** in your home directory to see the file. The file, if it exists, can specify keyboard mappings, windows to open when X starts, and similar configuration information.

Some desktop managers, notably KDE and GNOME, have their own configuration directories. Look for these in your home directory; they are also hidden because they start with periods: .kde and .gnome.

NOT STARTING X

If you opted to start X automatically when your computer boots up, you don't have to worry about using the startx command, because you'll automatically get a graphical login screen and will be taken immediately into X Windows when you log in. That's fine in most cases, but there are times you may want to start at the console prompt. For example, if you change your video card, you'll have to reconfigure X. Your new card probably won't be compatible with your old X Windows configuration, so you might have to start up in a non-graphical mode to configure it.

Personally, I prefer to start in non-graphical mode because sometimes I want to do some work from the console prompt and don't need X open. If I'm configuring a new system, for example, I usually rebuild the kernel to suit my needs, and then reboot. I don't need X up to do the kernel rebuild (though you can rebuild it from X, and I'll show you how in Chapter 6), and I don't want to wait for X to load and unload.

If you decide you don't want to start in X, you can tell it not to stop. Check your distribution's documentation for specific information on how to do this, but here's a common method:

1. Using a text editor, open /etc/inittab.
2. Locate the line that says id:5:initdefault:.
3. Change the line to read **id:3:initdefault:** (change the **5** to **3**)
4. Save the file.

After the system reboots, it will not immediately start X Windows. For those who care, that's because we've changed the runlevel from 5 (multiuser-capable with X Windows) to 3 (multiuser capable in console mode). Easy, huh?

CHANGING APPEARANCES

Now that you're familiar with ways of configuring and starting X Windows in Linux, it's time to get to the fun stuff: Tweaking the look and feel of your desktop. There are many different window managers and thus many different ways of making things look just the way you want them, but I'll describe common changes for the two commonly used and widely distributed desktop environments: KDE and GNOME.

KDE Control Panel

I'm partial to KDE, and I think it's the best choice for users who are used to the Windows interface. This revelation may spark hot fires of protest from the many GNOME supporters out there, but that's just a chance I'll have to take.

The tool used to configure KDE is known as the KDE Control Center. It's similar in principle to the Windows Control Panel, though it looks a little bit different. The Control Center, as shown in Figure 5-3, has a panel on the left-hand side with a hierarchy of options. The contents of the right-hand panel change to present you with the configuration choices for the selected option.

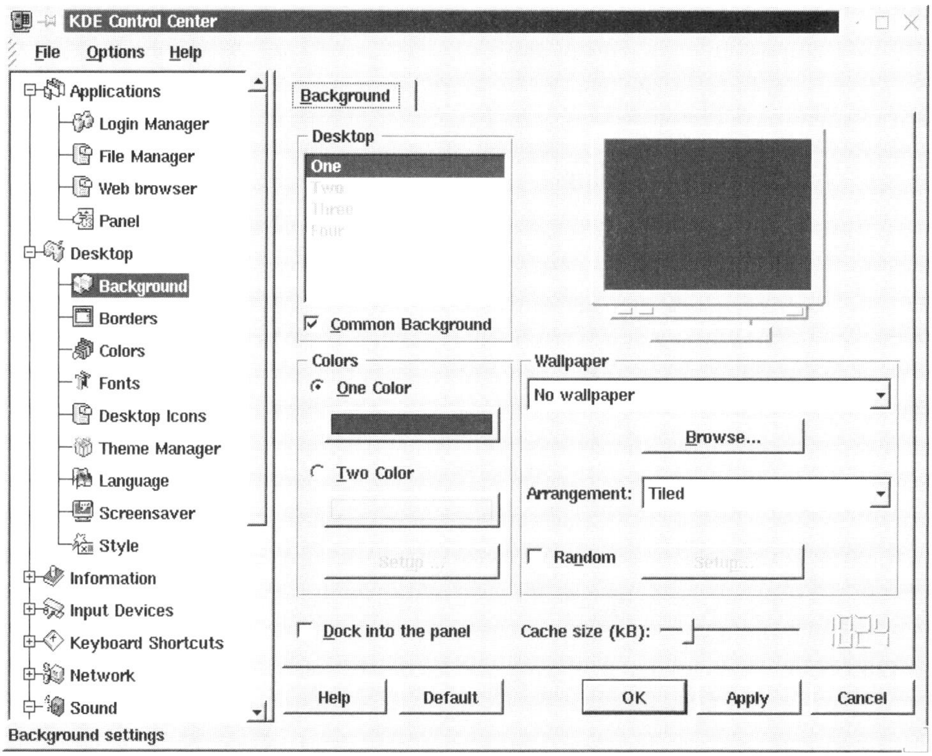

Figure 5-3. Configure KDE's look and feel from the Control Center

While the options on your version of KDE may vary slightly from those shown in Figure 5-3, the basic choices are the same. You can expand and contract subitems in the left-hand panel by double-clicking on the plus and minus symbols next to their parent items.

Applications

This set of options applies to some of the main applications included with KDE, including the K Desktop Manager (KDM), the K File Manager (KFM), KFM's web browser, and the Panel (which is similar in function to the Windows Taskbar).

Login Manager   The Login Manager controls the KDM login screen and its related operations. This login screen only appears if you run KDM on your system (which is usually only when you opt to start Linux in graphical mode rather than from a console prompt). The Login Manager options are only available if you run the KDE Control Panel as the root user, because this menu contains security-related settings. There are several tabs with different available configuration options.

The Appearance tab allows you to configure the greeting screen users see in the graphical KDM login screen. You may also set the logo KDM displays at login by selecting a file or dragging one over the existing image. Another option is to make the login screen's GUI look like Windows or the Common Desktop Environment (CDE), which would be more familiar to users of other flavors of Unix than to most Windows users. You can also set the login screen's language from this tab. For most users, there's not much point in tweaking these settings much, but if control over the login screen's appearance appeals to you, knock yourself out.

The Fonts tab's simple interface allows you to select the standard login screen's greeting font, as well as the font used for login failures and the font used for other text on the login screen. Like I keep saying, if you like being able to configure things, Linux is for you.

The Background tab allows you to select the background used with the login screen (which can be different from the background you use for your standard desktop, which I'll discuss shortly). You can set the background to a solid color, or a horizontal or vertical blend of colors. You may also set the login screen to use wallpaper, and there are many placement options.

The Users tab enables you to determine which of the Linux user accounts are shown from the login screen. You have the option not to show any accounts, which I'd recommend for servers and other higher-security systems (sure, if they know Bob's password and he's got an account on the system, they'll be able to get in, but at least you'll make them go through the trouble of thinking of Bob's account name and realizing they know that password). You can also include or exclude as many of the system and user accounts as you wish. It's handy to have the list of accounts displayed on login if there's reason to have multiple people or multiple accounts signed on separately.

The Sessions tab provides control over the system's shutdown process. The KDM login screen can allow users to shut the system down, and if you don't want just anybody to be able to do that, you'll want to make sure this option's settings are configured securely. You can prevent shutdown from the login screen, allow anyone to shut the system down from the login screen, or limit shutdowns to the root user or to the console prompt. For convenience' sake, I recommend one of the latter two options if you'll be using KDM.

The Sessions tab also allows you to determine what happens when a user requests a system shutdown or restart. While these options normally point to normal commands, you can change things to suit your needs. For example, you might write a script to send you an email before the system goes down, and then point the shutdown command to that script.

The final option on the Sessions tab gives you the option of starting up X with other window managers. You can configure the list of window managers to match those you've installed or that you want to use so that you can change your window manager from the login screen.

File Manager   This item allows you to configure the appearance of KDE's File Manager. There are three tabs with different configuration options. The first is the Font tab, which allows you to set the relative font size (small, medium, or large), and to set the standard font, the fixed-pitch font, and the character set used (for language-specific character sets).

The Color tab gives you control over the File Manger's background color, the normal text color, the color of URL links (such as web and ftp site links), and the color of links you've already followed. You may also tell the File Manager to underline links and to change the color of a link when the mouse pointer moves over it. The last setting on this tab sets the File Manager always to use these color definitions, even if another option is specified from within the File Manager.

The Other tab sets some miscellaneous options. You can allow individual settings to apply to individual URLs (so that the File Manager has a distinct look when you point it to different URLs). A second option may be useful for Windows users: Causing the "tree view" in the left-hand side of the File Manager to follow along as you click through folders in the right-hand side of the File Manager. This isn't what everybody likes, but if you want to see the directory structure around the current directory, it's quite useful.

The other options on the Other tab indicate the names of the terminal program and the text editor that are launched from File Manager when you request to do so. If you have a favorite editor or terminal program, you might as well configure File Manager to use it, too.

Web Browser   KDE's File Manager is integrated with a browser that allows you to use the same tool to peruse files on your computer, other computers on your local net, ftp sites, and even web sites. The Web Browser option gives you control over some of the browser's settings.

The Proxy tab is useful if you use a proxy server to access the Internet. You may select different proxy servers or ports for HTTP and FTP proxies, and you may also enter a list of hosts or domains that should not be accessed through the proxy server (which is useful when accessing an intranet).

The HTTP tab gives you some degree of control over the HTTP data you receive with the browser. You can indicate the languages you wish to accept, using "*" for all languages, "C" for the current language, or the two-letter abbreviations found on the Login Manager panel's Appearance option. You may specify the character sets the browser will accept from HTTP servers, and you may tell the browser to assume that all data it receives from HTTP servers is HTML unless the server explicitly says otherwise.

Using the User Agent option, you can configure the browser to masquerade as a different type of browser. For example, if a web site only turns on certain functionality if it determines you're using a Netscape browser or Internet Explorer, you won't see that functionality using the File Manager's browser functions. But from this screen, you can tell the browser to tell that web site it's one of those browsers. Of course, you have to know what the identification string the remote server is expecting, but if you do, this can be very helpful.

Finally, you can use the Cookies tab to enable or disable the use of cookies by the browser. If you enable cookies, you set a default policy to accept all cookies, ask about all cookies, or reject all cookies. In addition to this default policy, you may configure domain-specific settings to set non-standard policies for specific domains.

Panel   The KDE Panel and Taskbar can be configured from this option. Its first tab, cleverly labeled Panel, allows you to set the locations of the Panel and Taskbar. (The Taskbar is similar to the one in Windows, except that it only shows the open applications, while the Panel contains the status information, menus and "swallowed" applications also wedged onto the Windows taskbar.) You may also set the size of the Panel and its icons to tiny, normal, or large, depending on your monitor size, eyesight, and desire for desktop real estate.

The Options tab includes settings for enabling "tooltips" on the Panel menu, and the delay time between when the mouse pointer moves over the menu item and when the tooltip text pops up. It also controls whether the Panel and Taskbar automatically hide themselves when not in use, whether hiding and unhiding is animated, and how long they must be out of use before hiding.

The Options tab also allows you to customize the Panel a bit, by showing Personal entries or menu folders first in the menu. The current time may also be shown in 24-hour time (the default), A.M./P.M. notation, or in "Internet beats." If you don't know what an Internet beat is, you won't want to set your Panel clock to use it. As far as that goes, you may not want to set the Panel clock to use it even if you do know what an Internet beat is.

The Desktops option allows you to display and name from one to eight separate desktops. These desktops can be selected from the Panel and are one way of keeping your desktop uncluttered. For example, I've got a few systems with multiple desktops named after my servers. On each of those desktops, I've got processes running, showing the current load on its namesake server and other pertinent information. If I want to check on a particular server, I click on that desktop's icon in the Panel, and I've got the information. You may also set the desktop icons' width from this screen.

The History option gives you the chance to edit your "Personal" menu (the menu entries that are specific to your user account). If you are logged in as the root user, you may also edit the "Shared" menu (the customized menu entries shared by all user accounts). You may adjust the maximum number of recent folder and file entries displayed in the "Recent" menu.

There are several other options on the History screen, giving you control over display of "dot files," the Shared, Personal, and Recent menus, sorting rules, and the terminal application that runs when you open a folder while clicking the shift menu.

Desktop

This set of options is similar to what's found in the Colors, Desktop Themes, and Displays control panels in Windows, give or take a few items. The exact options available to you will depend on your installation of KDE, but I'll describe the most frequently used options.

Background   From this screen you can select a single background to use with all your virtual desktops, or you can give each one a different look (which can be useful for remembering which one's which as you flip between them). You can set the background to a single color or to a blend or pattern using two colors. You may also prefer to use an image as wallpaper; most distributions include a variety of wallpaper images, and of course you may add your own and control how it's displayed.

You may also set the wallpaper to random mode, which swaps the image out periodically (you can control what's selected and how frequently it changes). There's an option to add a display icon to the desktop panel for quick reconfiguration, and you can set the background cache size high if you use large wallpaper files on each desktop, or small if you prefer simple one-color backgrounds that don't require much memory.

Borders   If you've got multiple desktops enabled, one way you can switch between them is by enabling active desktop borders from this screen. The active borders sense when you move the mouse to the edge of the screen and leave it there for a delay you specify, and they'll switch to the next display. You can further configure the behavior of this desktop switching by telling KDE to move the mouse pointer to the center of the new desktop.

Another option on this screen allows you to set the snap zones for borders and windows. The snap zones define an area around the edges of desktop borders and windows within those borders. If you move a window within a snap zone of another window or of the desktop border, the desktop manager will place the window with its edge exactly touching its neighbor. This is nice for the anal retentive types among us.

Colors   If you've used the Colors control panel on your Windows PC, this screen will be easy to navigate. You can select from a set of predefined color schemes (and as with Windows, the results are previewed within the control panel). If you prefer, you can set the desktop colors by choosing each "widget" (window feature, such as title bars and window text) and setting its color individually. You can also set the overall contrast of the desktop colors you've chosen.

Fonts   This screen gives you the power to set the fonts used in different parts of the KDE desktop. You may select the typeface, enable bold or italics, set the size, and determine the character set used for each of four types of fonts used on the KDE desktop: The general fonts, fixed-pitch fonts, panel buttons, and the panel clock.

Desktop Icons   From this screen you can control the way icons are displayed on the desktop. To start with, if you want your icons spaced more closely or further apart than they started out, you may set the size of the vertical and horizontal grids to which they snap.

By default, icons on the KDE desktop are displayed with their text label on an opaque background. This makes it easy to read the icons' labels, but it may not fit with your sense of aesthetics. If that's the case, you may enable transparent text (which is really setting icon labels on a transparent background). You may also control the "icon foreground color" (really the foreground color of the icon's label) and the "icon background color" (which, if it's not transparent, is the background color of the icon's label).

Finally, by default, "dot files" are not given desktop icons, even if they're in the desktop folder. If you'd like to see icons for files with names that start with a dot, you can enable the hidden file viewing feature for the desktop. Be careful what you ask for, though; depending on your configuration, this may add many icons to your desktop.

Theme Manager   The first tab under the Theme Manager option is the Installer tab. From this screen, you may select from the existing themes KDE already knows about, reset the desktop to being themeless (the default), add a new theme (perhaps one you've downloaded from kde.themes.org), or create a theme of your own.

The Contents tab gives you control over the parts of the desktop the theme manager may influence. This is nice if you really like a theme except for its sounds, or default file manager, or icons, or whatever.

Finally, the About tab gives you information about the theme you're currently using, including its designer, version number, and copyright information. The designer's email address is often listed, giving you the chance to heap kudos on the creators of themes you appreciate. While you're at it, shouldn't you drop a line to the writers of computer books you've enjoyed recently?

Language   This screen's useful for multilingual users. It specifies three languages that should be used. If the language listed as "First" is not available, the language listed as "Second" is used. Likewise, if the "Second" language isn't available, the one listed as "Third" is used instead. If you're as weak in other languages as I am, you can leave all three entries set to the "default" language, and you're set.

Screensaver   This is another familiar screen for Windows users. A nice selection of screensavers is included. My favorite is definitely the Black Screen of Death screensaver, which simulates lockup screens from several personal computer operating systems. I still laugh when I see it. I also like the one that looks like the characters streaming across the screen in the movie *The Matrix.* Some of the screensavers have setup options you can tweak; you can click the Test button to check out the results.

The Settings portion of this screen allows you to set the delay time before the screen saver starts. You may also enable password protection on the screensaver and cause the password you enter to be displayed as asterisks. You can set the screensaver priority, which indicates how much processor time it should be given compared to other tasks. If you've got an elaborate screensaver running on a server, be careful about making it a high priority task and stealing CPU cycles from real work.

Style   This screen allows you to configure a few odds and ends of the user interface. You may have screen widgets (such as checkboxes, dropdown lists, etc.) displayed in the Windows 95 style or in Motif style. I don't think the Motif style is very attractive, but you can decide for yourself. Note that in Motif, an unchecked box bulges out of the screen toward you, and a checked box is indented into the desktop.

Another option you may enable from this screen emulates a feature of the MacOS. You can opt to place a menu bar at the top of the screen; as on a Mac, this menu bar will apply to the currently active application.

You may also set KDE to apply its fonts and colors to non-KDE applications. This applies only to some applications, but for the X Windows applications KDE knows about, it makes things look a little more uniform and familiar.

Finally, you may set the sizes of several icons to normal or large. You don't have a ton of control, but you can adjust the size of the KDE Panel and its icons separately from the File Manager and desktop icons, and you may give an independent setting to all other icons.

Information

Unlike most of what we've seen in the KDE Control Center, the Information option does not allow you to change any configurations. It's simply a place where system information is displayed for your reference. Because the information is available from other sources, Table 5-1 shows what kind of information is shown from the Information option and other places you could look on a Linux system to find similar configuration information.

Most of the information can be found by looking at text files in the /proc subdirectory. While it's possible to have a Linux system without activating the /proc subdirectory, most commonly used distributions include it, and I'll assume you want to include it in the kernel we compile in the next chapter.

Samba is a program used to allow Windows systems and Unix systems to share files and printers. We'll discuss it more in Chapter 9, but if Samba is installed on your system, a program called smbstatus can be used to identify the server status.

Input Devices

This option affords you the opportunity to adjust your keyboard and mouse configurations. You may configure International Keyboard operations, adjust your keyboard settings, and fine-tune your mouse behavior.

International Keyboard   If you use multiple keyboards for multiple languages or layouts, this option helps you configure the active keyboards and the ways you select them. The

Control Center Option	Command-Line Resource	Description
Devices	/proc/devices and /proc/misc	Unix character, block, miscellaneous devices
DMA-Channels	/proc/dma	DMA channels in use and by what
Interrupts	/proc/interrupts	Interrupts in use and by what
IO-Ports	/proc/ioports	I/O ranges in use and by what
Memory	/proc/meminfo	Memory totals and usage
Partitions	/proc/partitions	Partition type list
PCI	/proc/pci	Known PCI devices
Processor	/proc/cpuinfo	CPU type and information
SCSI	/proc/scsi/scsi	SCSI bus and devices
Samba Status	smbstatus	Samba server information
Sound	/proc/sound	Sound devices
X-Server	X -showconfig	X version and configuration

Table 5-1.   KDE Control Center Information and Sources

General tab gives you the option of adding or removing keyboards from the current list, and specifies the key combination used for switching between the keyboards. The advanced options allow you to handle Caps Lock behavior for languages where this is problematic, and gives you the opportunity to pop up an international keyboard menu in context and to save keyboard behavior within KDE applications.

The Style tab provides color options for setting the appearance of the keyboard indicator button that appears on the desktop, while the Startup tab allows you to "autostart" the indicator button on the desktop, dock it into the KDE Panel, or place it in a location you choose.

Keyboard   After the International Keyboard option, this one's pretty tame. You can turn the autorepeat feature on or off (perhaps to avoid that beeping sound when you fall asleep with your face resting on the keyboard). You can also adjust the volume of the keyclick sound the computer makes as you type. If you use a keyboard with as much tactile and audio feedback as I do, this won't be necessary, but for some of those mushy keyboards, it's nice to hear that each keystroke was actually registered.

Mouse   With this option, you can adjust how much the mouse accelerates as you move it, and how far you have to move it before the acceleration kicks in. You can also switch the left and right buttons from within KDE, so if you have multiple users on one PC, and one of them prefers to mouse with a different hand, that person can configure the mouse behavior.

Keyboard Shortcuts

These options allow you to customize keystroke combinations to perform certain tasks. There are two screens available for shortcut configuration: Global Keys and Standard Keys.

Global Keys   This option allows you to set global keystroke combinations. By "global," KDE's designers are referring to actions that occur outside specific applications. Switching between desktops or bringing up the task manager are two examples of global actions. You can change the keystrokes used to perform these tasks from the desktop.

Standard Keys   By "standard," KDE's designers are referring to actions that are common to KDE applications. Within each KDE-aware application, the same set of keystroke combinations—defined by you from this screen—is available to perform the same set of tasks within the application.

Network

While you might expect some pretty grand features under this heading, there's only one default Network option. Most people I know don't use it, because it's annoying, but I've talked to a couple of Linux users who love Talk, so let's, uh, talk briefly about it.

Talk is a common Unix utility that allows networked users to chat with one another in popup windows on their systems. KDE allows you to adjust the way it initiates and responds to talk conversations. Configuring talk requires some work outside the KDE Control Center, though, so don't expect that you can configure the utility here. This option is only for configuring talk's behavior within KDE.

Sound

These options give you control over the noises your computer makes, both simple and complicated. While the Bell option is available on any computer with a built-in speaker, taking advantage of the System Sounds option requires a Linux-recognized sound card, proper software configuration, and speakers.

Bell   This option allows you to adjust the volume, pitch, and duration of the system bell sounds played through the built-in speaker. There's a test button so you can tweak personal workstations to be quiet and unobtrusive and servers to be loud and plaintive.

System Sounds   If you enable sounds on a Linux system with a configured sound card, various system events can generate the sounds you specify. This screen allows you to select the system event and then match a corresponding sound. If the built-in list of sound files seems too limited to you (and it probably will), you can drag and drop additional

.wav files from the KDE File Manager onto the sound list, where they'll become accessible for use with system events.

Windows

Miscellaneous windowing behavior is configured using the Advanced, Buttons, Mouse, Properties, and Titlebar options.

Advanced   From this screen, you can enable the combination of CTRL+TAB to walk through the virtual desktops you've defined on your system. You can set the ALT+TAB combination to cycle through windows on the current virtual desktop, or all of them. You can also configure ALT+TAB to pop up a window list if you keep ALT held down (this is "KDE mode"), or not to give a window list at all and simply bring up the next window in the sequence if you hold ALT down ("CDE mode").

The Advanced screen also allows you to give control of your right (third) mouse button to KDE, which is nice if you use mostly KDE applications, or to relinquish the button to other applications, which can be useful in some applications, which demand full control of the right mouse button.

The last configuration option on this screen are filters, which allow you to tweak the appearance of windows that meet certain criteria you select based on text that appears in the title bar. Wholesale changes aren't possible, but for windows that don't need lots of KDE-added decorations, these options can save a little space, something most programmers are keen to do.

Buttons   This option gives you control over placement of the control buttons in a window's title bar. For each of the options shown in Table 5-2, you can specify that the button be placed on the left side of the title bar, placed on the right side of the title bar, or omitted altogether.

Button Name	Description
Minimize	Same as in Windows: collapse the window to an icon
Maximize	Same as in Windows: expand window to fill the screen
Sticky	Keeps window stuck in place, even when you switch to another virtual desktop
Close	Same as in Windows: eliminates the window
Menu	Similar to Windows: drops down menu options for the window

Table 5-2.   KDE Window Buttons

Mouse   Use this option to control mouse behavior depending on the mouse pointer's location. You may define behavior for when the mouse passes over the frame or title bar of any window. You may also define behavior for when the pointer is over the inside of an inactive window. Separate behavior can be specified for situations where the ALT key is held down while the pointer is anywhere over a window.

Properties   One window property that can be configured using this option is how windows are maximized. If you wish, maximizing a window can cause it only to expand vertically. You may also tell KDE to display content in windows that are being resized or moved, which can be useful if you're resizing a window to fit something displayed in it. The rate of the window resizing can be adjusted here, from instantaneous to slowly animated.

The window placement policy is also set from this screen. The default window placement setting is Smart, which attempts to minimize window overlap and clutter. The Random option will drop windows haphazardly across the screen, while Cascade will overlap window interiors but not title bars. The Manual option means you click on the desktop each time a window opens to indicate where it should be placed. Finally, the Interactive setting attempts to use smart placement until an overlap threshold you set cannot be met, and then it forces manual placement for additional windows.

If you've used Windows most of your computing life, window focus probably isn't something you've given much thought. In Windows, a window is selected (that is, "given focus") by clicking on it. That window retains focus until another window is clicked on. In KDE, this behavior is known as Click to focus. But there are other focus options available from the Properties screen.

A more customary way for Unix users to configure focus is known as Focus follows mouse. This option gives focus to whatever window the mouse pointer is sitting over. This makes it easier to type text into a window largely obscured by another window with reference information, but it can also be frustrating because you really have to know where your mouse pointer is located at all times. If you don't like Click to focus, I recommend this option.

Another option is Classic sloppy focus, which is similar to the Focus follows mouse option but allows you to cycle focus through the windows using the ALT+TAB key combination. And the Classic focus follows mouse option is also based on the Focus follows mouse option, but it strictly removes focus from a window if the mouse pointer leaves the window. This means that if the pointer isn't above any windows (perhaps resting over the desktop), no window has focus.

Titlebar   Going on the theory that controlling every last bit of the interface is better than not having any control, the KDE designers included the options to adjust the display of the titlebars. For example, you can alter the alignment of the window titles from the Windows-looking left alignment to center or right alignment. You can adjust the color gradient in the titlebars or use "pixmap" images to give the title bars a three-dimensional effect.

Another setting on this screen allows you to tell KDE what to do when you double-click a titlebar. You can also turn on title animation, which scrolls the title text back and forth if the window isn't wide enough to display the whole title at once. I find this more distracting than useful and tend to turn it off.

Giving GNOME Good Garb

Despite my preference for KDE, GNOME (pronounced "guh-nome") is highly configurable, widely used, and completely open-source. GNOME comes with documentation that's worth reviewing to get acquainted with the workspace; GNOME's creators use some potentially unfamiliar terminology to describe various features of the desktop environment.

While KDE uses its own window manager by default, GNOME is often paired with different window managers. Red Hat 6, for example, used the Enlightenment window manager, while Red Hat 7 uses Sawfish. That means there are two places you can go to tweak different aspects of your desktop layout: The GNOME Control Center and the window manager's configuration tool.

GNOME Control Center

The first place you can tweak your GNOME configuration is using the GNOME Control Center. By default, this tool can be found on the GNOME Panel at the bottom of the desktop—it's the one with a toolbox icon, as shown in Figure 5-4.

The Control Center itself is the window open in the lower right part of the desktop shown in Figure 5-4. Notice that on the left side of the Control Center is a list of settings (the Desktop Editor setting is selected in Figure 5-4). These settings are small configuration applications GNOME calls applets. Configuration using the Control Center entails selecting the applet you want to alter and then adjusting the settings shown in the right part of the Control Center.

The applets are modular, so you may have more or fewer in your Control Center, depending on what software you have loaded. I'll describe the options available for the applets installed with Red Hat 7. For each applet, there will be the buttons to temporarily "Try" the new settings you've added, "Revert" to the previous settings, "OK" to accept the changes permanently, "Cancel" to exit without saving changes, and "Help" to open the online documentation.

Desktop   The Background option allows you to set the background color and wallpaper image used on your desktop. You can choose from a simple single-color background, or you can setup a slightly more sexy, horizontal or vertical gradient from one color to another. You can also select an image to be used as your wallpaper, and specify that the image be tiled, centered, scaled with the same aspect ratio as the original, or scaled to fill the desktop.

The Panel option controls the behavior of the GNOME panel and its contents. The panel is the toolbar at the bottom of the GNOME desktop. It is the launching point for multiple menus, applications, and even serves as a "docking station" for miniaturized

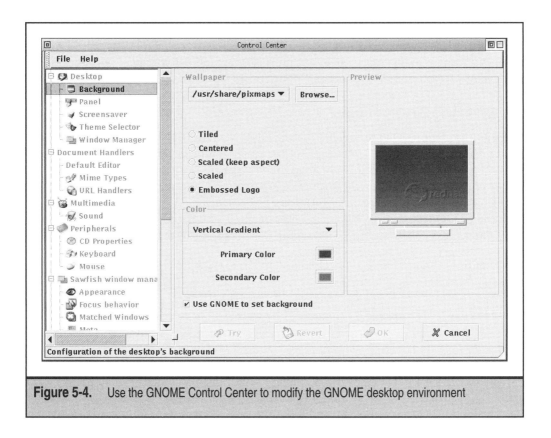

Figure 5-4.   Use the GNOME Control Center to modify the GNOME desktop environment

applications. From this applet, you can control the animations used with the panel, add texture to panel icons, control movement and spacing of panel objects, adjust menus, and enable or disable tooltips and key bindings. My favorite option in this applet is the Large Icons setting on the Menu tab, which makes the icons visible on screens with high resolutions.

The Screensaver option allows you to select a screensaver from a fairly large list, and then set its options. Options include

▼ The time that must elapse before the screensaver kicks in

■ Whether the current user's password will be required to turn the screen saver off

■ The relative priority of the screensaver task compared to others on the system (you don't want your screensaver sucking processing power from a server . . . you're not running an OpenGL screensaver on an NT or Windows 2000 server, are you?)

▲ The power management settings for systems with power management enabled

My favorite screen saver is "bsod," which treats you to Windows-like "Blue Screen of Death" error messages, as well as Mac-, DOS-, and Amiga-based error screens. I'm slowly learning not to fibrillate when I see the blue screen, but it still makes me laugh every time I see it.

The Theme Selector allows you to choose some pre-configured desktop looks. These range from the subtle to the unreadable, though most are pretty good. You can select from a list of available themes, and the major features of the desktop design are previewed below the list, so you can get an idea of what the whole desktop would look like. You can also adjust the user font from this applet.

The Window Manager applet allows you to select the window manager GNOME uses. Unless you've got a reason to use one of the others (Red Hat also includes *twm*, and others are available), I'd stick with the default, Sawfish. You can click a button here to edit the configuration, but I'll discuss configuration of the Sawfish window manager later in the chapter. Note that there are window managers that completely mimic Windows, if you like that sort of thing.

Document Handlers   The Default Editor option sets the text editor that's associated with editable documents. You might think of this choice the same way you would think about associating .txt files with Notepad or Write in Windows. Linux just comes with far more text editor options than Windows does, because programmers tend to be finicky about their editors. So you can choose from a wide range of editors here, and when you double-click on an editable file, it will open in the editor you selected.

The MIME Types applet is similar to the File Types function in Windows: It associates file extensions with applications. You can indicate how any given file type (based on its extension) should be handled for opening, viewing, and editing. You can also associate an icon with a given extension so you can recognize it more easily from within file managers.

The URL Handlers applet controls the way URLs are handled from within GNOME. It works much like the Mime Types applet, but instead of dealing with file extensions, it deals with URL listings. In Red Hat 7, Netscape is the default handler, while the GNOME help browser is specified for man pages, info files, and ghelp files.

Multimedia   The Sound applet is slightly more useful: It's like the Sounds Control Panel in Windows. From the General tab, you can enable sound for GNOME and for GNOME events. From the Sound Events tab, you can associate specific sound files with specific events in the desktop manager or within certain programs. So if you really need Homer Simpson saying, "Doh!" when an error message comes up, you can set it up. Then give yourself a pat on the back for increasing your productivity.

Peripherals   The CD Properties applet controls the way GNOME reacts when CDs are inserted in a CD-ROM drive. You may configure the system to automatically mount CD-ROMs that are inserted. You can tell the system to automatically start any auto-run CD-ROMs that are inserted. And you can force the file manager to open when a CD-ROM is inserted. You can also specify the command that should run when audio CDs are inserted. By default, GNOME plays the audio CD using the gtcd application. Enable audio CDs autoplay from this applet, put in an audio CD, and check out this great tool.

The Keyboard applet configures your keyboard's autorepeat and audible click settings. You can enable autorepeat on the keyboard (which sends, for example, a bunch of spaces if you rest a magazine on your space bar) and then specify the repeat rate and the delay period before the autorepeat takes place. You can also enable keyboard clicking, which produces an audible tone when you press a key. Turn up the volume in the applet and use autorepeat to make yourself sound like a 500 word-per-minute typing maniac.

From the Mouse applet, you can specify the hand with which you'd like to use the mouse (so GNOME can swap the left and right button definitions). You can also set an acceleration rate for the mouse cursor and a threshold speed that the mouse has to reach before the acceleration kicks in.

Session   The Startup Hint applet allows you to turn the login hint window on or off. The hints can be fairly tiresome if you're familiar with GNOME, but you may find them helpful for a time. If you wish, you can replace the tips with responses from the fortune command, which taps a large database of comments, stories, quotations, and cookie-style fortunes. Another option for login messages is to have the message of the day presented.

The Startup Programs applet is similar to the Services Control Panel in Windows NT and Windows 2000. You can specify non-GNOME programs that start up when GNOME starts up, you can browse the list of currently active programs, and you can set the system to prompt to save changes you make, or automatically save the changes.

User Interface   The Applications applet is very cool. It gives you control over the way menus, toolbars, and status bars behave in GNOME-compliant applications. These objects are controlled via the checkboxes shown in Figure 5-5.

In GNOME-compliant applications, menus can be dragged away from their usual locations and placed elsewhere. The menus can have contoured borders. Individual menus may be torn off and dragged elsewhere as standalone windows (simply select the dashed line at the top of a menu when this option is enabled). And individual menu items can have associated icons.

Likewise, the status bar at the bottom of a GNOME-compliant application can be configured here. If you enable status bar interactivity, some bars will use their own windows. If a status bar includes a progress meter, you can display on either the right or left side of the bar.

Finally, toolbars can also be personalized. Enable toolbar detachment and moving if you wish. Select contoured edges ("relieved") for toolbars and the buttons on them. Activate lines separating toolbar items if you like. And enable the text labels for toolbar icons if that'll be useful to you.

The Dialogs applet gives you control over the way dialog boxes are displayed in GNOME. First, it allows you to specify how buttons in dialog boxes are placed: By default; left- or right-justified; spread out; or on the edges of the boxes. Next, the applet lets you decide whether dialog boxes with common buttons (the "OK" button, for example)

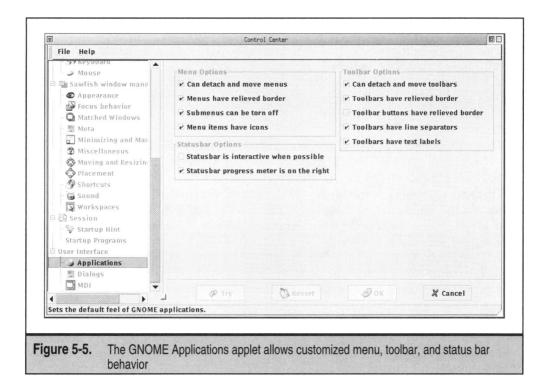

Figure 5-5.   The GNOME Applications applet allows customized menu, toolbar, and status bar behavior

will use icons with the text labels. You may also choose to have messages from information-only dialog boxes displayed in the status bar instead of in dialog boxes.

You can also determine the default dialog box positioning, which can be specified by the window manager, centered, or placed where the mouse is currently pointing. You may indicate whether you want button hints treated like other windows or handled specially.

And just for those of us who have used Windows too long, there's an option to place dialog boxes over their applications whenever possible. This is not standard X Windows behavior, but it's what many of us are used to because of Windows. It's a much nicer way of making your interface work.

The last applet, MDI, controls the way multiple documents are displayed within a GNOME-compliant application. You may select Notebook style, which gives each document open in an application its own tab; Toplevel, which shows the active document until you close that document; and Modal, which displays one document at a time but allows you to switch between multiple open documents. If you choose Notebook style, you may also specify where in the application the tabs will be displayed.

Sawfish Configurator

The Sawfish Configurator is the tool used to edit the window manager GNOME uses by default. The distinctions between the settings made to the desktop environment (GNOME) and to the window manager (Sawfish) aren't that important for our purposes, but in general the GNOME Control Center changes GNOME-compliant applications and the ways they relate, while the Sawfish Configurator changes the appearance of the windowing system features.

The Configurator may be opened from the GNOME Control Center using the Desktop - Window Manager applet, as I described earlier. When the Configurator opens, you will see a window similar to the one shown in Figure 5-6.

There are 11 options on the left-hand side of the Configurator window. Each of these allows you to control particular aspects of the Sawfish configuration. For the most part, these options control basic windowing functions, such as appearance, focus, movement, resizing, and placement.

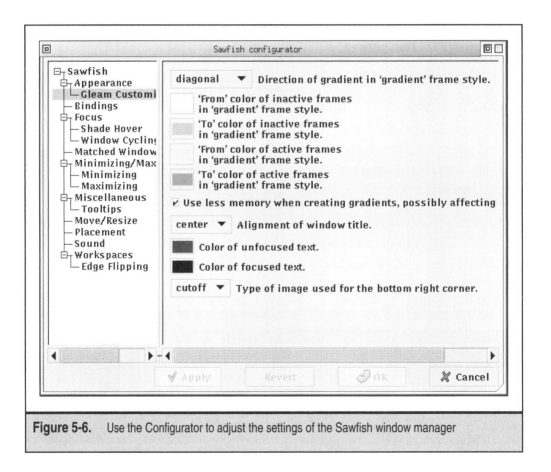

Figure 5-6.   Use the Configurator to adjust the settings of the Sawfish window manager

The Appearance option allows you to select the theme you wish to use for the windows created on your GNOME desktop. The Appearance settings describe how windows look when they're active and inactive: colors; fonts; and custom features. The concept behind the Focus Behavior option may be less familiar.

In Windows, a single window that's already open on your desktop gets "focus" when you click on it. In other words, if you click on a window, the cursor becomes active in that window. It's familiar behavior. In the X Windows world, though, that's not necessarily considered desirable behavior. Sometimes a Unix user wants to be able to type in a window without clicking on it. One situation in which that might be useful is when you're entering data from one window into another. It's sometimes easier to have the source window open to a large size and sitting on top, and have only a line or two of the destination window open—just enough room to type.

So you get a choice in Linux. The Focus Behavior option tells Sawmill how to give focus to a window. Focus is primarily granted on the basis of what the user is doing with the mouse. The Microsoft Windows interface grants focus to a window when you click on any part of it. Other options include granting focus to a window when the cursor enters it, or taking focus away from a window when the cursor leaves it. If it's not immediately apparent how these are different, you can select a setting, then click the Try button to see how it works and decide whether you like it.

The Matched Windows option is a very handy tool that allows you to specify rules by which certain windows get special placement, focus, or appearance. The rules cover everything from "all windows running on a particular system" to "only windows with this name." To set up a new rule, you click the Insert button, select a criterion, and click on a window. That window's characteristics are reflected in the resulting rule.

The Meta option gives you some input into how much complication you want to deal with while using the Configurator. You may select from three target options: novice; intermediate; and expert. If you select the novice setting, you'll sometimes see fewer options because Sawmill will hide more advanced configuration issues from you. The expert setting, on the other hand, brings everything out into the open.

The Minimizing And Maximizing option deals with the mechanics of minimizing and maximizing windows. The Miscellaneous option adds other random customizations and gives you control over *tooltips*, the little snippets of information that pop up, for example, when you leave the mouse pointer over a menu item or toolbar icon. And not surprisingly, the Moving and Resizing option gives you control over how windows behave when they are moved and resized.

The Sound option allows you to enable, disable, and control sounds linked to window events. I've found this functionality extremely irritating; while it's initially cool to have the Star Trek sliding door sound when you minimize a window, the effect grows old fast. The desktop event sounds configured in GNOME are less annoying.

The Workspaces options control the way multiple and virtual desktops are displayed. Both these settings give you more desktop real estate, but they accomplish that objective in different ways.

Adding more than one column or row to the display expands the total area of your desktop beyond the amount you can see at one time. Instead of having one monitor's worth of information on your desktop, you can have four monitors' worth (by configuring Sawmill with two rows of two columns). The viewable area of your desktop becomes a portal through which you can reach part of the whole desktop. When you move your mouse to the edge of the screen, the view changes to show the next virtual screen.

Another way of giving you more desktop room is by creating separate desktops, which are called *workspaces*. Instead of being connected to one another, these are distinct desktops. The two methods can be combined; for example, you can have three separate desktops, each equal in area to four monitors.

If this doesn't make sense, a little experimentation goes a long way to help clear up the distinctions. The options are easy to configure, and you can see the results in the GNOME Panel at the bottom of the screen, which shows which desktop, and which part of a virtual screen, is active. In fact, the best recourse with all of these options is to experiment with things until you like what you see. And if you don't like the look of one desktop, there are more where it came from!

CHAPTER 6

Step 3:
Compile a
Kernel

Having chosen to embark on your computer- and life-improvement project of detaching yourself from the Microsoft collective, you have installed Linux and have configured X to work and look the way that makes you happiest. Now it's time to undertake the next important step in the migration program: Decide to turn your system over to the power and flexibility of a customized kernel.

Do you want to use amateur (ham) radio, ISDN, Token Ring networking, or SCSI tape drives? Add them to the kernel. Could you care less about power management, symmetric multiprocessing, or 3Com network cards? Pull them out of the kernel. Can't decide what you'll want later? Rebuild the kernel as often as you like, create modular options for devices or features you don't need yet, or build multiple kernels and see which one works best.

WHY COMPILE A KERNEL?

It's a good question. After all, if all has gone well with your Linux installation so far, why go poking around in the holiest of holies? What's to be gained?

First and foremost, what's to be gained is a Linux installation that's tailored to your system and the tasks you're giving it. The Linux distributions generally install a multi-purpose kernel that can handle a whole class of machines. But if you know what kind of hardware you're using, why should you be chewing up memory with a bunch of preloaded drivers that you're not using?

As far as that goes, maybe there is other functionality you'd like to investigate on your system. Perhaps you'd like to set your Linux system up as a router now that it has proved itself by staying up for a while. You may have to compile a kernel with routing functionality built in . . . or it may be firewalls, or a new SCSI card or a peripheral or who knows what.

Perhaps the best reason to build your own kernel, though, is to take advantage of the improvements being made by kernel programmers around the world. This isn't a matter of grabbing random bits of code from random sources; the latest stable kernel version, which is likely to be newer than the version that came with your distribution, is available from **http://www.kernel.org**. The latest development version, with the latest features (many of which are still in process), is also available at that site. You can keep track of what the developers are talking about by reading the Kernel Traffic summary available at **http://kt.linuxcare.com**. These outstanding weekly summaries do a fine job of boiling down the technical discussions and the human interactions on the linux-kernel mailing list.

For what it's worth, building a kernel isn't difficult. It can take some time, especially if you're using an older, slower system. And it can lead you into a little trouble, particularly if you forget some essential drivers or features. But in my experience, it's far easier than avoiding Microsoft junk mail, for example. So count your blessings, and let's get going.

HOW TO COMPILE THE KERNEL

All you're doing when you compile the kernel is building a program. You don't have to write any part of the program yourself, but you do have to tell it what options you want to use. As with any other software, once this program (the operating system kernel) has been built, you have to install it to make it run.

In this section, we'll focus on the process of building the kernel; I'll save a discussion of what exactly you should build into the kernel for later in this chapter. For now, let's start by making sure we've got a fresh set of kernel files and that they're ready to go.

Pre-Tidy Things

The default location for your original Linux kernel source files is a directory known as /usr/src/linux. This directory is sometimes a logical link (see Chapter 3 if you're unfamiliar with that term) to a version-specific directory. Consider the following directory listing:

```
millerm@romans:/usr/src> ls -l
total 12
lrwxrwxrwx   1 root    root      12 Feb  9 06:29 linux -> linux-2.2.13
drwxr-xr-x   3 root    root    4096 Feb  9 06:28 linux-2.2.13
drwxr-xr-x   3 root    root    4096 Feb 11 02:35 linux-2.2.14
drwxr-xr-x   7 root    root    4096 Feb  9 06:33 redhat
```

In this /usr/src directory, for example, there are two subdirectories for Linux versions (2.2.13 and 2.2.14), and a logical link to one version (2.2.13). While you can keep multiple versions of the kernel sources this way, it's a better idea to leave the /usr/src/ directory tree as your installation left it. Instead of modifying the contents of that tree, you can create your own directory structure in a subdirectory of your home directory.

To update the Linux kernel, you can download the latest version from the Internet; while some distributions have download locations on their own web sites, you can also go to www.kernel.org to find past and present kernels, both production and developmental. Once you've downloaded the source file to your home directory, decompress it using the appropriate tool.

The smallest files (which will download fastest) are those with the .bz2 extension. To decompress them and expand them from the archive file, use commands like these (using the name of the file you downloaded):

```
millerm@romans: ~> bunzip2 linux-2.4.0-tar.bz2
millerm@romans: ~> tar xf linux-2.4.0-tar
```

This will create a directory structure in the directory where you ran the tar command. Change into the **linux** directory, which is the top level of the Linux source tree. From here, run **make mrproper,** as shown here:

```
millerm@romans: ~> cd linux
/home/millerm/linux
millerm@romans: ~/linux> make mrproper
```

This command cleans up residual files that might have been left behind by previous attempts to build the kernel, so you'll get disk activity and see many rm -f commands scroll down the screen. When the Linux command prompt returns, you're ready to move on to the next step.

Kernel Configuration

The next step is to configure the kernel, which means telling it which features you want to include, which you want to omit, and which you wish to build as modules. There are three main ways of performing this task: Using a prompt-driven command-line interface; running a text-mode utility that gives you menus of kernel options; or executing an X Windows application that gives the process a GUI.

make config

The bare-bones approach to configuring the Linux kernel is to use the **make config** command. This runs a script that gives you the opportunity to set each option, one by one. The interface is a purely text-based affair, and the process is entirely linear; if you make a mistake, you'll have to rerun the **make config** command until you get the options the way you want them.

On the other hand, **make config** will run on the most bare-bones installation of Linux; it requires neither X Windows nor even the text-mode libraries that give **make menuconfig** its relative user-friendliness.

When you run **make config**, some script messages will appear, followed by some actual configuration information and your first choice:

```
millerm@romans: ~/linux> make config
rm -f include/asm
( cd include ; ln -sf asm-i386 asm)
/bin/sh scripts/Configure arch/i386/config.in
#
# Using defaults found in .config
#
*
* Code maturity level options
*
Prompt for development and/or incomplete code/drivers (CONFIG_EXPERIMENTAL)
[N/y/?]
```

As the asterisked lines indicate, this first option falls within the "Code maturity level options" group. While there's only one choice to make in this group, other option groups offer many selections. Some will prompt you for further options only if you enable a higher-level feature; for example, you won't be offered drivers for particular ISDN devices if you decline to turn on ISDN support.

Manually Editing the Config File

There is a fourth option for performing kernel configuration, which is manually editing the configuration file used to compile the kernel. This file is ordinarily linux/.config, but because the **make mrproper** command deletes this file, it's already toast if you've followed the instructions in the previous section. That's okay; there's a copy in linux/arch/i386/defconfig that you can copy to the usual location.

The .config file is just a text file listing the options available in the kernel version you're building. If an option is not set, it is preceded by a pound sign and followed by the phrase "is not set," as shown here:

```
# CONFIG_EXPERIMENTAL is not set
```

If an option is set, there's no pound sign, and instead of the phrase at the end, there's an equal sign and either a "y" or an "m", depending on whether the option is to be included in the kernel or built as a module:

```
CONFIG_BINFMT_AOUT=m
CONFIG_BINFMT_ELF=y
```

The option names that appear here aren't the human-friendlier versions you get in the different configuration tools, so unless you have some idea of what you're doing, they may be too cryptic to work with. I haven't included those tags in tabular form in the "What to Compile into the Kernel" section that follows, but you can always consult the exhaustive list in linux/Documentation/Configure.help, which includes all the tags and descriptions of most of the tags.

If you wanted to, you could edit the whole .config file by hand, but that's really a waste of time. It's also useful to know how to edit the .config file if you use **make config**, which doesn't let you go back and change things if you make an error. Your knowledge of the .config file also allows you to save a .config file you know works so that you can use it for future reference or to rebuild a particular version of the kernel later if you wish to. In either case, you'd copy the .config file you like to linux/.config on the target machine and use the command **make oldconfig** to accept the .config file settings.

The three choices for the first option are indicated in the square brackets. You can tell that the CONFIG_EXPERIMENTAL option shown in the example above is disabled by default because the "n" is capitalized. If you wish to enable the option, enter **y**. If you want more information about the choice you're given, enter a question mark. A brief piece of explanatory help text is provided for most options.

Other options offer another choice, allowing you to select **m** to indicate that you don't want to include the feature in the kernel, but feel you're likely enough to use it that you'll build it as a module that can be loaded into the kernel as needed, and unloaded if it isn't. There are also a few options that expect you to choose a numeric value or a word as input; these will offer you the appropriate options when they appear.

When you get to the end of the process, you'll see a message like this:

```
*** End of Linux kernel configuration.
*** Check the top-level Makefile for additional configuration.
*** Next, you must run 'make dep'.
```

The "top-level Makefile" the message refers to is linux/Makefile, which is a master configuration file for the kernel build. You don't really need to look at this file, and you shouldn't be tweaking it directly anymore (in times past, one had to do so to enable certain new functions, such as SMP, in this file). We'll discuss the **make dep** command in the "Make the Kernel" section, but for now, let's consider some alternatives to a plain **make config**.

make menuconfig

This option is preferable to **make config** in most circumstances, not only because it's a little more aesthetically pleasing, but also because it allows you to change your mind gracefully. The kernel features are grouped together in a set of menus (thus the name of the command, as I'm sure you noticed) that you can navigate as you need to; this means you don't have to wade through every configuration option, which is nice.

To initiate this configuration utility, run the command as root:

```
root@romans: linux> make menuconfig
```

This will likely generate some messages on the console before a window similar to the one in Figure 6-1 opens.

Navigating the menus is easy; use the cursor keys to move to a menu item and then press ENTER to open the menu. Each menu item is preceded by a pair of square brackets, which signify a feature that must be included or excluded, or by a set of less-than and greater-than signs, which indicate that the feature may be modularized. Move to an option you wish to alter and press the spacebar to toggle through the options. An asterisk indicates that the option is selected, while an "m" indicates that the option is to be built as a module. If there's nothing between the brackets, the option will not be included in the kernel you're building.

In the menu shown in Figure 6-2, Kernel support for a.out binaries will be excluded from the kernel, while Kernel support for ELF binaries will be included and Kernel support for MISC binaries will be made into a module.

When you have configured the kernel functionality as you see fit, select Exit from the bottom of the Main Menu. When you're asked if you wish to save the configuration, select Yes and press ENTER. You're ready to move on to the "Make the Kernel" section.

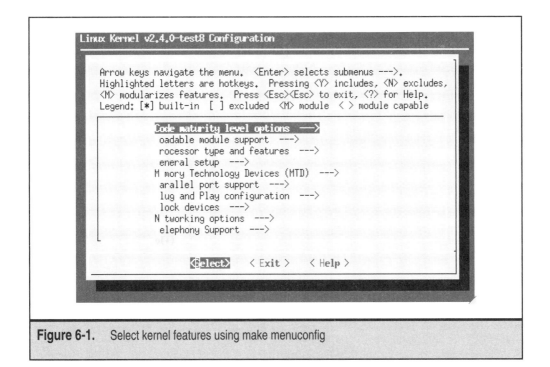

Figure 6-1. Select kernel features using make menuconfig

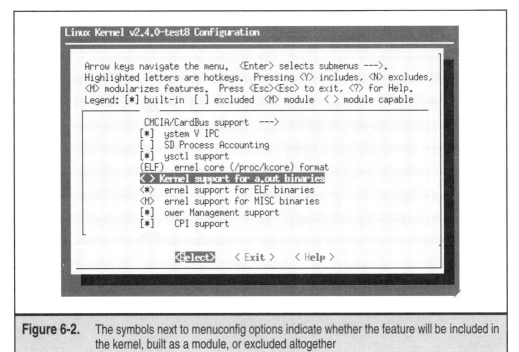

Figure 6-2. The symbols next to menuconfig options indicate whether the feature will be included in the kernel, built as a module, or excluded altogether

make xconfig

Although this is the nicest-looking of the three options, it requires you to have X Windows up and running. That's not a big deal for most people, as the major distributions all allow you to configure and run X Windows out of the box, but it does limit you if you've opted for a server installation without X Windows. (That's one reason you might want to configure a kernel on one system before transferring it to another system.) The xconfig Main Menu is shown in Figure 6-3.

Click on a menu button to open a window showing the lower-level menu. As shown in Figure 6-4, there are radio buttons for most of the options in these menus, though some options have a drop-down list of choices or a box in which you can enter a value.

When you've finished configuring the kernel, click on the Save And Exit button from the Main Menu, and you're ready to continue building the kernel.

Make the Kernel

Once you've used one of the methods of creating and editing the configuration file, you're ready to move on and create the new kernel. The next three steps can be lumped together on the command line, like this:

```
millerm@romans: ~/linux> make dep ; make clean ; make bzImage
```

The semicolons separate three commands, and the shell will respond by executing them one at a time. I'll go ahead and explain them one at a time, too.

Linux Kernel Configuration		
Code maturity level options	SCSI support	File systems
Loadable module support	IEEE 1394 (FireWire) support	Console drivers
Processor type and features	I2O device support	Sound
General setup	Network device support	USB support
Memory Technology Devices (MTD)	Amateur Radio support	Kernel hacking
Parallel port support	IrDA (infrared) support	
Plug and Play configuration	ISDN subsystem	
Block devices	Old CD-ROM drivers (not SCSI, not IDE)	Save and Exit
Networking options	Input core support	Quit Without Saving
Telephony Support	Character devices	Load Configuration from File
ATA/IDE/MFM/RLL support	Multimedia devices	Store Configuration to File

Figure 6-3.   The make xconfig option runs under X Windows

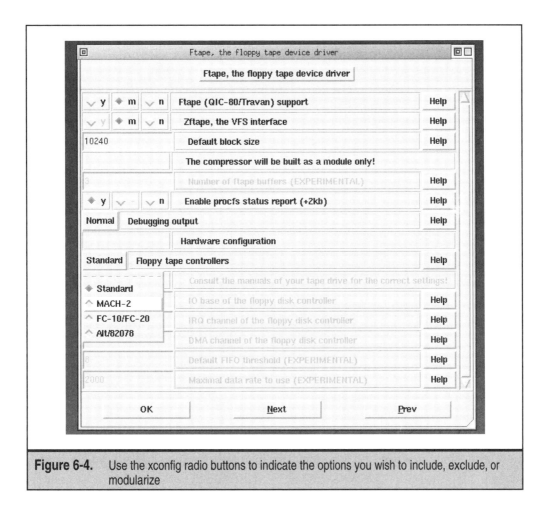

Figure 6-4.   Use the xconfig radio buttons to indicate the options you wish to include, exclude, or modularize

make dep

The first of the three options is **make dep**, also known as **make depend**. As the name indicates, it determines dependencies among the Linux files for the kernel you're building. If you enable the option to Set Version Information For All Symbols On Modules, the **make dep** process also determines the version information for the modules you build. More information is available in linux/Documentation/kbuild/commands.txt.

make clean

As the name implies, this option cleans out existing files where the new ones will be created. While it's not always necessary to do this, it won't hurt, so do it.

make bzImage

This step is where the kernel itself is actually compiled, and it's the one that takes the lion's share of the time in the process. When the shell gets to this command, it uses the configuration information you've given it to build a new kernel file. On Intel-based systems, this file is created as linux/arch/i386/boot/bzImage. For small kernels, you can use the **make zImage** command, but unless you're sure the kernel is going to be quite dinky, it's easiest just to use the bzImage option.

Many messages will scroll across your screen as your system compiles the kernel. When the process is complete, the system will show you the size of the file you've created. Cackle loudly, or scream, "It's alive! Alive!" at the top of your lungs, and then continue to the next step, in which we'll install the kernel.

Install the Kernel

In the last step, we created a file known as linux/arch/i386/boot/bzImage. This is the kernel file that we want our system to use, and to do so, we have to instruct the boot loader to use it.

Most distributions use LILO as the boot loader, and you can identify the current location of the kernel by viewing the /etc/lilo.conf file. Look for the first line that says "image=" for an entry like this one:

```
image=/boot/vmlinuz-2.2.12-20
```

Sometimes the vmlinuz file may be found in the root directory: /vmlinuz. Wherever that file is currently located, that's where you want to put the new kernel file. You'll have to use the *su* command to become the root user first. You don't have to give the vmlinuz file the same name as its predecessor (it's best that you don't, in fact, unless you know the new one's going to work, and even then you might want to use a more accurate name):

```
root@romans: /> cp ~millerm/linux/arch/i386/boot/bzImage /boot/vmlinuz-2.2.14
```

make bzdisk

Another useful option is the **make bzdisk** command. If you use this command in place of the **make bzImage** command, the kernel you create will be written to your first floppy drive (the equivalent of your A: drive in Windows). This disk can then be used to test a kernel without tweaking the existing configuration, or to boot the system in an emergency.

If you use this option and wish to boot from a floppy disk, you won't need to follow the kernel installation procedure that follows. Simply reboot the system with the floppy disk in its drive (and the computer's BIOS set to boot from the floppy drive).

This command copies the bzImage file just created to the /boot directory, where its name will be "vmlinuz-2.2.14" to help us remember what version it is. Now that it's in the right place, we can edit the /etc/lilo.conf file to update the image line so that it points to the new kernel.

When the /etc/lilo.conf file has been edited, we're ready to tell LILO to update its configuration information. This is a simple process (but you still have to be the root user):

```
root@romans /> /sbin/lilo
Added Linux *
```

You may see a slightly different message telling you which kernel(s) were added, depending upon the label tags specified in the lilo.conf file. Regardless, you're now ready to build any modules you specified during the configuration process.

NOTE: If you're running Corel Linux or another distribution from a Windows partition, you're likely using loadlin, another boot loader. When you build a new kernel on a loadlin system, you simply go into Windows and overwrite the existing file named vmlinuz with the bzImage file you just created (rename bzImage to **vmlinuz**.)

Make Modules

When you're configuring the Linux kernel, you have the option to include many options as modules rather than placing them into the kernel. Each module can be loaded and unloaded separately; in older days, Linux required you to tell the kernel what to load or unload, but module loading is now automatic if you build support for the kernel module loader (kmod) into the kernel.

To build the modules, simply run this command:

```
millerm@romans ~/linux> make modules
```

This will create the modules you requested during the configuration process. It will not install them, however, so there's a second step you must take (this one must be performed as root):

```
root@romans ~millerm/linux> make modules_install
```

This command copies the completed modules to a subdirectory of /lib/modules/ that corresponds to the kernel version. That's all there is to it; the modularized features of Linux are now available on an on-demand basis.

WHAT TO COMPILE INTO THE KERNEL

It's fine for me to tell you to compile a kernel. It's fine for me to tell you how to do it. But the first few times I built a Linux kernel, I wished I had a little more hand-holding than I did. If you're adventuresome, have a little time, and don't mind reading the extensive help information, there's plenty of information available during the config process (regardless of the config tool you use). You should be able to get everything you need and exclude the stuff you really don't want without too much trouble.

But for those who do want a little more assistance, this section will describe the options, focusing on the ones you're likely to want and glossing past the ones that aren't as likely to be useful. Just to warn you, I'm working with a test version of Linux 2.4, and I'm leaving out anything that's experimental. If you've got a different version of the kernel, you might find somewhat different options. And if you'd like to try experimental kernel code, you're on your own.

I've populated the tables in this section with the descriptions of the options, which tend to change a little from version to version of the kernel. I have also omitted experimental options, most laundry lists of hardware-specific device drivers, and many options that are only useful if you select an option I don't recommend. Most of these options have help text available in all three configuration tools, however, and if you're interested in an option I haven't explained in detail or covered in a table, consult this text to help you make your decision.

NOTE: Use common sense when following my suggested settings. If I haven't recommended enabling the driver for hardware you use on your Linux system, for example, go ahead and enable it. These suggestions are general-purpose and won't suit every situation.

Code Maturity Level Options

This option allows you to include partially developed features or drivers included with this version of the kernel. Unless you have to use hardware that only has experimental drivers, or wish to test these features, there's no reason to include them. If you do include them, you risk the usual dangers of using potentially incomplete code. Suggested config settings are shown here.

Setting Name	Recommended	Safest If Undecided
Prompt For Development And/Or Incomplete Code/Drivers	N	N

Loadable Module Support

These options allow you to determine how to handle pieces of the kernel code that are compiled as modules rather than built into the kernel. The options are shown here.

Setting Name	Recommended	Safest if Undecided
Enable Loadable Module Support	Y	Y

Setting Name	Recommended	Safest if Undecided
Set Version Information On All Module Symbols	N	Y
Kernel Module Loader	Y	Y

Activating the Enable Loadable Module Support feature allows you to compile certain kernel options as modules. These modules aren't included in the main kernel; they can be loaded into and removed from the kernel that's currently running on an as-needed basis. I'm going to recommend making certain options into modules, so please do enable loadable module support.

The Set Version Information on All Module Symbols title is a grandiose way of saying, "let me use modules from another kernel with the kernel I'm building." This is useful if you want to load a module someone built with another version of the kernel, or if you want to load a module that wasn't part of the Linux kernel code at all. This doesn't happen terribly often, and because we're going to be making modules for the kernel we're building, you shouldn't need it unless you get modules from other people.

The Kernel Module Loader option builds into the kernel the ability to load modules as needed. This is a great feature because you don't have to load the modules yourself. Kmod, the process that handles loading of modules, can also be configured to remove unused modules. See the kmod documentation in linux/Documentation/kmod.txt for more information about how to do this.

Processor Type and Features

These options allow you to customize the kernel to reflect your computer's CPU type. The general rule is to choose settings that reflect no more functionality than your system supports. In other words, if you use processor settings from a previous generation of chips, you're much more likely to be successful than if you select options that exceed your computer's specs. Obviously, you can get the best performance by specifying the options that line up best with your exact system settings. The suggested settings for these options are shown below.

Setting Name	Recommended	Safest If Undecided
Processor Family	The one matching your CPU	386
Intel P6 Microcode Support	N	N
Model-Specific Register Support	N	N
CPU Information Support	N	N
High Memory Support	Off	Off
MTRR (Memory Type Range Register) Support	Y	Y

Setting Name	Recommended	Safest If Undecided
Symmetric Multi-Processing Support	Y if multiple CPUs	N

The help text associated with the Processor Family selection explains which processors belong to which families. You can successfully choose a processor family equal to or older than the family used in your system (if you've got a Pentium III, for example, you can use the most appropriate setting, PPro/6x86MX, or an earlier setting, such as Pentium, 486, or 386.) This might be useful if you're sharing a kernel between multiple systems and want to use the lowest common denominator or if you're uncertain about what type of CPU you're using (tsk, tsk).

The next three options are not likely to be widely useful; the Intel P6 CPU Microcode Support option allows updates to be made to the processor microcode for the Pentium Pro processor and its successors. The Model-Specific Register Support and CPU Information Support settings allow access to specific processors on SMP systems.

The High Memory Support settings depend on whether your system's RAM exceeds 1GB. If you have RAM totaling 1GB or less, select Off. If you have more than 1GB but less than 4GB, select 4GB. If you want to use more than 4GB RAM, select 64GB.

The Memory Type Range Register (MTRR) feature showed up in the Pentium Pro processor and offers performance gains for systems using those chips and their successors. Some non-Intel CPUs can use this feature as well, so if you have a recent CPU, it's worth enabling MTRR Support.

The Symmetric Multiprocessing Support option provides support for multiprocessor machines. Disabling this option means the system will use only 1 processor, even if it has more. Enabling symmetric multiprocessing (SMP) will work on multiprocessor machines, regardless of the number of CPUs.

General Setup

These options are a bit of a hodgepodge, covering everything from PCI bus behavior and general parallel port support to the binary file formats understood by the kernel and Advanced Power Management (APM). The suggested settings are listed next.

Setting Name	Recommended	Safest If Undecided
Networking Support	Y	Y
SGI Visual Workstation Support	N unless you have an SGI system	N
PCI Support	Y	Y
PC Access Mode	Any	Any
PCI Device Name Database	Y	Y
MCA Support	N unless you have an MCA bus	N

Setting Name	Recommended	Safest If Undecided
Support For Hot-Pluggable Devices	Y	Y
PCMCIA/Cardbus Support	Y	Y
System V IPC	Y	Y
Bsd Process Accounting	N	Y
Sysctl Support	Y	Y
Kernel Core (/Proc/Kcore) Format	ELF	ELF
Kernel Support For A.Out Binaries	Y	Y
Kernel Support For ELF Binaries	Y	Y
Kernel Support For MISC Binaries	Y	Y
Power Management Support	Y if laptop	Y
ACPI Support	N except laptops	Y
Advanced Power Management BIOS Support	N except on laptops	N

The Networking Support option doesn't just enable networking with other computers using Ethernet cards or dialup connections, it also allows certain inter-process communications that use internal network connections. Just enable this option, okay?

On the other hand, if you're using a Silicon Graphics Inc. (SGI) Visual Workstation model 320 or 540, enable the SGI Visual Workstation Support option and seek professional medical help.

The PCI Support option is required if you have a PCI bus in your system. Because most computers currently do have PCI buses, it's best to enable this option. How does one set the PCI Access Mode? Most PCI-based systems include intelligence in the computer's BIOS to detect and configure PCI cards. Because certain computers don't do this very well, you can tell Linux how to identify the PCI peripherals: With the "Direct" mode, which bypasses the BIOS, the "BIOS" setting, which consults the BIOS, or with the "Any" mode, which tries the first method and uses the second method if the first proves unsuccessful. The PCI Device Name Database gives somewhat intelligible names to each of the PCI devices on the system, storing them in /dev/pci.

The Microchannel Architecture (MCA) bus is rarely seen these days as IBM's MCA-based PS/2 computers grow ever older. But in the unlikely event that you're trying to run Linux on such a system (an endeavor I don't much support), you can enable the MCA Support option.

On the other hand, hot-pluggable drives, which are disk drives that can be added and removed while the system is running, are becoming more and more common. Being able to swap hard disks while a system is running allows administrators of high-availability systems to replace drives without taking the system down, which can be a very useful skill indeed. If you have hot-pluggable disk drives, enable the Support For Hot-Pluggable Devices option.

The PCMCIA bus is widely used on laptop computers, though it's also possible to equip desktop machines with PC Cards as well. Enable the CardBus Support option if you want to be able to use 32-bit CardBus cards on your Linux system.

The System V IPC option is required to let certain processes talk with one another. While it's not necessary for every piece of software you might run, it's a good idea to include this functionality nonetheless.

The BSD Process Accounting option allows some programs to track usage information about different processes. Unless the system is configured to record this information, and to make it available, it won't do you much good.

The Sysctl support option gives you control over how the kernel behaves without actually changing the kernel. Only certain parameters can be altered; these can be found in the /proc/sys/ directory and are documented in the linux/Documentation/sysctl/ directory.

The Kernel Support For A.Out Binaries option is retained for backwards compatibility; a.out is an out-of-date format used in earlier versions of Linux. Still, until it has gone away for good, I suggest that you continue to build a.out support into the kernel, just in case. Note that *a.out* is still the default name for C executable programs; if you compile a program under a recent version of Linux, however, the binary file will be in ELF format (even though it's still called a.out).

The current format used for Linux binary files (program files and libraries) is known as the Executable and Linkable Format (ELF). You need to enable the Kernel Support For ELF Binaries option to run Linux. The a.out format is disappearing from the scene as more programs use the ELF format.

The Kernel Support For MISC Binaries option allows the Linux kernel to launch certain program files automatically when it recognizes their type. Examples of these binary files are Java programs that need to be run in an interpreter, and DOS executables that need to be run through the dosemu DOS emulator. Additional documentation on this format is included in linux/Documentation/binfmt_misc.txt.

Enable the Power Management Support option if you're configuring Linux on a laptop or another system with power-management hardware. There are two primary standards for such hardware; you'll want to enable either ACPI Support or Advanced Power Management BIOS Support, depending on which one your system uses. In my experience, ACPI generally works better. There are several additional settings to configure if you enable APM support.

Memory Technology Device (MTD) Support

This option allows Linux to access a variety of solid-state storage devices, most of which are used with embedded systems and other special applications, rather than desktop systems and servers. Unless you know you have an MTD, there's no need to enable this option.

Setting Name	Recommended	Safest If Undecided
Memory Technology Device (MTD) Support	N	N

Parallel Port Support

The Parallel-Port Support option enables Linux to use devices connected to the parallel port. While printers are commonly attached to parallel ports, many other peripherals, including a variety of disk drives, can use a parallel port connection. In a server environment, where printers are often directly network-connected rather than attached to computers, you may not need to activate your parallel ports. On the other hand, Linux makes a pretty fine print server and can save you a few bucks on an external print server device, so small environments especially may want to activate this option.

Setting Name	Recommended	Safest If Undecided
Parallel Port Support	Y	Y
PC-Style Hardware	Y	Y
Use FIFO/DMA If Available	Y	N
Support Foreign Hardware	N	N
IEEE 1284 Transfer Modes	Y	Y

If you're using a PC-compatible computer, and you activated parallel port support, you should select the PC-Style Hardware option. If you know your parallel port has a FIFO chip for accelerated parallel port communications, you can enable Use FIFO/DMA If Available. A few non-PC computers supported by Linux also use these parallel ports. If you have a non-PC-based system, you should select the Support Foreign Hardware option to enable the non-PC-style parallel port.

Finally, if you have a fairly recent system, you may have a bi-directional parallel port that complies with the IEEE 1284 standard. Enabling the IEEE 1284 Transfer Modes option allows you to make use of the Enhanced Parallel Port (EPP) or Extended Capabilities Port (ECP) functionality on your system. If you leave this option disabled, an EPP or ECP will still work as a standard printer port.

Plug and Play Configuration

Plug and Play (PnP) is a mechanism by which devices are identified for the system, and system resources are allocated for the devices. Enabling this feature allows the kernel to identify and manage PnP devices. The available options are shown here.

Setting Name	Recommended	Safest If Undecided
Plug And Play Support	Y	Y
ISA Plug And Play Support	Y	Y

Enable the Plug And Play Support option to turn on PnP support in the kernel. ISA bus devices can be identified to the system using the ISA Plug And Play Support feature.

While ISA cards aren't very common anymore, you may still have some; if you're not sure, I suggest you enable this feature.

Block Devices

This category includes the variety of storage devices and interfaces. The list of supported block device options is shown here.

Setting Name	Recommended	Safest If Undecided
Normal PC Floppy Disk Support	Y	Y
XT Hard Disk Support	N	N
Parallel Port IDE Device Support	N	M
Compaq SMART2 Support	N	M
Mylex DAC960/DAC1100 PCI RAID Controller Support	N	M
Loopback Device Support	N	M
Network Block Device Support	N	M
Logical Volume Manager (LVM) Support	Y	M
LVM Information In Proc Filesystem	Y	M
Multiple Devices Driver Support	Y	Y
Linear (Append) Mode	M	M
RAID-0 (Striping) Mode	M	M
RAID-1 (Mirroring) Mode	M	M
RAID-4/RAID-5 Mode	M	M
RAM Disk Support	N	M

Unless you don't have a floppy disk drive, you should enable the Normal PC Floppy Disk Support option. Even if you don't have a floppy drive, I'd suggest including it as a module. The XT Hard Disk Support option allows you to make use of ancient (IBM XT-era) disk controllers; most of these predate the 386, so you're very unlikely to have a system that uses one. The Parallel Port IDE Device Support option allows you to use an IDE device, such as a hard disk, tape drive, or CD-ROM drive, that connects to the parallel port. If you don't have such a device, you certainly don't need to enable this feature.

The Compaq SMART2 Support and Mylex DAC960/DAC1100 PCI RAID Controller Support options allow you to make use of these popular RAID controllers. Unless you're using a server with these devices, you can leave both options disabled.

In the context of the Loopback Device Support option, a loopback device is a file that can be treated like a disk partition or a disk in a removable drive. There are cases where people want to access disk images (such as a diskette image or ISO 9660 CD-ROM image) this way, but most folks can pass on this option.

The Network Block Device Support option enables an infrequently used method of sharing disk drives via TCP/IP, but using a more standard mechanism, such as NFS, is a better choice. Disable this option.

The Logical Volume Manager (LVM) Support option provides the ability to access virtual disks and partitions using a series of abstracted volumes and devices. You can clump multiple partitions and devices together into a group, and then subdivide this logical group into sets of logical volumes. It's a fairly flexible way of dealing with multiple partitions and disks, but it's a little complicated unless you're really interested. If you enable this option, you should also enable the LVM Information In Proc Filesystem feature, which provides access to the LVM management data via the /proc/lvm directory. If you're interested in LVM, be sure to see the linux/Documentation/LVM-HOWTO document for more information.

The Multiple Devices Driver Support option is a more traditional way of allowing you to address multiple hard disks as one logical drive. Just as software-based mirroring and other redundant array of inexpensive drives (RAID) options are available under Windows, they're available under Linux if you enable this option. Note, though, that the management of software RAID systems isn't as effortless in Linux as in Windows NT and 2000. Whether you merely combine two or more disk partitions or want to use RAID level 0, 1, 4, or 5, you should enable this feature.

Because this enables software-based multiple device support, you don't need to use this option to address a hardware RAID card. Hardware RAID is a better option if you can afford it, but if not, you can use the software version under Linux. Read more about software RAID in the Software RAID mini-HOWTO, which is usually found in the /usr/doc/ tree. For the very latest versions of HOWTO and mini-HOWTO documents, see **http://www.linuxdoc.org**, where you can browse or download documents to your heart's content.

▼ **Linear (Append) Mode**   Linear or append mode refers to combining multiple disk partitions into a single logical device to expand available space. From a storage capacity perspective, the inexpensive, high-capacity drives available today make this feature somewhat unnecessary, but from an ease of management perspective, it's nice to have the option to add another disk without pulling the old one out. All the same, I'd probably pass on the option or compile it as a module.

■ **RAID-0 (Striping) Mode**   Disk striping writes data across multiple disks to minimize the delay introduced by asking a single drive to write a chunk of data. Allowing two or more drives to divide the task of writing the data (writing consecutive bits of data across the array) improves performance. It doesn't, however, improve reliability, because there's no redundancy built into the system. So although it's fast, if you lose one of the disks from the striping set, you lose the whole set of data. So I wouldn't recommend RAID 0.

- ■ **RAID-1 (Mirroring) Mode**   RAID-1 doesn't stripe the data across multiple devices; instead, it writes the data to all the devices in the array. This makes it fast for read operations and about the same speed as a single drive for write operations. As long as a single hard disk remains intact, though, a system with mirrored drives can keep operating even if all the other drives conk out. This is a good, reliable mode of operation, so I'd suggest enabling this option or compiling it as a module.

- ■ **RAID-4/RAID-5 Mode**   These methods combine the data striping features of RAID 0 with "parity" data, which allows the system to continue operating if a single drive fails. And while I've had multiple drives from a RAID set fail at once, these methods are generally seen as offering the best combination of performance and failure resistance. RAID 4 sets aside a single drive to store the parity data, which provides the ability to rebuild the data should a disk fail. RAID 5 achieves the same result by striping the parity data across all the drives in the array. This is an efficient way to combine a set of disks for capacity and fault tolerance, and I'd suggest that you enable the option or compile it as a module.

- ▲ **RAM Disk Support**   Unless you have a reason to use a RAM disk (as with Windows systems, this is a mechanism by which part of the system's memory is accessed like a disk drive), there's no reason to enable this option. You can always select M to make it a module. RAM disks are often used during Linux installation, so they're enabled in the kernel that comes with most distributions.

A RAM disk is theoretically a good way of improving performance (by loading a program into a RAM disk, you may largely avoid touching the hard disk; since RAM is dramatically faster than disk, this is a good thing). However, Linux attempts to use available RAM to cache frequently accessed data, so the performance gains you would see from RAM disk use will generally be minimal.

Networking Options

This set of options deals with the type of networking features you plan to use rather than the hardware you plan to use. There are many options here, but most of them are not necessary for standard server or workstation operation. My recommended settings are shown here.

Setting Name	Recommended	Safest If Undecided
Packet Socket	Y	Y
Packet Socket: mmapped IO	N	N
Kernel/User Netlink Socket	Y	Y
Routing Messages	N	Y
Netlink Device Emulation	Y	Y

Setting Name	Recommended	Safest If Undecided
Network Packet Filtering	N except on systems used as Internet gateways	N
Socket Filtering	N	N
Unix Domain Sockets	Y	Y
TCP/IP Networking	Y	Y
IP: Multicasting	N	N
IP: Advanced Router	N	N
IP: Kernel Level Autoconfiguration	N except on systems relying on BOOTP or RARP servers	N
IP: Tunneling	N	N
IP: GRE Tunnels Over IP	N	N
IP: TCP Explicit Congestion Notification Support	N	N
IP: TCP Syncookie Support (Disabled Per Default)	N	N
The IPX Protocol	N unless you use IPX/NetWare	M
Appletalk Protocol Support	N unless you use AppleTalk	M
Decnet Support	N unless you use DECnet	M
802.1d Ethernet Bridging	N	N

Certain applications don't need to use an external networking protocol to communicate with a system's network devices; instead, they use the Packet Socket mechanism. While you may not know whether you'll be using these programs, it's best to assume you'll want to and enable this function. The Packet Socket: mmapped IO option is intended to accelerate input and output in the packet socket mechanism; disabling this option won't hurt anything, and it may be safer.

The next option enables a socket for communications between the kernel and applications running outside the kernel (in what's known as user space). You must enable the Kernel/User Network Link Driver option to use the routing messages feature and advanced routing, as well as a few other functions. If you expect to use the Linux system for which you're building the kernel strictly as a workstation, file, or print server, this option probably isn't necessary. But if you intend to use it as a network device, such as a router, DNS server, etc., enable it.

The Routing Messages option allows you to create a "character special file" called /dev/route in which the system will place some routing information. If you enable this option, you must log on to the system as root and use the mknod program to create /dev/route using this command:

```
root@romans \> mknod /dev/route c 36 0
```

This command may seem a little cryptic, but it's just telling Linux to create a special file called /dev/route, that the file is a character special file (it gets written to one character at a time), and that its identifying "major number" is 36 and its "minor number" is 0. The major and minor numbers identify the function of the special file to the operating system; a current list of the device files defined this way is located in the kernel Documentation directory (usually linux/Documentation/devices.txt).

If you enabled the Kernel/User netlink socket above, enable Netlink Device Emulation as well. It won't even be an option if you disable the netlink socket.

It's a truism these days that there are more crackers (by which I mean malicious hackers, not unrefined people from rural areas) with more time on their hands than there are system administrators, let alone network security experts. Given that reality, you have to think of network security the way we think of securing a house or a car: You can't really expect to achieve impenetrability, but you want to avoid being too attractive to the bad element, and you certainly don't want to make it easy for them to take or trash things.

That is actually related to the point at hand, which is that a simple, relatively low-powered Linux machine can function as a network firewall, given the proper configuration. While there are Linux-based products available that provide this functionality with prettied-up administration options, one may also configure things manually, and one way of doing this is by enabling this option in the kernel.

A network firewall allows you to isolate certain networks using a set of rules that defines which traffic is permitted and which is denied. The firewall supported by this kernel configuration option is a packet filter, which means that the firewall can permit and deny packets based on where they come from, where they're going, and the packet type.

If you want this Linux system to act as a packet filtering firewall, Enable Network Packet Filtering. Disable this option on ordinary workstations and servers. If you enable it, a submenu called IP: Netfilter Configuration will appear near the end of the Networking options menu. You'll want to open that submenu and enable the first two options: Connection Tracking and IP Tables Support. The other two options are for backward compatibility and shouldn't be necessary if you're setting up a new Linux system.

The Socket Filtering option allows programs outside the kernel to filter the packets that travel through specific sockets. These filters can be configured and passed to the kernel for individual sockets, but this option is really targeted to programmers. So leave this option disabled unless the contents of linux/Documentation/networking/filter.txt give you enough information to do something with it.

Enable the Unix Domain Sockets option, which allows various Linux programs to talk to each other. This option should be enabled even if you don't plan to network a system, because it allows interprocess networking—communications between applications on the same machine.

Everyone should enable the TCP/IP Networking option, which gives you access to TCP/IP networking on the Linux system and is used by some applications to communicate within the local host. In other words, there's not much reason *not* to enable this option. There are several additional options that become available when you enable TCP/IP.

Multicasting is a type of networking used to make communications from one-to-many or many-to-many computers more efficient. While standard unicast networking sends data from one network node to another, multicast sends the data from a network node to several specified addresses, meaning the data doesn't have to be resent to each recipient individually. This reduces the amount of network traffic required to get the data to all destinations.

This is useful for functions such as video broadcasting over the network, stock quote updates, and use of the IP Multicast Backbone (MBONE), which uses the Internet for distribution of multicast data. Most people don't need this functionality, so disable IP: Multicasting unless you've got a use in mind.

IP: Advanced Router is a parent option that allows configuration of several sub-options related to using a Linux system as a router. If you're building a kernel for a system you intend to use to route data between multiple networks, enable this option to get access to the child options. Otherwise, leave it disabled.

Enable the IP: Policy Routing suboption to allow a Linux-based router computer to be able to use routing rules based on the source address. Unless you enable this option, the router will only use the destination address when determining how to route any given packet. If you'll be running this kernel on a router, enable the option. Otherwise, don't bother.

The IP: Equal Cost Multipath option allows you to set up more complicated routing rules. Unless you enable this option, when a packet is routed, there's only one path it can take to its destination. If you enable this option, you can allow multiple paths to the same destination. These paths have equal cost, which is to say that none of them is automatically considered preferred over the others. Unless you know you'll need this, disable this option.

If you enable IP: Use TOS Value As Routing Key, the type of service (TOS) values associated with IP packets can be used to determine the route each packet will take. This allows you to select different types of networks to carry data with different needs, as specified by each packet's TOS information. Unless you know you'll need this, disable this option.

If you enabled the advanced router, you should also enable IP: Verbose Route Monitoring, which provides detailed routing log messages. This is one way of identifying improperly configured machines on the network or illicit attempts to gain access to your network.

For large networks with complex routing tables, you can make routing more efficient by enabling IP: Large Routing Tables. Smaller networks (the kernel help information suggests fewer than 64 entries) don't need this feature enabled.

IP: Kernel Level Autoconfiguration should be enabled on Linux systems that boot off the network rather than from a local disk. The autoconfiguration option initializes each system's networking functions using BOOTP or RARP. If you're installing this kernel on a diskless workstation, enable this option and either IP: BOOTP Support or IP: RARP Support, depending on whether your network uses the BOOTP protocol or a RARP server.

Enable IP: Tunneling only in the unlikely event that you need to encapsulate IP packets within IP packets, which is only useful if you're trying to spoof an address for good or ill. If you need it, you can also enable IP: GRE Tunnels Over IP to support generic routing encapsulation (GRE), which is used to help IPv6 and the far more commonly used IPv4 coexist on the same networks. The help text for this option notes that this can be useful for communicating with Cisco routers, which prefer the GRE tunneling to the standard Linux IP tunneling.

Enable IP: TCP Explicit Congestion Notification Support if you plan to use Explicit Congestion Notification (ECN) is a method of identifying and responding to network congestion on TCP/IP networks. If you're rolling out a network on which the router and most or all of the connected workstations use ECN, this can be useful—instead of dropping data packets when the network is congested, an ECN-equipped router tells the stations on the network to talk slower so it can keep up. If you have no plans to use ECN, you don't need this option.

IP: TCP Syncookie Support (Disabled Per Default) employs a defense mechanism known as "SYN cookies" to prevent a particular denial-of-service attack known as "SYN flooding." By using SYN cookies, the system can determine which users should be able to connect to the host system while the SYN flooding is taking place.

If your system will be accessible from the Internet, it's a good idea to enable this option, but as the name indicates, simply selecting the option before a kernel build isn't enough to turn on the SYN cookies. To do that, use the following command after you've compiled and installed the kernel:

```
root@romans /> echo 1 >/proc/sys/net/ipv4/tcp_syncookies
```

If you are using a multivendor environment with Novell NetWare servers, and would like to intercommunicate using their (formerly) native IPX protocol, enable The IPX Protocol. SPX support is in the experimental stage as I write this, so the extent of your application connectivity may be limited, but for basic networking functionality, including access to files and printers, IPX will serve admirably. Of course, if you have no NetWare, it's very unlikely you'll need IPX.

If you do enable IPX networking, you have the option of giving your Linux host an internal IPX network address to allow socket-level communications using the IPX: Full Internal IPX Network option.

If you have networked Macintoshes using Ethertalk or (heaven help you) LocalTalk that need to see your Linux box, enable Appletalk Protocol Support. You'll have to use the netatalk program, which is available from **http://www.umich.edu/~rsug/netatalk/**, to enable file and print services for AppleTalk-based Mac clients. And if you have to support communications with Digital Equipment Corp. systems using DECnet, you should enable the DECnet Support option. Otherwise, leave both these options alone.

The last networking option is for *802.1d Ethernet Bridging*. This feature allows a Linux system with multiple network cards to act as a bridge between Ethernet networks. As data packets come into the system's network card from one Ethernet, the system can check to see if that packet is destined for the bridged Ethernet, and if so, it will send the data onto that network over the other network card. Unless you mean to turn your Linux system into a network device, you don't want to do this.

Telephony Support

This option allows use of Quicknet Technologies, Inc.'s telephony cards, which allow you to make telephone calls by combining access to the plain old telephone system and the Internet. Unless you have one of the Quicknet products, don't enable this option, as indicated below. If you do, see the associated help text and **http://www.quicknet.net/** for more information.

Setting Name	Recommended	Safest If Undecided
Linux Telephony Support	N	N

ATA/IDE/MFM/RLL Support

Setting Name	Recommended	Safest If Undecided
Enhanced IDE/MFM/RLL disk/cdrom/tape/floppy Support	Y if IDE in use	Y
Use Old Disk-Only Driver On Primary Interface	N	N
Include IDE/ATA-2 DISK Support	Y	Y
Use Multi-Mode By Default	N	N
PCMCIA IDE Support	N	Y
Include IDE/ATAPI CDROM Support	Y	M
Include IDE/ATAPI TAPE Support	M	M
Include IDE/ATAPI FLOPPY Support	Y	M
SCSI Emulation Support	N	Y
CMD640 Chipset Bugfix/Support	Y	Y
CMD640 Enhanced Support	N	Y
ISA-PNP EIDE Support	N	N

Setting Name	Recommended	Safest If Undecided
RZ1000 Chipset Bugfix/Support	Y	Y
Generic PCI IDE Chipset Support	Y	Y
Sharing PCI IDE Interrupts Support	N	N
Generic PCI Bus-Master DMA Support	N	N
Boot Off-Board Chipsets First Support	N	N
Other IDE Chipset Support	N	N

Enable the Enhanced IDE/MFM/RLL disk/cdrom/tape/floppy Support option, which provides the full set of controls for IDE devices, which are ubiquitous enough that you should support them. If you've got an all-SCSI system, I'd still recommend building this option as a module. It's just too convenient to have the ability to throw in an IDE CD-ROM drive, hard disk, or tape drive without rebuilding the kernel.

Disable the Use Old Disk-Only Driver On Primary Interface option except in the unlikely event that you've got a really old hard disk interface for your first IDE drive *and* you have newer devices on secondary or later IDE interfaces.

Enable the Include IDE/ATA-2 DISK Support option unless you don't have IDE hard disks, in which case you should still build the module. Even if you're a SCSI bigot like me, you might want to connect an IDE drive at some point.

Enable the Include IDE/ATAPI CDROM Support option. If you don't have an IDE CD-ROM, build the option as a module. More than once I've temporarily connected an IDE CD-ROM to a system, and it's very nice to have the module available. While you're at it, build the Include IDE/ATAPI TAPE Support option as a module unless you already have an IDE tape drive or expect to add one. You should be able to disable the Include IDE/ATAPI FLOPPY Support option unless you have an ATAPI floppy drive, an LS-120 diskette drive, or an IDE ZIP drive.

Disable SCSI Emulation Support unless you know one of your IDE ATAPI drives is not supported natively by Linux. SCSI emulation is about making your IDE device look like a SCSI device, not about allowing you to access SCSI devices from an IDE system.

The remaining options mostly relate to support for specific IDE chipsets. If you know the chipset in use on your system, you can enable support for it and exclude the other options. If you're not sure about your IDE support, though, you can still configure your system relatively easily by enabling the top-level support options:

▼ CMD640 Chipset Bugfix/Support

■ ISA-PNP EIDE Support

■ RZ1000 Chipset Bugfix/Support

■ Generic PCI IDE Chipset Support

▲ Other IDE Chipset Support

Enable any additional hardware-specific options that are appropriate for your system.

SCSI Support

This option enables support for SCSI devices on the Linux system. If you know the system for which you're building the kernel has no SCSI host adapters or devices, and if you're not planning to add any, you can disable this option. Assuming you do have SCSI devices on your system, my option suggestions are shown here.

Setting Name	Recommended	Safest If Undecided
SCSI Support	Y	Y
SCSI Disk Support	Y	M
Maximum Number Of SCSI Disks That Can Be Loaded As Modules	40	40
SCSI Tape Support	M	M
SCSI CD-ROM Support	Y	Y
SCSI Generic Support	M	M
Enable Extra Checks In New Queuing Code	N	Y
Probe All LUNs On Each SCSI Device	N	N
Verbose SCSI Error Reporting	Y	Y
SCSI Logging Facility	N	Y

If you have SCSI devices on your Linux system, enable the SCSI Support option. You can specify support for particular types of SCSI devices separately. The first such option is SCSI Disk Support. This refers to hard disks using the SCSI interface, so if you have one or more, enable this. The next option sets the Maximum Number Of SCSI Disks That Can Be Loaded As Modules; the default of 40 is a fine setting for most of us, and it's not necessary to make the number close to the number of disks you're actually using.

Enable SCSI Tape Support if you have or plan to add a SCSI tape drive, and of course, you should enable the SCSI CD-ROM Support option if you have or plan to add a SCSI CD-ROM drive. Less obvious is the SCSI Generic Support option, which includes a hodgepodge of devices that don't fit into the other categories, including SCSI-based scanners and CD-R devices.

The Enable Extra Checks In New Queuing Code may not be an option in the version of the kernel you have available; it exists in the preliminary version to help identify problems in the SCSI code. If it's an option, enable it. The Probe All Luns On Each SCSI Device function is needed only for certain SCSI devices such as CD jukeboxes that have multiple SCSI Logical Unit Numbers (LUNs).

Enabling the Verbose SCSI Error Reporting option makes the SCSI-related error messages more verbose, and therefore more likely to be understood (ergo more useful). That's generally a good thing, so I say go for it. I'd only enable the SCSI Logging Facility option if you're having system problems and suspect that something in the SCSI bus is to blame. This is one of those options that must be enabled in the kernel and then turned on after the kernel is compiled and installed. Use this command:

```
root@romans /> echo "scsi log all 0" > /proc/scsi/scsi
```

This will capture all SCSI activity for future reference and troubleshooting. Identify your SCSI problem and then stop logging using this command:

```
root@romans /> echo "scsi log none 0" > /proc/scsi/scsi
```

There are two submenus available from this menu, each of which allows you to select the correct SCSI hardware for your system. Use the SCSI Low-Level Drivers menu for desktop and server systems, and select the driver or drivers you need to include to support your SCSI cards. For laptop systems using PCMCIA-based SCSI interfaces, the PCMCIA SCSI Adapter Support should be just the ticket.

I2O Device Support

This option is pretty easy to figure out: If you have any I2O devices, enable support for them here. If you don't have any I2O devices, don't enable support. The I2O architecture is intended to simplify the creation and use of device drivers, and to improve their throughput. For more information about I2O, including a list of products that use it, see **http://www.i2osig.org**.

Setting Name	Recommended	Safest If Undecided
I2O Support	N	N

Network Device Support

Unless you don't plan to network a Linux system, you should enable this option. While there are some methods of networking a Linux box without enabling this option, they're obscure (to most Windows administrators, at any rate) and I don't recommend them. However, I also don't recommend enabling more of these device support options than you really need. Below is a summary of my suggestions for the options selectable from the main menu.

Setting Name	Recommended	Safest If Undecided
Network Device Support	Y	Y
Dummy Net Driver Support	Y	Y
Bonding Driver Support	N	M
EQL (Serial Line Load Balancing) Support	N	M

Setting Name	Recommended	Safest If Undecided
Universal TUN/TAP Device Driver Support	N	M
General Instruments Surfboard 1000	N unless you use this product	N
FDDI Driver Support	N unless you use FDDI	N
PLIP (Parallel Port) Support	M	M
PPP (Point-To-Point Protocol) Support	Y	Y
SLIP (Serial Line) Support	N unless you must use SLIP	N
Fibre Channel Driver Support	N unless you use SLIP	N

Note that there are several submenus that can be reached from the Network device support page. These give technology-specific options, virtually all of which are device drivers for networking products that use these technologies:

▼ ARCnet devices

■ Ethernet (10 or 100Mbit)

■ Ethernet (1000 Mbit)

■ Wireless LAN (non-hamradio)

■ Token Ring devices

■ Wan interfaces

▲ PCMCIA network device support

Although the Dummy Net Driver Support option doesn't do much except in systems that only use Serial Line Internet Protocol (SLIP) dialup networking, it doesn't hurt to include it in your kernel. It provides a dummy network address for use when the machine isn't dialed into the network. This address just keeps applications from getting confused when the system is offline. Enable it.

The Bonding Driver Support option is a method of connecting systems together using more than one Ethernet connection. For example, you might want to connect a web server and the database server that it accesses using two 100MB Ethernet cards instead of just one. This process is known as *bonding* in the parlance of the Linux kernel, and enabling this option will allow it to happen. You also need multiple Ethernet cards and support for this feature on the computer or network equipment you're connecting to the Linux system you're configuring. This would be a rare occurrence, so most folks can disable this option.

EQL (Serial Line Load Balancing) Support is a funky feature that allows you to use two modems connected to a single system to improve network throughput. If the host you're dialing into can support this feature, it's a way of making SLIP and PPP connections rival ISDN speeds. More information is contained in linux/Documentation/networking/eql.txt. Most people don't have this type of configuration and can disable this option.

The Universal TUN/TAP Device Driver Support option allows you to configure a character special file that is treated like any normal Point-to-Point or Ethernet device. The file can be configured and accessed like a normal NIC. While this is kind of cool, it's not the type of thing that most Windows administrators are looking for. So disable the option. And unless you use the General Instruments Surfboard 1000 cable modem, don't enable that option.

If your Linux system uses a Fiber Distributed Data Interface (FDDI) NIC, enable the FDDI Driver Support option. While FDDI's dual ring redundancy and relative efficiency makes it a good backbone technology, its expense and the myriad of high-speed Ethernet options available make it relatively uncommon. So unless you've already got FDDI installed, don't bother with this option.

The Parallel Line Internet Protocol (PLIP) allows you to connect two PCs via the parallel port. But consider that you can purchase 10/100 Mbit Ethernet cards for $10 each before you get too excited about using the parallel port to transfer data. Why not network the systems instead? Disable the PLIP (Parallel Port) Support option.

The Point to Point Protocol (PPP) is used to connect systems using dialup lines. It's more recent than SLIP (the next option) and is a better option if you get to choose between the two. If you'll be dialing up (or being dialed up) for network access, enable the PPP (Point-To-Point) Support option. If you're using a modem for remote access, as most people do, you'll also want to enable the PPP Support For Async Serial Ports option that appears once you enable PPP.

The Serial Line Internet Protocol (SLIP) is another dialup protocol used to network systems over dialup lines. If PPP access isn't available to you (shame on your ISP or clients if that's the case), you can opt to enable SLIP instead by turning on the SLIP (Serial Line) Support option. If you do enable SLIP, you might as well also enable the Compressed SLIP (CSLIP) protocol, which allows compression of the packet headers to improve performance and the "Keepalive and linefill" options, which improve reliability on poor dialup lines. Don't enable 6-bit encapsulation unless the system you connect to requires it.

Amateur Radio Support

Do you want to attach amateur radio equipment to your Linux system? Then enable the Amateur Radio support option, read the HAM-HOWTO and the AX25-HOWTO documents, select the appropriate drivers, and continue with the kernel compilation. The rest of us will disable this option and slowly back away.

Setting Name	Recommended	Safest If Undecided
CONFIG_HAMRADIO	N	N

IrDA Subsystem

If you're building a Linux kernel for a system with an infrared port (most often, a laptop computer) and you wish to use Infrared Data Associations (IrDA) communications while using Linux, you must select this option. If you do so, you'll have several protocol options to choose from.

The IrLAN protocol allows you to connect systems via an infrared Ethernet. The IrCOMM protocol allows you to emulate a serial port over an infrared link. The IrLPT protocol allows you to set up the Linux box to print to a printer with an infrared port, but in server mode, it also allows you to use the Linux box as an infrared print server, giving access to a locally-connected printer to other infrared-equipped systems.

For further details on what's involved in using infrared connections on Linux systems, consult the IR-HOWTO document. An extremely brief document is available with the kernel in linux/Documentation/networking/irda.txt. More information can be found at **http://irda.sourceforge.net**. In most cases, people don't bother with infrared communications, and should set this option as shown below.

Setting Name	Recommended	Safest If Undecided
IrDA Subsystem Support	N	M

If you enabled the IrDA subsystem support, you should also enable the corresponding Infrared-Port Device Drivers. If you have enabled IrDA, you should enable the following options as well:

▼ IrTTY IrDA Device Driver

▲ IrPORT IrDA Device Driver

The remaining options enable support for specific IrDA chipsets and serial port dongles. Enable the appropriate one(s).

ISDN Subsystem

If you use an ISDN card in a system for which you're configuring a Linux kernel, you can enable this option to turn on ISDN support. This doesn't apply to ISDN modems and other devices that connect using another type of port, but internal ISDN devices may be supported. Most of the options in this section are device-specific drivers, so if you choose to enable this feature, you should choose the appropriate device support options. The driver for the widely-used Siemens chipset is known as HiSax and works with quite a few ISDN devices.

The non-device-specific ISDN options, such as support for synchronous PPP, require you to know what the ISDN device on the other side of the connection can support. Consult the help text and linux/Documentation/isdn/README for more information about ISDN configuration. Most people won't need ISDN support, and can disable the ISDN Support option.

Setting Name	Recommended	Safest If Undecided
ISDN Support	N	M

Old CD-ROM Drivers (Not SCSI, Not IDE)

If you're unfortunate enough to have a CD-ROM drive that uses a non-standard connection (that is, not IDE or SCSI), you may find support for it in this section. Enable the Support Non-SCSI/IDE/ATAPI CDROM Drives option and select the appropriate proprietary CD-ROM device to enable it under Linux.

If you're not sure which of these drivers your CD-ROM drive should use, you can consult the driver descriptions in linux/Documentation/cdrom/. Files in this directory give detailed information about the devices that correspond to the available drivers. Or be like the rest of us: Leave these options disabled and go buy yourself the dirt-cheapest IDE CD-ROM drive you can find.

Setting Name	Recommended	Safest If Undecided
Support Non-SCSI/IDE/ATAPI CDROM Drives	N	N

Input Core Support

These options allow you to use USB Human Interface Device (HID) products, particularly keyboards, mice, digitizing tablets, and joysticks. These options are used with character special device settings to make the USB devices available system wide. If you have USB capability on your system and think you might make use of it, enable all the options. If your system doesn't have USB ports, disable everything.

Setting Name	Recommended	Safest If Undecided
Input Core Support	Y	M
Keyboard Support	Y	M
Mouse Support	Y	M
Horizontal Screen Resolution	Depends on digitizer resolution	1024

Setting Name	Recommended	Safest If Undecided
Vertical Screen Resolution	Depends on digitizer resolution	768
Joystick Support	Y	M
Event Interface Support	Y	M

Character Devices

Character devices include virtual terminals, serial ports, mice, certain tape drives, and an assorted cast of other minor characters. My configuration suggestions are shown here.

Setting Name	Recommended	Safest If Undecided
Virtual Terminal	Y	Y
Support For Console On Virtual Terminal	Y	Y
Standard/Generic (8250/16550 And Compatible UARTs) Serial Support	Y	Y
Support For Console On Serial Port	Y	Y
Extended Dumb Serial Driver Options	N	N
Non-Standard Serial Port Support	N	N
Unix98 PTY Support	N	N
Parallel Printer Support	Y	M
Support For User-Space Parallel Port Device Drivers	M	M
QIC-02 Tape Support	M	M
Intel i8x0 Random Number Generator support	N	N
/dev/nvram support	N	N
Enhanced Real Time Clock Support	N except on SMP systems	N
/dev/agpgart (AGP Support)	N	N
Direct Rendering Manager	N	N

You should definitely enable the Virtual Terminal option, which allows the Linux system to be able to access multiple consoles from one keyboard and monitor. See Chapter 3 for a more detailed description of virtual consoles, which allow you to have multiple terminal emulators available. By toggling between these terminals, you can initiate multiple interactive console sessions, which can be convenient.

For example, you could start the kernel compilation process on one virtual console and then switch over to another virtual console to check your email. This isn't a big deal to those of us who are used to Windows NT and 2000, which multitask just fine. Linux can do it without the GUI, however, which means less overhead on the system and less likelihood of crashing (remember, Microsoft moved the video drivers into the kernel mode to improve performance starting with NT 4.0). You don't need to have X Windows running or even loaded to be able to switch screens like this.

The Support For Console On Virtual Terminal option should be enabled for normal workstation or server operation. This tells Linux that the system console should be displayed and controlled from a monitor and keyboard connected to the system. That means the set of virtual terminals you enabled in the previous option is the standard mechanism for human interface with the system. So why would you ever select something else? If, for example, you had a management console connected to several server serial ports, you might want those servers to convey information and receive instructions via those serial ports instead of the virtual terminals. I haven't personally used this configuration, and I doubt you will. So just enable this feature, okay?

Enabling the Standard/Generic Serial Support option enables standard serial ports, while disabling it disables standard serial ports. "Standard" serial ports are found on most PCs; nonstandard hardware includes devices such as boards used to add multiple additional serial ports. Unless you want to disable your serial ports altogether (a common thing to do on servers that don't have modems, UPS monitoring devices, or other hardware connected to the ports), or use nonstandard hardware, you ought to enable this option.

If you decided you want the system console messages—errors and other system messages—sent over a serial port, perhaps to a management console or to a printer, you should enable the Support For Console On Serial Port option. If you do so, you'll have to add a line to the LILO configuration file, /etc/lilo.conf, that looks like this:

```
console=ttyS1,9600 console=tty0
```

The first command specifies that the console messages will go to the second serial port (the numbering starts with 0, so 1 is the second port) at 9600 baud. The second command indicates that the default console is the first virtual console, but the serial port is still active. This configuration could be used to track the actions of system crackers, because they can cover their tracks elsewhere, but they can't erase printouts of system messages. For more information, see the file linux/Documentation/serial-console.txt.

Enabling the Extended Dumb Serial Driver Options setting allows you to select from the five dumb serial driver options that follow. Unless you expect to need one of these options (none of which are needed with most configurations), disable this option. On the other hand, if you have hardware that adds more than the four standard serial ports (known as COM1-COM4 in the Windows world), you should enable the Support More Than 4 Serial Ports option. Otherwise, disable it. If your serial port hardware allows more than one serial port to use the same IRQ, you can enable the Support For Sharing Serial Interrupts option. Otherwise, disable it.

The Auto Detect IRQ On Standard Ports option allows the kernel to select the IRQs used with your serial ports. But like the option name says, this isn't a safe thing to do (the ramifications of a bad guess can be problematic). So leave this option disabled. The Support Special Multiport Boards option refers to are serial boards with special monitoring ports used for failure warnings and the like. The kernel can support this feature if your hardware uses it. Otherwise, disable this option. Setting the Support The Bell Technologies HUB6 Card option isn't brain surgery: If you have one of these Bell Technologies cards, enable the option. If you don't, disable the option.

If a system for which you're building a kernel doesn't just use the standard serial ports, you'll want to enable the Non-Standard Serial Port Support option. Otherwise, disable the option. If you've got intelligent serial port hardware, enable this option and the option that corresponds to the hardware you're using. See the help text for the available hardware-specific options to see what devices are supported; there are multiple options available for several vendors. One additional option in this group enables synchronous HDLC communications for devices that support it.

Unless you know you need the Unix98 PTY Support feature, leave it disabled. This option exists because the GNU C library known as glibc 2.1 or libc-6.1 supports the Unix98 naming standard for pseudo-terminal devices. Previous versions of glibc followed the naming scheme that followed the example of BSD UNIX, so this option will only work if you've got the libc-6.1. You can check this by issuing the following command:

```
root@romans ~> ls -l /lib/libco.so.*
```

This will show the name of the current libc version, which will be a link to the GNU library. On a Red Hat 7 system, for example, the result of the previous command looks like this:

```
lrwxrwxrwx   1 root   root    14 Sep 29 18:23 /lib/libc.so.6 -> libc-2.1.92.so
```

If you enable the Unix98 PTY Support, you can also adjust the maximum number of the pseudo terminals from 0-2048. The default of 256 should work fine unless many users will be connecting to the system.

If you have one or more parallel ports to which you plan to connect one or more printers, enable the Parallel Printer Support option. While many people use inexpensive print server units that connect a printer to a network, it can be simpler to connect the printer directly to a computer, especially in small environments. And if you're installing Linux for a home system and don't happen to have a print server sitting around, this can be useful. If you use a serial port to connect your printer, or if you're building the kernel for a system without a connected printer, it's fine to disable this option.

If you have a QIC-02 tape drive, enable the QIC-02 Tape Support option. Otherwise, don't bother. If you do enable the option, you also have the option of enabling runtime configuration of the tape drive. See the associated help text for more information.

Watchdog Timer Support

Selecting these options allows you to set up a watchdog, which checks to see if the watchdog file is open, and if so, if it has been touched within the last minute; if it has not been, the system is rebooted. The idea here is that as long as the system's running properly, the watchdog file is modified periodically. Thus, if the file hasn't been altered in the last minute, the system must be on the fritz.

On a system that must be available as much as possible, you can enable the watchdog before a task that you think might lock up the system, and disable it afterwards. This process works best with a watchdog card you put in the system, but there's a software-only solution available as well. If you're interested, check out the information in the help text as well as the documents that come with the kernel: linux/Documentation/watchdog.txt and linux/Documentation/pcwd-watchdog.txt.

Activate the Intel i8x0 Random Number Generator Support if your system uses an Intel i8xx series motherboard. It won't be the end of the world if you have one of these boards and don't activate this feature, so if you don't know what chipset your motherboard uses (it often indicates the chipset as the system starts booting up), leave this feature deactivated.

Enabling the /dev/nvram Support option allows you to make use of the battery-backed memory in a PC's real time clock (RTC). There are only 50 bytes available here, and while this might be a cool little trick for a hacker, it's not wise for normal folk and administrators to be twiddling around in this area. Don't do it.

If you are building a kernel for an SMP system, enable the Enhanced Real Time Clock Support option. The RTC in your PC can also be used on uniprocessor machines, but I wouldn't suggest enabling this feature unless you're supporting multiprocessor machines. There is an associated character special file called /dev/rtc to which clock status information is written. To create that file, run the following command:

```
root@romans /> mknod /dev/rtc c 10 135
```

For more information about this option, see the associated help text and linux/Documentation/rtc.txt.

If you're using a system with an AGP-port 3D graphics card, you can enable /dev/agpgart to provide full AGP support for the card. As I write this, there isn't much support for this functionality, but that's likely to change. You should also enable the Direct Rendering Manager and the Direct Rendering Infrastructure (DRI) chip option that applies to your video card.

Mice

This set of options allows you to specify the specific type of non-serial mouse in use on your system. Most of these options are getting more rare; I still have a Microsoft Inport bus mouse and interface card, but it's languishing in a closet. Once PC manufacturers started widespread use of the PS/2 port, the proprietary bus mice listed here didn't stick around very long. Most people will want to enable the PS/2 Mouse Support option to access their PS/2 port mice, and will leave the rest of the options disabled.

However, if you have an older, proprietary bus mouse, or a TI Travelmate laptop or IBM PC110 palmtop, enable the corresponding option instead of the PS/2 mouse. For more information about these other devices, read the help text and the Busmouse-HOWTO.

Joysticks

If you have a joystick, enable the Joystick Support option, and make sure you enabled the Input Core Support option mentioned earlier. The rest of us will disable the option, shake our heads and get back to work (or continue playing games with mouse and keyboard). If you enable joystick support, you'll also need to enable the driver that matches your joystick hardware. If you're not sure what type of joystick you have, or yours doesn't appear to be listed, your best bet is to try the classic PC analog driver. May the force be with you.

For more joystick information, read the option-specific help text and these documents: linux/Documentation/joystick.txt and linux/Documentation/joystick-parport.txt. Quite an extensive array of products is supported, so you should be able to toast some foes without any trouble.

Ftape, the Floppy Tape Device Driver

Only enable the Ftape (QIC-80/Travan) Support option if you have one of these tape drives. I'm not a big fan of these devices, but they tend to be inexpensive, and that's certainly a motivating factor for many situations. So disable this if you don't use a tape drive on the system for which you're building the kernel, or if you've got a full-fledged IDE or SCSI tape drive. If you use a QIC-80 or Travan tape drive that fits the option description or is in the associated help text, enable this option. If not, it's fine to disable the option. Even if your tape drive doesn't connect to the built-in floppy drive controller, it may be controlled using the "floppy tape device driver" if it comes with its own proprietary interface card.

Enable the option if your tape drive is connected to your floppy disk controller, and set the additional settings to match your hardware. Read linux/Documentation/ftape.txt for more information.

PCMCIA Character Device Support

If you have a system that uses a 16-bit PCMCIA serial or modem card, or a 32-bit CardBus serial or modem card, activate this feature. For non-laptop users, it's pretty rare to see

PCMCIA cards in use (although it does happen). If your laptop uses a PC Card modem, you should activate this feature; otherwise, leave it off.

Multimedia Devices

If you're building a kernel for a system equipped with audio/video capture or manipulation cards, FM radio cards, or similar devices, you might investigate the options available here. This isn't an area of Linux that's very mature yet, but some information is available in a directory of its own: linux/Documentation/video4linux/.

I wouldn't very enthusiastically recommend Linux for doing audio-video work at this point unless you are a hacker or have access to hacker time. That opinion is likely to change as a little more time goes by, but there's much more selection on other platforms in terms of hardware and software available for the tasks. If you do enable Video For Linux, enable the appropriate hardware-specific driver as well. See the option-specific help text for more information about each driver.

Setting Name	Recommended	Safest If Undecided
Video For Linux	N	M

Filesystems

This set of options allows your Linux system to read (and often, to write) to a variety of different filesystems. While there are certain filesystems that should always be enabled (the Linux default file system type, ext2, and the standard CD-ROM filesystem, ISO-9660, come to mind), there are a number of other filesystems that may be useful in a mixed environment; you'll have to decide which are worth building into the kernel or compiling as modules, and which you don't expect ever to need. My suggestions are shown here.

Setting Name	Recommended	Safest If Undecided
Quota Support	Y	N
Kernel Automounter Support	N	N
Kernel Automounter Version 4 Support	Y	Y
DOS FAT fs Support	Y	M
MSDOS fs Support	Y	M
VFAT (Windows-95) fs Support	Y	M
Compressed ROM File System Support	N	N
Simple RAM-Based File System Support	N	N

Setting Name	Recommended	Safest If Undecided
ISO 9660 CDROM File System Support	Y	Y
Microsoft Joliet CDROM Extensions	Y	Y
Minix fs Support	N	M
NTFS File System Support	M	M
OS/2 HPFS File System Support	N	M
/proc File System Support	Y	Y
/dev/pts File System For Unix98 PTYs	N	N
ROM File System Support	N	N
Second Extended fs Support	Y	Y
System V And Coherent file System Support	N	N
UDF File System Support	Y	M
UFS File System Support	N	N

The Quota Support option allows you to set restrictions on ext2 filesystem disk usage for each account on the system. While disk quotas weren't built into Windows until the release of Windows 2000, if you've administered other network operating systems, such as NetWare, you may be familiar with quota management. The basic idea is that by specifying a maximum amount of disk space that a user can consume, you can prevent a small number of users from filling a shared partition with data, leaving no space for anything or anyone else.

Having worked in Information Systems departments for years, I consider this essential functionality for a network server, so unless you're the only user on the system, I suggest that you enable this option and read the Quota mini-HOWTO.

If you're going to be running on a distributed network with other Unix or Linux systems, enable the Kernel Automounter Version 4 Support option, which automatically mounts disk partitions (they can be on local drives, but this is generally most useful for network drives) as they're needed. This behavior is fairly transparent in Windows, and if you don't enable it, you'll feel a little peeved when you have to manually mount remote devices periodically. The Linux version of the automount concept unmounts the devices after the timeout you specify.

Adding support to the kernel isn't enough by itself; you'll have to start the automount daemon and indicate the partitions that you want automatically mounted. For more information, read the Automount mini-HOWTO document.

If you're going to run a dual-boot system or have left a DOS or Windows 9x partition on your Linux system, you'll definitely want to enable the DOS FAT fs Support option.

It's a good idea to enable it anyway so that you can read DOS diskettes and the like. When you enable this feature and one or more of the options that follow it, you allow Linux to read file allocation table (FAT) partitions transparently. Support for compressed drives isn't built into these options.

Enable the MSDOS fs Support option to give you access to plain old DOS partitions used by MS-DOS or Windows. This option allows you to access old-style FAT partitions with the standard 8.3 short filenames. It also gives you the option of using the next option, UMSDOS. The umsdos: Unix Like File System On Top Of Standard MSDOS fs option gives Linux the ability to run from an existing DOS partition. If you installed a distribution to an existing Windows system without creating a Linux partition, you'll need to enable this option. For example, the Corel Linux installation described in Chapter 4 runs from an existing Windows partition, and while this degrades performance, it's one way to try Linux without severely re-doctoring your system. If you've got an installation like that one, enable this feature and read linux/Documentation/filesystems/umsdos.txt. If you don't run Linux from a Windows partition, disable the option.

If you're running Linux on a Windows dual-boot system or left a Window FAT partition with long filenames intact on your Linux system and want to access the files contained on it, enable the VFAT fs Support option and read linux/Documentation/filesystems/vfat.txt. If you don't plan to access any Windows FAT disks with long filenames, you won't need this feature, but I'd still recommend that you compile the VFAT option as a module, because you just never know when it'll come in handy.

The Compressed ROM File System Support option is for use with the cramfs filesystem, which is a read-only filesystem mostly useful with embedded systems, and less applicable for desktop, laptop, or server systems. You can disable support for this feature.

Enable the ISO 9660 CDROM Filesystem Support option to be able to access CD-ROMs from your Linux system. This should be a no-brainer unless you don't plan to have a CD-ROM drive on the system for which you're building the kernel, and even then I'd suggest building this as a module. Joliet is Microsoft's extension to the standard ISO filesystem for CD-ROMs. It allows long filenames to be stored on and read from CD-ROMs. Whether you currently have any Joliet CD-ROMs or not, it's a good idea to enable the Microsoft Joliet CDROM Extensions option or at least compile it as a module so you'll be able to read them if you get them.

Minix is an educationally focused operating system that was an inspiration for Linux; Linus Torvalds wrote Linux in part because he wanted more functionality than Minix offered and he didn't like its license restrictions. He based some of the original Linux functionality on Minix; among those was the minix file system. It's unlikely that a Windows user coming to Linux at this stage of the game will need Minix compatibility, but you might get a Minix floppy from an aging operating system hacker, and you might need to use a "rescue" diskette that uses the Minix filesystem. I haven't had any problems, though, just disabling the Minix fs Support option.

Although there is experimental support for read-write access to NTFS partitions under Linux, this is a somewhat better option for real-life environments with data you care about. If you're migrating a server or workstation from Windows NT or 2000 to Linux, you can enable the Windows NT NTFS Support option to allow read-only access to the data on local NTFS partitions. Whether you use this access to migrate the data to a native Linux partition or just leave read-only access until the data is no longer needed is up to you.

IBM's long-lived, little-used replacement for DOS and Windows, known as OS/2, uses a filesystem called HPFS (for High Performance File System). If you've got a local disk with an HPFS partition you want to access, you can enable the OS/2 HPFS Filesystem Support option. If you're not an OS/2 user, don't bother.

I've mentioned the /proc filesystem several times in this chapter as well as in Chapter 3 and Chapter 5. In brief, it's a virtual filesystem from which you can read system information. It can be very useful to get the information it stores, and some programs need it to exist, so please do enable the /proc Filesystem Support option.

If you enabled Unix98 PTY support from the Character devices menu described earlier, enable the /dev/pts Filesystem For Unix98 PTYs option. I suggested that you disable that option, though, so unless you've got a reason to support the latest naming standard for pseudo terminals, disable this option too.

The ROM Filesystem Support option isn't often needed in everyday life; it exists to allow very small kernels that only load this filesystem initially, and then load additional filesystems as needed. The most common application of this functionality is Linux distribution installation disks, though it's possible to use it for other features. Most of us aren't likely to do so, though, so disable this option.

The second extended filesystem, better known as ext2, is the most commonly used filesystem on Linux systems. Unless you're running Linux from a Windows partition (on a Corel Linux system you installed without creating a Linux partition, for example), you should absolutely enable the Second Extended fs Support option, and I'd suggest you enable it even if you're running Linux from one of those UMSDOS partitions. The help text for this option helpfully points out the existence of the Ext2fs-Undeletion mini-HOWTO. It also points out some additional tools for tweaking or viewing ext2 partitions.

Unless you need to be able to read disk partitions from these operating systems, there's no need to enable the System V And Coherent Filesystem Support option. If you have an SCO, Xenix, or Coherent disk you need to access, you can do so by turning on this feature.

The Universal Disk Format (UDF) is a filesystem standard currently used primarily with DVD and CDROM devices. UDF is necessary for DVD-ROMs, and can also be used with CD-R and CD-RW drives to perform "packet writing." This standard is intended to be faster and more space-efficient than the ISO9660 filesystem traditionally used on CD-ROMs. If you want to read from DVD-ROMs or from CD-R or CD-RW discs that use UDF, you should enable the UDF Filesystem Support option. Read the linux/Documentation/filesystems/udf.txt file for more information about Linux-based UDF tools, and see Adaptec's DirectCD (**http://www.adaptec.com/products/faqs/directcd.html**) for an example of use of UDF on Macs and Windows-based systems.

UFS Filesystem Support enables the filesystem used in a number of BSD-derived versions of Unix, including FreeBSD, NetBSD, NextStep, OpenBSD, OpenStep, SunOS, and

Solaris. If you have disks from these systems you need to access locally, enable this option. Most people won't need to worry about this.

Network Filesystems

In the last set of options, you enabled the local filesystems you'll be using. In this set of options, you can specify network filesystems you wish to be able to access. These include commonly used filesystems such as Unix's NFS, Microsoft's SMB, and Novell's NCP, as well as a less-known filesystem known as Coda. While I list default suggestions for these options below, you should enable the ones you think you'll need for your environment.

Setting Name	Recommended	Safest If Undecided
Coda Filesystem Support	M	M
NFS Filesystem Support	Y	Y
Provide NFSv3 Client Support	N	N
Root Filesystem On NFS	N	N
NFS Server Support	N	M
Provide NFSv3 Server Support	N	Y
SMB Filesystem Support	Y	M
Default Remote NLS Option	Your NLS language code	Leave it blank
NCP Filesystem Support	M	M

Enabling the Coda Filesystem Support option allows your system to access Coda servers (if you use additional software to do so). Coda is a network filesystem that's similar to NFS, but including a number of significant enhancements, and much less widely used. I suggest that you build the Coda support as a module so that you have it as an option, but it's not likely to be necessary. For technical information about Coda, read linux/Documentation/filesystems/coda.txt and look at the web addresses referenced for the user software.

Enable the NFS Filesystem Support option so that you can connect to other Unix systems using the Network File Sharing (NFS) protocol. Although NFS has some problems, it's widely used and supported and is the de facto standard for mounting drives across a network of Unix machines. Even if you've only got one Linux computer and no other Unix systems, I think it's a good idea to compile in NFS support, especially because I think you'll end up with more than one Linux box. They're addictive. For more information on NFS, you can read the NFS-HOWTO document, which gives quite a bit of information, including interesting information about NFS security problems and a few things to do to make things more secure.

There is a newer version of NFS out there than the v2 that the preceding option enables. If you are in an environment built around NFS v3, you can enable the Provide NFSv3 Client Support option to access NFS v3 servers. If that's not the case in your environment (in mine, for example, the NFS servers will negotiate v2 or v3 on a per-client basis), leave this option disabled. If you're setting up a diskless workstation booting from an NFS partition across the network, enable the Root File System On NFS option. Otherwise, run away from it, screaming and pulling your hair, if any.

The previous NFS kernel options dealt with client functionality; they allow a system to access remote disks using the NFS protocol. The NFS Server Support option allows you to load NFS server functionality into kernel space. There are user-mode programs (programs outside the Linux kernel itself), notably nfsd, that allow you to do this, and while they're slower, they're also more mature and tend to be more common. Still, if you want to try this tool, enable this option and read the NFS-HOWTO document for more information. Otherwise, disable the option. If you want your Linux system to be an NFS v3 server, enable the NFS Server Support option as well.

Microsoft uses the Server Message Block (SMB) protocol for communications between Windows products. If you wish to mount Windows shares from a Linux box, you should enable the SMB Filesystem Support option. This isn't the same as Samba, the program that allows the Linux system to advertise disk and printer shares to Windows systems; I'll discuss Samba in Chapter 9.

In my environment, it's not necessary for the Linux systems to access Windows shares (we try not to keep anything important on Windows systems). However, I realize that most people may not be as fortunate as I am, so if you'd like access Windows shares from the Linux system, enable this option and read the SMB-HOWTO.

The NCP Filesystem Support option is similar to the SMB filesystem support option, but it allows access to NetWare volumes using Novell's NetWare Core Protocol (NCP). If you don't have NetWare servers on your network, disable this option (and the Network Filesystems options that follow, all of which are NetWare-related). However, if you want to read NetWare server volumes from the Linux system for which you're compiling the kernel, enable this option. That is, if you want this Linux system to act as a NetWare client, you should enable this option.

Although most people (including me) won't need to enable NetWare client support on their Linux system, the NetWare OS is dear enough to my heart that I'll quickly mention the suboptions related to NCP filesystem support. Enable the Packet Signatures option to improve security on your NCP network. Disable the Proprietary File Locking mechanism unless you know your NetWare-aware applications can use the file locking mechanism.

The Clear Remove/Delete Inhibit When Needed option should usually be enabled; it allows you to alter the Delete Inhibit and Rename Inhibit flags on NetWare files. The Use NFS Namespace When Available option is also usually desirable, as it enables NFS-style mixed-case filenames on NetWare volumes that support it. While you're at it, enable Use LONG Namespace If Available, which makes use of the OS/2 namespace on NetWare volumes that support it.

Unlike the NFS namespace, the OS/2 namespace does not support mixed-case filenames. Enabling the Lowercase DOS Filenames option displays in lowercase all filenames on a volume with the OS/2 namespace. The Allow Mounting Of Volume

Subdirectories option gives you the option of mounting subdirectories on NetWare volumes. Otherwise, you'll only be able to mount volumes from the top of the volume structure.

NDS Authentication Support is a useful feature if you want to authenticate your Linux box in an NDS environment. See the help text for a warning about the root user's ability to read the session key when this option is enabled. The Native Language Support (NLS) section that comes later in the configuration (and in this chapter) allows filenames to be displayed using appropriate character sets on client systems. It's a good thing, so enable Allow Using Of Native Language Support. And then enable Symbolic Links And Mode Permission Bits so you will be able to create symbolic links and manipulate execute permission bits on a NetWare volume from a Linux client.

Partition Types

These four options give you the ability to access disk drives partitioned from other operating systems. This is mainly of use if you have one of these drives installed on the system for which you're building a Linux kernel, which will be rare for folks moving from a Windows environment. Enable any that correspond with the origin of the disks you wish to access, but I'll assume you won't be doing this.

Setting Name	Recommended	Safest If Undecided
Advanced Partition Selection	N	N

Native Language Support

This set of options allows you to access files on certain partitions using native language characters. Activate the character sets that correspond to the languages you wish to use. For example, my computers and their files are located with their users in the United States. While some of us speak other languages at home, we use English to communicate with each other and with our customers. So I enable Codepage 437, which corresponds to the U.S. and Canada DOS character codepage, and NLS ISO 8859-1, which corresponds to North American and most Western European languages. The Default NLS Option should be set to the best default language for your situation; in mine, the iso8859-1 setting works just fine.

Console Drivers

The options in this section allow you to configure the drivers used to display the Linux console. The first option is one everyone will want to enable (it's good to have a console, it really is). I'm not as enthusiastic about the second option, at least for use by recovering Windows addicts.

Setting Name	Recommended	Safest If Undecided
VGA Text Console	Y	Y
Video Mode Selection Support	Y	Y

Enable the VGA Text Console option, which allows you to access the Linux text-mode console from any VGA-compliant system. I consider this a mandatory option, even on systems I don't expect to need to access from a local console display. Naturally, I think you should agree with me.

For people who do a great deal of work at a plain console prompt, the Video Mode Selection Support option is a definite plus. It allows you to specify the video mode used for the console screen. Instead of having one default resolution setting, you can vary the setting to fit more rows and columns of characters. I use this on systems that are mainly touched from the console, and you may decide you like it, too. However, I don't think it's widely useful for people migrating from the Windows world. If you're interested, enable this option and add this line to your /etc/lilo.conf file (remember to run /sbin/lilo afterwards):

```
vga=ask
```

This will prompt you for several resolution options when you start the system. Select the one you want and make a note of the corresponding code. If it looks good to you, you can edit the line you added to /etc/lilo.conf, replacing the "ask" argument with the four-digit code. Rerun /sbin/lilo and restart the system, and you're good to go.

Sound

While Linux provides support for a large number of sound cards, many users have found sound support somewhat difficult to configure. Many distributions include tools to make sound configuration simpler; Red Hat, for example, includes a text-mode utility called sndconfig. You can just run the command (as root), and Linux can automatically find and configure your sound card.

Setting Name	Recommended	Safest If Undecided
Sound Card Support	Y (if you use a sound card)	M

For server-class machines, I don't see a point in including a sound card at all, and I recommend leaving the Sound Card Support option disabled. If you want sound on your workstation (or a server, for that matter), go ahead and enable this option, then find the device-specific driver that corresponds to the sound hardware on your system. More information is available in the Sound-HOWTO, and in the help text for each option.

Note that many sound cards fall under the OSS Sound Modules option, so if you don't see your sound card in the initial list, be sure to enable the OSS option and look at the rest of the list.

USB Support

The Universal Serial Bus (USB) is a relatively new way of attaching peripherals to a personal computer. Although it has been around for a few years, USB still isn't overwhelmingly utilized in PC hardware, but this seems to finally be changing. In fact, it's possible to purchase "legacy-free" systems that eschew PS/2, keyboard, serial, and parallel ports in favor of more flexible USB ports. The USB connector takes less room than do standard serial or parallel connectors, so that's an advantage in many ways.

If you use USB ports and peripherals, you can tell the kernel to include support for them. While most of the USB support options are specific to the types of devices you use, there are a few general settings you should be able to figure out independent of your hardware.

Setting Name	Recommended	Safest If Undecided
Support For USB	Y if you use USB ports and devices	M
USB Verbose Debug Messages	N	N
Preliminary USB Device Filesystem	Y	Y

Enable Support For USB if you want to use USB devices. There's no need to turn on USB Verbose Debug Messages unless you're doing troubleshooting of the USB code, but if you enable USB, you should also enable the Preliminary USB Device Filesystem, which populates the /proc/usb directory with information about your USB bus and the devices connected to it.

You must enable one of the USB Controllers options; systems with Intel chipsets are most likely to use one of the UHCI drivers, while systems without Intel chipsets are most likely to use the OHCI driver. Select additional device support as appropriate for your menagerie of USB devices, and you're done.

Kernel Hacking

This last option is supposed to be used for kernel hacking; it provides key combinations using the SYSRQ key found on most current keyboards (the key also known as PRINT SCREEN). These key commands can give you control of the system even when the kernel's not behaving as it should.

The trouble is that most of these actions should really only be taken on a system that's being used for testing. You don't really want your production system being unintentionally rebooted, its processes stopped and restarted, or all programs killed in the current virtual terminal.

Setting Name	Recommended	Safest If Undecided
Magic SysRq Key	N	N

So I recommend that you do not enable this key. If you're really curious, though, I suggest that you read the linux/Documentation/sysrq.txt and decide for yourself whether to activate the magic key.

MANAGING MULTIPLE KERNELS

The ability to make customized kernels may lead you to wonder whether you can configure multiple kernels and make use of different ones at different times. Happily, the answer is yes. In many cases, creating a single kernel and loading additional modules when you need them is perfectly adequate. For example, if you have a laptop and want different devices loaded depending on whether you're on the road or in your office docking station, you can build the network and parallel port support as modules and load them only when you're docked and have a network card and printer.

However, there are circumstances where multiple kernels are a better option. Naturally, if you're going to be testing multiple kernel builds, it's a good idea to be able to back out of the changes you're making, and having access to multiple kernels is a good way of doing this. When certain distributions install themselves onto a multiprocessor system, they provide access to two kernels; one for normal SMP activities, and one for uniprocessor mode for troubleshooting.

So how do you make use of multiple kernels on a system? You instruct your boot loader to point to different kernel files and give yourself an opportunity to select one. The sample /etc/lilo.conf shown below configures the boot loader to prompt the user to enter one of two kernels: The standard kernel, stored in /boot/vmlinux; or the test kernel, stored in /home/millerm/bzImage.

```
boot = /dev/sda   # boot from the master boot record
                  # of the first SCSI drive
prompt            # prompt for the correct kernel at boot
delay = 15        # 15-second delay
linear            # It's a big SCSI drive

image = /boot/vmlinux   # the primary bzImage file
  root = /dev/sda1      # the root partition
  label = Linux         # the name used to select this kernel
  read-only             # mount root read-only initially

image = /home/millerm/bzImage   # a second bzImage file
  label = TestKernel            # the name used to select this kernel
  root = /dev/sda1              # the root partition
  read-only                    # mount root read-only initially
```

Some of the options shown in this example need to be changed on your system; the drive names and partition numbers, for example, need to correspond to your configuration.

You might want to change the delay time if you're slow on the draw (I tend to start doing something else when I reboot and sometimes forget to select the kernel I want during the delay...but a longer delay irritates me, so 15 seconds is a good compromise for me).

Naturally, you can't just point an "image" label at any old file; the kernel you want to use needs to be located there. And don't forget that you *must* run "lilo" as root to incorporate any changes you've made:

```
root@romans /> /sbin/lilo
Added Linux *
Added TestKernel
```

The asterisk indicates that the kernel labeled "Linux" is considered the default. The system will boot up with the default kernel unless you select another kernel from the prompt before the delay period passes (if a delay has been set in /etc/lilo.conf). To select a kernel that's not the default, type its label at the LILO boot: prompt as the system comes up. If you forget the name you want, press the TAB key while the LILO boot: prompt is visible, and a list of the configured labels will appear.

LILO CONFIGURATION FROM LINUXCONF

In the remaining chapters of this book, I'll demonstrate different types of system configuration and management tasks. Many of these tasks can be automated on Red Hat and derivative systems using a tool called "linuxconf." While the tool simply provides a graphical front end to the text-based utilities and files you would otherwise have to manipulate manually, it does provide a framework from which an experienced Windows system administrator can often work more comfortably than at the command line.

And although I've described the contents of the /etc/lilo.conf file, the truth is that you may not have to manually edit the file at all if linuxconf is available to you. So in this section, I'd like to explain how to run linuxconf, and how to use it to configure LILO.

Running linuxconf

Because linuxconf is a system configuration utility, you'll need to run it as root. That means you should log on as root or use the su command to become root. (Don't forget to use the exit command to become a regular user again when you're done.)

Run linuxconf from a console prompt or in an xterm using this command:

```
root@romans: /> /bin/linuxconf
```

If you're at a console prompt, a full-screen, text-mode interface will appear. If you are in X Windows, a graphical interface will appear. A panel on the left-hand side shows a tree of configuration options, and the detail window on the right side shows the settings available for the selected option. In Figure 6-5, the LILO tree has been expanded in the left-hand panel, and the LILO defaults option has been selected.

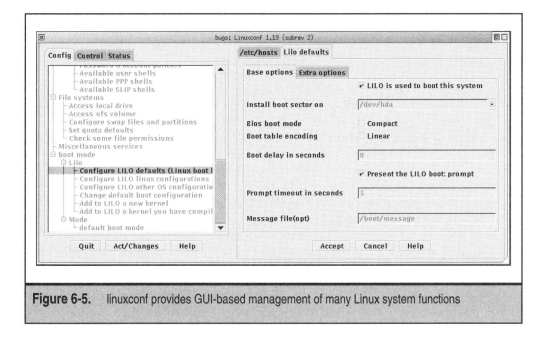

Figure 6-5.   linuxconf provides GUI-based management of many Linux system functions

Configuring LILO Defaults

As Figure 6-5 indicates, the LILO options that would ordinarily have to be typed into /etc/lilo.config are available with online help, drop-down lists, radio buttons, and other graphical crutches. This makes linuxconf an especially useful tool for the novice Linux administrator, since it gives you an idea of what your options are.

The Base options tab shown in Figure 6-5 allows you to enable or disable LILO as the system's boot loader (using the LILO Is Used To Boot This System button). You can indicate where LILO should install the boot sector, which in Figure 6-5 is set to the MBR on the first IDE hard disk, /dev/hda.

The Compact boot mode setting is supposed to reduce boot time, but I've never bothered to use it. The Linear boot table encoding setting, on the other hand, is useful for large SCSI drives, and I've had good results using it with large IDE drives as well.

You can set the boot delay if you want to configure a wait time before LILO starts booting, which I've never found particularly useful. Check the radio button to cause the LILO boot: prompt to appear (by the way, in Figure 6-5, the Compact and Linear buttons are deselected and the Present The LILO boot: Prompt button is selected; Windows users sometimes have trouble telling which is supposed to be which).

The timeout time is the duration the LILO boot: prompt is displayed before the system is booted using the default kernel, and the entry in the optional Message File box should point to a text file used to display a message at boot time.

NOTE: If you keep selecting menu options from the left-hand panel, the right-hand display area will become quite cluttered. It's nice to keep things tidy using Quit or Cancel to close configuration tabs you're not using, or Add or Accept changes you want to make.

Configuring Extra Options

The LILO defaults option in linuxconf also has an Extra Options tab, on which you can find several less frequently used LILO options. However, the first entry, which allows you to enter a "root partition," is a useful one. The value in this box should be the device name of the root partition (such as /dev/hda5). Another commonly used option is the Read Only selection for boot mode, which starts the system with its partitions mounted read-only to start with (you want this; the system will set them to read-write once the system is up and the partitions have been checked).

If you use a ramdisk, there are options for setting its size and for enabling an initial ramdisk (as described earlier in this chapter). You also have the option to set the VGA mode to something other than the default resolution. You can enable password protection on the startup process, and you can add other boot options (see the LILO HOWTO for more information).

Checking Configurations

The linuxconf menu also includes an option for viewing LILO Linux Configurations. If you select this entry from the left-hand panel, you will see a list of boot configurations showing each one's label, the partition it boots from, and the name and location of the kernel it boots. This is handy for keeping tabs on what's going on with your LILO configuration.

To add additional linux configurations, click the Add button and provide the information requested, including:

▼ Label

■ Kernel image file

■ Root partition

■ Ramdisk size (if any)

■ Boot mode

■ VGA mode (if any)

■ Boot options (if any)

■ Initial ramdisk (if any)

▲ Password (if any)

You can also look at the list of LILO Other OS Configurations to see the label and boot partitions for the non-Linux operating systems LILO knows about. To add an unlisted operating system, click Add and provide the label and boot partition.

Adding a Kernel

To add a new kernel, start linuxconf and select A New Kernel from the Lilo menu. This will open a window like the one shown in Figure 6-6.

In the Kernel Image File box, enter the path and filename where the kernel image is located. In Figure 6-6, the kernel is sitting in the directory where we initially created it, ~/linux/arch/i386/boot.

The next choice you have is whether to add the new kernel as the default startup option (but retain the existing kernel as an option), to replace the current kernel with the new kernel, or to add the new kernel as an option, leaving the current kernel as the default. In Figure 6-6, the last option has been selected.

Next, tell linuxconf what label you'd like to give this kernel option, and indicate where you want it to reside. In the example shown in Figure 6-6, the label is TestKernel and the kernel will be copied to /boot/linux-2.2.14.

The rest of the options are the same as you'll see when you add an existing configuration to LILO; I suggest you indicate the root partition and specify that the system will boot up read-only initially, but you should be able to leave the other boxes blank.

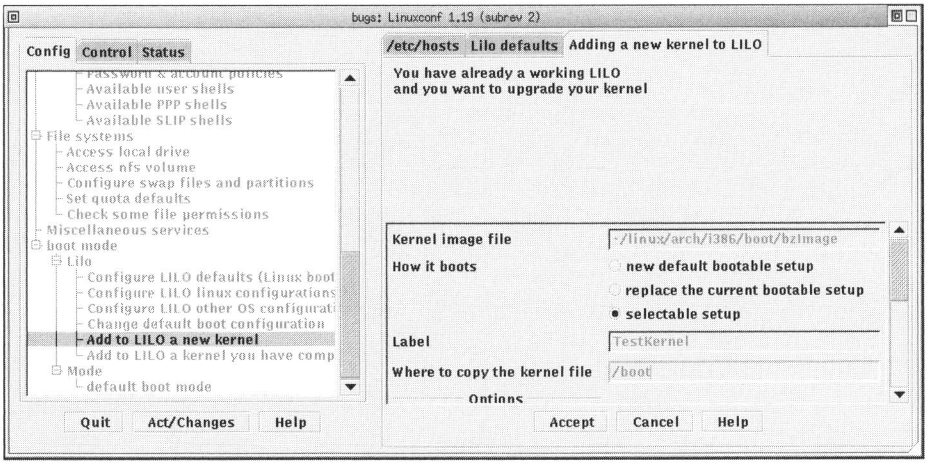

Figure 6-6.   Use linuxconf to configure LILO to use a new kernel

Activating Changes from linuxconf

Be sure that on each window in which you made changes that you click the Accept button. Once you've done that, click the Act/Changes button in the bottom left corner of the linuxconf window. This will bring up a System Status tab that will ask you if you want to preview the changes to be made or just activate them (you can also quit without making the changes by clicking the Quit button in the lower left-hand corner). It can be instructional to see what changes linuxconf has made, so if you're interested in learning more about how Linux works, have a look at that.

When you've seen all you want, click the Activate The Changes button to start the system updates required to implement the changes you've requested. In some cases you will be prompted to confirm actions linuxconf is taking; others will run without further ado.

Once the kernel update has taken place, you can restart the system to take advantage of the new features you've added or of the space you saved by eliminating features you weren't using. And since we've started looking at linuxconf, let's continue by using it to configure Linux to run on a network. We'll do that in Chapter 7, coming up next.

CHAPTER
7

Step 4:
Connect to a
Network

Now that you've cooked up your own kernel, you're ready for life in the Linux fast lane. In the next nine chapters, we will blitz through the details of system configuration and administration of Linux systems. We can go quickly from here because the most popular Linux distributions include convenient configuration tools that will help you tweak the operating system and supporting applications to suit your needs. Naturally, I'll explain underlying details so that you know what the system is doing, but I'll use Linuxconf, the GUI-based system configuration tool that comes with Red Hat and derivative distributions, as a framework.

Having progressed this far, you're ready for the fourth step in breaking the Microsoft habit—connecting your Linux system to a network. While most distributions, including Red Hat, allow you to configure networking during installation, it seems to be a truism that on networks, things change. So you've really got to know what to do if you need to alter your network in some way that will influence your Linux system configuration. So without further ado, let's hop to it!

BASIC HOST CONFIGURATION

While it's possible to use other mechanisms, such as editing the configuration files manually, or using third-party mechanisms such as Webmin (**www.webmin.com**), it's common for administrators to use the linuxconf tool to perform network configuration. You need to be the root user to run linuxconf, so become root and start the program:

```
root@romans: \> linuxconf &
```

While you can run this tool outside of X Windows, I wouldn't recommend it. It's not very attractive in full-screen text mode, and some of the controls are a little hard to remember (for example, in the text version of linuxconf, you use CTRL-X to open a drop-down list of options, which I don't consider very intuitive or memorable; in fact, I only remember it because I try to remember which of those x-ing keystroke combinations gets me the drop down list).

From within X Windows, though, it's easy enough to use. As shown in Figure 7-1, there's an expandable list of options in a panel on the left-hand side of the screen, and in the right-hand side are the choices available for the options you've selected.

In the course of this chapter, we'll be looking at options that fall under the Networking branch of the Config tree (the two top entries in the left panel shown in Figure 7-1). We'll start by doing the basic host configuration found, not surprisingly, under "Basic host information."

Set Host Name

This is the entry shown in Figure 7-1. Type the system's qualified hostname (that is, its name plus domain name) in the Host Name box on the Host Name tab.

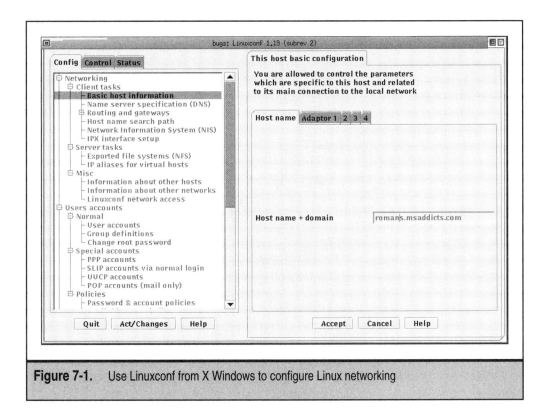

Figure 7-1.   Use Linuxconf from X Windows to configure Linux networking

Configure NICs

There are four other tabs visible in Figure 7-1. The first is labeled Adaptor 1, while the other three are numbered 2, 3, and 4. These tabs allow you to set the network adapter-specific information, as shown in Figure 7-2.

As you can see in Figure 7-2, there is a radio button indicating that the first network adapter is enabled. For each adapter you wish to activate in the Linux system, be sure this radio button is depressed.

The second option on the adapter pages indicates whether the system is using a static IP address (the Manual option), getting its IP address information from a DHCP server (the Dhcp option), or getting the IP information from a BOOTP server (the Bootp option). All three will work; you just have to decide which is appropriate for your purposes.

The next field allows you to specify a name and domain name for the machine; for systems with a single network card, this should be the fully qualified hostname (hostname plus the domain name). If you have multiple network cards, you can give the host a different name for each interface. The optional aliases field that follows provides you the opportunity to alias the machine name to something more manageable; with

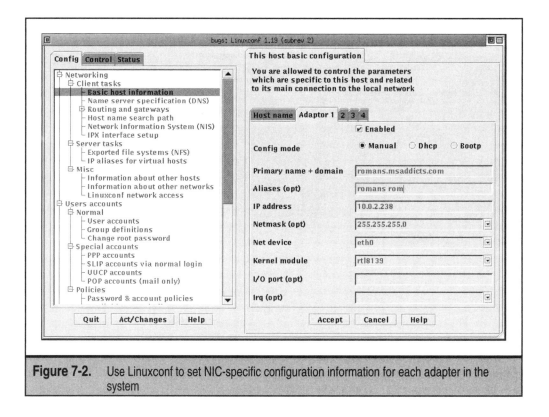

Figure 7-2.   Use Linuxconf to set NIC-specific configuration information for each adapter in the system

servers named after New Testament books, I like to have little three-letter aliases to make things easier to type.

Specify the correct numeric IP address for each network adapter on the next line; if you omit the optional netmask setting, your netmask will be presumed not to create subnets. If you want to use a custom netmask to subnet your network, you can enter the mask here (note that the Linuxconf help for this page largely consists of a table of oft-used subnet netmasks).

The Net Device is the standard interface name used by the network card being configured. For standard Ethernet devices, the first network card is known as eth0 (and the second as eth1, the third as eth2, etc.). Other device types are possible, though, so if you have an ARCnet or Token Ring network, don't despair. Well, go ahead and despair, but not because Linuxconf can't find a net device for you. It can.

The Kernel Module entry allows you to tell Linuxconf which networking device driver you'll need. This information is used to load the device driver if it has been created as a module rather than included in the kernel. The list should include all the entries known to your installation of Linux, so if you need a module that isn't listed, you should go back to Chapter 6 and go through the kernel configuration process and build a new kernel containing the driver, or make the driver as a module.

The last two options allow you to specify the I/O port and IRQ settings used on your NIC; for newer cards this is rarely necessary, so unless you think you have to, you can try running without setting these options.

Manual Host Configuration

Duplicating this configuration process by manually editing files isn't difficult, but the file locations may vary somewhat between distributions. In later sections of this chapter, I'll tell you how each Linuxconf option alters the underlying Linux configuration files, but to simplify the introduction of Linuxconf, I've deferred that explanation for these basic options. If you want to make the changes manually, there are several files you'll want to manipulate using your preferred text editor.

/etc/hosts

This file contains a list of known IP addresses and the names of the corresponding hosts, but for now we're primarily worried about the hostname of the machine we're configuring. For it, we need a loopback entry and an address for each active network card:

```
#
#  DM hosts file
#  11-24-2000 MJM
#
127.0.0.1    localhost
10.0.2.238   romans.distinguishingmark.org       romans rom
```

If you have a "real" network-addressable IP address for a system, associate the hostname with that address instead of the loopback address.

Note also that the file has some comments; they're a little more cryptic than they might be, but they do tell me the last time I touched the file, which is useful because I've got a terrible memory.

/etc/sysconfig/network

This file contains a little more information than we've configured yet in Linuxconf, but we'll go ahead and look at it anyway. While you should put the hostname and address in the /etc/hosts file, you should also include the hostname in the /etc/sysconfig/network file:

```
NETWORKING=yes
FORWARD_IPV4=false
HOSTNAME="romans"
GATEWAY="10.0.2.254"
GATEWAYDEV="eth0"
```

This file simply tells us that IP networking is enabled on this system, that it's not configured as a router, that its hostname is romans, and that it's pointing to the gateway (router) at 10.0.2.254, which it can reach using the eth0 device.

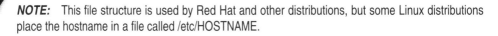

NOTE: This file structure is used by Red Hat and other distributions, but some Linux distributions place the hostname in a file called /etc/HOSTNAME.

/etc/sysconfig/network-scripts/

The configuration information specific to the Ethernet cards is contained in this directory. Actually, if you take a look in the directory, you'll see a variety of files, including configuration files for PPP and loopback interfaces, as well as scripts for managing the different interfaces.

For the moment we're only interested in the configuration of the Ethernet adapters, though. For the configuration data entered under "Basic host information," we could instead go to the file /etc/sysconfig/network-scripts/ifcfg-eth0. The first few lines of this file allow us to set the information we need:

```
DEVICE="eth0"
BOOTPROTO="none"
IPADDR="10.0.2.238"
NETMASK="255.255.255.0"
ONBOOT="yes"
```

Additional network cards can be configured using the sibling files with the appropriate "ethX" names.

NOTE: This file structure is used by Red Hat and other distributions, but some Linux distributions place the Ethernet configuration information in a file known as /etc/rc.d/rc.inet1.

NETWORK PROTOCOLS AND ROUTING

There are several networking options available beyond the basic configuration of an IP client. In this section, we'll look at some of the more advanced IP configuration options, focusing on how to get the host to recognize remote systems and networks. Linuxconf also allows us to configure the host to run IPX, so we'll look at that option as well.

Name Server Specification

One way an IP-based system identifies other systems is by referring to a Domain Name Server (DNS). The Web works because a fabric of DNS servers maintains records showing which IP addresses correspond to the addresses we enter; even on a smaller scale,

Displaying Network Card Information

While Linuxconf is a nice front end for configuring your network card, it's helpful to have information about the current status of your network connections. The /sbin/ifconfig command is useful for this purpose.

Because ifconfig is in the /sbin directory, it can't be run by regular user accounts, so you'll need to become the root user before running it. You can specify a single interface to view (e.g., by running **ifconfig eth0** to look at the first Ethernet card only), or you can look at all the interfaces. Running **ifconfig -a** will display the status of all cards, active or inactive, and produces output that looks similar to this:

```
eth0      Link encap:Ethernet  HWaddr 00:40:C7:87:4E:69
          inet addr:10.0.2.238  Bcast:10.0.2.255
Mask:255.255.255.0
          UP BROADCAST RUNNING MULTICAST  MTU:1500  Metric:1
          RX packets:337630 errors:0 dropped:0 overruns:0 frame:0
          TX packets:298470 errors:0 dropped:0 overruns:0 carrier:0
          collisions:40010 txqueuelen:100
          Interrupt:10 Base address:0xd400

lo        Link encap:Local Loopback
          inet addr:127.0.0.1  Mask:255.0.0.0
          UP LOOPBACK RUNNING  MTU:3924  Metric:1
          RX packets:5037 errors:0 dropped:0 overruns:0 frame:0
          TX packets:5037 errors:0 dropped:0 overruns:0 carrier:0
          collisions:0 txqueuelen:0
```

Notice that the ifconfig information contains several sometimes-useful tidbits, including the type of interface being described (in this case, Ethernet and Local Loopback), the NIC's hardware address, IP addresses, the network broadcast address, netmasks, status information, and some metrics.

Check the man page (using **man ifconfig**) for more information on what can be done with the ifconfig command. One handy thing to note is that this is one way of enabling promiscuous mode on a NIC, which may be necessary for doing network sniffing. You can also use ifconfig to set a NIC to receive all multicast packets.

DNS is a useful option for networks large enough to make maintenance of the hostnames a headache.

Whether you're pointing to an internal DNS server to access company hosts, your ISP's DNS server to access Internet hosts, or both, you'll probably want to enable and use DNS on your Linux systems. Enabling DNS in Linuxconf just requires you to select the Name Server Specification from the Config-Networking-Client Tasks tree. This will bring up a window that allows you to enable DNS (check the box to indicate that "DNS is required for normal operation").

Once DNS is enabled, you can enter your host's domain name and up to three DNS server addresses. You may also add additional domain names to search if your network spans a number of domains and you may need to access servers across these domains. Click Accept and you're done setting up DNS.

The Linuxconf interface is a front end to the /etc/resolv.conf file. While the DNS Usage option is for Linuxconf's benefit only, the other changes you make will be visible in the resolv.conf file, which includes lines like these:

```
domain prolificinc.com
search stdcells.com
search standardcells.com
nameserver 10.0.2.1
nameserver 10.0.2.254
```

Default Gateway

The default gateway is simply the router that this system will depend upon to send data located outside the local network. To configure this option in Linuxconf, select Defaults from the Config-Networking-Client Tasks-Routing And Gateways tree. Enter the gateway's IP address in the Default Gateway field.

If you want the system you're configuring to act as a router, you can check the Enable Routing box on the Defaults screen. Unless you've configured the system to be a router, however, you shouldn't enable this option.

You can also examine the /etc/sysconfig/network file to find (and change, if you wish) the current default gateway, which is defined on a line as follows:

```
GATEWAY="10.0.2.254"
```

Other Routes

If you want to designate other ways of getting off the local network, you can specify other routes to get to specific networks or hosts. You can also configure the system to recognize multiple logical IP networks running over the same physical network.

All three of the options described next manipulate a file known as /etc/sysconfig/static-routes. If you wanted to manually edit this file, you could do so; once the changes have been made to your satisfaction, you don't have to reboot the system; you can simply restart the networking processes using the command /etc/rc.d/rc3.d/S10network reload (assuming you're in normal multiuser mode, known as runlevel 3).

Displaying Routing

There are several sources of networking status information available on a Linux system. If you enabled the /proc filesystem in the kernel, you can examine the files and subdirectories in /proc/net for information that might be relevant to something you're doing. On the other hand, if you're looking for quick and dirty routing information, you can check out the **/bin/netstat** command.

Netstat is a useful tool for determining routing information, identifying enabled and active sockets, and viewing network interface statistics. To view the current routing information, you can use the **netstat -r** command, which produces output similar to this:

```
Kernel IP routing table
Destination     Gateway         Genmask         Flags   MSS Window  irtt Iface
10.0.1.1        galatians.disti 255.255.255.255 UGH       0 0          0 eth0
10.0.2.238      *               255.255.255.255 UH        0 0          0 eth0
nt-net.dm.org   *               255.255.255.0   U         0 0          0 eth0
127.0.0.0       *               255.0.0.0       U         0 0          0 lo
default         10.0.2.254      0.0.0.0         UG        0 0          0 eth0
```

Notice that in this example, there are several destination hosts and networks specified, with a few different gateways and several other bits of information available. The Destination column shows the target host or route. The first entry in the output is 10.0.1.1, a host that has been specially configured to be reached via a custom route.

The Gateway column shows how information gets to a specified destination from the host you're working on. So to get to 10.0.1.1, this routing table indicates that the gateway is a host whose name starts with galatians.disti.

The Genmask entry indicates the level of the routing rule. Simply put, the portions of genmask that are set to 255 show which part of the address in the Destination column needs to match the destination of a packet to be routed. If that doesn't make sense, let me try it this way: In the output, notice that the two hosts listed, 10.0.1.1 and 10.0.2.238. For these rules to be invoked, all four segments of the destination address must match the Destination setting for these rules. If they don't match, the next rules are consulted until one is found that applies. So if a packet is destined for 127.82.82.12, it will be sent to the loopback address at 127.0.0.0, because the genmask only compares the first portion of the two addresses.

More information on netstat, including how to use the -t option to show TCP socket information and how to use the -i option to show interface statistics, can be found on the man page (**man netstat**).

To Networks

If there are networks you wish to access without using the primary gateway, you can use the Other Routes To Networks option to configure the correct gateway. For example, my company has a separate network for customers who come for training or to make use of our on-site systems. Rather than have the primary systems access this network using our main router, we've configured each system to recognize that the network is connected through the firewall that separates the production network from the customer network.

Setting this up in your own environment is not at all difficult using Linuxconf. Simply select the Other Routes To Networks option from the Config-Networking-Client Tasks-Routing And Gateways tree. On the tab that appears are fields for the name or IP address of the gateway (router) to use to access the destination network, the destination network number itself, and the desired netmask, as shown in Figure 7-3.

Notice that the destination network number ends with a .0 address. This is how you tell Linux that the whole network can be reached via this gateway. To reach a specific host instead, see the "To hosts" section, which is next.

Your entries in the Linuxconf table populate the /etc/sysconfig/static-routes file. In the following line, the network 10.0.1.0 can be reached via 10.0.2.240.

```
eth0 net 10.0.1.0 netmask 255.0.0.0 gw 10.0.2.240
```

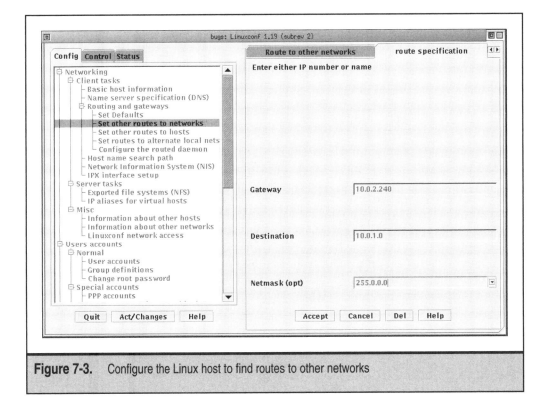

Figure 7-3.   Configure the Linux host to find routes to other networks

To Hosts

If you need to tell the host you're configuring how it can access a specific host on another network, you can do so using the Other Routes To Hosts option from the Config-Networking-Client Tasks-Routing And Gateways tree. This configuration is very straightforward; you simply indicate the address of the gateway that knows how to reach the destination host, and then enter the destination host's IP address.

This is useful when there are multiple routers connected to the local network and you want to be sure that the traffic to the designated host goes through the designated gateway.

The Linuxconf front end modifies the /etc/sysconfig/static-routes file with one line per host you specify. In this example, the system can reach 10.0.1.1 via the gateway at 10.0.2.240:

```
eth0 net 10.0.1.1 netmask 255.255.255.255 gw 10.0.2.240
```

To Alternate Local Networks

There's one more option that fits into this treatment of other routing options, but it's a little different from the preceding two. An alternate local network is an IP network that is logically different (it has a different network address) but runs on the same physical network (it shares a hub or is on the same physical wiring as the main network). If your network is structured this way, don't fear; you can use the Routes To Alternate Local Networks option from the Config-Networking-Client Tasks-Routing And Gateways tree to add the additional local networks.

You'll have to specify the network number (remember that this will end with at least one .0 to indicate that it's the whole network) and the network interface used to access this network, and you can specify an appropriate netmask for each network you specify.

The changes made in Linuxconf are used to update the /etc/sysconfig/static-routes file; the following line indicates that the system can reach any host on the 10.0.3.0 network via the second NIC (eth1).

```
any net 10.0.3.0 netmask 255.255.255.0 gw eth1
```

Routed Daemon

The routed daemon is a process used to maintain routing tables using the Routing Information Protocol (RIP) information, which allows dynamic routing. RIP is used to ascertain how many gateways must be traversed when data takes a particular route from one host to another. By comparing this count of "hops," the hosts on a network can determine the most expedient way of getting from one place to another.

In small environments with a very small number of interconnected networks, this isn't important, but in more complex environments, where there may be many different ways of delivering data from one host to another, it can be quite useful.

But while this option configures the routed daemon, it's not likely that this daemon will be enabled on your system. It's not well loved by most networking folks, who often prefer gated. Still, you have the option to use routed, and your Linuxconf choices are simple.

If you are configuring a host that will not do any routing (including almost every system with a single network card), you can enable the option to listen to routing information only. Since these hosts don't do any routing, they shouldn't have anything to say on the subject. If, on the other hand, the system you're configuring does do routing, you should enable the Export Your Default Route option instead. This tells your system to announce its services and updates the dynamic routing tables via RIP.

The changes made using the Linuxconf front end are stored to the file /etc/sysconfig/routed. This file contains two variables that are read when routed is started:

```
EXPORT_GATEWAY="no"
SILENT="yes"
```

Name Service Search Path

The next option is telling the Linux host how it should go about getting hostname information. There are three sources of this information available for configuration:

▼ /etc/hosts file

◼ DNS server

▲ Network Information System (NIS) server

Using the Host Name Search Path option from Linuxconf's Config-Networking-Client Tasks tree, you can specify which of those three sources the host you're configuring consults. You can also set the order in which they're consulted. Simply indicate whether multiple IP addresses might be assigned for a single host, then select the option that orders the name service resources the way you want them.

The order you designate is reflected in the /etc/host.conf file, which contains two lines:

```
order hosts, bind, nis
multi on
```

The first line lists the name service resources in the order they'll be consulted, and the second line indicates that the system can deal with multiple IP addresses for a single hostname.

NIS Configuration

If your network includes NIS servers (and if it doesn't, there's no point in consulting them in the "Name Service Search Path" section described above), you can configure the Linux host's NIS client settings from the Network Information System (NIS) option in the Config-Networking-Client Tasks tree. Enter the NIS domain and the NIS server address or name in the fields provided.

The changes made to the underlying system files by the Linuxconf front end are reflected in two files. The first one is /etc/sysconfig/network, which has an NISDOMAIN entry set equal to the domain name you specify:

```
NISDOMAIN="prolificinc"
```

The other change is made in the /etc/yp.conf file. "YP" refers to "yellow pages," a predecessor to today's NIS that is also supported by Linux. The yp.conf file includes a ypserver entry pointed to the NIS server you specified:

```
ypserver 10.0.2.3
```

IPX Configuration

If you need the Linux system to be able to use the IPX protocol, you can configure the IPX protocol settings using the IPX Interface Setup option from the Config-Networking-Client Tasks tree. There are three tabs on which you can set IPX-related networking options: Config; Adaptor 1; and Internal net.

Config

If you need IPX enabled, make sure the Enable IPX Networking radio button is enabled. The two additional options allow the system to autoconfigure itself to select the correct interface and frame type for the network.

Linuxconf makes changes to an underlying system file based on the options you choose. This file is /etc/sysconfig/network, which includes a variety of network settings, including these three IPX-related entries:

```
IPX="yes"
IPXAUTOPRIMARY="off"
IPXAUTOFRAME="off"
```

In these lines shown, IPX has been enabled, but the automatic configuration of the frame types has been disabled. In most cases, a Linux system being configured to read files from a NetWare server will be able to use the "on" settings for the two IPXAUTO options.

Adapter 1

If you wish to select your own frame types and network numbers, you can do so using this tab, as shown in Figure 7-4.

Each section of this tab allows you to configure a frame type that may or may not be active on your network. If you're an experienced NetWare administrator, these options will be easy to set. If you're not, you should really only opt for this type of configuration if the autoconfigure option on the Config page doesn't work.

You should enable as many of the four listed frame types as you need to connect to NetWare servers on your network. The default frame type used on NetWare servers has

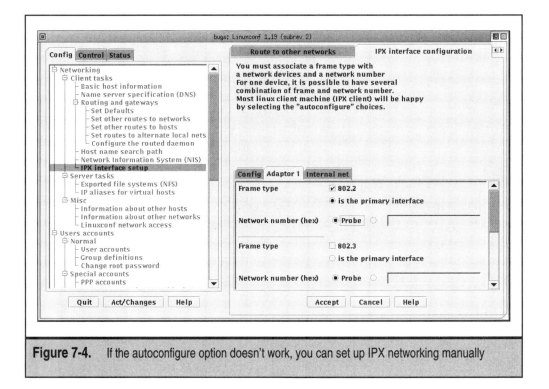

Figure 7-4.   If the autoconfigure option doesn't work, you can set up IPX networking manually

changed over time, but I have seen NetWare 3.x servers still in operation using the old 802.3 frame type, so be sure you know the details of your own situation.

You can designate one of the frame types as the primary interface on the adapter by selecting its "is the primary interface" radio button. While I've had good luck probing for the IPX network number, you can also specify the network number yourself.

The Linuxconf front end to the adapter settings modifies lines in /etc/ifcfg-eth0. There are three lines for each frame type. The first indicates the IPX network number for the interface (if one was specified—if not, the value is omitted and the IPX network number will be probed). The second line indicates whether the frame type is active on the specified NIC, either Yes or No. The third line indicates whether the frame type is the default for the specified NIC, either Yes or No. While all four frame types may be active, only one should be set as the primary.

```
IPXNETNUM_802_2=""
IPXPRIMARY_802_2="yes"
IPXACTIVE_802_2="yes"
IPXNETNUM_802_3=""
IPXPRIMARY_802_3="no"
IPXACTIVE_802_3="no"
```

```
IPXNETNUM_ETHERII=""
IPXPRIMARY_ETHERII="no"
IPXACTIVE_ETHERII="no"
IPXNETNUM_SNAP=""
IPXPRIMARY_SNAP="no"
IPXACTIVE_SNAP="yes"
```

These lines activate Ethernet_802.2 and Ethernet_SNAP, making 802.2 the default frame type for the interface.

Internal Net

This tab gives you the opportunity to configure the host-specific internal network number and the primary network node number. For systems that aren't doing any IPX routing, which ought to be most of them (what on earth are you doing routing IPX with a Linux system, for heaven's sake?), you won't need to configure these entries.

When you configure these options, the changes are reflected in the /etc/sysconfig/network file, which has two entries related to the internal network configuration options:

```
IPXINTERNALNETNUM="195948557"
IPXINTERNALNODENUM="0"
```

Note that in the first line, the IPX internal network number has been converted to binary format from the hexadecimal format in which it was entered (and in which it's commonly displayed on NetWare systems).

DIALUP NETWORKING

If your Linux system will be using a dialup connection, you have three types to choose from. Newer versions of Linuxconf (including the one that ships with Red Hat 7) allow you to configure any of these three types in exactly the same way you configured the network card. You simply define additional network adapters for each type that's relevant. So, for example, if you configured your Ethernet card as Adapter 1, you can add your PPP connection as Adapter 2.

Older versions of Linuxconf have a PPP/SLIP/PLIP option on the Config-Networking-Client Tasks tree, where you'll see the currently configured connections and can edit them, remove them, or add additional definitions. Clicking on an existing definition will bring up its configuration details; you can view or change these details or delete the definition altogether from this menu.

If you click the Add button to create a new dialup networking connection, you're given a choice of the three types available: Point-to-Point Protocol (PPP); Serial Line IP (SLIP); or Parallel Line IP (PLIP). Most everyone these days has access to and uses PPP, but we'll briefly look at SLIP and PLIP as well, just in case you're one of the unfortunate few.

PPP

When you select a PPP interface, you'll see a configuration page like the one shown in Figure 7-5. Enter the phone number you dial to establish a PPP connection, and make sure to set the modem port properly (/dev/ttyS0 equates to COM1, /dev/ttyS1 equates to COM2, etc.). If your PPP connection supports PAP authentication, check the box. Then enter the login name and password you wish to use to establish contact. You can click Accept to use the default PPP configuration, or click Customize to further tweak the settings.

If you do opt to customize the PPP connection settings, you'll be given four tabs to choose from: Hardware; Communication; Networking; and PAP. These contain settings you should already know about, including line speed, modem initialization and dial strings, timeout values, and IP addresses for the local and remote hosts. The changes made on these pages are included in the file /etc/sysconfig/network-scripts/ifcfg-ppp0 (for the first PPP connection; the second would be in the same directory as ifcfg-ppp1). Sample contents of this file are shown as follows.

```
DEVICE="ppp0"
ONBOOT="no"
USERCTL="no"
MODEMPORT="/dev/ttyS0"
LINESPEED="115200"
PERSIST="yes"
DEFABORT="yes"
DEBUG="yes"
INITSTRING="ATZ"
DEFROUTE="yes"
HARDFLOWCTL="yes"
ESCAPECHARS="no"
PPPOPTIONS=""
PAPNAME="rootabega"
REMIP="10.4.0.4"
NETMASK=""
IPADDR="10.0.2.2"
MRU="1444"
MTU="1444"
DISCONNECTTIMEOUT="831"
RETRYTIMEOUT="5"
BOOTPROTO="none"
```

The modem dial string, including the phone number, can be found in /etc/sysconfig/network-scripts/chat-ppp0. And the PAP password, if configured, is stored in /etc/ppp/pap-secrets. None of these files can be read by non-root users, so they're relatively secure.

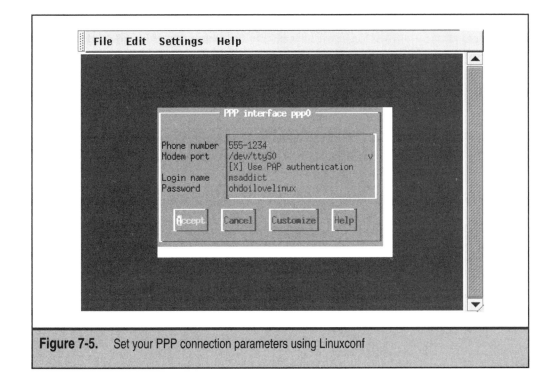

Figure 7-5. Set your PPP connection parameters using Linuxconf

SLIP

The process of configuring a SLIP connection is virtually identical to the PPP process, but instead of populating the ifcfg-ppp0 and chat-ppp0 files, Linuxconf creates or modifies /etc/sysconfig/network-scripts/ifcfg-sl0 and /etc/sysconfig/network-scripts/chat-sl0 (for the first SLIP connection, naturally). PAP is not an option under SLIP, so there are no PAP-related features accessible from Linuxconf or in the files themselves.

PLIP

The process of configuring a PLIP connection is very similar to the process of creating a SLIP connection, but this time Linuxconf creates or modifies /etc/sysconfig/network-scripts/ifcfg-plip0 and /etc/sysconfig/network-scripts/chat-plip0 (for the first PLIP connection). Because PLIP is used over parallel lines, there are no phone numbers or modem settings to fiddle with.

NFS FILE SERVICES

NFS file services are the Linux world's most common solution to the question, "How can David access files on my machine?" While you may not want David to access your files, there may be another computer on your home or office with which you'd like to share files. If you've used Unix before, you're probably familiar with NFS, and NetWare servers have long been able to offer their disk volumes as NFS shares. If you wish to make portions of a Linux system accessible to other Linux systems, or to other Unix users, or to Windows users already running NFS access programs like WRQ's Reflection suite, you'll need to export the file systems using the Exported File Systems (NFS) option on the Config-Networking-Server Tasks tree.

Selecting this option gives you the chance to add or modify what your Linux system allows others to see. To modify an existing NFS export, just click on it from the list given; to create a new one, click the Add button, which brings up a tab like the one shown in Figure 7-6.

In the screen shown in Figure 7-6, the path to be exported is listed as /home. You can enter which ever directory you wish, as long as it's local to the system you're configuring. If you export the root directory, for example, other users will have access to every part of your system, because the root directory (/) is the parent or ancestor of every other directory on the system. Ordinarily, you don't want to be quite that friendly.

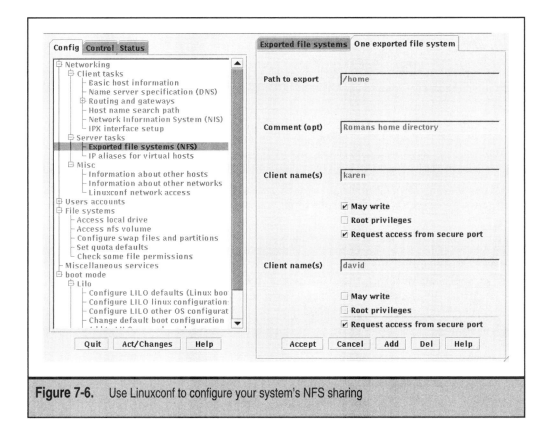

Figure 7-6.   Use Linuxconf to configure your system's NFS sharing

Just as you don't need to create a share for your C: drive if you just want people to get to a certain folder in your home directory, you don't need to export your whole Linux file system if you just want people to access a particular area. It's better instead to determine the directories you wish others to be able to access, and designate them individually.

If we return to the screen shown in Figure 7-6, the /home directory (and its subdirectories, by the way) is being exported to two client machines, karen and david. Notice that I said two machines; unlike the Windows paradigm, which provides a user with access to certain shares, NFS gives certain machines access to the exported paths.

Notice as well that the karen machine has been granted write permission to the NFS export, and the david machine lacks this access. While karen can read and write to the /home directory and its children, david may only read from the directory. Neither user has been granted root privileges in this directory (NFS isn't the most secure access method and I'm not excited about granting root privileges this way).

The Translate Symbolic Links option expands the path of a symbolic file link to include the full path from the root directory, even if the root directory isn't what is being exported. I haven't had cause to use this and it makes me just a little edgy. The Request Access From Secure Port option, on the other hand, is intended to make sure that NFS client requests will only be accepted from privileged ports (less than port 1024). Enable it.

These options are incorporated into the /etc/exports file, which is the master list of NFS export directories on the system. Here's a sample:

```
/home karen(rw) david (ro,all_squash)
```

This line almost exactly duplicates the settings created from the Linuxconf screen shown in Figure 7-6. The remote system karen has been granted read and write access to the /home directory on the system being configured. The remote system david has been granted read-only access to the /home directory. The all_squash option is one I've added by hand. It prohibits users coming from david's machine from having user rights to the target system. You can read about this option and a few others on the man page for the exports file; to read all about it, just execute the following command:

```
man exports
```

VIRTUAL HOSTS

I wouldn't call this a frequently used feature, but you can easily configure your Linux system to respond to a number of different IP addresses. This can be useful, for example, if you want to run a system as a web server that responds to multiple IP addresses and serves up different domains and pages depending upon the requested address. While much of that functionality is configured in the web server software, the fundamental IP networking aspect can be setup in Linuxconf.

Simply select the IP Aliases For Virtual Hosts option from the Config-Networking-Server Tasks tree, and then click a network device to enter alternative IP addresses. When you do so, you'll see a screen like the one shown in Figure 7-7.

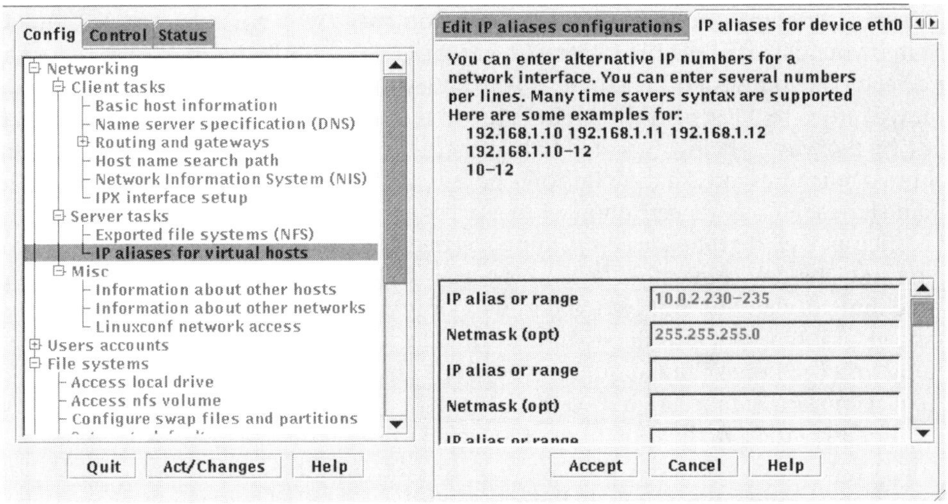

Figure 7-7.   Linuxconf allows you to easily enter multiple ranges of alternative IP addresses for a host

Using this interface, you can enter a large number of IP addresses individually, or as described on the Linuxconf screen in Figure 7-7, you can enter a whole range of addresses in a variety of ways. This makes it easy to set up noncontiguous IP addresses all on the same host.

The IP Aliases For Virtual Hosts information can be viewed or configured manually in a series of files in the /etc/sysconfig/network-scripts/ directory. For the first network card in the system, the first range of addresses is specified in ifcfg-eth0:0. Based on the information entered in Linuxconf in Figure 7-7, that file's contents would look like this:

```
IPADDR="10.0.2.230-235"
NETMASK="255.255.255.0"
```

There will be another file known as ifcfg-eth0:1 if you specify a second range, and so on. If there are multiple network cards in the system, they'll each have their own set of IP alias files numbered the same way.

ADDITIONAL LINUXCONF CONFIGURATION

There are three additional types of network configuration that can be performed from within Linuxconf. The local list of hostnames can be edited. The networks the Linux system knows about can have names associated. And you can enable Linuxconf access across a network.

Hosts File

To edit the local list of hostnames, select Information About Other Hosts from the Config-Networking-Server Tasks tree. This will bring up a window like the one shown in Figure 7-8.

If you click the Add button, you're presented with several fields to fill to describe the new host. You must enter the host's primary name and domain name, as shown in the examples in Figure 7-8. You have the option of adding aliases for the system name next (and let me take this chance to encourage you to alias the system to its name *without* the domain name, even if you don't use any other aliases). You must enter the host's IP address, and you are allowed to add a comment if you wish. For networks larger than a few machines (I define "few" as "a number small enough to allow me to retain basic user and hardware information for more than a week or two"), I like to note the machine's primary user or function and its CPU type and RAM size. This makes for a large entry, but it helps me compensate for the loss of brain cells damaged while jubilantly butting heads with other men at sporting events. But perhaps I'm over-sharing.

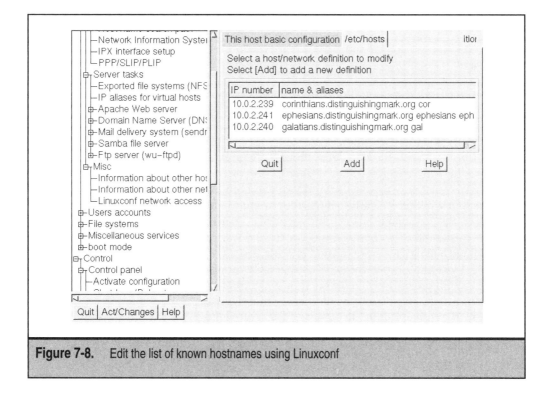

Figure 7-8.   Edit the list of known hostnames using Linuxconf

The file you're editing by using this Linuxconf option is the /etc/hosts file we discussed earlier in this chapter, and it should be familiar to most Windows network administrators. It contains the various hosts the system knows about without outside help from DNS or NIS servers. While an abbreviated version appeared in the Basic Host Configuration section, I'd like to include a somewhat larger example here to illustrate a few things.

```
#
#  DM hosts file
#  5-24-2000 MJM
#
#  loopback
#  --------
127.0.0.1     localhost
#
#  old testament net
#  -----------------
10.0.1.1      genesis.distinguishingmark.org       genesis gen
10.0.1.2      exodus.distinguishingmark.org        exodus exo
10.0.1.3      leviticus.distinguishingmark.org     leviticus lev
#
#  new testament net
#  -----------------
10.0.2.238    romans.distinguishingmark.org        romans rom
10.0.2.239    corinthians.distinguishingmark.org   corinthians cor
10.0.2.240    galatians.distinguishingmark.org     galatians gal
```

While this file is not long (it only describes five other hosts), it includes a fair amount of information, some of which isn't placed in the file by Linuxconf. First, it has comments at the beginning of the file—indicated by the pound signs—that tell what it is, when it was last changed, and who changed it. For this reason, I prefer to use a text editor to manipulate the /etc/hosts file manually, though the Linuxconf option works just fine. Comments like the ones shown are handy when you're trying to figure out who messed up the file and when, but they're also useful if you print out a copy and are trying to figure out what it is and whether it's remotely current or should be tossed into the recycling heap.

Second, the "localhost" entry, as I mentioned earlier, is not cross-referenced to the system's hostname. Third, the hosts on the two separate IP networks, 10.0.1.0 and 10.0.2.0, have been logically separated and include a comment indicating what they are. Of course, I've chosen a naming scheme that isn't very helpful, so perhaps the comments aren't as elucidating as they could be. If that's your gut response, fantastic! Go thou and don't do likewise; comment your files better than I have.

Finally, the fully qualified hostname appears first after the IP address, and the host's aliases follow. That order isn't strictly necessary, but it's nice. Don't forget the aliases, though, as they make life much easier when you're accessing multiple systems, especially ones named like these are.

Named Networks

Linuxconf also allows you to associate names with IP networks using the Information About Other Hosts option from the Config-Networking-Server Tasks tree. When you click on this entry, you'll be shown a list of the currently named networks (if any). Click on an existing network to modify or remove the name, or click the Add button to add a new network name.

You must enter the network's primary name and domain name, but you can add aliases as well. You must enter the network's IP address, remembering that it's a network and must end in .0, and you may include a comment. It's not at all necessary for you to use network names, but they can also make things easier to remember or reference. Any network names you select must be unique (from each other and from host names).

These entries are stored in the /etc/networks file, which is another one I prefer to edit by hand. In the next example, there are two networks listed by their formal, fully qualified names, then their IP addresses, and finally their aliases.

```
#
#   DM network file
#   5-25-2000
#
ot-net.distinguishingmark.org      10.0.1.0    ot
nt-net.distinguishingmark.org      10.0.2.0    nt
```

Linuxconf Remote Access

Linuxconf is easy to use, all the more so because you can use it to remotely manage other systems. Naturally, this has some security ramifications, and you only want to allow this functionality from within the relatively safe confines of an internal network. All the same, it's handy not only for managing remote systems, but for enabling web-based host administration, even locally.

To get started, select Linuxconf Network Access from the Config-Networking-Server Tasks tree. If you select this option, you can click the box to Enable Network Access. If you decide to do this, I recommend enabling the Log Access feature as well so you can see what machines have originated requests for Linuxconf, and track what they have done.

Once this initial setup is done, you can add multiple hostnames or networks that are authorized to access Linuxconf remotely. Once you've configured access for the systems or networks, click the Accept button, move to one of the systems you've given access, and try accessing the Linuxconf features remotely. This can be done by pointing a web browser (even the web-savvy KDE File Manager will do) to **http://*hostname*:98/**, where the *hostname* is the name of the machine you've been configuring in Linuxconf (the IP address will work, too). You should end up with a screen like the one shown in Figure 7-9.

The underlying file that Linuxconf modifies based on your entries is known as /etc/conf.linuxconf. While there are some items unrelated to remote access, the relevant part is easy to find: It follows the [netaccess] tag. In the following example, remote access has been allowed for any host on the network 10.0.2.0, and access will be logged in /var/log/htmlaccess.log.

```
[netaccess]
htmlaccess.from 10.0.2.0
htmlaccess.dolog 1
htmlaccess.enable 1
```

You can view the contents of the htmlaccess.log file using one of the **pager** programs, such as **more** or **less**, and if you only care about very recent entries, you can use the **tail** program instead to view the end of the file. (Use the **man** command to view manual

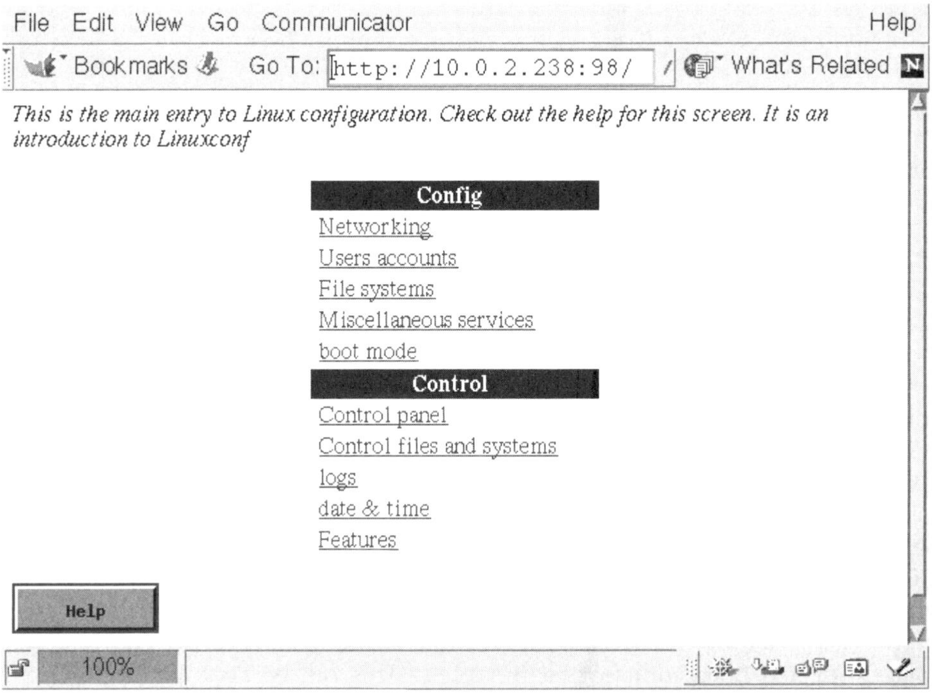

Figure 7-9.   Use a web browser to remotely configure a system using Linuxconf

pages for each of those commands if you're unfamiliar with them.) If the remote access has been used, the log file will include messages that look something like this:

```
Dec 28 09:43:00 admin.prolificinc.com Request: ok,==Networking/
Dec 28 09:43:06 admin.prolificinc.com Request:
ok,==Networking/ok,==Linuxconf==network==access/
Dec 28 09:43:07 admin.prolificinc.com File request: images/redarrow.gif
Dec 28 09:43:07 admin.prolificinc.com File request: images/Accept.gif
Dec 28 09:43:07 admin.prolificinc.com File request: images/Add.gif
Dec 28 09:43:15 admin.prolificinc.com Request:
ok,==Networking/ok,==Linuxconf==network==access/
Dec 28 09:44:14 admin.prolificinc.com Request:
ok,==Networking/ok,==Linuxconf==network==access/add,0/
```

The log information tells us that someone from the system known as admin.prolificinc.com accessed the Linuxconf system on Dec 28, and made a change to the Linuxconf network access settings on the system we're monitoring. I hope it was somebody we knew!

CHAPTER
8

Step 5:
Manage Users
and Groups

You have progressed far, seeker after Linux knowledge. And your next task is one that all recovering Microsoft users must face: Now that your system is in operation, how do you set it up for user access? There are several ways of managing users and groups on a Linux system, and we'll explore a few of them in the course of this chapter.

MANAGING USER ACCOUNTS

Remember that Linux is a multiuser operating system, which means that whether it's running on a system used as a workstation or a server, it was designed to be accessed by multiple people. It's less like the Windows 9x family of products, which have a flimsy user login mechanism, and more like the Windows NT/2000 family, which more tightly integrates the concept of multiple user accounts.

What this means for you is that user accounts are a necessary part of Linux administration, whether you're running Linux on a standalone system at home or as a server in your office. If your organization is growing, or you have lots of turnover in your workplace or love life, you may have lots of administration to do. So let's talk about how to add, change, and delete user accounts.

Adding Users with Linuxconf

Linuxconf is a pretty painless mechanism for adding user accounts. Using the full-screen text mode interface, the GUI under X Windows, or the web browser interface, you can view the current user accounts and add more as needed. When you click the Accept button to finish adding the account, you'll be prompted to enter the account's password. Before you get to that point, though, there are four sets of account information that Linuxconf can handle: basic account information, password management parameters, mail settings, and account privileges. We'll discuss each in turn.

Base Information

The base information is the fundamental set of data required when creating the user account. There are eight pieces of information that Linuxconf is interested in getting, but only the first three are required:

▼ Enabled?

■ Login name

■ Full name

■ Group

■ Supplementary groups

■ Home directory

■ Command interpreter

▲ User ID

Base Information in Linuxconf   The first thing Linuxconf wants to know is whether the account you're creating is active. You can create an account that is disabled by deselecting this option. This might be useful if you're preparing the system for a batch of new users and you don't want a bunch of accounts sitting open and idle before the users get access to the systems. (Working in the Silicon Valley, I also find this option useful when creating an account in advance for a new employee scheduled to start imminently, but who may at any time between agreeing to start and actually starting, receive and accept an outrageously better offer.) The login name is simply the account name; in the example shown in Figure 8-1, the login name is "karen". The full name is used for human identification purposes; when people have similar or cryptic account names, it's very useful to have real names associated with them.

The optional information includes the account's primary group membership (in the example, this is the sickeningly mushy "sweetie-pies") and any additional groups in which the account shares membership. I'll discuss groups more in "Managing Group Accounts" later in this chapter.

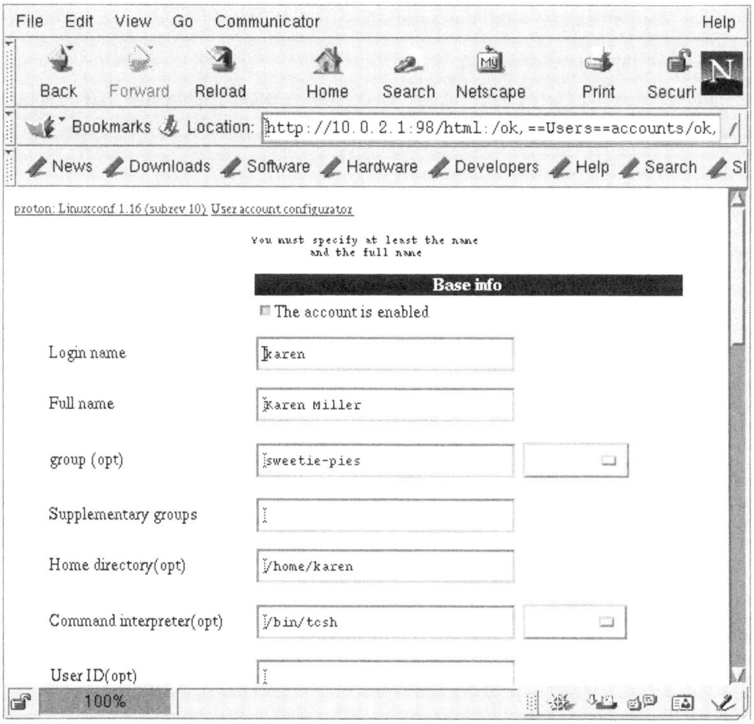

Figure 8-1.   Use Linuxconf to enter the base information required to activate a user account

The user's home directory comes next; you'll want to set aside a place for home directories, and the /home directory is traditionally used for this purpose, though there are a variety of different ways of approaching this issue. The command interpreter is the user's default shell; I'd recommend using **/bin/bash** unless you or your user have a strong preference for another shell (in Figure 8-1, Karen appears to prefer /bin/tcsh).

You can also set the numeric user ID if you want to; if you do not make an entry here, the system will allocate the next available ID number, which may be fine for you. I like to allocate ID numbers based on a user's department or job description, so I generally opt to set the user ID myself.

Base Information Storage   The information you're entering in Linuxconf goes into Linux configuration files that can be viewed and manipulated directly. The base information goes into the file /etc/passwd, which stores user account information. Some lines extracted from a Linux system's /etc/passwd file are shown below:

```
albers:GEHgcXOY/x5PQ:501:100:Daniel J. Albers:/home/albers:/bin/tcsh
dedood:n2eboLEFKhJAg:502:100:Paul de Dood:/home/dedood:/bin/tcsh
brianl:0GVDfwU1WnIw2:503:100:Brian Lee:/home/brianl:/bin/tcsh
demo:NgjZqSUhcobjs:605:200:Demo:/home/demo:/bin/tcsh
```

The first entry in each of these four lines is the login name (the colons separate the different entries). The second entry is a password hash code, but we'll talk more about them later. The next entry is the user ID, and the number that follows it is the user's primary group ID. The user's full name comes next, followed by their home directory and shell. You can edit most of this information manually to good effect, but the password field is more complicated. You can't enter a password here and have it work; all you can do is delete the whole password.

You also have the option of using command-line tools to create user accounts, which allow you to create scripts that can automate creation of large numbers of users. The **useradd** and **mkpasswd** commands are quite valuable for this purpose: **useradd** creates a new user with the attributes you specify, and it allows you to maintain defaults for all users it creates; **mkpasswd** generates a random password with a number of characters you specify. Check their man pages for more information.

Password Parameters

The next set of user account options set the password parameters for the account. These include

▼ The number of days a new password must be retained before it can be changed

■ The number of days a password can be retained before it must be changed

■ The number of days advanced warning users get before the account expires

■ The number of days until the account expires

▲ A set expiration date

These options are similar to the ones available with network operating systems from Microsoft and Novell; they give you some control over the password policy and the life-span of user accounts.

Mail Settings

The next option in the Linuxconf user account addition process is to set up mail forwarding and aliases for the new user. The message redirection is stored in the user's home directory, in a file called *.forward*. If mail is delivered to that user's account, it is forwarded on to the destination specified in the .forward file. The alias information is stored in /etc/aliases, which correlates actual user account names with email aliases.

Privileges

The next group of user account settings relates to system administration permissions that may be granted on a per-account basis. This stuff isn't the kind of thing you want to allow every Johnny Punchclock and Judy Drone to do, but it's useful for allocating a subset of the system administration tasks to certain individuals without giving them the all-powerful root password. The administration privileges are grouped into four sets: general system control; service control; miscellaneous control; and user account configuration.

General System Control   In the first category are the heavy-duty control items. Ordinarily you won't want to grant these types of controls to anybody (after all, if you're going to let them shut the system down, you may as well give them the root password). These privileges include

- ▼ Permission to use Linuxconf
- ■ Permission to activate configuration changes
- ■ Permission to shut down the system
- ■ Permission to change the network mode
- ■ Permission to view the system logs
- ▲ Equivalence to the superuser (root)

Now, by all that is beautiful and holy, don't ever just grant these abilities to users without considering why you're doing so. Make sure there's a darn good reason and no other way of accomplishing what must be done.

Services   This section groups together management of some add-on services. Granting access to one or more of these services allows the user to configure them from Linuxconf (assuming you allowed them to use Linuxconf in the "General System Control" section) and to start, stop, and restart the processes:

- ▼ Apache administration
- ■ Mail to Fax manager
- ▲ Samba administration

Miscellaneous   Granting this privilege allows the user to modify the message of the day, a text message that appears whenever someone logs into the system. This message is saved into the /etc/motd file and can be edited manually if you prefer.

User Accounts   Use this set of privileges to give a user the ability to manage one or more of these types of other accounts:

▼   POP accounts

■   PPP accounts

▲   UUCP accounts

Changing User Information

Changing any of the information entered in Linuxconf is as simple as selecting that user from the list and making any desired modifications, from disabling the account to changing the user's default shell, to altering the user's privileges.

Another way of accomplishing the same task is by using command-line utilities. As root, you can alter all the basic user information using the **usermod** command:

```
usermod -u 701 -g 101 -d /home/karenm -m -c "Karen Miller" -l karenm karen
```

In this example, the account "karen" is renamed to "karenm;" its user ID is changed to 701; its primary group is changed to group 101; the home directory is changed and the contents of the current home directory are moved into the new one; and the user comments are changed to reflect Karen's married name.

The user can make changes to their own personal information as well. For example, the user account comments, which include the user's full name, office location, office phone number, and home phone number, can be altered using the **chfn** command:

```
chfn -f "Karen Miller" -o 428B -p x346 -h myob
```

And if a user just needs a new shell, the **chsh** command may be used:

```
chsh -s /bin/bash
```

The list of available shells is stored in /etc/shells; this list may viewed directly or from Linuxconf or using the command **chsh -l**. A user may not use **chsh** to change the shell to one that's not listed in /etc/shells; **chsh** will generate an error message if this feat is attempted.

Removing User Accounts

The process for removing user accounts from Linuxconf is quite simple; just go into the User Accounts area, select the user you wish to delete, and click the DEL button. Buh-bye, user. This action will give you the option of leaving their home directory intact, archiving its contents, or deleting them. But as usual, there are other ways of doing this. For example, there's a command-line utility called *userdel* that can delete a user's account (and optionally, all the files in their home directory). You can also edit the /etc/passwd and /etc/shadow files directly—just delete the lines defining the user account to delete the account. Removing the home directory and mail spool file (found in /var/spool/mail) can be done manually from the command line or an X Windows file-management tool.

However, deleting the user account and the files in the home directory aren't the only things you should think about doing. For example, the user may have created files elsewhere on the system. If you delete the account that owns those files, you'll have to change their ownership. You can tell that a user account has been pulled out from under a file when you see a directory listing that includes information like this:

```
-rwxr-xr-x    1 502     customer     388    May 13 12:40 tasks.sh
```

In the places where you'd ordinarily expect the owner's name, the number 502 appears instead. Apparently the account that corresponded to user ID 502 has been deleted. What to do now? It's certainly possible that you'll just want to remove the file, but if you want to assign it to another user, you can do that easily using the **chown** command:

```
root@romans: /home/demo> chown broadcom tasks.sh
```

The command listed above changes the owner account for the tasks.sh file to the user named broadcom. You could also do this for all the files in a directory. Check the man page for more information about **chown**.

MANAGING GROUP ACCOUNTS

The primary reason groups are used on Linux systems is to be able to give a set of people access to files. While group membership can be used for a variety of other tasks, file ownership is the most common reason for their existence, and in many installations, it's the only reason for their existence. Let's take a closer look at why and how to create them, and how to modify and remove them.

Group Account Philosophy

Recall from Chapter 3 (or go have another look, if your lecithin intake isn't adequate or you've eaten too many meals, as I have, prepared in aluminum pans) that file and directory ownership and access is figured three different ways. Each file or directory has a user account owner, a group account owner, and a set of permissions that apply to the rest of the world.

This is an adequate way of enabling or disabling access to the systems (something I'll discuss more in Chapter 14). It does require you to think a little bit about where to place files and who to put into groups, lest you find yourself hopelessly entangled in a mass of cryptically named groups with uncertain purposes. There are a few things you should know about group creation before you start.

User Accounts Have One Primary User Group

Each user account has an associated primary user group. This means, for example, that if a user creates a file, by default their user account becomes the user owner and their primary group becomes the group owner.

User Accounts Can Be Members of Many Groups

Having a primary group does not prevent the user from being a member of another group. Or another. Or another. A user can be a member of one, some, or every group. Just because you *can* make a user part of every group, though, doesn't mean you *should* do so. Your approach should be to limit groups to users who have a need to join.

Groups May Be Group Members

This allows you to make large groups out of smaller groups. For example, if the Sales and Marketing department consists of the three organizational groups, Sales, Marketing, and PR, there's no need to add each group member to both groups. Create the subgroups first, and then make those groupnames members of the s_and_m group (or whatever you choose to call Sales and Marketing on your system).

User Groups Can Be Password-Protected

But in networks I've seen, group passwords are rarely used. End users seem to be fully challenged by having and remembering their account password; add too many more passwords and they'll start forgetting things like their home address and phone number, Aunt Genette's birthdate, and which restroom they're supposed to use. That's generally considered a bad thing. This doesn't mean you shouldn't use password protection for groups, but be sure you think the ramifications through.

User Groups Should Have Sensible Names

While I've seen networks with poorly chosen user account names, badly named user groups seem much more prevalent. I've always assumed this is because user names are generally related to the users' real-life names, and this dose of reality keeps the administrators a little more in touch. But group names are often created for a set of people united conceptually rather than organizationally.

Because groups are most often used for access to files and directories, then, consider using group names that reflect this purpose. For example, if /home/departments/ap needs to be accessed by some, but not all the people in three different departments, it might be sensible to call the group access_home_ap and include only the people who need to access those directories. The "access" groups easily convey both their function and the specific area to which they provide permissions.

The bottom line is to think about what you need to do before doing it. Group management isn't any more difficult in Linux than other operating systems, but like the others, it works best if the rationale is given some brain cycles before the keystrokes are made.

Creating Groups

Creating groups in Linuxconf is a simple matter. Go to the Group Definitions option and click the Add button. Enter the group's name and the numeric group ID you wish to use (which should be a number greater than 100 if you'll be adding user accounts to the group). Enter the names of any members who will not be listing this group as their primary group. This information will go into the /etc/group file, where each group name is listed in the form: *username:password:group ID:members*. For example

```
access_payroll::814:dedood,jones
```

This line defines the "access_payroll" group, which has no password (there's nothing between the first and second colons), has the group ID number 814, and includes users dedood and jones, for whom these are alternate groups, not the primary group (primary groups are specified on a per-account basis in the /etc/passwd file).

The directory section of the Group Addition dialog box makes its changes to the /etc/conf.linuxconf file. It allows you to specify whether each primary user of the group should have a different directory created, and if so, what their parent ("home base") directory should be. You may also specify the default permission settings for these home directories (see Chapter 14 for more information on file and directory permissions).

Adding and Removing Users

Users may be added to the groups when you create either the users or the groups, as described, or later. You may use the Linuxconf interface and add users to the Alternate Members field (or remove them), or if you prefer, you can use a text editor to add or remove members from the appropriate lines in the /etc/group file and the /etc/gshadow file.

MANAGING THE ROOT ACCOUNT

As I hope I've already made clear, the root account is special. It's not a user account, and nobody should be using it as a primary account. Some administrators go to great lengths to make use of the root account difficult by selecting harsh terminal color schemes, not enabling productivity features such as command completion and command history, or other unfriendly measures.

I don't think that this is necessary in most cases, and there are downsides to each of these solutions. For example, some people feel that the root user shouldn't have any customized shell files or other niceties, and this is a reasonable perspective, because we don't want to make it easy to run unnecessarily as the root user. On the other hand, having command completion can prevent errors from being introduced by the human being who's logged in as root.

Because root is all powerful on a Linux computer, a person can accidentally delete far more than they ought to, or restart the system at the wrong time, or fall into a myriad of other slipups that crop up in my nightmares. To help you avoid these problems, I'd like to make a few suggestions for using the superuser properly and avoiding unnecessary use of the superuser.

Using Root Properly

The first part of managing the root account is being sure you're using it properly. Windows administrators and home users of NT or Windows 2000, many of whom are accustomed to using the Administrator account much of the time (I confess to leaving my NT server consoles logged in as Administrator far too often), should take this opportunity to break themselves of the habit. There are a few ways of doing this.

Know Why You're Using Root

Why are you logged in as root right now? What task are you performing, and do you really need to be root to do it? There are good reasons to be root, of course. Viewing log files that are off limits to other users, killing recalcitrant jobs that won't respond to their owners, and scheduling cron jobs to execute tasks periodically are examples of things that are appropriate for root to do.

Don't Kill Root

I shouldn't have to tell you this, but please don't ever delete the root account. You can recognize it in the /etc/passwd file; it should be the first entry and will look something like this:

```
root:x:0:0:root:/root:/bin/bash
```

Don't delete that entry. Don't kill it from Linuxconf or another management tool. Be nice to the root account. Say nice things about it when you use it. Press the keys gently when you're entering its password. Don't hurt it.

Relinquish the Root Password to as Few People as Possible

I've worked in environments where executives insisted on having the superuser passwords on all the systems in the company, and it always made me nervous, especially as I spent time helping them recuperate from some mortal wound they'd given their own desktop systems. Now, being an executive doesn't necessarily make you a bonehead (though there may be a correlative, rather than causal, relationship between the two states), and there are plenty of management employees who are capable of handling the root account.

In the spirit of the "Know Why You're Using Root" section above, though, you have to ask yourself why each person who wants the root password should have it. And while you may not be able to tell your managers you won't give them the root password, you should be able to define a restricted-access policy that makes sense for your organization.

And if you're concerned about the number of people who have root password access, you might try the passive-aggressive approach: Change the root password and inform only the people who actually need it. If somebody else comes to ask why they can't get in, say, "Gosh, I just changed it because we were concerned that it had been compromised. What did you need to do as root?" If this doesn't work, give them my email address and I'll give them what for. Heh, heh, heh.

Know How to Recover Root

Having few people know the root password means it's possible that the sad day will come when nobody knows the root password. At the rate system administrators change jobs these days, the likelihood of losing the root password is fairly high. So what do you do if you need to administer a system whose root password has been trashed?

This is where a boot floppy comes in very handy. Some distributions will also allow you to boot into a non-installation version of Linux right from the installation CD-ROM. Either way, you'll want to insert the appropriate disc or diskette and have everybody log off the system. Make a note of the location of the /etc directory; normally, it is not placed on a different partition from the / directory, so use the **mount** command to determine the partition that is mounted as /etc or /. Make a note of it.

If a non-root user can shut the system down gracefully, use the **shutdown -h now** command to do so. If mortal users don't have this power, check and see whether mere mortals can unmount any of the partitions on the system. If this doesn't work either, issue the **sync** command a few times to make sure the disk contents are up to date and not hanging out in a cache somewhere (after everybody's off the system and there aren't any active processes running). Then hold your breath, and while wincing, use CTRL-ALT-DEL from the console to reboot the system.

Boot from the floppy or CD-ROM, which will mount its own root directory and file structure, and importantly, use its own account definitions. Login as root and use the **mount** command to mount the hard disk partition containing your normal /etc directory. For example, if /etc is on the /dev/sda1 partition, you can use the command:

```
mount /dev/sda1 /mnt
```

This makes the contents of the /dev/sda1 partition visible on /mnt. You should be able to change into the /mnt directory and find the /etc directory. Edit the passwd file contained there by deleting the text between the first two colons on the root account's line, so that it looks like this:

```
root::0:0:root:/root:/bin/bash
```

Now edit the shadow file in the same directory by deleting the text between the first two colons on the root account's line. Restart the system, and you should be able to log in as root without a password. Change that situation quickly using the **passwd** command, and for heaven's sake, put the new password in your safe or something.

This exercise should also give you an idea of why it's important to maintain physical security over your systems. Given a floppy disk and access to the system, you've just changed the root password. Sobering, isn't it?

Avoiding Unnecessary Use of Root

Making appropriate use of root isn't just a matter of using it correctly, it's also a matter of not using it incorrectly. And there are some options for you if you wish to avoid using root when there's not a good reason.

Give a Reasonable Amount of Access to User Accounts

This is a pretty simple concept. If you give users or groups enough access over their own directories, you won't need to get Big Brother Root involved to help them out. Or if you give certain trustworthy users membership to groups that give them management authority over certain files and directories, they'll be able to take care of needs in those areas without constant reliance upon you.

On the other hand, opening up system areas to user access is likely to make you need to use root to fix problems that users cause unintentionally. So the principle is to give autonomy to users in their designated areas, and keep a stranglehold on all other areas.

Use Root Alternatives When Possible

Think about how you're using the root account and find ways of performing the same tasks without logging in as root. For example, most systems don't allow normal users to mount the disk partitions, which is appropriate. But it also means that from time to time the root user might have to remount a remote partition (when a network connection has been down, for example). One way of eliminating direct root intervention from this scenario is to use the automounter to remount partitions that get lost this way. Check the man pages on the **autofs** command for more information about using the automount features.

Another way to work around use of the root account is by using a tool designed for the purpose. One such utility is *sudo*, which allows normal users to perform a "superuser do" as permitted by the real superuser. If your distribution doesn't include sudo, you can get it from **http://www.courtesan.com/sudo/**. Basically, you edit a file called /etc/sudoers to indicate who is allowed to perform superuser-like tasks, and you can lock down precisely which commands and options may be executed.

Don't Give Root User Account Features

The general principle here is that the root account isn't a user account. Nobody is using the superuser account as their personal account, so it doesn't need certain types of functionality. It doesn't need to use a cool window manager or the corresponding configuration dot files. It certainly doesn't need to use electronic mail; while system messages will sometimes be mailed to root, it's easy enough to edit the /etc/aliases file to forward mail for root to the user account of the system administrator.

MANAGING SPECIAL FUNCTION ACCOUNTS

The special function accounts are those used by users on PPP, SLIP, UUCP, and POP connections. If your system is acting as a server for one or more of these services, you can use Linuxconf to configure user access to each one.

PPP Accounts

If your Linux system will be acting as a server for PPP clients, you can use the PPP Accounts option in Linuxconf to manage the PPP accounts separately from the rest of the user accounts. The same pieces of information are needed for PPP account information as for standard account creation. While configuration and troubleshooting of a PPP system falls outside this book's scope, there's plenty of information available to help you if you're interested. I suggest you start with the PPP-HOWTO document and the Linux Administrator's Guide.

Base Information

As the screen in Figure 8-2 illustrates, there are few differences between the interface for entering the basic user information whether creating local user accounts or PPP accounts.

As you might expect, there are fields for entering the login name, full name, home directory, and user ID. All these pieces of information will be stored in the /etc/passwd file, as with any user account. The differences can also be seen in Figure 8-2, however. Notice that the primary groupname is set to **pppusers**, and the command interpreter (the shell) is set to **/usr/lib/linuxconf/lib/ppplogin**. This script controls what happens when a PPP account is used.

Password Parameters

The password parameters for a Linuxconf-based PPP account are identical to the ones available for standard user accounts. Like other user accounts, the PPP account password settings are stored in /etc/conf.linuxconf.

Mail Settings

You probably won't be surprised to find that the mail settings for a PPP account are the same as those for the normal user accounts described earlier in this chapter. The information you enter here will be stored in the .forward file in the user's directory and in the /etc/aliases file.

SLIP Accounts

If you will be hosting SLIP accounts on the Linux system, you can use Linuxconf to configure the SLIP accounts. These accounts differ very little from the normal user accounts, but like the PPP accounts, they have their own primary group name and command interpreter lines.

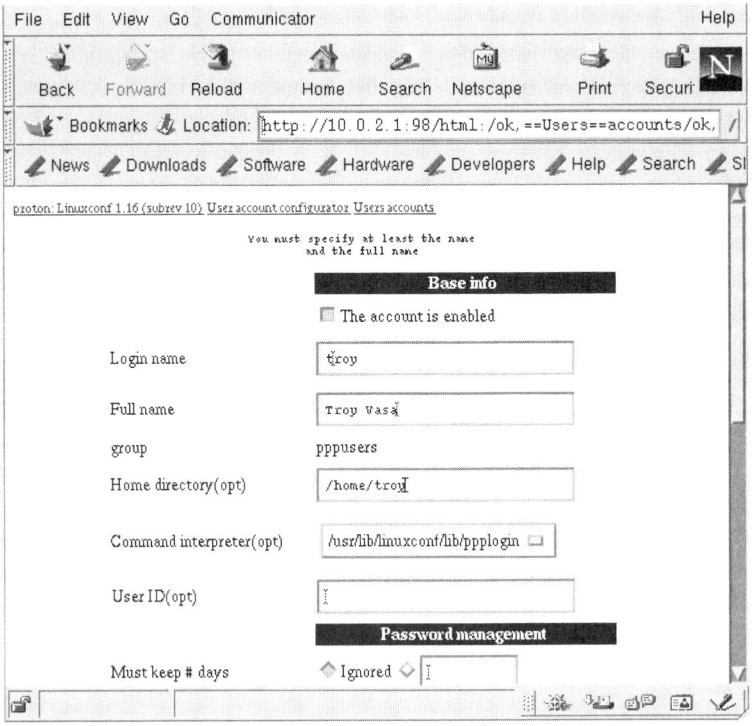

Figure 8-2. Set the basic user information for a PPP account in Linuxconf

In the SLIP version, the special group for these users is known as **slipusers**, and the default command interpreter is **/sbin/diplogin**. This special shell performs the configuration of the modem and interfaces so that a SLIP connection will be established.

There is a configuration file known as /etc/slip/slip.hosts that gives you control over the addresses assigned to the login names used on your system, providing a layer of security for the SLIP connection.

UUCP Accounts

Unix-to-Unix Copy (UUCP) is a method of providing basic dialup network functionality. You're most likely to run into the Taylor UUCP implementation, which is described in some detail in the UUCP-HOWTO. The Linuxconf interface for creating UUCP users is similar to the one used for normal accounts, PPP accounts, and SLIP accounts.

One way the UUCP user configuration is different is in the primary group assigned, which is always **uucp**. Another difference is that there is no shell defined, because everything the UUCP user boils down to a job transferring data from one system to another. The last difference is in the default home directory, which is normally /var/spool/uucppublic. The configuration files for the UUCP setup can be found in the /etc/uucp directory.

If you don't have an existing need for UUCP, I wouldn't recommend implementing it; while many Unix users are quite familiar with it, Windows administrators might as well stick with PPP for dial-up connections.

SETTING ACCOUNT POLICIES

The last user-account-related configuration options to which we need to turn our attention are the general policies that dictate how accounts are validated, which shells are usable, and what information should be given to users when they log in.

Account Policies

The system account policies include two major types of information: rules for validating the passwords when they are created or changed, and default account management rules. While you can specify the account management settings for individual users when they're created, you can also configure the system's default settings as you want them.

Password Validation Rules

There are several of these rules, and while some of them are familiar to administrators of other network operating systems, some are unique to Unix and Unix-like environments. These options can be seen in the top half of Figure 8-3, which shows the web-based Linuxconf interface to the Password & Account Policies option.

You can use these options to make your passwords more difficult to guess by making them longer and increasing the number of required non-alphabet characters. If you enable the Private Group option, each user will be assigned to a corresponding group created at the same time (with the same name as the user account). Disabling this option causes users to be added to a single group by default; you can change that group when you create the user.

If you don't like the standard /home directory being the default base directory for your users, you can change that base directory to the location you specify. This may be useful in particular when your users have home directories on a different system than the one on which you're creating accounts.

The Creation Permissions option may seem a little oblique to Windows administrators without Unix experience. It simply means that when the new user's home directory is created, access permissions need to be assigned. The value shown in Figure 8-3, 700,

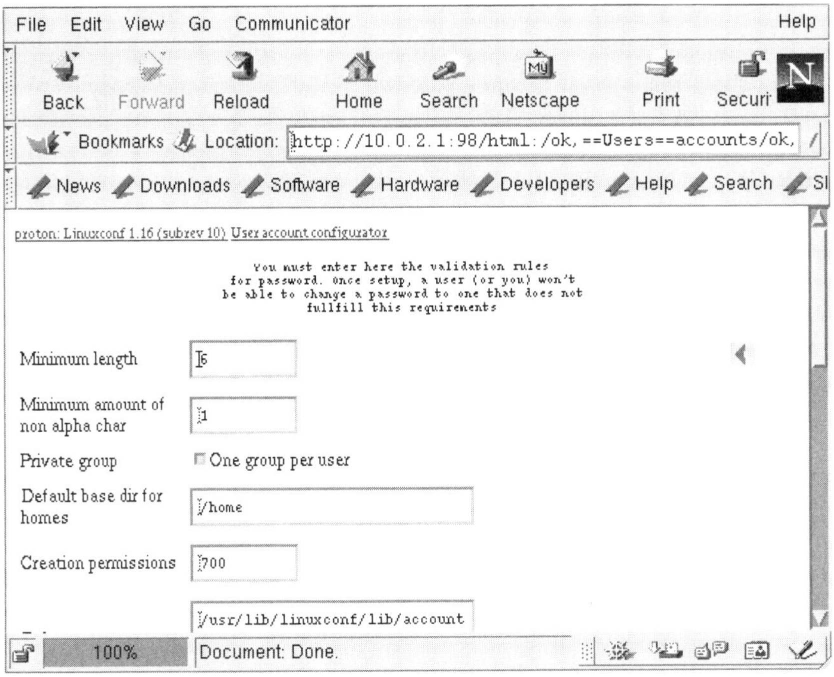

Figure 8-3.   Set default password and account policies from Linuxconf

corresponds to full access for the individual who owns the directory and no access for other users. This is a reasonable default for home directories; the corresponding directory listing might look like this:

```
drwx------    4 karen      spouses      4096 May 15 10:23 karen
```

The Delete Account Command is the command that's executed when you tell Linuxconf to delete an existing user account. There's a default script for this task, but if you want to modify it or replace it completely, you can do that. After all, this is Linux you're using! Similarly, the Archive Account Command points to the script executed when you choose to archive an account before it's deleted. The default script compresses the contents of the user's home directory into a file in the /home/oldaccounts directory.

The last two fields in this section allow you to specify commands to be performed after a user account is created or before a user account is deleted. There are several things you might decide you want to do when you create a new user, including activating scripts on other systems or adding the user to databases or other applications. And you may want to write a script to inform some users of the impending demise of a user account and the files in its home directory. You get to decide what you want to do in these situations, and you can write a shell script to perform whatever tasks you think necessary.

Account Management Defaults

For systems with password-shadowing enabled, which you should, the default account management settings can be configured in this area. These options are similar to the ones you can set on a user-by-user basis, but they apply to each user who doesn't have another value specified.

The Must Keep # Days option sets the amount of time a user must keep a password before it can be changed. The Must Change After # Days is the number to set if you require your users to change their passwords regularly (that is, if you prefer them to write the password down rather than keep for eight years the one they remember). The Warn # Days Before Expiration setting tells the system to warn the user some number of days before the account is due to expire. Account Expire After # Days sets accounts to expire a set number of days after their creation, while the Standard Account Duration option designates a specific default expiration date for all accounts. Unfortunately, that last option is expressed in days after January 1, 1970, so it's not easy to read at a glance. These settings are stored in /etc/conf.linuxconf.

Setting Default Shells

The Available User Shells option allows you to add or subtract from the list of shells available for users. The Linuxconf front end modifies the list of accepted shells found in /etc/shells, so if you want to narrow the list of possibilities, or expand it to include a great new shell, you can do that from here or by editing that file directly.

Message of the Day

This simple option allows you to designate a message to be displayed to each user when they log into the Linux system. Whether you're announcing scheduled downtime, a company potluck, or that someone's headlights are on, this can be useful from time to time. This message is found in the /etc/motd file, which you can edit directly or programmatically if you prefer.

CHAPTER
9

Step 6: Mingle with Microsoft, Network with Novell

You've got your users installed and configured now, and you're ready to commence with the internetworking. That's Step 6 in our recovery program: Make a list of Microsoft and Novell systems and establish contact with them all. This being a book on overcoming Microsoft by using Linux, it shouldn't surprise you that I plan to show you how to connect with Microsoft users and servers. But there's still quite a lot of NetWare out there, despite my best efforts in the 1996 classic *Migrating from NetWare to Windows NT*.

So in this chapter we'll focus on getting you access to data wherever it might be: an existing partition on your Linux system's hard disk; a Windows client station or server; or a NetWare client or server.

TRANSFER FILES FROM A LOCAL DISK

If you're converting a system from another operating system to Linux, you may have retained a partition containing your DOS or Windows programs and data. A great feature of Linux is its ability to handle these filesystems—to the point of allowing you to mount such partitions and access them seamlessly from Linux. You also have the option of accessing other file systems, such as Windows NT's NTFS and OS/2's HPFS, on a read-only basis. Either way, you can move the data as you see fit if it's on a Linux-readable partition on your Linux system.

The details of that process are entirely up to you, and the low cost-per-gigabyte of disk storage these days gives you some flexibility with how you can approach the task. Four years ago, I would have spent quite a few words suggesting ways of paring down your current data set so that you could start fresh and new after eschewing Microsoft. Today, my suggestion is to drop a few more bucks on large disk drives (even 30GB drives don't cost much now), use them to create new homes for your data, mount up the old drives, and move the data. No muss, no fuss.

Transfer FAT and VFAT Data

So you thought you'd test Linux on your old Windows9x system. And you've got Linux running and it isn't causing you any problems. And you're thinking, "My stars and garters, if only I had access to the My Documents folder while I'm running Linux. I'd never have to boot up that other inept, proprietary, bloated operating system again." If you're thinking something along those lines (though I realize that few people who aren't my late uncle actually use the term "my stars and garters"), I've got good news for you. What you're asking to do is easy. And it can be done without trouble from any MS-DOS partition or Windows 9*x* partition.

DOS FAT Partitions

If the partition you want to access is an old MS-DOS-style partition with the stylish 8.3 filenames, you can access it by telling Linux that you want to get to a partition of type msdos or umsdos. You'll also have to know the name of the device the partition resides on, and the number of the partition (for example, /dev/sda1).

From the Command Line   To mount a DOS partition that is the first partition on the first SCSI drive, you could use the following command:

```
root@romans /> mount -t msdos /dev/sda1 /mnt/dosdrive
```

This command simply tells Linux to mount the filesystem on the /dev/sda1 partition at the mount point /mnt/dosdrive (that directory must already exist, by the way), using the filesystem type msdos (umsdos also works).

After the filesystem on the partition is mounted, its contents can be accessed from the Linux system in the directory /mnt/dosdrive. Mounting the partition there is roughly equivalent to calling the C:\ drive /mnt/dosdrive instead: All the files and directories from the DOS partition are accessible in this directory, using their same names and the same relative paths.

Mounting a DOS-formatted floppy disk works the same way:

```
root@romans /> mount -t msdos /dev/fd0 /mnt/floppy
```

Many current distributions conveniently pre-create the /mnt/floppy mount point for you.

From Linuxconf   Because there's inevitably more than one way to do things in Linux, and because we've been using the Linuxconf tool to GUIfy other system administration tasks, and because the header immediately preceding this paragraph implies the use of Linuxconf, you might guess that Linuxconf may be used to provide access to a local DOS partition. You would be right.

The Access Local Drive option in the Linuxconf Config-File Systems tree allows you to view, add, and remove local drive mounts on the system. To mount your DOS partition this way, click the Add button to bring up the configuration screen shown in Figure 9-1.

The Base filesystem information is straightforward. You type the partition name in the Partition field, select a partition type from the list provided (for a DOS partition, the correct type is msdos), and specify the mount point you wish to use. Unlike the command-line interface, Linuxconf will let you know if that mount point doesn't already exist and will ask if you want it to create the mount point for you.

The General Options section is a friendlier interface to a variety of settings that can be specified when a filesystem is mounted, as shown in Table 9-1.

The last two options described in Table 9-1 theoretically enable quotas on the partition (you must enable quota support in the kernel to get it on the filesystem). This option isn't necessarily used by your system, though. There should be a file called quota.user in the filesystem's root directory so that user-based quotas work. The quota.group file in the same directory should help make group-based quotas work.

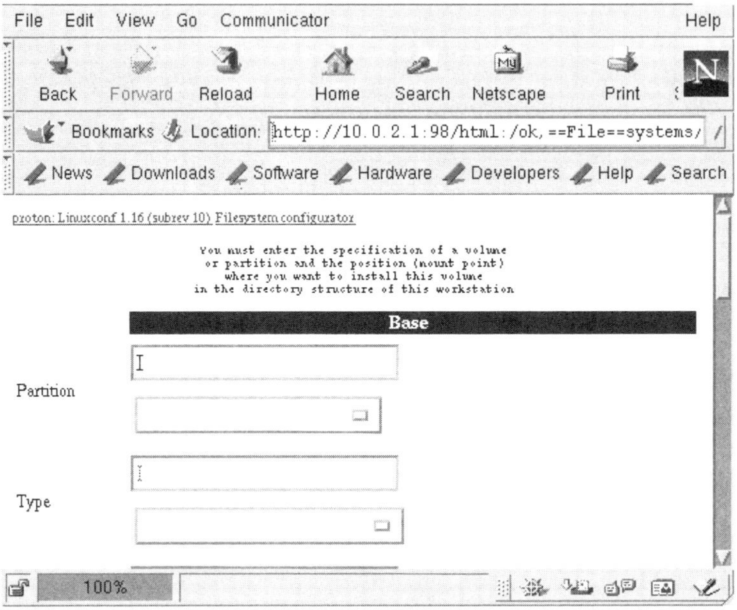

Figure 9-1.   Mount a DOS partition from Linux using Linuxconf

The other two options are the Dump Frequency and fsck Priority. The entries you make in these fields correspond to columns in the /etc/fstab file and are used to indicate whether the partition should be included in a system dump (one type of backup) and when the filesystem integrity should be tested.

If you set the dump frequency to 0, the filesystem on this partition will be excluded when a system dump is performed. If the frequency is set to 1, the partition will be included in system dumps. Partitions on hard disks should generally have a dump frequency of 1, while swap partitions and partitions on removable media should have a frequency of 0.

The fsck Priority setting tells Linux when to check the filesystem on startup. Swap partitions and partitions on removable media don't need to be checked, so they can be given a priority of 0. The root partition should be checked first, so set its priority to 1. Other priorities that you wish to check can be given a 2; they will be checked after the root partition. View the man pages for fsck for more information on how it works.

User, Permission, and Translation Options   One difference between FAT and multi-user filesystems like the ones used by Linux and Windows NT is that FAT filesystems don't in-

Linuxconf Option	Mount Command Flag	Description
Read only	ro	Prevents all users from modifying the contents of the filesystem
User mountable	user	Allows normal users to mount the filesystem if it's unmounted (doesn't require root)
Not mount at boot time	noauto	The filesystem isn't automatically mounted when the system starts up
No program allowed to execute		Prevents execution of programs from this filesystem (especially useful for securing user-mountable removable drives)
No special device file support	nodev	Prevents the use of special devices on this filesystem to improve security
No setuid programs allowed	nosetuid	This option prevents processes running under an assumed user ID from exercising the special privileges of that ID on this filesystem
User quota enabled	usrquota	Theoretically enables user-level quota restrictions on the filesystem
Group quota enabled	grpquota	Theoretically enables group-based quota restrictions on the filesystem

Table 9-1.   Linuxconf Filesystem General Options and Mount Command Options

clude the concept of file ownership. Because DOS and early Windows systems were designed for use by a single person, file ownership was irrelevant.

When you've got multiple users on a system, though, it's handy to be able to acknowledge ownership to a user and group to allow more flexibility and security. So if you mount a single-user filesystem such as msdos or vfat on your Linux box, how are these multi-user elements handled?

I'm glad you asked. Linuxconf gives you the opportunity to configure the elements using DOS Options or (U)Msdos And Hpfs Options, depending on the Linuxconf interface you're using. Either way, you get fields for:

▼   The default user ID assigned to own all files and directories in the filesystem.

■   The default group ID assigned to own all files and directories in the filesystem.

- ■   The default permissions to be set on these files and directories

- ▲   The translation mode used to reconcile the different ways the operating systems treat the end of a line of text.

Each of these options, shown in Figure 9-2, corresponds to a configuration option in the mount command or the /etc/fstab file.

The Default User ID is the user ID number of the user account that will have ownership of the files and directories. The Default Group ID is the group ID number of the group account that will be given ownership of those files and directories. The Default Permission setting is the three-digit sequence indicating the owner, group, and "world" permissions.

The Translation Mode options take a little more explaining; they don't allow you to view an English language file in, for example, Deutsch. A Windows text file indicates the end of a line using the ASCII carriage return character followed by the ASCII line feed character. On Linux (and other Unix) systems, the end of a line in a text file is specified with the line feed character alone. Thus, if you open a file in Linux after you edit it on a

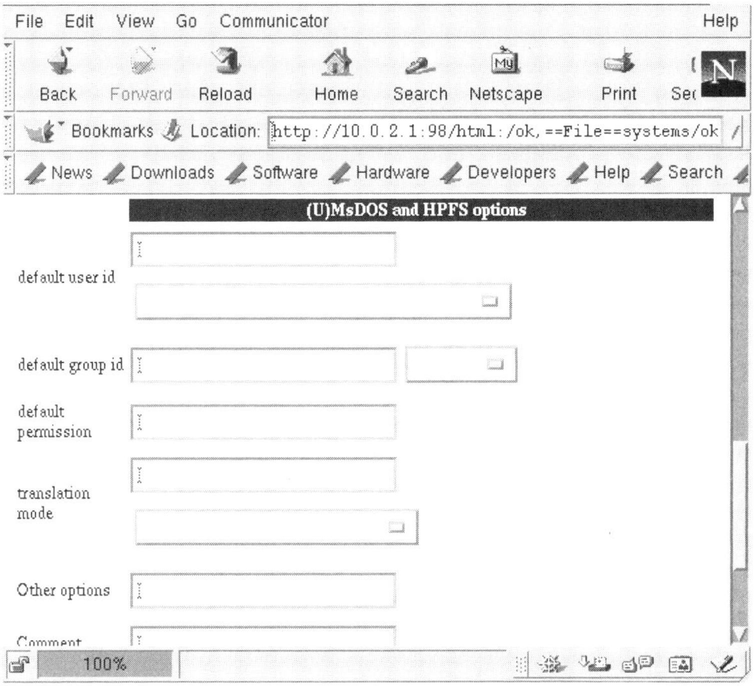

Figure 9-2.   Linuxconf provides a front end for setting default ownership, permissions, and file translation for a FAT or VFAT filesystem

Windows system, you'll find that at the end of each line there is a ^M sequence. It'll drive you insane if you let it, so this option is supposed to help translate for the two systems so that neither one gets short-sheeted.

There are three options for the translation mode field: Binary; Auto; and Text. The Binary setting performs no translation on the files. The Auto setting attempts to match the file's extension with a list of known program, archive, layout, and graphics extensions. If the extension doesn't match one of those options, it's assumed to be a text file and is translated. The Text setting translates each and every file, even ones that could be assumed are binary files.

While Auto is reasonably safe, the best course of action is to avoid using the same files on both systems any more than possible. If you want to share files on a dual-boot system, that's fine, but otherwise, go ahead and move the files over to a native ext2 filesystem. And then select the Binary option.

Here's an example of what a line in the /etc/fstab file might look like once you've configured these options:

```
/dev/sda2   /mnt/windoze   vfat   rw,conv=binary,uid=504,gid=501,umask=700   1   0
```

In this case, the vfat filesystem on /dev/sda2 will be mounted in the /mnt/windoze directory with read-write access allowed. Files and directories will be owned by the user whose ID is 504 and the group whose ID is 501, and the default permissions for those files and directories will be 700, which gives full read, write, and execute permissions to the owner user account and prevents access from everyone else. The filesystem at /mnt/windoze will be included in a system dump, and will not be touched with fsck.

Linuxconf offers two more fields: one is a comment field you can use to remind yourself what you're doing with the filesystem you're configuring; the other is a generic Other Options field that's included because there are other options that can be fed to the mount command. Check the man pages for mount and fstab for more information.

Windows VFAT Partitions

The later Windows 9x partitions use the VFAT filesystem, which added support for long file names. Mounting a VFAT filesystem from the Linux command line is very similar to mounting a FAT filesystem; only the partition type is different:

```
root@romans /> mount -t vfat /dev/sda2 /mnt/windoze
```

Performing the same task with Linuxconf is identical to the process used to mount a FAT filesystem, with the obvious exception that you must specify the VFAT type.

Move Read-Only Data

If you're configuring a Linux system that contains a hard disk with partitions that can only be read (not written to) from Linux, have no fear. If the partition uses NTFS, you're in luck; just be sure you included support for reading from the filesystem when you built the kernel.

There's little difference between moving data from these partitions and from the FAT and VFAT filesystems I just described, except that the Linuxconf interface isn't going to give you the **ntfs** filesystem type as an option. That's okay, though, you can just enter it into the text field rather than selecting from the drop-down list. And of course, you can always edit the /etc/fstab file directly.

CONNECT TO MICROSOFT SYSTEMS

If you are more interested in keeping some of your Microsoft systems running than in assimilating them into your Borg-like collective of Linux servers, do not fear. Many of us feel and share your pain, and due to the magnificent work of the Samba development team (**www.samba.org**), there's an answer for us.

Samba is a tool that uses the Server Message Block (SMB) protocol common to Microsoft operating systems to allow users on Unix and Linux systems to share resources with users on Windows systems. A very small number of my company's computer users only have Windows machines, but through the magic of Samba, they can access the Unix-connected printers, and the Linux users can access the Windows-connected printers.

While this book was written using Microsoft Word running on a PC running Windows, the files were saved to my Linux system exclusively. I mean, I don't mind using a bloated and inefficient word processor, but I refuse to let Windows trash any more of my files as it takes its periodic tumble, mumbling feebly into its LifeAlert unit, "I've fallen, and I can't get up!"

So I've configured Samba for my networks, and I'd like to take the opportunity to show you how to configure it for yours. Additional information on the subject can be found in the SMB-HOWTO document.

Configure Samba for Your Environment

The Samba configuration occurs in the /etc/smb.conf file, which is a large but heavily commented file; if you know what you're doing, you can edit it directly. If you know what you're doing, though, I wonder why you're reading this chapter of this book. Don't you have someone to flame?

In this section, I'll go through the steps of using Linuxconf for general Samba configuration, setting up home shares, printer shares, disk shares, and netlogons. You're welcome to join me, whether you're an erudite expert, one of Microsoft's many malicious, marketing myrmidons, or just learning Linux. Start by pointing Linuxconf to the Samba File Server option in the Config-Networking-Server Tasks tree.

CAUTION: At this time, direct Linux access to NTFS partitions from Windows 2000 systems does not function properly. While you may safely access these partitions using Samba, using the kernel code may damage the data. Earlier versions of NTFS should be readable, but Windows 2000 makes changes to the NTFS filesystem that Linux doesn't handle. The overall status of NTFS support in future kernel releases in uncertain, as it lacks a maintainer at this time.

Setting Defaults

If you select Defaults from the Samba File Server option, you'll be presented with a set of basic server configuration information. These options include basic configuration information, password policies, access rules, network settings, account utilities, and other features.

Base Configuration   Your first decision is whether you wish to make the Linux passwords or the SMB passwords the primary list. Choose Synchronize SMB From Linux Passwords if you want the passwords maintained using /etc/passwd, or the Synchronize Linux From SMB Passwords option if you prefer to have the primary password resource be /etc/smbpasswd. Of course, you can select both options to have the passwords synchronize no matter where they're changed.

The next configuration step is to enter the server description that appears in the domain or workgroup's list of hosts. You can enter a static text string, but you can also include some of the variables supported by Samba—the **%h** option to give the hostname and the **%v** option to give the Samba version number seem the most useful. Figure 9-3 shows the result of entering the following line as the server description string on the system named proton:

```
Linux Samba Server %v on %h
```

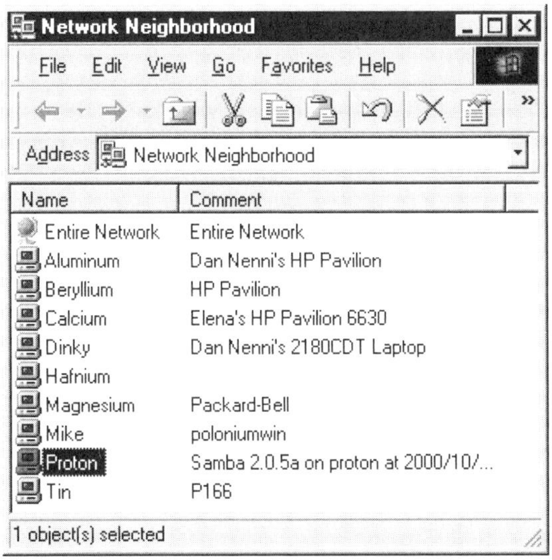

Figure 9-3.   Linux or Windows? They may only know if you tell them

The next field in the Linuxconf configuration is the workgroup to which the system will belong. If you will be connecting your Linux system to an NT or Windows 2000 domain, you can specify the domain name in this field instead of a workgroup.

The Netbios Name and Netbios Aliases are optional entries. The NetBIOS name of your Samba-equipped Linux system defaults to the hostname, but if you need to make it different, you may do so here. If you wish to create virtual NetBIOS hosts, you can add the system's aliases in the appropriate field.

Password Settings   The password settings control the way in which users are authenticated when they try to access the Samba system. If you enable the Encrypted Password Required option, client systems must pass encrypted passwords to be able to access the system. This is fine for Windows 98, fully Service-Packed Windows NT 4.0, and Windows 2000 systems, which default to using encrypted passwords. You'll have to enable password encryption on any Windows 95 systems that need to access the Samba server if you enable this option.

The Authentication Mode option allows you to select the authentication method from a list of four choices:

- ▼ User
- ■ Server
- ■ Domain
- ▲ Share

The user authentication method, which is the default, requires each user who wishes to access the Samba system to have an active account on the system and enter the correct password for that account.

The server authentication method seems the same to the user, but instead of the Linux system doing the password authentication, it points to another server to perform this function. If you select this option, enter the NetBIOS name of one or more NT servers you trust for this task in the Password Server field.

The domain authentication method also points to another system to perform user authentication, but instead of being another server, it's domain controller. This involves making sure the Password Server field is set to the NetBIOS name of the domain primary domain controller (PDC), making sure the Workgroup field contains the domain name, and starting Samba as described in the "Run Samba" section that follows.

Once the Linux box is running Samba, you'll have to tell it to join the NT domain by issuing the **smbpasswd** command with the **-j** option; in the next example, the system is attempting to join a domain known as PROLIFIC:

```
smbpasswd -j PROLIFIC
```

Once your system has joined the domain, you'll have to be sure to add user accounts for each domain user who wants to access resources on the Samba server. More information on this configuration, and links to tools that help creating these accounts, can be found at your nearest Samba mirror site, in the directory samba/docs/ntdom_faq/page6.html.

The share authentication method allows users to access system resources on a share-by-share basis. This means that a privileged password, not a user/password combination, is used to gain access to each such resource.

Because certain Microsoft operating systems aren't very careful about the case of passwords, the Password Level field exists to give the Linux system (which cares very much about the case of the passwords) a little leniency in interpreting the password's case. The value in this field represents the maximum number of digits in the Unix password that can be capitalized.

Setting this figure isn't really a science; on one hand, you want to include enough digits to allow for a normal amount of mixed-case digits. On the other hand, if you want the passwords to be secure, you must minimize the amount of "play" that's allowed between what the user enters and what the correct answer should be. If you want more information on this field, check out the Linuxconf help file, which gives some good examples.

The Passwd Program field is where you can enter a customized password entry script. The default value in this field is /bin/passwd %u, which runs the standard passwd authentication program for the user who is making the connection. It's certainly possible that you would want to create your own script, but I wouldn't recommend it for now. The default should work well.

Finally, the Allow Null Passwords Account option allows you to provide or prevent access to accounts with null passwords. If you care even a little bit about security, don't enable this option. If you don't care about security…well, I wash my hands of you.

Access Privileges   The Allow Hosts and Deny Hosts fields allow you to enter lists or groups of hosts or networks that are specifically allowed or denied access to the system. Enter a single hostname, or a whole list separated by commas. Enter an IP address, a network number, or a set of network numbers (e.g., "10.0."). Use the argument EXCEPT to indicate one or more addresses from the specified range that should be excluded from the allow or deny rule.

If you leave these fields blank, the system's default behavior is to allow access from anywhere (subject to authentication as you configured it in the Passwords section, of course). If there's overlap between the two fields, the tie goes to the Allow Hosts rule. Uncle Samba is apparently softhearted.

Network Settings   The OS level controls the priority of the Samba server with respect to network browsing. If you want Microsoft systems on your network to remain the browsing masters, you can leave this option set to 0. If you want the Samba system to become the master browser, you can increase this option to 33 or higher, which should give the Samba system priority. The Samba documentation suggests setting this value to 65 if you want to ensure that it's the master browser.

If you want your Samba system to be the local master browser, enable the Preferred Master option. If you want the Samba system to be the master browser for the whole domain, enable the Domain Master option. Be sure you coordinate this setting with the selections you've made on other Samba servers and on NT systems in the same local network and the domain as a whole.

The Remote Announce option is used to cause the Samba system to announce itself to remote networks—potentially even using different workgroup names. I have not worked in an environment in which this has been necessary, but if it sounds appropriate for your needs, review the help information in Linuxconf and knock yourself out.

If you know what you're doing and want to enable a single Samba system on your network to be a WINS server, you can check the box to Enable Samba As A Wins Server. Otherwise, if you use WINS, enter the name of the existing server in the WINS Server field.

Samba ordinarily is only enabled on the first NIC in your Linux system. If you want it to be active on other NICs, you should enter the IP addresses of those cards, separated by spaces, in the Interfaces field.

The Name Resolve Order option defines the method for resolving host names. Enter as many of the four methods as you wish, in the order you want them used, and separated by spaces. The options are described in Table 9-2; by default, they are all consulted, in the order shown in the table.

Automatic Account Scripts   Under certain conditions, it may be useful to allow the Samba server to create and delete Linux user accounts. A user account is useful if there isn't one for a user who has been authenticated by the Windows network. These circumstances must all be true to prompt the automatic creation of an account:

▼ Authentication mode must be user or domain.

■ The specified server or domain controller must authenticate the user.

■ The user must not already have an account on the Linux system.

■ Script must exist and take the argument %u, which becomes the account name.

▲ The English word for the day of the week must end in "y".

Option	Description
lmhosts	Consult the /etc/lmhosts file to resolve hostname to IP address.
host	Use the Linux systems' normal host lookup methods as specified in the /etc/nsswitch.conf file.
wins	Check with the defined WINS server, if any.
bcast	Try a broadcast on each NIC to check for the host on the local subnet.

Table 9-2.   Mix and Match Samba Name Resolve Order Methods

Okay, that last requirement isn't mandatory, but the others are. By default, there's no script set, so the user won't be added on the fly. Linuxconf comes with a single script option that you can select (or use as the basis for a script of your own). It looks like this:

```
/usr/sbin/adduser -s /bin/false -g popusers -c "smb account %u" %u
```

This creates a user with minimal functionality on the Linux side of the Samba box (no shell and a minimal-rights primary group) that can access Samba resources, depending on how you've configured them. This allows you to add a user on the Windows side and not have to worry about duplicating the process on the Linux side.

Automatic account deletion, on the other hand, ensures that a user account that is disabled on the Windows network is also removed from the Linux network. The stars and planets don't have to be properly aligned for this to happen (well, no more than usual, anyway), but the following conditions must be true:

▼ Authentication mode must be domain (because server authentication doesn't provide a definitive statement that an account has been deleted).

■ The specified domain controller must return an error code indicating that the user no longer exists in the domain.

▲ The delete script must exist and take the argument %u, which represents the account name to be deleted.

The default is to include no such script, so automatic deletion is not enabled. However, you may select the default option from Linuxconf, which looks like this:

```
/usr/sbin/deluser %u
```

This is a simple script: Given the user represented by %u, remove that user's account and the contents of their home directory. The moral of the story: Don't accidentally delete a user from the NT domain if you enable this option, or you'll be in for double account restorations.

Other Features   This last set of default options is a bit of a hodgepodge of Samba functionality. The Guest Account option allows you to specify a Linux user account used when public access is allowed to a Samba resource. If you allow public access to disk or printer shares, you should enter an account name with few privileges; the "nobody" account is a reasonable choice.

The Dead Time option should be set to the number of minutes of inactivity you want the Samba system to allow before it disconnects a Samba client that has no files open. The default value, 0, does not connect such users. Depending on the number of users you have vying for server resources, a value ranging from 10 to 30 seems reasonable. Most clients will reconnect seamlessly, so it's good to set a value here.

The Debug Level determines the amount of logging that's done by the Samba system, which could be useful for debugging or troubleshooting. The higher the number, the more detail is logged. Don't worry about this option; setting it to 0 won't be a problem.

The Default Service option allows you to provide some type of service to those who request a service that can't be found. See the Linuxconf help text for a little more information about this option, but the idea is that instead of giving users an error message when they try to access a service that isn't available, you can give them read-only access to some public area. Think of the warm fuzzies they'll feel when they don't get an error message. On the other hand, think of the confusion this will engender when they ask for a printer and get a directory of press releases.

If you enable the Show All Available Printers option, every printer defined in the /etc/printcap file may be browsed by default. And the WinPopup Command is a command the Linux server is told to run when it receives a WinPopup message. The help text suggests a method for conveying this information to the Linux user that simply pulls the message into an X Windows text editor. I'm not a big fan of WinPopup messages, so I just leave this field blank.

Fun with Samba Variables

I've mentioned the %u and %h variables you can use to tailor Samba scripts and messages. Variables like these make it possible to automate many tasks or make them specific to a user, a protocol, a group, a system, or one of the other entities represented by these variables. Here's a more exhaustive list, complete with short descriptions (more information can be found using the **man 5 smb.conf** command.

Variable	Description
%a	Attempts to recognize the remote system's OS architecture
%d	Current server process id
%g	User %u's primary group
%G	User %U's primary group
%h	IP hostname of the Samba system
%H	User %u's home directory
%I	Client machine's IP address
%L	Samba server's NetBIOS name
%m	Client system's NetBIOS name.
%M	Client system's IP hostname
%N	NIS home directory server
%p	Service's home directory
%P	Current service root directory
%R	Negotiated protocol level
%S	Current service name
%T	Current date and time
%u	Current service user name
%U	Desired client session user name
%v	Samba version number

Configuring Users' Home Shares

This set of options is used to configure sharing of home directories (which can be handled separately from other disk shares). You can tailor this feature to meet your particular needs by setting access from hosts, enabling and disabling individual users, and configuring scripts.

You have two initial configuration steps to take, though. First, enter a useful description of the home shares in the Comment/Description field. People don't always see these share descriptions in real life, but they're still nice to have. The **%h** option to include the Samba server hostname can be useful here.

The second thing to do is decide how much you want to enable and advertise the share. Most of the time, if you're creating a share, you'll want to enable it by selecting the This Share Is Enabled option. But sometimes you might want to take a share offline, and you can do that by deselecting this option. You can also make the share visible to users browsing the network by enabling the Browsable option. In some cases, disabling this option provides a small amount of additional security by making the share less of an attractive nuisance enticing users to go where they're not supposed to go.

Home Share Access   The Public Access option enables password-free access, opening the home shares to perusal by anybody who can browse the SMB network. Of course, their access level is defined by the Guest Account setting described in the Other Features option.

The next option is Writable, which, if enabled, allows users to create files and directories in the home directories, subject to their effective permissions. There's nothing wrong with making home directories writable (that's usually what they're there for), but I'd be careful configuring public access via a guest account if you enable writing to the directories.

The Allow Hosts and Deny Hosts settings configure Samba to accept or reject the hosts or networks you specify in the same way the same entries worked in the "Setting Defaults" process described earlier. Adding entries here allows you to create exceptions to or exclusions from the default rules you already laid down.

Home Share Users   The first user-related option allows you to specify a list of users who might access the system. This sounds more useful than it is, I'm afraid. This isn't really an effective method for restricting access to the system; instead, it serves as a sort of guest list to the Samba server to help identify user names that might be associated with the password that has been given. This doesn't seem to be necessary if you're using recent Microsoft operating systems, but older ones may not pass the user name Samba is expecting.

If you desperately want to make the user list a security method, you can enable the Only User May Connect Feature, which restricts access to the users specified in the list (you may specify users by listing an NIS or Linux group they're part of; just append the @ symbol to the beginning of the group name and add it to the list).

The Write List option overrides the Writable setting above; by listing a user or group in this field, you allow the user (or all group members) write access to the home shares.

This option is usually best reserved for system administrators, who can revel in their mighty systemwide powers!

The Valid Users field lists the users who are allowed to login and use the service. Unlike the User List field, which checks the password being provided for a match with any password corresponding to any user in the list, a "valid user" must give the password that matches their username.

There's also the Invalid Users, who are not allowed to login to the service at all. It's not a bad idea to add the names of defunct user accounts to a group (I like the name "deadpile"), and then sticking that groupname here, preceded by a "+" to specify that it's a Linux groupname, or an "@" to look for an NIS group first, and then for a matching Linux groupname. If a name appears in both the valid and invalid lists, the tie goes to being valid, because Samba is such validating software.

Setting Max. Connections to a value greater than 0 (the default) allows you to limit the number of active simultaneous connections. Users who attempt to connect to the service after the maximum limit has been reached will be denied. Samba uses lock files stored (by default) in /tmp/samba to keep track of these files.

Populate the Read Only User List field with the names (or groups of names, preceded by an "@" or "+" symbol) of users who should not have write access to the home directories, even if the Writable option is set.

Home Share Scripts   Sometimes it's useful to execute a script whenever a user logs in or logs out from the system. There are four fields in which you may enter the scripts:

- ▼ **Setup command**   Runs when someone connects to the service.

- ■ **Setup command (root)**   Runs as root when someone connects to the service.

- ■ **Cleanup command**   Runs when someone disconnects from the service.

- ▲ **Cleanup command (root)**   Runs as root when someone disconnects from the service.

The help information in Linuxconf gives examples of such scripts, including ones verbatim from the man page for smb.conf. I haven't found these very useful, but I have used these features to perform some user upgrades and to move them from one system to another. If executing a script at connect or disconnect times seems useful to you somehow, see what you can do with it!

Configuring Printer Shares

Configuring printer shares is quite simple. Select the Default Setup For Printers option from the Config-Network-Server Tasks-Samba File Server tree. Enter a description for the share; the default All Printers is pretty easy to understand, but you can always throw in a %h for good measure, if you wish.

To enable access to the printers share, make sure the This Share Is Enabled option is selected. If you don't mind just anybody printing, you can enable the Public Access option. Personally, I prefer that people log into a real account if they access *anything* on my networks. But do what you think is best.

Performing netlogon Setup

This set of options is used when the Samba system is acting as a login server for the domain. You can get to this portion of the configuration by choosing Netlogon Setup from the Config-Network-Server Tasks-Samba File Server tree. Enter a name for the share in the Netlogon Share Title field, and be sure the This Share Is Enabled option is selected.

Specify the directory in which you'd like to keep the netlogon file in the Directory To Export field. You may also specify a logon script, path, drive, and home relative to this exported directory.

Logon Script   Specify a Microsoft-style logon script to run when the user logs in. This script can be either a .bat file or a .cmd file, just like you'd use on a Microsoft server. Indeed, it should be formatted using a DOS-based editor to ensure that the file uses the redundant Microsoft carriage return/linefeed commands to end each line.

The script can contain NET USE statements to map network drives, or perform any other tasks you're used to including in your Windows login scripts. You can use the %u, %g, or %m variables, for example, to create user-, group- or system-specific logon scripts.

Logon Path   Use this field to designate the directory in which Windows 9*x* profiles are stored. Don't make put this in the home share tree; give it a place of its own. The client systems will reference the user.dat and user.man files, and will load their Desktop, Start Menu, Programs, and Network Neighborhood folders from the path you indicate here.

Logon Drive   Use this field if you have Windows NT or 2000 workstations that need to know what drive letter to use to connect the home directory. The format is the drive letter and a colon (e.g., h:).

Logon Home   Specify the user's home directory here. The default entry is

```
\\%N\%U
```

This sets the home directory to point to the directory named for the user account on the home directory server. If your home directory is located in a different directory structure, change this field to reflect that.

Configuring Disk Shares

You can setup non-home disk shares by selecting Disk Shares from the Config-Network-Server Tasks-Samba File Server tree in Linuxconf. Departmental or project shared space may be configured this way, for example.

You begin disk share configuration by giving the share a name and a description so that users will know what the share is for. Enable the share by checking the This Share Is

Enabled box, and make the share visible from a network browser by checking the Browsable box.

The Inherit Settings From Share option gives you the chance to use an existing share as a template for a new share; the new share will use the existing share's configuration settings by default, but you may change settings in the new share as you see fit.

The Directory To Export is the path from root to the directory that will be treated as the top level of the disk share. As with any disk share, you want to make sure you pick a directory deep enough in the tree that users won't be able to branch over into places they shouldn't be. Creating a disk share of the / directory on a Linux system is not the safest thing to do, for example.

Disk Share Access   Enable the Public Access option to allow anyone who can browse the SMB network to access the disk share. The public access level is defined by Samba's guest account setting. If this option is selected, you can also enable the Guest Access Only to force all users to access the share as guest users. The Writable option allows users to create files and directories in the share, subject to their effective permissions.

As with the home shares access options, the Allow Hosts and Deny Hosts fields allow you to enter lists or groups of hosts or networks you wish to allow or deny access to the system. Enter a list of hostnames or IP addresses separated by commas, and/or a set of network numbers. The EXCEPT argument may be used to indicate one or more addresses from the specified range that should be excluded from the allow or deny rule.

If you leave these fields blank, the system's default behavior is to allow access from any system. If there's overlap between the two fields, the tie goes to the Allow Hosts rule.

Disk Share Users   The only difference between the user configuration required for the home directory share and other disk shares is the Admin Users field. This field should contain the names (or the group name containing them) of the users who should have Administrator access to the share. These users will enjoy unrestricted access to the share, and will be equivalent to the superuser on the share, so don't make just anybody an Admin user.

Disk Share Scripts   With the exception of the Magic Script field, these scripts are identical to the ones described in the home share section. The first four fields contain the scripts that run: when someone connects to the service; as root when someone connects to the service; when someone disconnects from the service; and as root when someone disconnects from the service.

The magic script is a script that can be opened from a client station; when it is closed, the script is executed on the server. This feature is experimental in the version of Samba I'm working with, so I suggest you take the Samba team's advice and don't rely on this feature!

Disk Share Features   There are some interesting miscellaneous options contained in the Features section of the Linuxconf configuration tool for Samba disk shares. For example, the Force User and Force Group options allow you to specify a single user and group.

Any user who connects to this disk share will access the share as the forced user and/or group. This makes it easy to control access to simple shares—you need only worry about one user account on the Linux side!

The Don't Descent option (which should really be called Don't Descend, but there are quite a few typos and odd word choices throughout the Linuxconf interface and help system) allows you to specify directories that users will not be able to descend into, presumably because those directories are too deep or not appropriate for user access. Two examples given in the smb.conf man page are the /dev and /proc trees, and it is difficult to see how the contents of these system directories is of any use to the Windows users connecting through Samba. Just enter the directory names, separated by commas, and they'll be displayed as empty when viewed through the disk share.

Configure the Guest Account (This Share) if you want to specify a particular user account used for public access to the share. The Magic Output setting allows you to specify a file to which output from the Magic Script will be written. This value defaults to the name of the magic script with a .out extension. And the Max. Connections setting limits the number of simultaneous active connections permitted for the share. Users who attempt to access the share after the limit is reached are kicked out of the inn and are lucky to find space in the stables.

Run Samba

If you've plowed through all that Samba configuration, you're ready to take on a simple task for a change. (Actually, there are a number of additional options not covered by Linuxconf, so if you're looking for functionality that isn't covered, check out the smb.conf man page and the **samba.org** web site.) So you'll be happy to know that the actual running of the Samba process is quite simple.

Running Samba on a Red Hat or derivative distribution just means making sure the process gets started. You can see whether it's running by using the /etc/rc.d/init.d/smb script and checking for the Samba server status, like this:

```
root@romans /> /etc/rc.d/init.d/smb status
```

If the Samba server is running, it will tell you so, and it will give you the process ID numbers for the related processes:

```
smbd (pid 18934 18919) is running...
nmbd (pid 18930) is running...
```

On the other hand, if the server isn't running, the smb status command will return something more like this:

```
smbd is stopped
nmbd is stopped
```

In case you're wondering, the smbd process is the part of Samba that serves up resources, while the nmbd process provides NetBIOS name services from the Samba server. You can check their man pages for more information about each, but we'll be manipulating them indirectly, using the **smb wrapper** program found in the /etc/rc.d/init.d directory.

To get a stopped Samba server running, you tell the smb script to start things up:

```
root@romans /> /etc/rc.d/init.d/smb start
```

You should get good news from your server in response:

```
Starting SMB services                            [OK]
Starting NMB services                            [OK]
```

If you want to shut down the Samba server, you'll issue the same command, replacing the **start** with **stop**. And to restart the server—perhaps because you manually edited the smb.conf file and want the changes to be reflected in the way the server is running—you can issue the **smb restart** command, which stops the processes and then starts them again.

To ensure that the Samba server is started each time you reboot the Linux system, use the /usr/sbin/ntsysv tool. This is a full-screen text-based tool that shows you the services available on your system and allows you to select the ones that will be started at boot time. This is a convenient way of ensuring that the startup files are properly synced. Figure 9-4 shows that the smb service is indeed enabled at startup on my Samba server.

Troubleshoot Samba

While there's not enough room in this book to give you a full explanation of how to troubleshoot any of the services we'll be discussing, the Samba service is vital to Linux administrators with a Windows client and server legacy. So allow me to point you to the documentation on the Samba web site. As I write this, there is a Samba diagnosis procedure available for your use; go to the Samba server mirror nearest you, follow the Documentation link, and from the Other Documentation section of the page, find the Diagnosing Samba link.

But because most of my problems have been solved in just a few steps, I'll give you a quick rundown on a few of them here. If they're not enough to locate and solve your problem, do try the web site, which includes information on how to use some of the Samba utilities I haven't mentioned.

First: Check the smb.conf File for Errors

Although the Linuxconf interface will detect certain errors when you attempt to enter incorrect settings, it's a good idea to check the smb.conf file to make sure that it's doing what you think it's doing. And while you're checking, you might make some changes by hand.

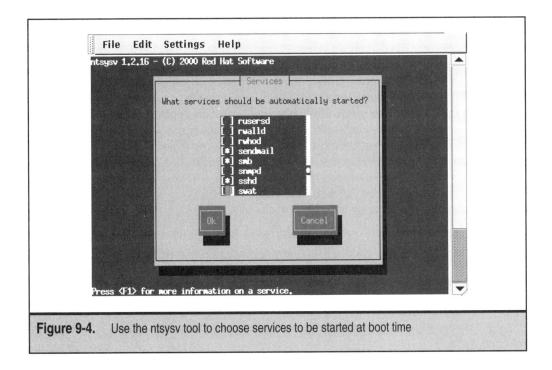

Figure 9-4.   Use the ntsysv tool to choose services to be started at boot time

As I mentioned earlier, this file is quite long, and while it's extensively commented (with a great deal of information available on the man page, as well as in this chapter), it's not necessarily easy to trap every error, especially when you're working with Samba for the first time. Fortunately, the good Samba folks have provided a script to check the smb.conf file for internal consistency. To run the tool, just tell it where the smb.conf file is located:

```
root@romans /> /usr/bin/testparm /etc/smb.conf
```

The program will keep you apprised of its status as it runs:

```
Load smb config files from smb.conf
Processing section "[homes]"
Processing section "[printers]"
Processing section "[home]"
Processing section "[netlogon]"
Loaded services file OK
Press enter to see a dump of your service definitions
```

If you press ENTER, testparm will give you a breakdown of the options you've selected for each section; it's a little like reading the smb.conf file without comments.

Deal with Password Encryption

If you're having trouble reaching a Samba server from Windows 2000, Windows NT 4.0 patched to Service Pack 3 or later, Windows 98, or Windows 95-OSR/2, but you can reach it from earlier Microsoft operating systems, the culprit is most likely clear text passwords. Earlier Microsoft products use them; later ones won't do it by default.

You'll have to decide for yourself whether password encryption, which brings with it passwords saved to disk in ways that aren't perfectly secure, or clear text transmission, which may allow passwords to be captured over the wire, is better for your situation. I lean toward enabling clear text passwords from the client stations, but this can be an irritating step to have to take with each new system if you don't have an effective means of automating the process for each client platform in use.

Use Unencrypted Passwords   If you decide to enable unencrypted passwords, use the regedit command appropriate to the platform, and change the value specified in Table 9-3 to enable the Windows system to transmit clear text passwords.

Samba Password Encryption   If you opt to enable password encryption on the Samba server, follow these steps:

1. Add the following line to the [global] section of the smb.conf file

```
encrypt passwords=yes
```

OS	Registry Key	Name and Data
Win 2000	[HKEY_LOCAL_MACHINE\ SYSTEM\CurrentControlSet\ Services\ LanmanWorkStation\ Parameters]	"EnablePlainTextPassword"=dword:00000001
WinNT 4.0	[HKEY_LOCAL_MACHINE\ SYSTEM\CurrentControlSet\ Services\Rdr\Parameters]	"EnablePlainTextPassword"=dword:00000001
Win 98	[HKEY_LOCAL_MACHINE\ System\CurrentControlSet\ Services\VxD\VNETSUP]	"EnablePlainTextPassword"=dword:00000001
Win 95	[HKEY_LOCAL_MACHINE\ System\CurrentControlSet\ Services\VxD\VNETSUP]	"EnablePlainTextPassword"=dword:00000001

Table 9-3.   Enable Unencrypted Passwords on Microsoft OSes

2. Red Hat stores the smbpasswd password file in /etc/smbpasswd. Make sure the file is only readable by root by using this command:

```
root@romans /> ls -l /etc/smbpasswd
-rw------- 1 root     root    208 May 12 14:01 smbpasswd
```

If the file permissions don't match the ones you see in that line, use this command to correct them:

```
root@romans /> chmod 600 /etc/smbpasswd
```

3. Populate the smbpasswd file. There's a shell script to do this from the /etc/passwd file, but I prefer the control of adding users intentionally (perhaps now is a good time to have your users rectify their accounts so you can clear out the unnecessary ones?). The smbpasswd program does this without much fuss.

```
root@romans /> smbpasswd -add karen honeybunny
```

This command is easy to figure out: It adds a user named karen with the oh-so-sticky password honeybunny. You can script these additions from a list of your user accounts and some nice, industrial strength passwords.

4. Now you can allow the users to modify their passwords by enabling the special set user ID permission on the /etc/smbpasswd file:

```
root@romans /> chmod u+s /etc/smbpasswd
```

You should be able to use the encrypted passwords on your Samba server and its clients now!

Ensure Printers Are Recognized

Perhaps I'm jumping the gun by pointing this out, since I haven't discussed printer configuration yet. But in the interests of keep all the Samba information in one place, here's a simple way of making sure Samba can recognize the printer names you think it should: Use the testprns program. Give this little tool the name of the printer you're trying to access, and the location of your Linux system's printcap file, and it'll tell you if Samba knows how to use the printer. (We'll talk about the printcap file in Chapter 10.)

```
millerm@romans /> testprns lj4500 /etc/printcap
```

In this example, I'm trying to determine whether the printer I think is called lj4500 can be accessed using the information in /etc/printcap. If it can be, I should see this message:

```
Printer name lj4500 is valid.
```

But if I've got the name wrong, I'll get another message:

```
Printer name lj4500 is not valid.
```

If that turns out to be the case, the reason I can't find the printer from the Windows client is that a printer of that name isn't known by the Linux system.

CONNECT TO NOVELL SYSTEMS

While connecting to Microsoft-based systems has taken up the majority of space in this chapter, I don't want to completely neglect Novell's NetWare. I'm far enough removed from my years toiling as a NetWare administrator that I feel pretty benign about the NOS, and it's also true that the company has been improving its product line since I've been away. You may have some NetWare systems that you'd like to access from your Linux stations. And if you have NetWare clients around, you may find that in certain circumstances it's easier to have your Linux system emulate a NetWare server than to go around changing each and every client. So in the interests of those in either situation, I'd like to talk about solutions to both problems.

Connecting as a Client

Connecting to a Novell server from a Linux client system is easy if you have the right tools. Perhaps loading the NFS namespace on your NetWare server volumes is the easiest way of doing this, but that's not an option for everyone. Thankfully, Red Hat provides the *ncpfs* package, which qualifies as the right tool for the job. If you included the IPX protocol when you built your kernel, and configured it using Linuxconf (as described in Chapter 7), you're sitting pretty.

Using ncpmount

If IPX is working properly on your system, you can use the **ncpmount** and **ncpumount** utilities to mount and unmount NetWare volumes from your Linux system. For example, if you wanted to access a NetWare server known as TITUS, you could use the following command:

```
root@romans ~> ncpmount -S TITUS -U supervisor /mnt/titus
```

This will prompt you for the supervisor password on TITUS; if you enter it correctly, you will be able to access the TITUS volumes from the mount point specified, /mnt/titus. For each volume on TITUS, there will be a separate subdirectory in the mount point.

There are many other options available when connecting to a NetWare server using ncpmount. Table 9-4 describes some of the more useful options, but you can check the man page for more detail.

By including the ability to do things like pass the password, ncpmount gives you the chance to completely script the connection between the Linux and NetWare system, though it naturally means you'll have to secure the script, especially if you plan to be using the NetWare Supervisor password.

Option	Description
-S servername	Name of NetWare server
-U username	Username for logging into NetWare server
-P password	Password for the NetWare user account
-V volume	Volume to mount (defaults to mounting all of them)
-b	Forces bindery-mode login on NDS servers
-u uid	User ID the mounted files are given
-g gid	Group ID the mounted files are given
-f mode	File permissions given on the mounted volumes
-d mode	Directory permissions given on the mounted volumes

Table 9-4. Common ncpmount Options

In addition to the **ncpmount** and **ncpumount** commands, there's the **nprint** command, which can be used to print jobs to a NetWare queue. Extensive NetWare bindery object manipulation tools are included with the ncpfs package, and there's even pserver, a program that allows you to feed NetWare print jobs to a Linux print queue. And all of this functionality costs you how much? What a beautiful thing free is, especially when free works well.

Using .nwclient

While the command line works just fine for infrequently made connections, and connection scripts are fine for scheduled connections, neither is very friendly to users who periodically want to connect to a NetWare server, but who don't want to be bothered (or can't be trusted) to use the command line.

For cases like these, ncpfs can use a user-specific file called .nwclient. This configuration "dot" file goes in a user's home directory and contains information about the connections they're likely to make.

The file may contain passwords, so it must be secured with file permissions set to 600. After you create the file, be sure to use the chmod utility to change the permissions to this level, which allows the owner (only!) read and write access to the file.

The file contains one or more lines containing a SERVER/USER combination, and optionally a password. Consider these contents of a .nwclient file:

```
TITUS/GARYSOTO
TIMOTHY/GARYSOTO redants
JUDE/GUEST -
```

The first line, which provides the default connection information, will attempt to connect to the server TITUS as user garysoto, and will prompt the user for a valid NetWare password. The first line could be invoked by a command like this one:

```
garysoto@james /> ncpmount /mnt/titus
```

The second line specifies a different server with the same username, and provides a password for that username. To connect to this server, the command might look like this:

```
garysoto@james /> ncpmount -S TIMOTHY /mnt/timothy
```

Finally, the last option uses the dash to indicate that no password is needed for the GUEST account on the JUDE server. Depending on your environment, a file like this could make life easier for your users or provide no advantage at all. You make the call.

Running as a Server

If explaining how to connect NetWare servers was on the periphery of this book's focus, it's pretty safe to say that NetWare server emulation is rather outside the boundaries. But this is a cool enough feature that it at least deserves a little mention. And because Martin Stover's NetWare-emulating mars_nwe package is included with Red Hat, you may be interested in trying it.

There are two easy steps required for setting up the mars_nwe package to emulate a NetWare server on your Linux box. First, you should configure the /etc/nwserv.conf file to meet your needs. And second, you need to start the service.

Configuring nwserv.conf

The /etc/nwserv.conf file exists by default if you have installed the mars_nwe package on a Red Hat server. It is extensively commented, so you should be able to follow the logic of the file layout. The following lines are an extremely abbreviated version that includes all the uncommented portion of the nwserv.conf file on the system I'm using:

```
# Define a read-only, all-lowercase SYS volume
1     SYS       /var/mars/nwe/sys     kr
# Define a read-only, all-lowercase, removable-media CDROM volume
1     CDROM     /mnt/cdrom2           kmr
# Define a HOME volume with all-lowercase filenames
1     HOME      /home                 k
# NetWare server name is ROMANS828
2     ROMANS828
# Autoconfigure internal network number and node
3     auto      1
# Auto-set net number and devices, set frame type and delivery ticks
4     0x0       *                     snap       1
# Don't save routes
```

```
5     0
# Claim to be NetWare 3.11 server
6     1
# Enforce universal password encryption
7     0
# Set the default UID and GID to 'nobody'
10    99
11    99
# Relate the SUPERVISOR user with a password and Linux account
12    SUPERVISOR                      nw-super    a8g3RT39A
# Relate login names between NetWare and Linux
13    WIINIKKA                        ian
# Don't use kludge to map Linux logins to NetWare logins
15    0
# Do simple sanity checks on startup
16    1
# Configure NetWare printing to Linux printer
21    LP              SYS:/PRINT/LP    lpr -Plp
# Set debugging information - kept recommended defaults
100   0
101   1
102   0
103   0
104   0
105   0
106   1
# Run nwserv as daemon, enable logging & append to logfile
200   1
201   /var/log/mars_nwe.log
202   0
# Take server down 15 seconds after down command is issued
210   5
# Issue broadcasts at 120-second intervals
211   120
# Log routing info every 5 broadcasts, rewrite logfile each time
300   1
301   /var/run/mars_nwe.routes
302   1
# No watchdogs
310   -1
# Define special station file ...
400   /etc/nwserv.stations
# ... but ignore it by getting nearest response to
```

```
# 'get nearest server request' *ever* given
401   0
```

Some of this configuration is arcane, but if you're familiar with NetWare server administration, none of it is particularly surprising. Once the configuration file is prepared, you're ready to start the server.

Running nwserv

To start the NetWare server emulator, simply run the /usr/sbin/nwserv program. If you set the program to run as a daemon on line 200 of the configuration file, this will run as a service and you won't have to think about it.

If you run the SLIST command from a NetWare-connected system, you should be able to see the Linux system advertising its services. You can even use **slist** from a Linux system running ncpfs; either way, you'll see your server listed something like this:

```
Known NetWare File Servers              Network      Node Address
-----------------------------------------------------------------
ROMANS828                               0A0002E      000000000001
```

Which means you're up and running!

To configure this service to run whenever the system restarts, use the same /usr/sbin/ntsysv tool I mentioned in the "Run Samba" section earlier in this chapter. The service you'll want to find and enable is mars_nwe.

CHAPTER 10

Step 7:
Enable Printing

In the last chapter, we discussed the process of integrating Linux into your Microsoft or Novell network. Part of properly integrating these networks is providing print services, and if your objective is to reduce or eliminate your need for those proprietary operating systems, you'll have to enable printing from your Linux systems.

And that brings us to Step 7 of the 12-step program: You must admit to yourself that Linux printing and print services are easy to configure. That simple step will allow you to provide all the print services you desire, will increase the efficiency of your network, and could very well bring about harmony among the nations. Email me if you need a more detailed explanation of the logic behind that conclusion.

In this chapter, then, we'll discuss how to configure printing on a Linux system, how to make that printing capability available from various client operating systems, and how to manage printers in a Linux environment.

CONFIGURE THE LPD DAEMON

The first step in our printer configuration process is to set up the line printer daemon (lpd). This is the program that runs in the background, listening for and spooling print jobs to the appropriate printers. As with other services we've looked at, there are ways of configuring lpd from GUI-based tools. However, I also want to explain some of the underlying changes that are made to the system when you use the GUI tools, so that you won't be insulated from what's really going on.

Running printtool

The Red Hat solution to the problem of printer configuration is a program called the printtool. This is a graphical tool that must be run by the superuser under X Windows. When you execute the **printtool** command, you will see a window similar to the one shown in Figure 10-1.

Printtool can help you configure four different types of printer connections under Linux. Printers that are directly connected to the Linux system (for example, via the parallel port) are configured as *local printers*. Printers connected to other Linux or Unix systems (including certain print server devices) are configured as *remote Unix printers*. You can also make use of printers that are connected to Windows and NetWare systems on your network, if they're ready for sharing.

Local Printers

Most of us connect local printers via the parallel port, and one nice feature of printtool is that it attempts to automatically locate printers connected to these ports. To add a new local printer, click the Add button from the main printtool screen. When you're prompted for a printer type, as shown in Figure 10-2, select Local Printer and click OK.

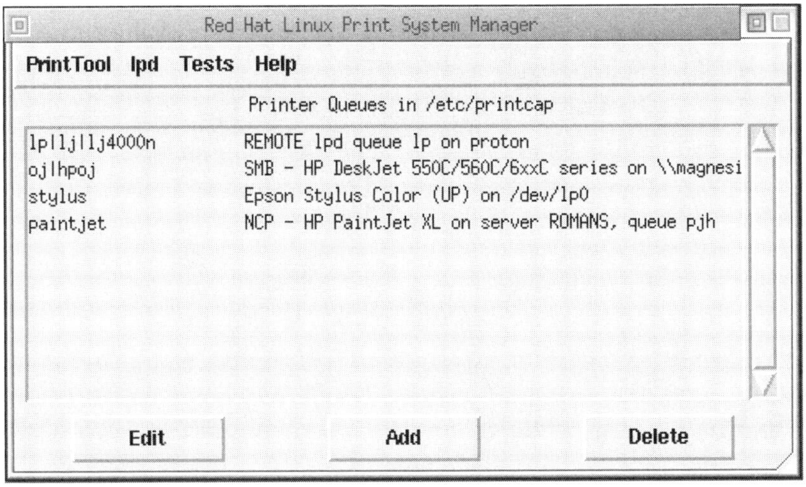

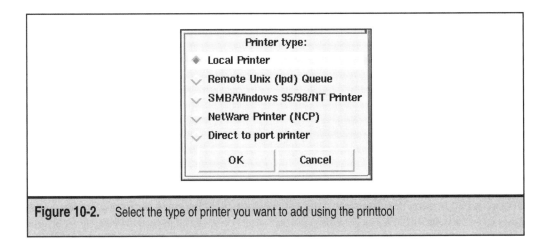

Figure 10-1.   Use printtool to configure printers under Linux

The printtool will tell you which printers it found on your system's parallel ports and allows you to edit several aspects of the printer's configuration. Figure 10-3 shows an example of the types of information you can specify to configure your particular printer.

Notice that the first field allows you to enter multiple names for the printer. Separate multiple printer names using the "pipe" symbol usually entered using the SHIFT key and

Figure 10-2.   Select the type of printer you want to add using the printtool

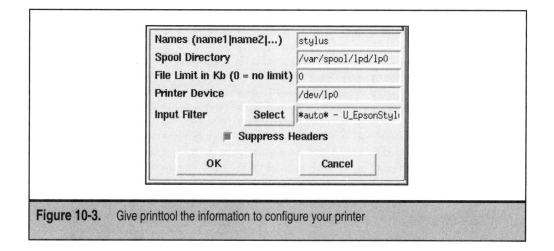

Figure 10-3.   Give printtool the information to configure your printer

the backslash key (SHIFT-\). The default printer on a Linux system is known as "lp," but the printer in Figure 10-3 has just one name, **stylus**. I'd suggest adding the pipe symbol and **lp0** as an additional name, based on the other entries in this example. I like naming printers something related to their manufacturer or to their function, but you can use whatever naming scheme you like.

The Spool Directory entry specifies where the print files are placed when a print job is being handled. The default location on Red Hat systems is in the /var/spool/lpd/ directory, with one directory for each printer. The printtool will create these directories as needed; you can change the default subdirectory name if you wish, and it will be fine.

The File Limit option gives you the opportunity to limit the size of jobs that can be handled. This is especially useful if you have a space problem on the partition that contains the /var/spool/ directory, as print jobs can be quite large. I've also seen obnoxious users literally attempt to make a system administrator's life difficult by pumping out a bunch of huge print jobs. Whether this happens intentionally or not, it's something to be aware of.

The Printer Device field should reflect the Linux device name of the printer that's connected. If you have a printer connected to the second parallel port, you'd want the entry in this field to be **/dev/lp1** instead of the **/dev/lp0** value shown in Figure 10-3. Remember that Unix starts numbering its devices at 0, while Windows starts device numbering at 1.

The Input Filter option allows you to specify a filter that tells your particular printer how to handle different types of files when you print them. If you click the Select button next to this field, you'll see a window like the one shown in Figure 10-4.

There are two main panels in the filter list shown in Figure 10-4. On the left-hand side is a list of printers and printer series, alphabetized mostly by manufacturer. The noteworthy exception to this alphabetization scheme is the Postscript Printer option. If you have a

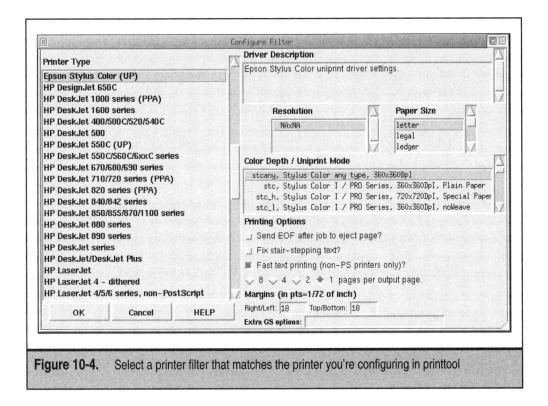

Figure 10-4.   Select a printer filter that matches the printer you're configuring in printtool

PostScript printer, that's the option for you. If you don't have one, scour the rest of the list for your printer.

If your printer isn't listed, you might look at your printer's manual or at the manufacturer's web site to determine whether the printer is compatible with a listed printer. LaserJet compatibility, in particular, is common these days. Once you've picked a printer type, click the OK button to return to the printer configuration screen.

The last option in this window is the Suppress Headers box. If you check this box, you won't get a header page that otherwise precedes each print job. On a local printer, those pages are usually quite unnecessary.

Remote Unix Printers

Configuring a remote Unix printer is very similar to configuring a local printer. Click the Add button and from the window shown in Figure 10-2, select the Remote Unix (lpd) Queue option. Configuration is nearly identical to the process used for the local printer, but instead of entering the local printer device, you enter a remote hostname and the printer queue name from that hostname.

The Remote Host field can contain an IP address or the name of a print server on your network; if you have a print server device that's addressable from Unix and Linux, like the HP JetDirect, you can specify the IP address for that device. The Remote Queue field is the name of the printer queue that has already been configured on that system. Consult your print server device manual for the name of the built-in queue name, if any.

Note that if you don't want to kill any more trees (or waste any more energy with unnecessary recycling) than necessary, you can also suppress headers on a network printer. I have been in environments where these header pages were very useful; the most common situation was when large numbers of people shared high-capacity printers. Once you've configured the settings on this screen, click OK to return to the main screen.

Windows/SMB Printers

There are several additional fields to fill out if you want to configure access from a Linux system to a Windows-based printer. As with the remote Unix printer, you can enter the print server's hostname in the Hostname Of Printer Server field. You may also add the IP Number Of Server if you desire. Enter the printer share name in the Printer Name field.

Access information for the printer is also entered from this screen. While it's best to access SMB printers that don't require a password, because the password is saved without encryption, it's possible to enter a username and password that have access to the share. Fill in the Workgroup field with the correct Windows workgroup name.

The rest of the information on this screen is the same as described in the "Local Printers" section. When you're satisfied with your entries, click the OK button to return to the main screen.

NetWare/NCP Printers

If you have a NetWare printer you'd like to access from a Linux system, you can configure it using printtool. While most of the information is identical to what I've described in the preceding sections, there are a few NCP-specific options. Please do note that the username and password are stored unencrypted on the Linux system, so don't use an account that has any useful access to anything but the printer.

The Printer Server Name in this case is the name of the NetWare server, and the Print Queue Name, not surprisingly, is the name of the NetWare print queue on that server. The User and Password fields specify the account required to gain access to that server and print queue.

Underlying Changes

Those configuration steps didn't seem very challenging, did they? That's because they weren't. The changes they make to your Linux system aren't very complicated, either. I still prefer making the changes from printtool if I'm setting up a new printer, simply because I'm less likely to make a configuration typo that way. But once I've got a system connected to the printer, it's easy to write a script to add the changes to other systems on the network. Sweet Linux eases the pain! The printtool changes two areas on your Linux system: The /etc/printcap file and the /var/spool/lpd/ directory.

/etc/printcap

This file contains the basic definitions for each printer you've defined on your Linux system. Most of the common information that printtool requests is found in this file, as this example shows:

```
##PRINTTOOL3## REMOTE POSTSCRIPT 600x600 letter {} PostScript Default {}
lp|lj|lj4000n:\
    :sd=/var/spool/lpd/lj:\
    :mx#0:\
    :sh:\
    :rm=prolific:\
    :rp=lj:\
    :if=/var/spool/lpd/lj/filter:
##PRINTTOOL3## LOCAL uniprint NAxNA letter {} U_EpsonStylusColor stcany {}
lp1|stylus:\
    :sd=/var/spool/lpd/lp0:\
    :mx#0:\
    :sh:\
    :lp=/dev/lp0:\
    :if=/var/spool/lpd/lp0/filter:
```

There are two printers defined in this example, and as the comment line preceding each one indicates, they were each created by printtool. The most common printcap arguments are shown in Table 10-1.

Notice that not all these entries are found in the previous examples; for instance, printtool only creates an accounting file entry (which gives you statistics on print queue

Argument	Description
sd	This printer's unique spool directory
mx	Maximum spool file size
sh	Suppress headers
rm	Remote machine name
rp	Remote printer/share name
if	Print filter
lp	Local printer device name
af	Accounting file

Table 10-1. Common Printer Configuration Arguments in /etc/printcap

usage) if it's pointing to a printer on an SMB or NCP server. If you're interested in more configuration options, they're exhaustively listed in the man page for printcap, **man 5 printcap**.

/var/spool/lpd/

The /var/spool/lpd directory is where most distributions place the lpd-related files. Indeed, this directory is referenced in two of the lines in the first /etc/printcap definition:

```
:sd=/var/spool/lpd/lj:\
:if=/var/spool/lpd/lj/filter:
```

The first line indicates that the printer's unique spoolfile directory is /var/spool/lpd/lj, and the second line sets the print filter (which is a script that determines what kind of file is being printed and how best to print it).

There should be a separate directory in /var/spool/lpd for each printer you set up. By default, printtool will suggest a name like /var/spool/lpd/lp0, which is fine. If you want to change the name to something else, you should use printtool to do so.

RUNNING PRINT JOBS

Now that you've configured your printers, it's time to get printing. While most Windows applications include a pretty transparent mechanism for printing (using the File | Print menu), the variety of interface designs on Linux applications, and the prevalence of text-mode tools, make it quite likely you'll just want to print a file from the command line or from a GUI file manager tool. No matter *how* you're accessing the print command, though, it's useful to know how to point to the right Linux printer from a Linux client, from a Windows client, or from a NetWare client.

From Linux

As with everything else in Linux, there are a few ways of printing. When you're printing from the command line, there are several utilities available for outputting files to your printer. When you're using X Windows, you can use those same command-line tools, or you can use the print functionality built into many applications.

Command-Line Printing

If you just want to output the contents of a file to a printer, you'll do just fine with the **lpr** command. The following command illustrates some of the most commonly used options for the **lpr** command:

```
millerm@romans ~> lpr -Plj4000n -#2 /etc/printcap
```

This command line prints the contents of the file /etc/printcap to the printer named lj4000n, making two copies. If you want to print to the primary printer (the first one listed in your /etc/printcap file), you don't have to specify the **-P** option, and if you want to print a single copy, you don't have to specify the **-#** option.

You can also set an environmental variable to indicate the default printer you wish to use. You'll have to check your shell's man pages to get the scoop, but for sh/bash shells, you can set this option from the command line like so:

```
[millerm@romans ~]# PRINTER=oj
[millerm@romans ~]# export PRINTER
```

Performing the same task in the csh/tcsh environment takes one statement:

```
millerm@romans ~> setenv PRINTER oj
```

You can check the current setting of your PRINTER environment variable using this command from either shell:

```
[millerm@romans ~]# echo $DISPLAY
```

The **mpage** utility is found on many systems; it allows you to specify the number of pages that are printed on a single piece of paper, giving you a little more control over your deforestation efforts. If you have a PostScript printer, **mpage** is quite convenient:

```
millerm@romans ~> mpage -4 -Poj /etc/smb.conf
```

This command will print four pages of text (reduced in size to fit and boxed for legibility) on a single sheet of paper. There are many additional options you can choose from; see the man page.

The **enscript** utility is another common tool for tweaking the output of a print job. You have even more control over how the output is displayed, and I've seen people go so far as to alias their favorite set of **enscript** options and use it as their default print command. Enscript can be invoked like this:

```
millerm@romans ~> enscript -2 -a2 -G -j -r /etc/smb.conf
```

These options, from left to right, tell enscript to print two columns per page, to print only the second page, to use a fancy (gaudy) header, to put borders around the columns, and to print the page in landscape mode. For large files, this can be a handy option, because the gaudy header gives you the date and time the file was modified, the filename, and the current page number.

X Windows Printing

Not every job requires you to issue a print command, though. For example, X Windows applications sometimes allow you to print from within their menu systems. One example is Netscape's Navigator, which is included with most distributions these days. When you select File | Print, you are shown a window like the one shown in Figure 10-5, which allows you to configure the underlying print command. In Figure 10-5, the print command is a simple **lpr**, and this works just fine.

Other tools have their own Windows-style printer interface, as exemplified by the K File Manager print menu, shown in Figure 10-6.

From Windows

Printing from Linux is fine if you're committed to a wholesale migration to open source platforms for workstations and servers alike, but chances are that you'll have Windows users left over, even if you migrate most of them. And of course, one reason Linux is a pleasure to use is its compatibility with other operating systems, including Microsoft's best efforts.

If you have configured the All Printers share in Samba (see Chapter 9 if that doesn't ring a bell), and you've configured the Samba server and the Windows clients to agree on whether or not to encrypt passwords, you can easily set up a Linux-connected printer share from Windows.

Add the Linux printer to your Windows system just as you would any other:

1. From the Start menu, select the Settings option.

2. Choose the Printers entry from the list of Settings.

3. Double-click the Add Printer icon, and click Next.

4. Select the Network Printer option and click Next.

5. Enter the server and printer name in the format

   *LINUXHOST**PRINTERNAME*

   If you don't recall the exact name, click the Browse button (or the Next button in Windows 2000) to browse the network for servers and printers.

6. Once you have selected the correct printer, click the Next button.

7. If the Windows system needs to load a driver for the printer you have specified, it will prompt you for the manufacturer name and model number of the printer. Click Next when you're done.

8. Indicate whether you want the printer to become your default printer, and click Next.

9. Some versions of Windows will ask if you'd like to print a test page; choose the option you want and click Finish.

You should now have an operational Windows printer definition that just happens to point to a Linux print server. It will appear in your Printers folder, just like any other printer. An example from a Windows 2000 workstation is shown in Figure 10-7.

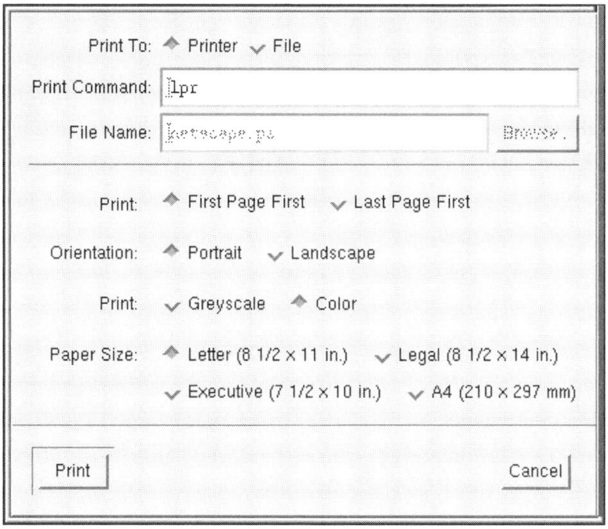

Print To: ◆ Printer ◇ File

Print Command: `lpr`

File Name: `netscape.ps` Browse.

Print: ◆ First Page First ◇ Last Page First

Orientation: ◆ Portrait ◇ Landscape

Print: ◇ Greyscale ◆ Color

Paper Size: ◆ Letter (8 1/2 × 11 in.) ◇ Legal (8 1/2 × 14 in.)
◇ Executive (7 1/2 × 10 in.) ◇ A4 (210 × 297 mm)

Print   Cancel

Figure 10-5.   Configure the print command used within Netscape Navigator

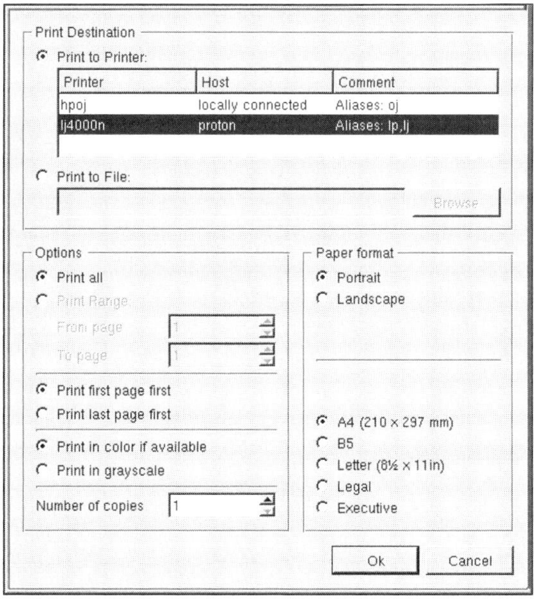

Print Destination

◉ Print to Printer:

Printer	Host	Comment
hpoj	locally connected	Aliases: oj
lj4000n	proton	Aliases: lp,lj

○ Print to File:

Browse

Options

◉ Print all
○ Print Range
  From page |1|
  To page |1|

◉ Print first page first
○ Print last page first

◉ Print in color if available
○ Print in grayscale

Number of copies |1|

Paper format

◉ Portrait
○ Landscape

◉ A4 (210 × 297 mm)
○ B5
○ Letter (8½ × 11in)
○ Legal
○ Executive

Ok   Cancel

Figure 10-6.   Use the familiar File | Print command in X Windows applications that support it

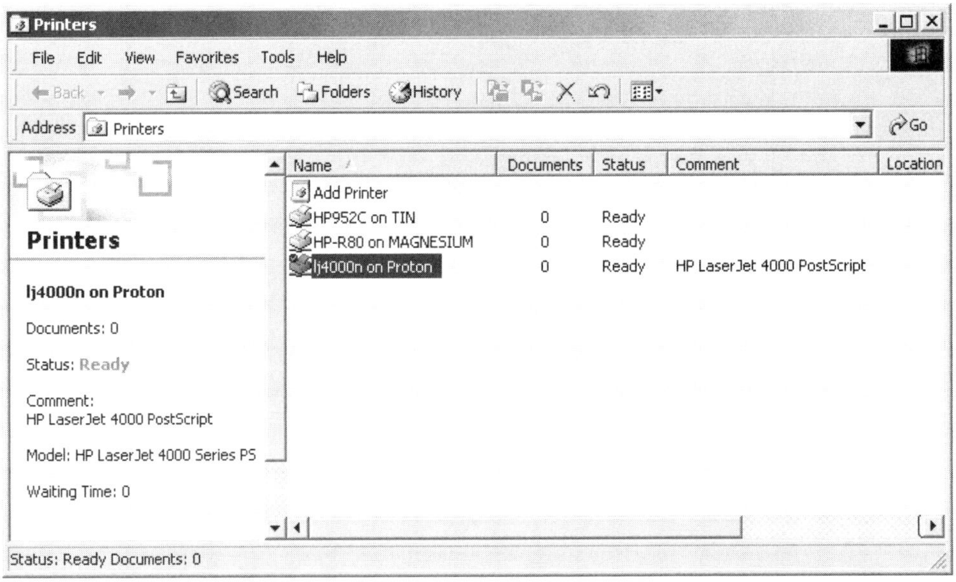

Figure 10-7. The Linux printer can be used by Microsoft systems on the network

From NetWare

If you still have Windows users connected to NetWare servers, and you set up your Linux server to act as a NetWare server, your clients should be able to point to the print queues as they would on any Novell NetWare server.

The pertinent area of the /etc/nwserv.conf file is 21, where you set up the queue name the NetWare emulation will advertise, the directory to which the print files are spooled, and the Linux print command used to print those files. These options should make a little more sense now than they did when you were reading Chapter 9 for the first time.

PRINTER MANAGEMENT

The obvious tool used for printer management is printtool. Printtool allows you to configure, edit, and delete print queues (which really makes up most of the print management you'll have to do...at least I hope so, for your sake). But it can also be used to start and stop the lpd daemon and to print test files to the print queues you've configured. There are other tools available for printer management, especially the classic Unix command-line utilities. I'll describe what's available to you in those programs, and then I'll give you some idea of what else is out there.

Standard Management Tools

The fundamental tasks that need to be performed for printer management include starting and stopping the print daemon (to implement configuration changes, for example), testing the queue, viewing the contents of the queue, removing some or all the jobs from a queue, and checking accounting information, if any. The following commands allow you to perform these tasks in Linux.

printtool

We've spent most of our time in this chapter working from the context of printer configuration done in printtool. Two functions I haven't talked about so far are printtool's lpd management and its testing capabilities.

Once you've made a change to a queue's configuration, you'll have to kill the current lpd daemon, which is running with the old configuration information, and restart it with the new configuration information. This can be done from the command line, but it's very easy to do using printtool. Simply go to the lpd menu within the printtool and select Restart lpd. That's all there is to it!

You can also test the queues on your Linux system from within printtool. Select one of the print queues from the main screen, and then go to the Tests menu and select either Print ASCII Test Page or Print Postscript Test Page. These options dump a text file or a Postscript file to the printer, so you can make sure your system can handle both types of data.

lpq

The **lpq** command allows you to examine the print spool associated with one of your print queues. If you wish to examine the printer that's currently defined as your default printer, you don't have to specify a name. On the other hand, if you want to specify a particular non-default queue, you can do so using the **-P** option, as shown in this example:

```
millerm@romans ~> lpq -l -Poj
```

This command will allow you to view the contents of the "oj" print queue. Notice that there's a **-l** option listed as well. This option tells **lpq** to provide a long version of the queue information. If you don't specify the **-l** option, **lpq** will give you a single line of information for each job queued on the system.

The **lpq** information includes things like who created the job, what its status is, its job ID. If there are no entries in the print queue, **lpq** will tell you that, too.

lprm

The **lprm** command removes a job from a print queue. If you've got a big job that's causing some problems, or if you realize you printed the wrong document, this command can be quite useful. The following example removes the last job spooled in the lj4000n print queue:

```
millerm@romans ~> lprm -Plj4000n
```

If the lj4000n printer were the default printer, it wouldn't be necessary to specify the -P option. If you have several jobs queued up, you can use **lpq** to identify the job ID for the print job you want to kill, and specify it on the command line to make sure that's the one that dies.

Sometimes it's useful to kill every job spooled in a queue, and that's possible as well. This is usually something the superuser will want to do, so in the example shown here, root has logged in and is killing every job in the default queue.

```
root@romans ~> lprm -
```

That hyphen is the option used to terminate print jobs with extreme prejudice. It's good when a process has gone haywire and is printing out a bunch of stuff it ought not. It's also good, by the way, if you want to irritate one of your system's pesky users. But you didn't hear that from me.

pac

This last option is more intriguing than obviously useful. It allows you to account for how many pages of printer paper (or feet of plotter paper) have been consumed by the users on the system. This information is only available if there's an accounting file **af** option specified in printcap for the printer you want to keep tabs on.

But if you enable that option, you can use a command like the following one if you find out that one of your employees is writing a book and is probably mowing through reams of paper printing drafts, feedback, and the like:

```
root@romans ~> /usr/sbin/pac -Plj4000n millerm
```

See the man page for **pac** if you're interested in learning more. The superuser has to run this job, so if you're wasting paper, do it as root. Whoops, did I say that out loud?

Other Sources of Information

There are plenty of other tools available for managing printers under Linux. I want to mention a couple that I've used and point you to a couple of potential sources for others.

Webmin is a full-featured, web-based, modular administration interface. It can help you add users and groups, or configure Samba or MySQL, or administer your printers. It's easy to install (and I'll show you how in Chapter 13) and use.

HP JetAdmin is available for many different platforms, and you may have used it on a Windows system. Whether you have or not, it's reasonably easy to configure, it doesn't appear to cause Address Resolution Protocol (ARP) storms anymore, and it works well if you use HP printers and print server devices. There's also a web-based interface available, but my mileage has varied with that product.

The web sites **http://freshmeat.net** and **http://sourceforge.net** are excellent resources for applications of all descriptions, and both have printer-related tools available. If you're looking for something you haven't seen from the other tools I've described, it might be worth your while to do a little browsing.

One last resource that I find quite useful is Grant Taylor's Linux printing web page, located at **http://www.picante.com/~gtaylor/pht/**. The Printing-HOWTO is quite good, and the database of Linux support for particular printer hardware is invaluable. If you've got a printer you're not sure about, check the database.

CHAPTER
11

Step 8:
Establish
a Web Server

If you have been using servers in a Windows NT or Windows 2000 environment, you may have had the opportunity to use Microsoft's Internet Information Services (IIS), which comes bundled with the operating system. With Linux, you have the opportunity to use the Apache web server, which hosted more than 60 percent of web sites, according to the September 2000 Netcraft survey (see **http://www.netcraft.com/survey** for the latest information). Apache is included with most Linux distributions, many of which automatically enable the server during installation!

Just as easy availability gave IIS a certain appeal on Windows servers, it makes Apache that much more appealing on Linux. It can also help you achieve Step 8 of our 12-step program: Establish a reliable web server. While you have other web server options available to run on Linux, we'll examine getting Apache running on Linux, plus ways of managing the service and your content.

RUNNING APACHE

Because most major Linux distributions include Apache, most people won't even need to install it. However, if you find yourself among the unfortunate few, you can leverage the tips in Chapter 13 to install a version of Apache from the Apache Software Foundation at **http://www.apache.org/**.

The issues we will tackle in this chapter include customizing your Apache installation to do what you want it to, starting, stopping, and restarting the web server daemon, and creating virtual sites on your web server.

Customizing the Web Server Using Linuxconf

Customizing an Apache web server can be accomplished a few different ways. There are some graphical management tools available (see **http://gui.apache.org/** for more information about these), and of course, you can always manually edit the underlying configuration files. Because we've been focused on using Linuxconf for system administration, though, it seems sensible to start by using it to customize our web server configuration.

While Linuxconf doesn't do everything, it certainly proves to be a useful tool to have hanging from your Linux administration belt. This proves true with Apache server management as well. As we go along, I'll point out where the options are being incorporated into the text-based configuration files so you have an idea of what's going on under the hood.

To get started, open Linuxconf from the command-line, from X Windows, or in a web browser. Traverse the Networking-Server Tasks-Apache Web Server tree, where you'll find the Apache configuration options.

Setting Web Server Defaults

To set the basic Web server information, select the Defaults option from the Apache Web Server tree. You should see a screen that is similar to the one shown in Figure 11-1.

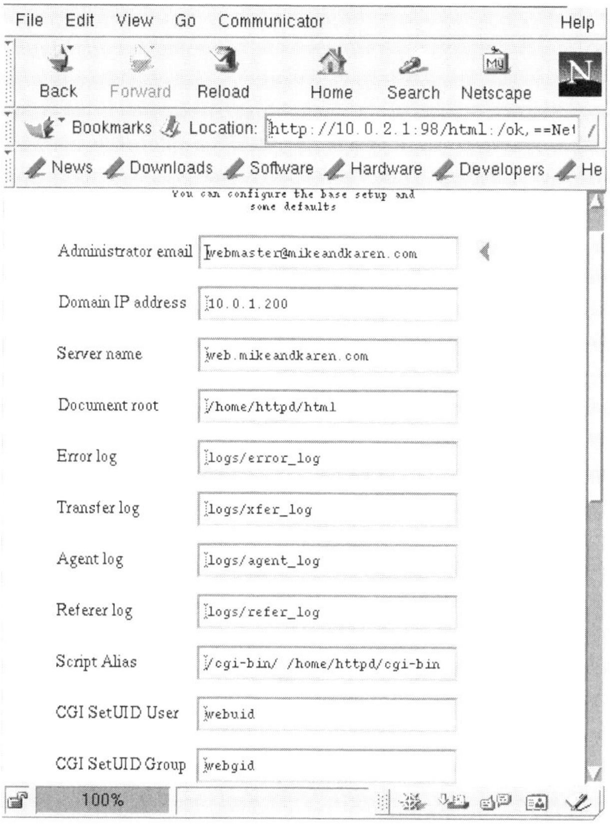

Figure 11-1.   Configure basic web server features from Linuxconf

Administrator Email   The first field allows you to set the web server administrator's email address, which is sometimes shown to web site users (when an error is encountered). While the customary approach for this field is to name that user webmaster within the server's domain (or primary domain), the configuration details are really up to you. Just be sure it's the address of someone who cares about errors users might receive, and that it corresponds to a real mail address or alias.

If you're interested in where this information goes, note that in Red Hat's installation of Apache, the address you enter here will be placed in the /etc/httpd/conf/httpd.conf file, on a line like this:

```
ServerAdmin webmaster@mikeandkaren.com
```

Other Linux distributions may put this configuration file in a different location; if it's not in that directory on your system, you'll have to check your documentation or do a search for the file to find it.

Domain IP Address   This field allows you to specify the IP address that multiple domains will be sharing on your web server. This should be an IP address, but you could also add a colon and a port number if you want to specify the hosts on a particular port. The address you enter here is added to /etc/httpd/conf/httpd.conf, as shown here:

```
NameVirtualHost 10.0.1.12
```

Server Name   While most systems won't require this entry, it's not a bad idea to set the server name to be the one you want. Depending on how your DNS records are set up, omitting this entry might make Apache select the wrong name for your server. While this is rare, you can avoid it by entering the fully qualified domain name of your server. This will be reflected in the /etc/httpd/conf/httpd.conf file in a line like this one:

```
ServerName www.mikeandkaren.com
```

Document Root   The document root is the directory you'd like to be the top-level location for documents provided by the server. Enter the full path from the server's root directory to the directory where the top-level files will be stored. This entry will be placed in the /etc/httpd/conf/httpd.conf file like this:

```
DocumentRoot /home/httpd/html
```

This is a typical address because it's how Red Hat and other distributions set up the Apache server. In this case, if a web client looked at www.mikeandkaren.com/index.shtml, they'd be pointed to /home/httpd/html/index.shtml on the Linux server.

Web Server Log Files   The Apache web server will gladly maintain several log files for you, allowing you to see what kind of errors, transfers, client browsers, and referring sites it notices. Each of these options may be specified separately, so you don't have to set any of them. The information can be useful, though, so I recommend setting them all, especially if you're snoopy like I am.

All these settings are assumed to be relative to the Apache server's ServerRoot (which is /etc/httpd in Red Hat and many other distributions), unless they begin with a slash, which indicates tat the entry is an absolute filename from the server's root directory (/).

The Error Log option allows you to specify the name of the log file for the server's error messages. The Transfer Log field specifies the location of the log file in which every access to the server is logged. The Agent Log is used to record the web browsers used by visitors to the web site. Finally, the delightfully spelled Referer Log stores the reference links that send visitors to your site from another one.

Using fairly normal configuration settings would result in the following lines being entered in the /etc/httpd/conf/httpd.conf file, with one exception. The AgentLog option below will quietly flush any information that comes its way into the Great Bit Bucket in the Sky, never to be seen again.

```
ErrorLog logs/error_log
TransferLog logs/access_log
AgentLog /dev/null
RefererLog logs/referrer_log
```

Script Alias   This entry is used to specify the relative and absolute paths to the directory where CGI scripts are stored. CGI scripts are programs used to provide dynamic content for the web sites. The two arguments to the ScriptAlias entry are the name of the CGI script directory relative to the web site's address and the name of the same directory in absolute terms (from the root directory of the Linux system).

```
ScriptAlias /cgi-bin/ /home/httdp/cgi-bin
```

CGI SetUID Options   These options set the user and group ID used when a CGI script is executed. While this defaults to the user "nobody," it's often preferable to create a new user and group expressly for the purpose of running scripts from the web server, which will make it easier to track—and lock down—access from the Web.

The CGI SetUID User sets the user ID, while the CGI SetUID Group sets the group ID. These are set to unique user and group names in the following example:

```
User webuid
Group webgid
```

Tuning   Why all these options are considered Tuning, I have no idea. The first option, Listen On Port, merely indicates the TCP port number on which the web server will await client requests. The default port, 80, is the right choice unless you've got a reason to make people use another port to reach your server. This doesn't seem like a tuning parameter, but here it is.

The Pid File entry also has nothing obvious to do with tuning, but is does specify the file in which the service writes its process ID number. This number is convenient for things like killing or restarting the server.

The Time Out field is used to specify the amount of time a client is given between the time it makes a connection to your server and the time it makes a request. If the client dawdles longer than the number of seconds specified in this field, they'll be disconnected, and taunted by castle-dwellers with outrageous accents. Well, they'll just be disconnected.

Finally, the Host Name Lookups option actually does give you some control over performance. If you enable this option, the server will attempt to resolve each client's hostname from its IP address. That sounds pretty cool, but what you sacrifice is response time, given the additional overhead that these DNS lookups can require and because the client doesn't get a response until the lookup has occurred. There are other ways of being a snoop, so you shouldn't have to enable this option.

Features These options can be enabled or disabled using the checkboxes next to them. All the options you enable will be placed on a line in the /etc/httpd/conf/httpd.conf file like this:

```
Options Includes ExecCGI Indexes
```

The seven options available in the Features section are described in Table 11-1, including the tag the option adds to the configuration file.

Configuring Subdirectories

Once you have set the server-wide options, you can customize the configuration of different subdirectories. Use the Sub-Directory Specs option from the Apache Web Server tree, and click on the Add button to set rules for a directory.

Option	Description	Tag
Server Side Includes	Enables processing of .shtml files and SSI tags	Includes
IncludesNOEXEC	Enable SSI without the #exec tag and prohibiting CGI execution from #include statements	IncludesNOEXEC
May Execute CGI	Enable CGI scripts	ExecCGI
Indexes	If there's no index.html or equivalent in a directory, serve clients a formatted index of the directory instead	Indexes
May Follow Symlinks	Allow client access via symbolic links	FollowSymlinks
Follow Symlink If Owner Matches	Only allow client access if the link and the target file have the same owner	SymLinksIfOwnerMatch
Multiviews	Client and server can negotiate displayed content language	Multiviews

Table 11-1. Descriptions of Linuxconf's Default Apache Options

Directory Path   This is just the path to the directory for which you want to override the default options. Specify this as an absolute address, starting with the root directory of the web server. For example, you might enter something like:

```
/home/httpd/html/hissingweasels
```

This addition will be made to the /etc/httpd/conf/httpd.conf file in the form of a Directory section. Each directory you add using the Sub-Directory Specs option will get its own special directory in the configuration file, and each will be denoted with tags like these:

```
<Directory /home/httpd/html/hissingweasels>
</Directory>
```

Between those two lines will be the options you specify on the rest of this configuration page, starting with the Features section.

Features   This list of features should be familiar; it's the same as the list shown previously in Table 11-1. If you want to allow or disallow a different set of features in particular subdirectories on the server, here's your opportunity. Each option you select in this section goes into an Options line between that directory's start and end tags.

Override Policies   This option tells the server which options can be overridden in the current directory based on the contents of a .htaccess file. These files are configuration ("dot") files nestled into the content tree of your web server. They allow you to set access to a directory without having to restart the web server.

If you plan to enable .htaccess files in the directory you're configuring, you can indicate the servicewide policies that the files can override. These options are listed on a single line in the appropriate directory sections. If you selected all the options Linuxconf provides, you'd create a line like this one:

```
AllowOverride AuthConfig FileInfo Indexes Limit Options
```

SSL Options   Secure Sockets Layer (SSL) configuration is a complex process, and while Linuxconf helps you enter some of the useful parameters, it does little to explain how or why to use them. If you know what you're doing, though, you can configure SSL for the current directory using the fields in this section.

The Cipher Suite field is where you enter the SSLCipherSuite string that specifies how the client connection is negotiated. The Require field populates the SSLRequire directive, which sets the rules for who gets access. The Options field sets the SSLOptions directive to enable various runtime options. The Verify Depth field fills the SSLVerifyDepth statement, which indicates how far removed the certificate can be without being invalidated. Set the SSL Require SSL box to enable the SSLRequireSSL flag. And finally, set the SSLVerifyClient level using the pull-down list next to the Verify Client field.

Don't worry if this set of options is a little mind-boggling. If you're not worried about running SSL, it's irrelevant. If you don't know how to run SSL, but want to, you should start by having a look at **http://www.modssl.org/**, where these options and others are described in as much detail as you could wish for. The changes you make in this Linuxconf section will be reflected in the /etc/httpd/conf/httpd.conf file like this:

```
SSLCipherSuite ALL:!ADH:RC4+RSA:+HIGH:+MEDIUM:+LOW:+SSLv2:+EXP
SSLVerifyClient 2
SSLOptions OptRenegotiate
SSLRequire %{REMOTE_ADDR} =~ m/^192\.76\.162\.[0-9]+$/
SSLRequireSSL
SSLVerifyDepth 2
```

Setting File Specifications

This set of options is identical to the set available for subdirectories. The only differences between the two are how you get there (the Files Specs option from the Apache Web Server tree), what it affects (specific files instead of specific directories), and the entries it makes in the /etc/httpd/conf/httpd.conf file (it creates a <Files> section). You can add as many specific files as you like, making each one's configuration unique if you wish.

Select Modules

This option allows you to enable additional modules in the /etc/httpd/conf/httpd.conf file. It's best to use this option if you know what you're doing, and quite frankly, if you know what you're doing, editing the file directly is an easier way to go. Many options are listed in the configuration file; you can comment out the ones you don't want to use, and uncomment or add the ones you want to use (assuming they've been compiled on your system):

```
# LoadModule speling_module      modules/mod_speling.so
LoadModule userdir_module        modules/mod_userdir.so
```

In this example, the delightfully named "speling_module" is inactive (it's commented out), but the "userdir_module" is enabled. The latter module, by the way, allows you to specify a root directory used when the client request contains a reference to a tilde-based ~username. This is considered basic functionality and is included by default. The spelling module isn't used as often because the overhead of looking for matches for misspelled or incorrectly capitalized requests can be large.

Manage Performance Features

Another fine set of options in the Apache Web Server tree allows you to set parameters for the web server processes that run on your Linux system. You can use these parameters to fine-tune your resource allocation, though for most systems, the defaults will be no problemo. To see those defaults, select the Performance option, which will bring up a configuration screen like the one shown in Figure 11-2.

There are three subsections in this window. The first allows you to set parameters related to the number of server processes. The second section relates to how long a connection is maintained. The extremely brief third section sets a different type of client timeout.

Number of Processes   The Start Servers field allows you to set the number of server processes the service starts with. In other words, when Apache is launched, how many web server processes are initially launched? Enter this number in this field, which is set to 10 by default.

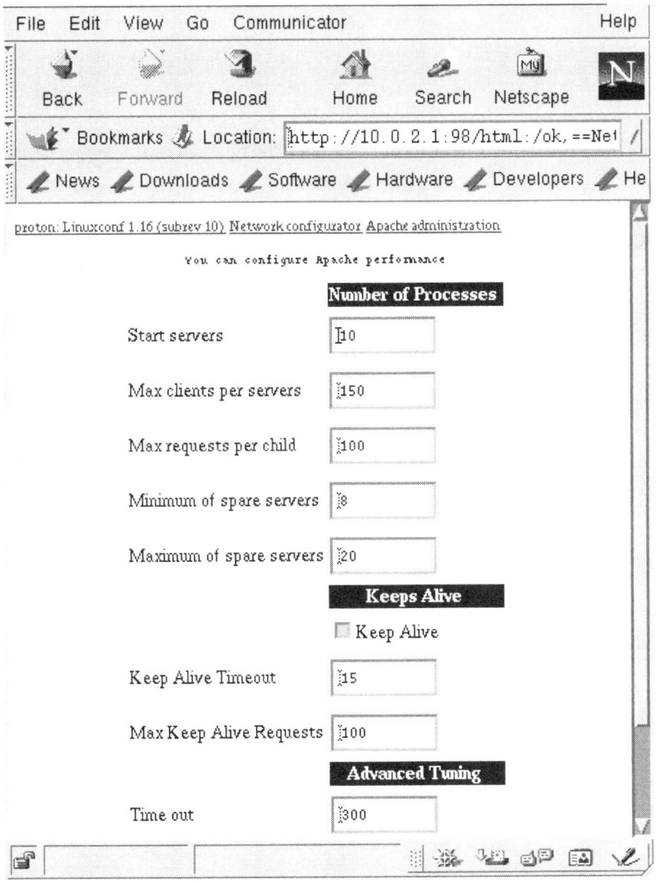

Figure 11-2.   Configure Apache server performance settings from Linuxconf

The second field, Max Clients Per Servers, allows you to set the maximum number of server processes for this web server. Because each user who connects to the web server uses a server process, this effectively sets the maximum number of simultaneous users.

The Max Requests Per Child field sets the lifespan of each server process, in terms of requests they handle. Like some type of insect, each process serves requests as needed, and when they've served 100 requests, they die. This isn't intended to be a biology lesson so much as a defense against memory leaks. By killing all processes after a certain amount of service, the server ensures that one leaky process can't sink the ship.

The Minimum Of Spare Servers is an awkwardly phrased field, but it's used to determine the minimum number of idling servers. If there are fewer server processes than the number set here, Apache will start additional processes until this parameter is satisfied. Think of these as analogous to the road crew workers who seem to just be standing there while others are working. The system is designed to include them so that it's ready for whatever happens.

You can't have a bunch of workers lollygaging around a job site, though, and likewise, you don't want a bunch of unused server processes sitting around. So the Maximum Of Spare Servers field allows you to designate the number of slugabeds it can stand. If the number of inactive server processes exceeds this value, Apache kills off processes until the number is accessible again. Just thinking about this made me work harder.

Keeps Alive   The Keep Alive option allows you to enable multiple user requests within a single connection. This is good because it prevents the user and server from having to re-establish a connection each and every time there's a new request.

If you enable the Keep Alive option, you can set two related parameters. The first is the Keep Alive Timeout, which is the number of seconds a connection is maintained before it is closed. If the client isn't making requests more frequently than this, the connection will be terminated. The Max Keep Alive Requests option sets the maximum number of requests in a single, persistent connection. Note that there's no sense making this number larger than the Max Requests Per Child set in the preceding section.

Advanced Tuning   Apparently there's not much need for advanced tuning, at least not the way Linuxconf has organized this module. The lone field, Time Out, allows you to set a maximum lag between the time a user establishes a connection and the time they make a request.

Setup Secure Socket Layer

The mod_ssl Configuration is the last option in the Apache Web Server tree. Configuring mod_ssl is beyond the scope of this book, but Ralf S. Engelschall's documentation on the subject, available on the Web at **http://www.modssl.org/docs/**, should give you all the information you need to know if you want to make use of this security module.

If you want to configure the SSL module, this is where you do it from Linuxconf. Some of the options mentioned earlier, in the "Configuring Subdirectories" section, are globally configurable here. Other options that are more relevant to the server-wide operations may also be set here.

Controlling the Server Daemon

Once you've finished configuring the Apache server, you should start or restart the server. Linuxconf will do this for you, but you may also do it yourself. You can use the following command to check the current status of the web server:

```
root@romans /> /etc/rc.d/init.d/httpd status
httpd (pid 31832 31831 31830 31829 31828 31827 31826 31825 31822) is running...
```

This response tells you whether Apache, the httpd daemon, is running, and if so, the process IDs for its processes. You can use the same command, substituting **restart** for **status** to kill the current processes and restart them with the new configuration information you've entered. You can also use the **start** and **stop** options to initiate and kill the processes separately.

If you want the web server to start automatically when the server boots up (or if you want to prevent it from doing so), you can use the /usr/sbin/ntsysv full-screen, text-mode utility described in Chapter 10. But I want to mention another way of accomplishing this task, this time from within Linuxconf.

Select the Control Service Activity option from the Control-Control Panel menu. You'll see a list of known services, and those that are currently running will say so. You can click on the name of a process—in this case, httpd—to open a control screen like the one shown in Figure 11-3.

As you can see in Figure 11-3, the Automatic Startup for this process has been enabled. That means the Apache service automatically starts on the server named Romans. There are buttons at the bottom of this screen that allow you to accept configuration changes you've made (in this case, the only option is to enable or disable the process at startup), or to start, stop, or restart the server. It's just another way of doing the same thing!

Setting Up Virtual Sites

Perhaps you noticed that I skipped over an option in the Apache Web Server menu in Linuxconf. The Virtual domains option is used to set up multiple domain names using a single Apache server. This can be useful for separating different projects, products, groups, functions, or people. It also allows you to do cool thinks like act as a web hosting service.

You can create virtual web sites using unique IP addresses, but I think it's easier to manage the virtual domains as aliases to a single IP address. Either way, you need to configure the DNS entries for the servers so users will be able to reach each virtual domain you create. In other words, just configuring Apache for virtual domains won't get most of your clients connected.

There are few differences between the basic Apache server configuration and the configuration of a virtual site. Instead of using the Defaults option again, of course, you select the Virtual Domains option. If you click the Add button, you can add a new virtual domain, or if there are existing virtual domains, you can click a name to view, edit, or delete that domain.

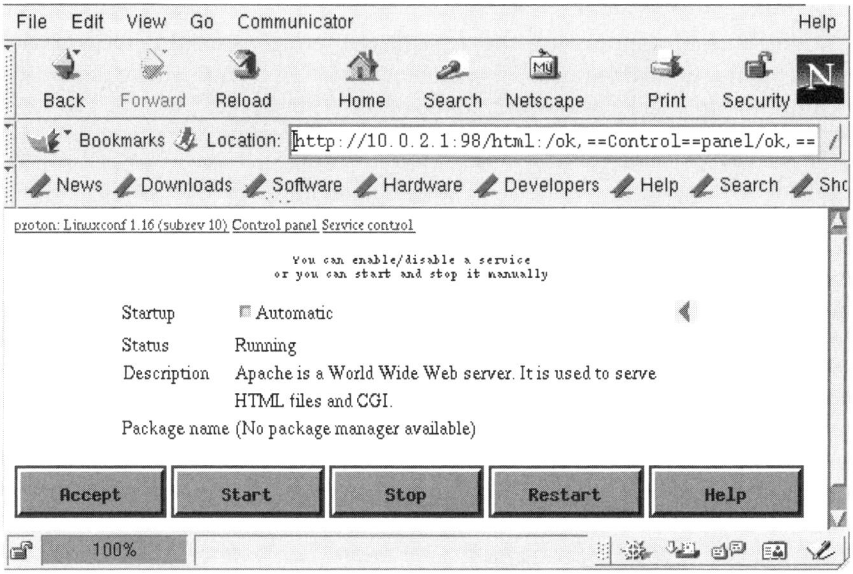

Figure 11-3.   Control individual processes from within Linuxconf

The virtual domain configuration screen is similar to the default configuration screen, with the addition of two extra fields. The Virtual Host Name is the name or IP address of this virtual host (duh!), which should be registered as a valid domain name in DNS or in all your users' host files or NIS domains. The other additional field is the Server Aliases field, which gives you the chance to enter aliases for your virtual domain, which should also be registered in DNS.

The other entries are identical to ones that you set for the main web server domain. You can also tweak the SSL settings for the virtual domain on this page. The changes you make will be added to a virtual server definition in the /etc/httpd/conf/httpd.conf file, which will contain entries like the ones shown here:

```
<VirtualHost 10.0.1.230>
ServerName www.foo.com
ServerAlias www.foo.net www.foo.org
</VirtualHost>
```

MANAGING CONTENT

There's not much to content management on a web server, regardless of the server software you're using. But I'd like to highlight a few of the basic tasks involved in maintaining a web site. From the placement of text and images, to enabling SSI and CGI features, to basic server status monitoring, it may be helpful to know the basics of how to manage the server you've set up.

Storing Text and Images

The most straightforward place to put text and images on an Apache server is in the document root you defined for the server or its virtual domains. You can create a directory structure to organize this content as you please, though I'm always surprised at how many people just dump everything into one directory.

But you're not limited to this linear directory tree. Don't forget, for example, that you can create logical links to other files or directories on the server or on a remotely mounted filesystem. This allows you to create links, for example, to user directories on a file server or from individual user workstations.

Consider the following contents of a document root directory:

```
drwxrwxr-x   8 root      web       4096 Mar 23 10:09 .
drwxrwxr-x  13 root      web       4096 Feb  9 16:03 ..
lrwxrwxrwx   1 millerm   users       17 Mar 13 08:50 .albers -> /home/albers/html
lrwxrwxrwx   1 millerm   users       14 Feb 27 14:35 .howto -> /usr/doc/HOWTO
lrwxrwxrwx   1 millerm   users       17 Feb 25 15:10 .jerryw -> /home/jerryw/HTML
lrwxrwxrwx   1 millerm   users       19 Feb 27 14:35 .mini -> /usr/doc/HOWTO/mini
drwxr-xr-x   2 root      root      4096 Jan 13 19:54 css
-rwxr--r--   1 millerm   users      973 Jan 22 10:47 customers.shtml
-rwxr--r--   1 millerm   users     4134 Mar 13 08:50 employees.shtml
-rwxr--r--   1 millerm   users      978 Jan 21 13:38 holidays.shtml
-rwxr--r--   1 millerm   users     2123 Feb 29 10:18 index.shtml
-rwxr--r--   1 millerm   users     6469 Mar 17 14:29 is.shtml
drwxr-xr-x   7 millerm   users     4096 Aug 16  1999 manual
drwxr-xr-x   3 root      root      4096 Feb 19 13:32 mrtg
drwxr-xr-x   3 millerm   users     4096 Feb  4 10:16 prolificinc.com
```

Notice that there are several "dot" files set up as links to other directories. These don't have to be dot files; I just think it's tidier to make them so. If the May Follow Symlinks option was enabled for this server or this directory in Linuxconf, those links allow quick and easy access to directories and systems outside the current tree. For example, the /home/albers/html directory could be NFS mounted from another system, but there's no need to include convoluted references in the HTML pages themselves; instead, they can refer to contents of the .albers directory, and the server will be able to get them there.

Enabling Server Side Includes

Another expedient option is to enable SSI, which gives you dynamic access to the files and programs on the host system. While this increases overhead because the server must parse each file for includes and execute them locally, it makes life pretty easy for those creating the web page content.

For example, using the "include file" directive, you can include a stock header and footer template to give your web pages the same look and feel. This ensures consistency; because you're not reusing the original code over and over, you're literally using the same code over and over. If you want to change the template, you only need to change one header file and one footer file.

Server Configuration

Enabling the SSI functionality on the server is straightforward:

1. Tell Apache to parse certain HTML files.
2. Designate the .shtml extension for parsing.
3. Enable parsing for the directory that will use it.

As you may have guessed, these things happen based on whether and where you enable the Server Side Includes option for the default configuration, specific files and directories, and virtual domains. Enabling SSI produces an option in the httpd.conf file, you may recall, called "Includes." But other underlying changes occur in a file I haven't mentioned yet, /etc/httpd/conf/srm.conf. This file contains some other features you might find interesting, such as the icons associated with different file types for directory listings.

For our purposes, though, the interesting part of the srm.conf file relates to telling Apache what types of files to handle. The two lines that should be included in the configuration file once you've enabled SSI are

```
AddType text/html .shtml
AddHandler server-parsed .shtml
```

The first line simply tells the web service that there's another type of html file and that it can be identified by .shtml extensions. The second line instructs the server to parse these .shtml documents for special strings that can be replaced by server-produced content. In both cases, you could manually tweak the system to use an extension that's not .shtml, but .shtml is the de facto standard.

Web Page Configuration

To include dynamic content in your web pages based on SSI, you need only use the .shtml extension for the page. This means the page will be parsed (so don't use this extension on pages that don't need server side includes, or you'll be wasting processing resources) for these includes. But what are they?

The include statement in a .shtml file is placed between comment brackets, as shown here:

```
<!--#config timefmt="%m/%d/%Y" -->
```

The **config** option allows you to configure how error messages, file sizes, and dates are displayed. This example sets the date's display format to print in the mm/dd/yyyy format. The following example actually prints the date in the format that has been specified:

```
<!--#echo var="DATE_LOCAL" -->
```

The **echo** command outputs the specified variable into the text of the HTML page, so it's useful for doing things like indicating the date a page was loaded. Even more useful is the **exec** command, which allows you to run a command on the server and dump its output into the HTML page. For example:

```
<!--#exec cmd="/bin/ls docs/*.pdf" -->
```

This option runs the **ls** command to give a listing of the PDF files in the docs directory. This information is placed into the HTML page where the include tag was invoked, so it might be useful to format output like that by using <PRE> and </PRE> tags around the include statement.

There is another version of the **exec** command that executes CGI scripts instead of standard system programs. Consider this example:

```
<!--#exec cgi="/cgi-bin/createaccount.cgi" -->
```

This option runs the createaccount.cgi script from the Apache server's cgi-bin directory. Note that neither of these options will work if the IncludesNOEXEC option was selected for this server or this directory.

You can output other useful information using SSI, including the size of a file:

```
<!--#fsize virtual="docs/prodocs.pdf" -->
```

The **fsize** option looks at a given file and returns its filesize; this is particularly useful if you want users to know how large a file is before they start downloading it. You can also include the last modification date of a file using a similar command:

```
<!--#flastmod file="index.shtml" -->
```

Notice that in the **fsize** statement, the argument is "virtual," while in the **flastmod** statement, the argument is "file." The reason is that in the **fsize** statement, the file is located in a different directory than the .shtml file with the **include** statement. If that's the case, either statement needs to use the "virtual" argument. In the **flastmod** example, the file is assumed to be in the same directory as the .shtml file.

To do the funky template voodoo I mentioned earlier, you need to use the **include** statement, which basically slurps in the contents of the file you specify into the .shtml file at the point you specify it:

```
<!--#include virtual="includes/head.txt" -->
```

In this example, there's a file (located in another directory—did you notice the "virtual" specification?) called head.txt. This file presumably includes the header information for the file that ensures its consistency with its brother and sister files.

There are several environmental variables that are populated automatically based on server and client information. You can print out the whole list at once using this command:

```
<!--#printenv -->
```

Simply working with the variables that are built in isn't enough fun, so you can set variables of your own using the **set** command:

```
<!--#set var="luser" value=$REMOTE_USER -->
```

Configuring CGI

We've already discussed how to enable a CGI directory using the Script Alias and May Execute CGI options from within Linuxconf. But I haven't actually explained the rationale for how to go about setting up your system for CGI scripting; I've only touched on the mechanism for doing so. There are three steps to enabling CGI with some modicum of security:

1. Point the Script Alias to the directory you will secure for CGI scripts.
2. Turn off CGI as a default option.
3. Configure the CGI directory to allow execution of scripts.

The first step is easily accomplished: simply set the Script Alias option for your server or virtual site to point to the directory you have in mind. This directory should be outside the server's document root so you can further limit access.

The second step is equally straightforward: just deselect the May Execute CGI option from the default or virtual server configuration page, and from any other directory you've defined.

The third step requires two substeps. The first is just to configure the CGI directory (the one you're pointing to in the Script Alias field). Use Linuxconf to do this, and be sure the May Execute CGI option is selected—preferably with no other options selected. Doing so will produce an entry in the /etc/httpd/conf/httpd.conf file that looks something like this:

```
<Directory /home/httpd/cgi-bin>
Options ExecCgi
</Directory>
```

This is fine, but the second substep is to make sure that you've enabled CGI scripts with the extensions you actually use. Check the /etc/httpd/conf/srm.conf file for the AddHandler line, and make sure it doesn't allow any more CGI extensions than you need. You can add an AddHandler line to your CGI directory definition in the httpd.conf file; it should contain only the extensions you plan to use. For example, if your CGI scripts all use .pl and .cgi extensions, you could simply add this line:

```
AddHandler cgi-script .cgi .pl
```

Monitoring Server Status

The last stop on our whirlwind tour of the Apache web server is some basic server monitoring. We've already talked about how to find out whether or not the httpd daemon is running. We can get a little more information from Apache's log files, and from the web-based server status information it provides.

Using Log Files

The four log files I mentioned earlier: the Error Log, Transfer Log, Agent Log, and Referrer Log, are a treasure trove of information for administrators who want to know who is accessing the system, what they're accessing, where they're coming from, and what problems they encounter.

While there are tools that put a pretty face on the log file (see, for example, **http://www.analog.cx/**), the raw material is not that difficult to read. Deciding what is important to notice may be another issue. The bottom line is that it's a good idea to define all four types of log files that Linuxconf knows about and to review them periodically as you see fit.

The Error Log is the most important file to review, because it may tell you about misconfigurations in httpd, or it may indicate that users are having some kind of a problem you haven't heard about directly. By default, this file is found at /etc/httpd/logs/ error_log.

In the example shown here, there don't appear to be any server configuration problems, but Apache warns us that the /usr/sbin/suexec tool will be used to execute programs from the web server. There are two errors flagged, though, indicating that somebody was looking for a file that doesn't exist.

```
[Sun Oct 22 04:02:04 2000] [notice] Apache/1.3.9 (Unix)  (Red Hat/Linux)
configured -- resuming normal operations
[Sun Oct 22 04:02:04 2000] [notice] suEXEC mechanism enabled
(wrapper: /usr/sbin/suexec)
[Thu Oct 26 10:40:15 2000] [error] [client 10.0.2.228] File does not
exist: /home/httpd/html/mrtg/mrtg-l.gif
[Thu Oct 26 10:40:46 2000] [error] [client 10.0.2.228] File does not
exist: /home/httpd/html/mrtg/mrtg-l.gif
```

Notice that both the client's IP address and the address they failed to look up are indicated, so you know not only who had a problem, but what the problem was. Not only that, but the help file flags this line with an [error] tag to help you distinguish it from the other messages.

Web-Based Server Status

If you're looking for more quick-and-dirty information of the "Is the server up and what's it working on?" variety, there's one more option I'd like to mention before we move on to configuring email. That option is a SetHander directive, and it looks like this:

```
<Location /server-status>
SetHandler server-status
order deny, allow
deny from all
allow from .prolificinc.com
</Location>
```

Add that option, restart the httpd daemon, and then point a browser to webserveraddress/server-status. You should see a screen like the one in Figure 11-4.

While this isn't the most glamorous display you're ever going to find, it's pretty useful for the mundane things you actually need to know. For example, you can see useful tidbits like the server version and uptime, the process IDs and what each process is doing, as well as a "scoreboard" showing the possible server processes (the rows of dots), which reveal what the system is doing. And that's quite enough for the moment.

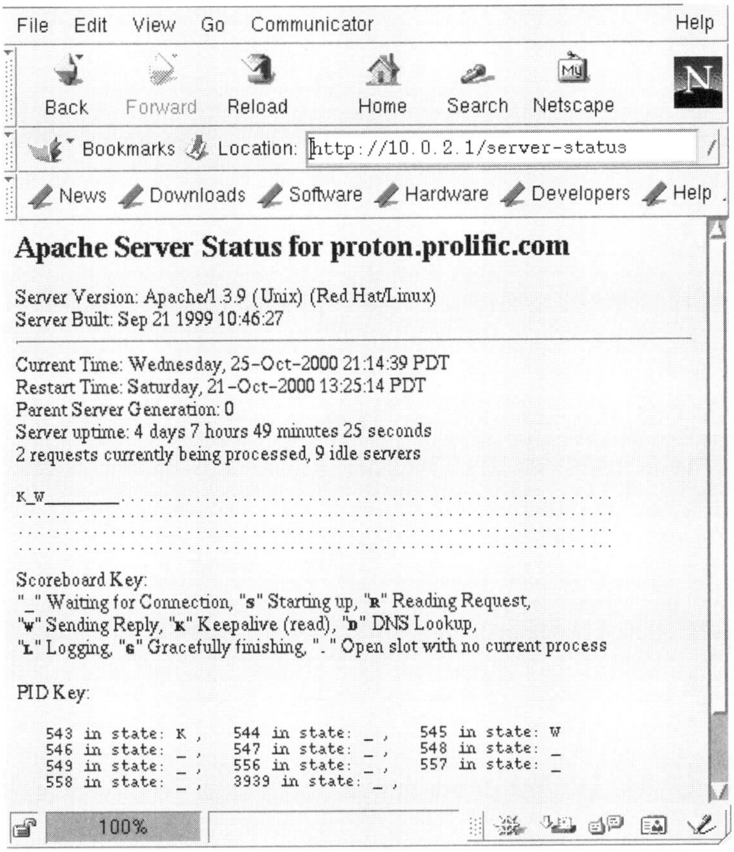

File   Edit   View   Go   Communicator   Help

Back   Forward   Reload   Home   Search   Netscape   N

Bookmarks Location: http://10.0.2.1/server-status

News Downloads Software Hardware Developers Help

Apache Server Status for proton.prolific.com

Server Version: Apache/1.3.9 (Unix) (Red Hat/Linux)
Server Built: Sep 21 1999 10:46:27

Current Time: Wednesday, 25-Oct-2000 21:14:39 PDT
Restart Time: Saturday, 21-Oct-2000 13:25:14 PDT
Parent Server Generation: 0
Server uptime: 4 days 7 hours 49 minutes 25 seconds
2 requests currently being processed, 9 idle servers

```
K_W_____...........................................
.......................................................
.......................................................
.......................................................
```

Scoreboard Key:
"_" Waiting for Connection, "s" Starting up, "r" Reading Request,
"w" Sending Reply, "k" Keepalive (read), "b" DNS Lookup,
"L" Logging, "G" Gracefully finishing, "." Open slot with no current process

PID Key:

```
543 in state: K ,    544 in state: _ ,    545 in state: W
546 in state: _ ,    547 in state: _ ,    548 in state: _
549 in state: _ ,    556 in state: _ ,    557 in state: _
558 in state: _ ,    3939 in state: _ ,
```

100%

Figure 11-4.   Enable the SetHandler server-status directive to enable web-based status monitoring

CHAPTER 12

Step 9: Manipulate Email

In the previous chapter, we did some Web server configuration and management. Now, those are pretty fun tasks. But when you set up a Web site, what happens? That's right, you need a place to put the spam that starts arriving. So in this chapter, we'll begin Step 9: Contact others via email.

The subject of email on Linux is an immense one; for example, the massive O'Reilly tome, *Sendmail, Second Edition*, exceeds 1000 pages. But I also want to mention some other tools people use for managing their mail, as well as end-user tools for reading and editing mail. So break out your jogging shoes, and let's get rolling!

CONFIGURING SENDMAIL

Sendmail handles the majority of the world's electronic mail. In its fullness, it is a vast, complicated system. But if you're looking for basic mail handling functionality, it's not difficult to get things set up properly. And Linuxconf makes configuring your mail domains and users a straightforward, GUI-based process. Of course, if you're looking for more information, that's available as well, including a fine document on configuring sendmail on Red Hat: **http://www.redhat.com/support/docs/howto/RH-sendmail-HOWTO/book1.html**.

Mail Domain Configuration

To begin configuring your mail system, start Linuxconf and navigate to the Mail Delivery System (Sendmail) option from the Config-Networking-Server Tasks tree. This brings up a menu of sendmail options, including these configuration items:

▼ Basic information

■ Special (domain) routing

■ Masquerading rules

■ Mail to fax gateway

▲ Virtual email domain

I'll not include options that you can safely ignore. Check out Bryan Costales' *Sendmail, Second Edition* if you're looking for more information about sendmail configuration than you find here.

Basic Information

Configure basic mail system settings from the Basic Information option, which includes basic mail connection information, messaging and DNS features, miscellaneous settings, and domain aliases.

Present Your System As   Ordinarily, mail coming from a user on a system will be addressed as user@machine.domain; for example, you might get mail from mjm@romans.msaddicts.com. But most of us prefer that the mail appears to be coming from the domain, without a machine specified. So in this field, enter the domain name as you want it to appear on outgoing messages.

Accept Email For   Enabling this option allows your sendmail server to accept mail that's addressed to its machine name and also mail addressed to its domain name. So whether you sent mail to mjm@romans.msaddicts.com or to mjm@msaddicts.com, if romans is accepting mail for the domain, it'll receive (and hopefully deliver) both.

Mail Server/Gateway   Enter the name of the server that will store the mail for your organization in the Mail Server field, and the name of the server responsible for forwarding mail to the rest of the network or the rest of the world. These may be the same system (they may even be the system you're configuring).

Mail Gateway Protocol   You'll have to decide which protocol is used to connect the system you're configuring with your network's mail gateway. The default is SMTP, which is pretty common (and makes a fine default), but if you know you have an unusual mail connection, one of the other choices may be more appropriate for your situation:

- ▼   esmtp Enhanced SMTP
- ■   esmtprem Expensive ESMTP (on demand links)
- ■   uucp-dom Recommended modern UUCP
- ▲   uucp Old UUCP

Enable Relay Control (Spammers)   This option enables a set of rules intended to prevent spam mailers from using the sendmail software to forward their mail from your system. You want to do what you can to avoid letting your mail servers become "open relays" for undesirable uses. Not only can the load bog down your server, it involves you in the despicable practice of wasting peoples' time and money with unsolicited commercial email they don't want.

Messages Size Limit   If you don't want your users to be swapping QuickTime videos with their friends and family, you can set a limit on the size of messages that go through the sendmail system. Of course, not being able to receive large useless files also implies not being able to receive large useful files as well, but you might want to set a limit anyway.

Process Queue Every   How often do you want the mail system to run through the mail queue? I like the default value of 1 minute, which gives snappy service from a dedicated mail server. If you're trying to use the system for other things, though, or are using an on-demand connection, you might want to space things out a little more.

Use Special Shell smrsh   The sendmail restricted shell (smrsh) is an alternate shell the mail system can use to reduce the risk of attacks during mail delivery. It restricts the commands that may be executed and how many commands can be executed during delivery.

Maximum Recipients Per msg   My first job out of college involved use of some Wang mini-computers that would crash fairly predictably if anyone sent a message addressed to the whole company. This was pretty useful information for some users, it seemed, because we had a few outages on some pretty fine spring days one year.

Sendmail can handle large numbers of mail messages, but you may want to prevent your users or spammers from sending to tremendously long lists of addressees at once. This might be useful in particular for ISPs, whose user lists are often accessible from the system and can be used to create provider-wide mailing lists.

DNS Features   The DNS options allow you to designate that a message needs to come from a source DNS can identify as valid, or that DNS should not be used at all. This latter option would mostly be useful for systems connected via UUCP, where DNS servers may not be available. Requiring DNS is considered by some a certain degree of protection against spamming, since spammers often use nonexistent domain names. However, you'll still get plenty of spam from forged return addresses from valid domains, so don't get too excited.

Deliver Locally to Users   If there are users on the system who have mailboxes on the sendmail server you're configuring, you can add their usernames to this field to have any mail sendmail receives delivered to those users locally.

No Masquerade from Users   Remember from the first field that we usually want our organization's email to be presented as coming from the domain, rather than from a particular system within the domain. Unfortunately, for default user accounts, such as root, making use of this Present Your System As setting can obscure vital information. If a root sends a message from a system in your domain, you'll want to know on which machine that root lives. If there are other accounts that need to be distinguished from each other, add their names here.

Trusted Users   Certain accounts need to be able to send mail using a different user ID than the one that's in the From line of an outgoing message. The three normal examples are the default accounts: root, which should be able to do what it wants; daemon, which is the account sendmail typically uses; and uucp, which needs to be trusted for UUCP messaging to work.

Special Routing db   This option should only be enabled if you need to enable special routing between domains, which we'll address shortly in the "Domain Routing" section. If you do enable it, you'll have to select the database format you'll use from the drop-down list.

Local Delivery Agent   You can leave this option set to Let Linuxconf Probe, which will allow the Linuxconf tool to determine the program used to deliver local mail on the system. Local mail is mail destined for a user on the same system.

Support Bogus Mail Clients   Enabling this option tells sendmail to bestow a little grace upon messages that come from mail sources that don't generate correct SMTP HELO commands, which are the introductory messages sent by a delivering system to a receiving system. In my opinion, you shouldn't have to enable this option. But I'm cold and callous, especially when it comes to SMTP.

Domain Aliases   If you want your email address to be valid across multiple domains, you can enter as many machine names (each with a domain name you wish to use) in the Aliases For Your System fields. Click the Add button to add additional fields in the unlikely event that three isn't enough.

Domain Routing

Special routing is only needed if you have some reason to use a non-default routing path. In other words, if you plan to use some type of alternate way of getting mail to a particular host, you should add a "special (domain) routing" record. Do that by selecting this option from the Config-Networking-Server Tasks-Mail Delivery System (sendmail) menu.

For each remote destination you want to designate, you should enter:

▼ The destination hostname

■ The hostname of the alternate mail system that will be used to deliver messages to that destination

▲ The mail gateway protocol used to deliver messages to that mail system

There's also a checkbox available here that allows you to use this entry as a template for *any* host in the same domain or one of its subdomains. You may override this template on a host-by-host basis by specifying special routing for particular additional hosts.

Masquerading Rules

In the context we're currently discussing, masquerading is rewriting a message's "from" information when it's being forwarded. This can be useful for fixing messages coming from systems that don't properly create the "from" address, or for making all outgoing messages appear to come from the same corporate domain, even if they originate from an internal domain.

To create a masquerade rule, enter the following information:

▼ The original from address that will always be rewritten (this can be a user address or just the @domain portion if the rule should apply to all users in that domain)

■ The new from address that the messages will receive (this can also be a user address or just the @domain portion if the rule should apply to all users in that domain)

▲ A comment explaining what you've done and why, so your successor understands what you were doing. Don't you think you'll get a promotion for the increased uptime and reduced expense your migration to Linux will provide?

Mail to Fax Gateway

Does the option of sending faxes via email appeal to you? Linuxconf can do some configuration of sendmail to this end. You may set up allowable calling zones, authorize certain email addresses to send fax messages, encrypted or otherwise, to numbers in those zones, and log these faxes.

There's a basic fax spooling script in the /var/lib/linuxconf/lib/ directory, and it can feed messages to a program called faxspool. This in turn prepares the messages to be delivered using the sendfax program. Check out the man pages for more information on these scripts. Other fax programs are available, and some of them may be more friendly than these programs.

Virtual Email Domain

If you want to add virtual domains to the email domains handled by the sendmail server, this option allows you to configure them. The help text is quite helpful for details on how to set up the DNS servers to support the virtual domains, but the sendmail server configuration is straightforward.

Each virtual domain is handled separately from the primary domain sendmail is servicing on the system. For each virtual server, you can specify the following information:

▼ The fully qualified virtual domain name (required)

■ A fallback destination for messages that don't match an alias or known user

■ If you leave this field blank, unmatched messages will be bounced. If you specify a domain (@domainname), the message will be sent to the same username at the specified domain. If you specify a specific user and domain (user@domain), the mismatched message will be sent to that user. If you specify a username by itself, the message will be forwarded to that user in the same domain name.

■ A starting user ID number for users in this virtual domain

■ A limit on each user's inbox size. Default is no limit (0).

■ Additional alias filenames (the first is /etc/vmail/aliases.domainname)

▲ Additional domains that should be virtualized to this same definition

Mail User Configuration

Getting the server ready to handle incoming and outgoing messages wasn't too tough, was it? The next step is to configure the system for your users. If mail is going to be delivered to local user accounts, you don't really have any user setup to perform. On the other hand, if you want to set up rules for how mail addressed to particular users is handled, you'll want to consider complex routing and aliases for your sendmail users.

User Routing

I skipped over Linuxconf's Complex (User) Routing option in the previous section, because it is used for configuring mail for particular users. In this case, the problem it's solving is this: What if you want to transfer mail from one server to another based on the destination user name *and* domain name?

For example, if you are hosting email for multiple domains on one sendmail machine, but want to have mail addressed to certain specific users delivered to different machines (bugs@somesoftwarecompany.com and bugs@crazyaboutentomology.com), you can do that from this option.

For each user, you'll need to specify

▼ The original recipient email address.

■ The new destination address for the recipient

■ Optionally, the fully qualified hostname of the destination server

■ The mail gateway protocol used to deliver the message to the new destination address

▲ A brief comment explaining what you're doing and why

User Aliases

The user routing option is needed when the user and domain name to which you want to forward a message are different from the original message's designated recipient. But if you just want to send the message to one or more users in the same domain, you can use the User Aliases option. To add these aliases, you need to fill in the following fields:

▼ The name of the alias.

■ The name of a program, script, or statement to pipe the mail through, if desired. This could be used to send the mail to a log file or to the bit bucket.

■ A file that contains a list of the users included in this alias, if desired. This is useful if you want to be able to (or want somebody else to be able to) edit the alias list from a text file.

▲ The names of users who should receive mail sent to the alias, if desired.

Virtual Domain Aliases

This option is identical to the preceding User Aliases option, but instead of being used in the primary sendmail domain, these aliases are established for the virtual domains you have created on your system. See the list of options above to see which fields to fill out.

MANAGING SENDMAIL

Although we're moving extremely rapidly through the process of setting up sendmail on a Linux mail server, since we've talked about it at all, it seems sensible to include a little information on how to maintain it. Two management issues we haven't discussed much previously are monitoring the mail queue and preventing spam.

Keeping Tabs on the Queue

You can view the contents of the sendmail queue from within Linuxconf. Go to the Config-Networking-Server Tasks-Mail Delivery System (Sendmail) tree and select the Manage The Mail Queue option, which will bring up a display like the one in Figure 12-1.

There aren't any messages queued up in Figure 12-1, and hopefully you won't have mail backed up on your system, either. But if you do get some messages queued up, and you wish to delete some, you can easily accomplish this by clicking on the message ID to open the message. Click the DEL key to delete the selected message.

Anti-Spam Measures

If you've got an email address, you're getting spam. And if you're running a mail server, you're probably getting quite a lot of spam. I've talked to administrators who say ten per-

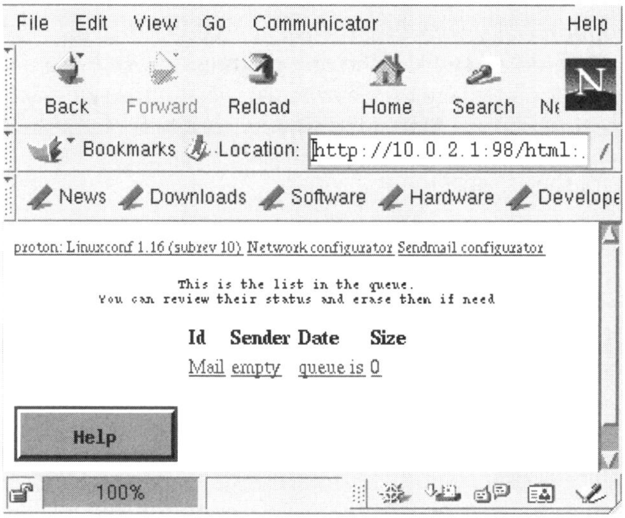

Figure 12-1. View contents of the sendmail message queue from Linuxconf

cent of their incoming mail is unsolicited commercial email, most of it with forged return addresses.

While there's not much that can be done to turn that flood into a trickle, there are some anti-spam features built into sendmail, and the Linuxconf allows you to configure these fairly easily. Thus, you can not only bounce mail from known offenders or suspect addresses or networks; you can also tell sendmail the specific domains and hosts for which it should be forwarding messages.

Rejected Senders

Use this option to filter out any messages from a particular email address, network address, or hostname, or any address in a domain. Enter into the Email Origin field the origin address you want to filter.

You may also add an error message to be sent when the message is bounced. Make it as pleasant or obnoxious as you desire. If you think the message will actually reach the recipient (most spammers forge addresses to avoid having to deal with this type of thing), you might consider some variation on this theme: "Thank you for your inquiry about our email editing services. Future messages we receive from you will be edited at a flat rate of $500 per message. For variations on this theme, and others, see Axel Boldt's Blacklist at **http://math-www.uni-paderborn.de/~axel/BL/blacklist.html#harsh**. While you're there, trace links back to his homepage and read his interesting, though unrelated, comparison of Germany and the U.S.A.

Relay For/To

The Relay For options restrict who can use this sendmail system as a mail relay. To specify a host or network numerically, select the 'Relay For' By IP option and enter the IP address (you can specify part of a complete address to permit use by the whole network, e.g., 10.0.1.). To specify the host or domain by name, select the 'Relay For' By Name option and enter the hostname or domain name.

The Relay To Hosts option limits the hosts and networks to which you will allow your system to transfer mail. If you normally use a single mail connection to an ISP or another corporate location, this could be the only entry you create.

ALTERNATIVES TO SENDMAIL

Don't get me wrong: sendmail will do the job. There are plenty of people out there who are experienced with it, and you shouldn't have any trouble getting outside help if you need it. The Mail-Administrator-HOWTO is one resource that discusses configuration of sendmail and other Mail Transport Agent (MTA) services. The Mail-HOWTO has some similar content. But neither document has much to say to hype up use of sendmail. So what other options are out there?

qmail

The qmail package is preferred to sendmail by many administrators, who feel that its ease of configuration and security make it clearly superior to sendmail. I don't feel at all strongly about qmail's superiority in those areas, and I'm inclined to think that you're best off using the package that came preinstalled with your distribution. However, you should investigate qmail if you expect to be managing mail and think sendmail's myriad options won't be worth the trouble, given that many of those options aren't accessible through Linuxconf. The primary qmail web site is at **http://cr.yp.to/qmail.html**.

exim

While qmail's primary strength is considered its security, exim is supposed to be easier to configure than either sendmail or qmail. Remembering that the mail system that's already installed on your system gives you an advantage, you still might want to investigate exim if you're considering doing more hands-on configuration of your mail system. Its primary web site is **http://www.exim.org/**.

Postfix

Postfix aims to be a competitor to qmail and is said to be faster than both qmail and sendmail (though unless you're handling large volumes of mail, performance shouldn't be a major issue). Consult the Postfix web site at **http://www.postfix.org/** for more information.

smail

This program is pretty much the granddaddy of sendmail's rivals. While it's easier to configure, it also offers fewer options and less scalability. Time appears to have passed smail by, so if you're interested, exim might be a reasonable substitute. There isn't a central smail web site, but there is an ftp site at **ftp://ftp.planix.com/pub/Smail**.

OpenMail

One of these tools is not like the others, and it's Hewlett-Packard's OpenMail. This package allows you to support PC client packages such as Microsoft Exchange and Lotus cc:Mail, running all the while on a Linux platform. HP offers a free trial period for this tool, but it's still commercial software. Read more about it at its main page: **http://www.ice.hp.com/cyc/om/00/index.html**.

USER MAIL AGENTS

It's all fine and good to have a mail server on your Linux box. But how do you read mail on a Linux system? There are many tools available, but three of the most commonly used Mail User Agents (MUAs) are elm, mutt, and pine.

elm

In my opinion, elm is a little bit like the vi text editor: They're both old and ubiquitous. Elm's interface is trim and straightforward, but if you want to do anything funky, you won't have any idea how to do it. All the same, for basic access to the Linux mail system, it's easy enough to use. Check out the web site at **http://www.myxa.com/elm.html**, and try running the program from the command line. Editing a message in elm uses the vi editor commands.

pine

The pine (Pine Is Not Elm) MUA is more powerful, and in my opinion, a little easier to use than elm. It's more menu-driven, for one thing, and your options are a little more clearly presented than with elm. It can also access POP and IMAP mailboxes, so you can use it to get to your Internet mailbox as well, whether that's local or at an ISP. It can also browse NNTP newsgroups. See the web site at **http://www.washington.edu/pine/** for more information, and try running it from the command line as well. Editing a message in pine uses the pico editor commands.

mutt

The mutt MUA is a mongrel tool that has taken some of the better features of the other mail tools, and adds a few of its own. I particularly like mutt's ability to use color, since I'm not stuck in front of a monochrome terminal. It also allows you to choose your favorite mail editor, which is nice for emacs aficionados. Consult the web site at **http://www.mutt.org/** for more information, and try running it from the command line.

POP MAIL

While the MUA programs described in the preceding section will work well for your Linux users, they won't do your Windows users much good. What will do them some good is enabling POP access on your mail server and pointing a POP-capable mail tool at that server. Those things are very easy to do.

Using Linux as a POP Server

Most Linux distributions come with a POP service of some kind. Red Hat can handle POP or IMAP connections, but you'll have to enable the service you want. Follow these instructions:

Open /etc/inetd.conf in a text editor, and find the lines that begin with pop-2, pop-3, and imap. They're probably all commented out; if you want to use POP to access the mail accounts, you can do that by uncommenting the line that starts with the pop-3 (just delete the pound sign). If you prefer to use IMAP, uncomment that line instead.

Once you've uncommented the line, you'll have to restart the inet daemon by running the following command:

```
root@romans /> /etc/rc.d/init.d/inet restart
```

Using Netscape as a POP Client

While there are other tools that can be used to access mail from POP and IMAP servers, Netscape's usually a good choice for users from the Windows world. The Netscape interface looks similar to what they're used to, and it's part of a program they probably have open anyway. Configuring the Netscape Messenger to access your POP server is very simple.

1. Start Netscape, and from the Edit menu, select Preferences.
2. Select the Mail & Newsgroups option.
3. Choose the Mail Servers entry, which opens the window shown in Figure 12-2.
4. From the Incoming Mail Servers section, click Add (unless there's already a server defined, in which case you can select it and click Edit).
5. In the General tab of the configuration window that appears, enter the name of your POP mail server.
6. Select the type of mail server. The pertinent choices are POP or IMAP.
7. Enter the name of the user's POP account on the server.
8. If you're dealing with an executive, check the Remember password box. Otherwise, lecture the user on the importance of password security.
9. Tell Netscape how often to check the POP mailbox; the default of 10 minutes should be fine.
10. Select the option to automatically download new messages as it notices them.
11. Click OK to return to the Mail Servers window.
12. Enter the name of the SMTP server (for outbound mail), and enter the user name if necessary.
13. Click on the Identity option and enter the user's full name.

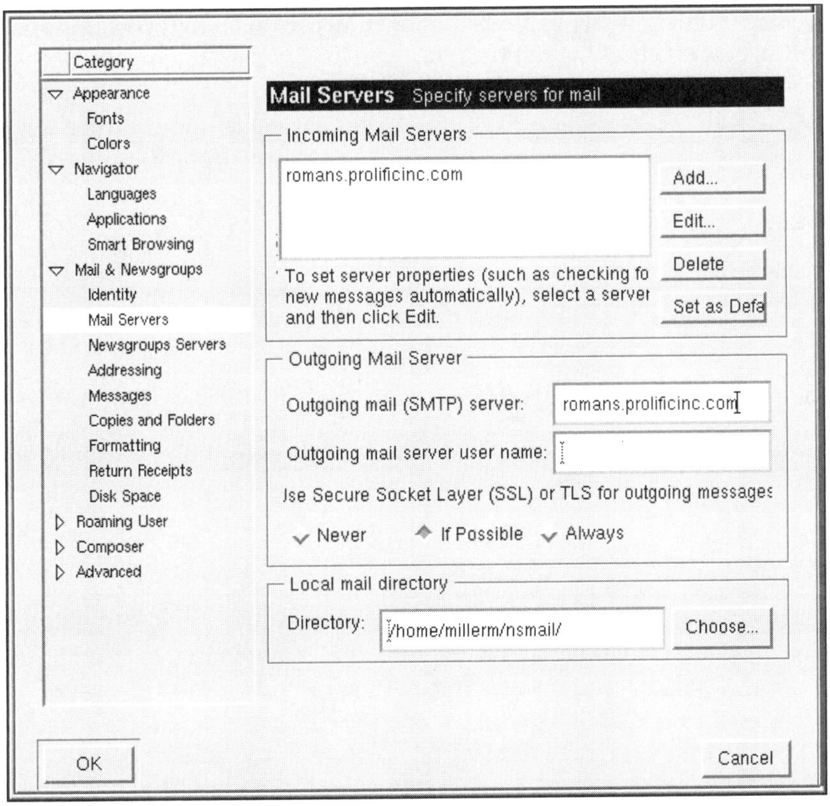

Figure 12-2.   Configure Netscape to use your POP mail server

14. Enter the user's email address and return address, if that's different.

15. Specify the name of the user's signature file, so they can create a clever file that's attached to each outgoing message.

16. Click OK, and you're done.

When you open Netscape's Messenger component, you'll have access to the mail account you configured. Click the Get Mail button to get new mail, and you should be sitting high and dry.

In the next chapter, we'll talk about how to add more software to your system. You may wish to apply that lesson immediately by checking for the latest version of Netscape from your distribution's maker or from Netscape itself (**http://www.netscape.com**).

While Internet Explorer has taken the brunt of the attack by script kiddies and crackers, there have been some security exploits demonstrated with certain versions of Netscape, too. So you're best off checking out the latest version.

CHAPTER 13

Step 10: "Make" More Software

In the last chapter, we looked into installing and configuring mail software. Not all of the tools I mentioned come with every distribution of Linux. So what do you do if you want some software that wasn't included with the distribution? You move to Step 10 of our Microsoft abuse recovery program, and continue to look for new software and promptly make it.

USING PACKAGES

While there are more involved ways of adding new software to your system, the most convenient method for most people is a *package manager*. This utility is a program that allows you to manipulate software that has been tidily wrapped up into a ... well, a package.

A package is composed of a set of files and some additional information; together, they tell your system where the files need to be installed, which other files are required to make these files run. The package system maintains enough information about the packages to allow you to do several useful things. One is safe removal of a package, because the system knows whether any other packages need a file. This is like an uninstall program that actually works.

Another fine feature of package managers is verification of one or all the packages on the system, because the system knows the packages that have been installed and the corresponding files that should be present.

Convinced that packaged software is a good thing? Whether you are or not, you might check out this section. We'll start by looking at the package options available to you, and then move on to package management tools and procedures.

RPMs and DEBs

There are two widely used package formats: RPM and DEB. RPM files are used by the many Red Hat derivative distributions (and, I'd better hasten to add, other distributions that are not derivative works), while DEB files are used by Debian and related distributions, including Corel Linux.

For our purposes, a package is a compressed set of files, stored along with additional information, which can easily be unpacked and installed by a user. RPM and DEB packages both do this, and while there are differences between the two formats, they both serve to make the process of installing and uninstalling software significantly easier. If you're really interested in the differences between the two formats, check out the information Joey Hess has provided at **http://kitenet.net/~joey/pkg-comp/**.

I don't think there's a compelling reason to use one type of package over another. I think you should choose the distribution you want to use and work with it. But you may find that one package type or the other is more useful to you, and if you're planning on building and distributing software, you may want to be able to support both formats.

Note that there are a couple more package options that I won't cover here. The first is SLP, which is used by the Stampede distribution (**http://www.stampede.org**). It aims to make packages less dependant on package managers, but it's not widely used, at least as I write this. The other isn't really a package, it's a compressed tar file, commonly known as a *tarball*. I'll discuss these files a little more in the "Compiling Source Tarballs" section of this chapter, but they lack the file dependency information that's included in what I consider a package.

Package Management

There's a dizzying array of packages available for use on Linux platforms, and two of the easiest ways to access and install them is through use of package managers. In recent chapters, I've been focusing on the Red Hat distribution's tools; naturally, because the popular Debian distribution and its ilk use a different package manager, you might find yourself having to (gasp!) ... read the documentation if you use one of the DEB-based distributions.

While I've generally gone from explaining the use of a GUI tool before explaining how to make the same kinds of changes from the command line, I'd like to reverse that sequence in this case. Automating package installation is very easily accomplished from scripts, and that requires a little understanding of the command-line functions.

If you find the command line completely frustrating, though, please skip ahead to the "Kpackage" and "GnoRPM" sections that follow. Those are standard GUI tools that come with the KDE and GNOME desktop environments, and they're extremely easy to use and are quite powerful. They just aren't designed for hands-free batch processing.

Command-Line RPM

Using the **rpm** command isn't difficult, and it's certainly extensively documented. See the man page and the documentation at **http://www.rpm.org**. The primary actions are easy to figure out, though. They're listed in Table 13-1.

RPM Option	Description
rpm –q	Query the RPM database
rpm –V	Verify installed files against original package
rpm –U	Upgrade or install package
rpm –e	Uninstall products

Table 13-1.   Basic RPM Command-Line Options

Querying   You can query your system for its RPM information, which can be useful for finding out what a package contains or for finding which package owns a file on your system. For example, to learn some basic information about a package you're considering installing on your system, you can use a command like this one:

```
rpm -qip webmin-0.78.rpm
```

This tells the **rpm** command that you're doing a query for package information, and that you're interested in the package file "webmin-0.78.rpm."

That's fine if you have the package file handy. But what you often want to know is: What package owns a file? To answer that question, you can issue a command like this:

```
rpm -qf /etc/sendmail.cf
```

That command tells you the name of the package that owns /etc/sendmail.cf, complete with version number information. But often, that information isn't enough to tell you what the package really is. So to see some basic information about the package that owns a file, use the **-i** option:

```
rpm -qif /etc/sendmail.cf
```

This is one of the more useful query commands, especially when you're first figuring out what's going on with your Linux system. But sometimes you want a list of all the files that came with a package, and you can find that information using a command like this:

```
rpm -qlf /etc/sendmail.cf
```

That format finds the package that owns the /etc/sendmail.cf file and then reports back a list of all files owned by that package. You could also specify a package name instead.

You can play around with the **rpm -q** options if you're looking for other information, or how to find it. But let me leave you one more command; this one produces lengthy output. It produces a list of all configuration files identified by all installed packages and formats them with the file permissions, ownership information, and size, as the **ls -l** command does:

```
rpm -qacv
```

Verification   Verifying a package means checking the files installed on your system against the contents of the package that installed them. It's a way of seeing what has changed, and in many cases, that change is fine. For example, configuration files almost always need to change, and you may change file permissions or ownership of certain files. But it's a good thing to be able to identify which things have changed and how.

To that end, the **rpm** command offers the **-V** option, which performs verification on a package or file—or all the installed packages. The brute-force method is to verify all packages, an operation that can take quite some time and may spit out quite a bit of output:

```
rpm -Va > rpm_verify.txt
```

Notice that the output from the rpm command is being redirected into the file rpm_verify.txt. This is a separate, optional step, but it's much easier to review the data in a file than streaming across your screen.

The output from the verification commands depends on whether there are differences between the data in the package and the files actually installed on your system. If there are no differences, there won't be any output. For each file that differs, however, there will be output that looks like this:

```
root@romans /> rpm -Vf /etc/sendmail.cf
S.5....T c /etc/aliases
```

The cryptic-looking characters to the left of the /etc/aliases file show three ways in which the file differs from the original package specification and provides us with a piece of information that helps us interpret the results.

The **S** means that the filesize differs from the original file's size. The **5** means the MD5 checksum for the file differs (which makes sense, since it appears the file contents have been changed). The **T** means the file has been modified from the original package date, which is also consistent with a file that has been changed. The **c** means that this file has been marked by the package as a configuration file, and therefore is likely to have been touched since the original installation. These values and the others (the periods in the example output indicate that the other values match the originals) are described in Table 13-2.

Installation   If you check the man page for the **rpm** tool, you'll find that there's a **-i** option that allows you to do package installation. So why am I suggesting that you use the **-U** option? It's been my experience that the fewer options I'm using infrequently, the more likely I am to remember the options I use frequently. And the **-U** option provides the dual functionality of installing packages that aren't already installed and upgrading packages that need upgrading.

The basic approach for applying this command to real life is pretty simple. Specify the package on the command line this way:

```
root@romans /> rpm -Uvh webmin-0.78.rpm
```

The **-U** option, as I mentioned, specifies the upgrade operation. The **vh** option, specified together in this context, causes the package name to be displayed next to a set of pound signs that are placed sequentially as the installation process proceeds. This gives you an idea of the progress being made if the package is large.

Output	Description
S	File size
M	Mode: file permissions and file type
5	MD5 sum
L	Symbolic link
D	Device
U	User
G	Group
T	Mtime
.	Matched original
c	Configuration file

Table 13-2.   RPM Verification Flags

You can use this option in a script to automate setup of a new system. For example, the following example installs or upgrades all RPM files found in the /home/rpm directory:

```
rpm -Uvh /home/rpm/*.rpm
```

If you maintain a directory of the packages you're currently using, you can ensure consistency across your Linux environment by scheduling a script with contents like the example shown. See Chapter 14 for more information on scheduling jobs.

Uninstallation   The uninstall option is also very easy to use. All you need to know is the name of the package (the package name, not the file name). You can use the query options to find that out if you need to and issue a command like this one:

```
root@romans /> rpm -e perl-Data-ShowTable-3.3-2
```

If another package depends on the module you're attempting to uninstall, rpm will inform you. Otherwise, the package will be blipped off your machine. If you want it back, reinstall it.

Kpackage

If you use the KDE desktop environment, you'll find that there's a nice tool known as kpackage that gives the **rpm** commands a graphical interface. If you prefer to use a GUI, and if you don't have to script what you're doing, kpackage is useful.

To run the kpackage program, issue the **kpackage** command from the command line after becoming the superuser. Or use the menu option from KDE; it can likely be found in the Utilities folder from the KDE button. You can browse through the packages installed on the system using the tree structure shown in Figure 13-1.

Installing packages   There are several ways to install a package from kpackage, but one of the most straightforward works like this:

1. Launch kpackage.
2. From the File menu, select the Open option.
3. Traverse the directory structure to the desired package file, select it and click OK.
4. Check the package information to make sure it's what you were after, as shown in Figure 13-2.
5. Make sure the selected options are correct: Upgrade, Replace Packages, and Check Dependencies are chosen by default, as shown in Figure 13-2, and this is usually what you'll want.
6. Click Install; the package will be installed, will be listed in the package tree, and will be available for use.

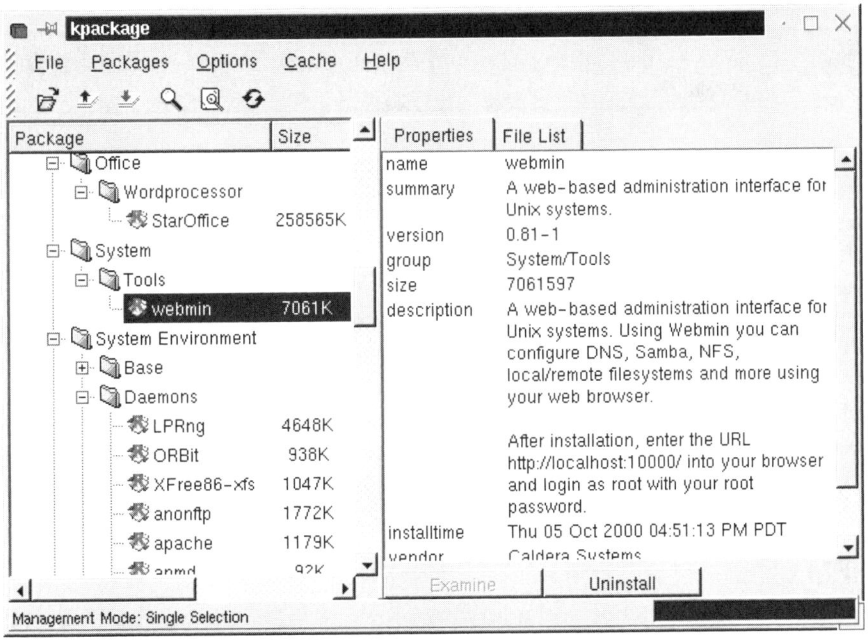

Figure 13-1.   KDE users can perform package management with kpackage

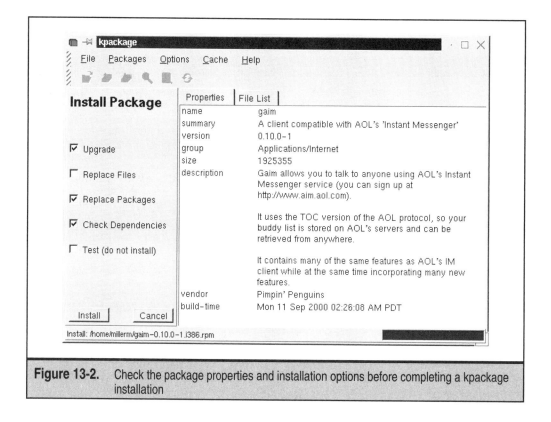

Figure 13-2. Check the package properties and installation options before completing a kpackage installation

Removing a Package If you select a package that has already been installed, you will have the option to uninstall it. The Uninstall button is found at the bottom of the left-hand panel, beneath the display of the file properties. Look back at Figure 13-1 if you're not clear where the button is located.

If you click that button, you can remove the selected package from your Linux system. When you do so, you're given several options, as shown in Figure 13-3.

The Use Scripts option enables the processing scripts that are part of the package; it's best to leave this enabled. Likewise, the Check Dependencies option is there to prevent you from pulling the rug out from another package, so you'll usually want to leave it enabled. The Test option, on the other hand, prevents the uninstall from occurring; it just goes through the motions so you can see if there are dependency problems.

GnoRPM

If you prefer GNOME to KDE, and many people do, you have another GUI-based package management tool: gnorpm. This is a standard tool for GNOME installations. Truth be told, if you install both KDE and GNOME on your Linux system, you can use either or both of these programs.

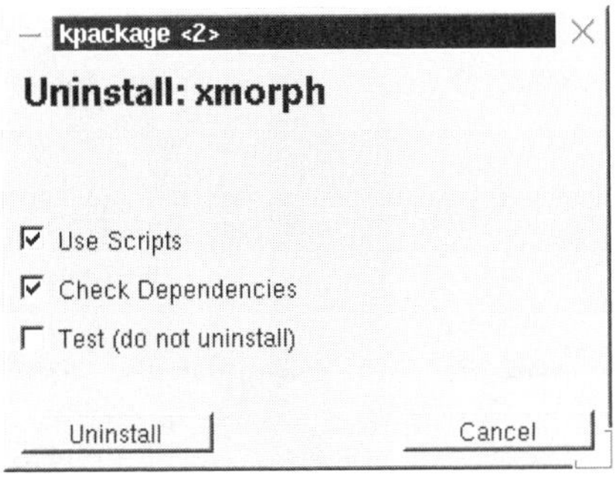

Figure 13-3.   Select the uninstall options when removing software using kpackage

When you launch gnorpm from the command line or from GNOME's System menu, you'll see a screen like the one shown in Figure 13-4.

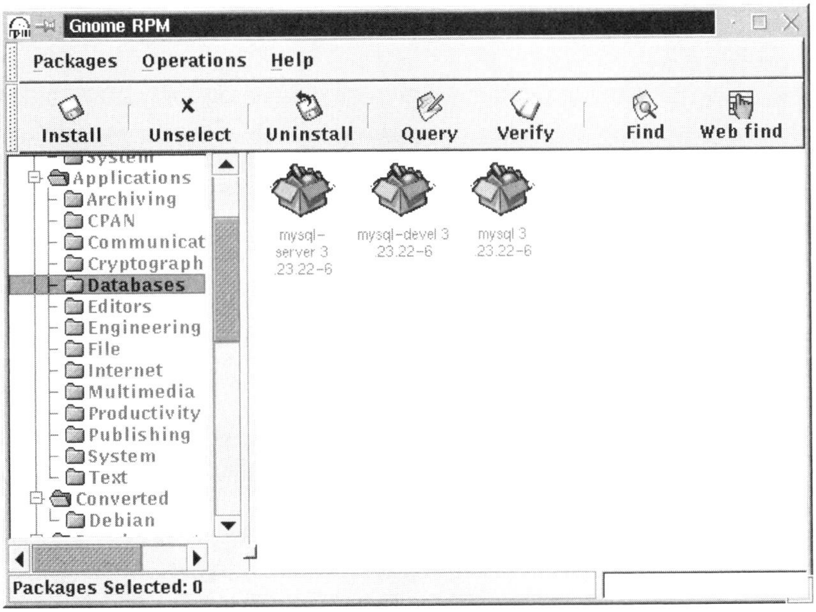

Figure 13-4.   GNOME users can perform package management from gnorpm

The tools are quite similar in many ways; if you use the graphical file-management tool for either environment, you can drag and drop package files from the file manager into the appropriate package manager, or you can use the menus or buttons to do the same thing.

One useful gnorpm button is the Web Find option visible in Figure 13-4. This option checks the known sources on the Web for new packages and updates to the packages you already have. Click the Web Find button, then look through the list of packages in the tree on the left side of the screen, as shown in Figure 13-5.

Notice that in Figure 13-5, the selected package is a viewer that converts Microsoft Office files to HTML. The package information is displayed on the right side of the screen, including a URL for the package's home page. This can be useful for tracking down updates, documentation, or someone who can help with a particular package.

Notice as well that in the left-hand panel's list of packages, those packages that have already been installed are noted. If there's an updated version available, the update will be displayed in another color (blue) to help you notice its availability.

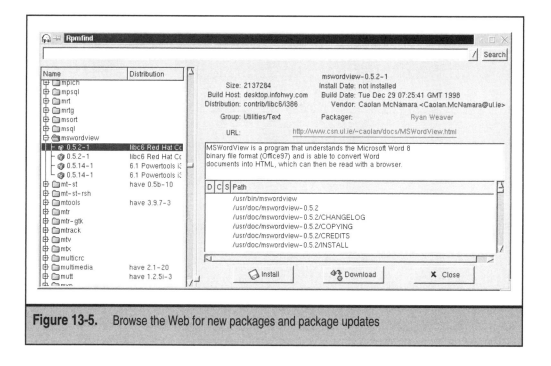

Figure 13-5.   Browse the Web for new packages and package updates

USING MAKE

You may not always be fortunate enough to find a package for the software you want to install, especially if you're interested in running the very latest versions that are available; such leading-edge software is rarely prepackaged for your convenience. That doesn't mean you're left out in the cold, though, because "making" programs isn't very hard.

By "making programs," I'm not talking about writing the programs on your own. Whether or not you feel comfortable doing that, you can build programs from sources other people have written. In fact, another reason to learn about the **make** command is because some software is distributed as source files. In other words, even if they're bundled in a package, the files still need to be built once they've been installed. If the distributor intended this to be the case, the RPM package will have the extension .srpm instead of the usual .rpm.

Source Tarballs

Most of the software you find on the Web isn't going to be packaged that way, either. Instead, it's usually wrapped up into a compressed archive file affectionately called a "tarball." You can usually identify these creatures by their extensions, which are usually one of these:

- ▼ .tar
- ■ tar.gz
- ■ .tgz
- ■ .tar.Z
- ▲ .tar.bz2

Tar Files

The first extension may be identifiable as the output of the **tar** command, which is short for "tape archive" but often has nothing to do with tapes. Basically, the **tar** command takes several files, with or without a directory structure, and encapsulates them into a single file. It's not unlike how a ZIP file works on PCs, or StuffIt files on Macs, except that there's no compression going on in the process. To create a tar file, you can issue a command like this one:

```
millerm@romans ~> tar cvf loveletters.tar ~/to_karen/letters/*
```

This is a common set of options; they indicate that the **tar** command should create, verbosely, a file named loveletters.tar, from all the files and directories found under my home directory in the directory to_karen/letters/.

It's fine to know that, but it's not exactly relevant to the task at hand, which isn't putting files into an archive, it's removing them. That's pretty easy, too:

```
karen@romans ~> tar xvf loveletters.tar
```

Karen can open the archive using these options, which tell the **tar** command to extract the archive file verbosely. Being able to create and open tar files is very useful, but it's not the whole story, because as I mentioned, these files aren't compressed.

tgz and gz Files

The compression part is where the other extensions come in. While Linux systems can use the **zip** and **unzip** commands to manipulate ZIP files for swapping with PC users, the gzip program is more widely used. The .tgz and .tar.gz extensions indicate that the file has been both archived by **tar** and compressed using **gzip**. To create a compressed version of the archive, I could use the file I already created:

```
millerm@romans ~> gzip loveletters.tar
```

This would produce a file called loveletters.tar.gz, and it might be dramatically smaller than the original file, depending on the data. But I don't have to go through two steps to perform this task; I can have the **tar** command call the compression utility at the same time:

```
millerm@romans ~> tar cvzf loveletters.tgz ~/to_karen/letters/*
```

This would produce a file called loveletters.tgz that is roughly equivalent to the .tar.gz file. That's not always true, but for our purposes, it's close enough, because either way, the compressed file can be opened the same way:

```
karen@romans ~> tar xvzf loveletters.tgz
karen@romans ~> tar xvzf loveletters.tar.gz
```

Either command fully decompresses the archive and extracts its files and directories.

Z Files

A less-favored compression option that's more often found on other Unix platforms is a pair of tools known as **compress** and **uncompress**. The compression on a "compressed" file isn't as great as the compression on a gzip file, but because some Unix systems don't include the **gzip** utility, **compress** may be more useful if you're sharing files with Unix users. The utilities work pretty much as you'd expect; to create an archive, you can use a command like this:

```
millerm@romans ~> compress loveletters.tar
```

This would produce a compressed file named loveletters.tar.Z. Undoing the compression is equally straightforward:

```
karen@romans ~> uncompress loveletters.tar.Z
karen@romans ~> tar xvf loveletters.tar
```

bz2 Files

Although there are other compression tools, the other you're most likely to encounter (and probably already have if you've built your own kernel) is the **bzip2** utility. You can use it just as you may have come to expect:

```
millerm@romans ~> bzip2 loveletters.tar
```

The output file would be named loveletters.tar.bz2. Undoing the bzip2 compression works similarly:

```
karen@romans ~> bunzip2 loveletters.tar.bz2
karen@romans ~> tar xvf loveletters.tar
```

Consider this example: I want to install Bluefish, a compact HTML editor with almost every feature I want. While there's a Debian package available for download from the Bluefish home page (**http://bluefish.linuxave.net/**), there's not an RPM. So I download a compressed tarball called bluefish-0.3.6.tar.bz2 and begin the installation process:

```
millerm@romans ~> bzip2 bluefish-0.3.6.tar.bz2
millerm@romans ~> tar xvf bluefish-0.3.6.tar
```

Now I'm ready to continue, so let's move on to talk about what's required to build the software once you've got it.

Building Software

Now that you know how to crack open the shell of the compressed file nut and can get to the tasty, tasty meat, what do you do? I beg, beseech, and implore you to do one special thing: Read any file that's named anything like "README," and any file named anything like "INSTALL." You'll often find files with those names in the base directory created when you expanded the archive

CAUTION: I'm not kidding. Read the information that comes with the software before you install it. I don't mean to be patronizing, but you really should know what the software's creator is trying to tell you before you go wildly inserting it into your pristine system.

Configure

While the installation process will vary from application to application, the most common first step involves some basic configuration. The software's designers usually try to keep things tidy by selecting default options that work for most people, but there's so much variation in the Linux world that it's possible you'll have to tweak some settings.

Sometimes the configuration step involves running a script; this is often called "configure," in a gesture that's both utilitarian and easily understood. Check any installation instructions for details, but running a script like this usually requires you to tell your shell where the file is located, even if you try to run it from the directory in which it's located.

To return to the Bluefish HTML editor example, I need to move into the directory created when I unpacked the archive, and run the **configure** script. (I know this, of course, because I read the INSTALL file.)

```
millerm@romans ~/cd bluefish-0.3.6
millerm@romans ~/bluefish-0.3.6> ./configure
```

The "dot-slash" notation tells the shell that the configure file is located in the current directory. Once the script has been launched, a variety of system checks are performed, and several files are created. We're done with the configuration step.

Installing Webmin via Tarball

Although systems that use the RPM package manager can easily install the Webmin program available from **http://www.webmin.com/**, I'd like to mention it as another example of a program that can be built. That's largely because I think it's an excellent tool for system administrators, regardless of how it's installed.

In the interests of making things interesting, Webmin doesn't use a configuration script called **configure**. Instead, it uses a script called **setup.sh**. So if you download the latest version of the Webmin package (at this time, that's Webmin 0.78), you can follow these steps to run the configuration script:

```
millerm@romans ~> cp webmin-0.78.tar.gz /usr/local
millerm@romans ~> cd /usr/local
millerm@romans ~> gunzip webmin
millerm@romans ~> tar xvf webmin-0.78.tar
millerm@romans ~> cd webmin-0.78
millerm@romans ~> ./setup.sh
```

This script will ask you a sequence of questions regarding your system, the software you have installed, and where that software is installed. Answer to the best of your knowledge, and grit your teeth while trying to remember why you didn't want to install it as a package. But soon the process will be over, and you don't have to use the **make** command.

Make

The next step is running the **make** command. This is not a hard-and-fast rule; each tool you build should be treated as its own entity, with its own set of installation steps. All the same, this is very often the next step.

Make is a program on your system that knows how to create a usable set of program files given some input files and some knowledge of your system. The configuration step is largely responsible for providing the input for **make**, and by running it now, you're telling it to go out and compile the files as it sees fit. While there are sometimes options you can use with the **make** command (remember the different options when building the kernel in Chapter 6?), that's often unnecessary.

Looking once more at the Bluefish example, I had run the configuration script, and the INSTALL file tells me that the next step is indeed to run **make**:

```
millerm@romans ~/bluefish-0.3.6> make
```

Notice that there's no "dot-slash" in front of the **make** command, which isn't located in the current directory. It is run from its home (usually /usr/bin/make), using the files in the current directory for instructions.

The **make** process can be time-consuming, but at least many gratifying messages scroll across the screen as it does its work. While you may not be able to understand what it's doing, it's a little visual reassurance that something is happening. When it's done happening, you'll get a pretty unassuming message and will be returned to the shell prompt.

Make install

The last step is installing the software you just built onto your system. That's a fairly automated process with most software you'll find, because the **make install** command will copy the files to the correct places on your system. Before you run **make install**, though, you normally need to become the superuser, because software usually ends up in directories that mortal users don't get to access.

The last step to the installation of the Bluefish software is to become root and run the **make install** command:

```
millerm@romans ~/bluefish-0.3.6> su
Password:
root@romans ~/bluefish-0.3.6> make install
```

More messages scroll across the screen, and once I'm at the shell prompt again, I use the **exit** command to become my mortal user self again. Now I can run the tool by issuing the following command from within an xterm:

```
millerm@romans ~/> bluefish
```

This brings up the Bluefish editor as shown in Figure 13-6.

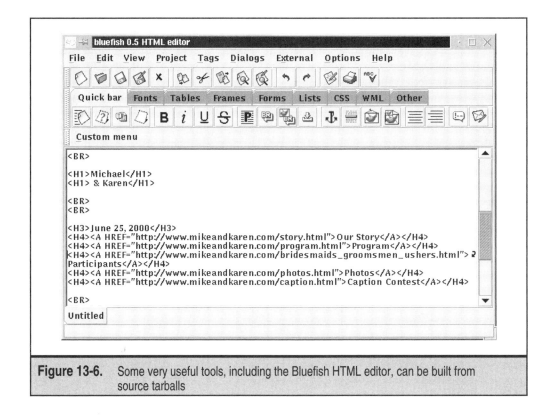

Figure 13-6.   Some very useful tools, including the Bluefish HTML editor, can be built from source tarballs

NEW SOFTWARE

So you know how you can build cool programs that other people have created. The next logical questions are twofold. First, how do you find these programs? And second, what if you want to make your own packages, either to distribute software you're writing, or to perform package-based system administration?

Finding Sources and Packages

The short answer to the first question is "the Internet." There's a treasure trove of software out there, and while there are plenty of pennies in sight, there are also many pieces of gold. Among the locations I suggest you look are these:

AppWatch	http://www.appwatch.com/Linux/
CNET	http;//download.cnet.com/downloads/0-10004.html?tag= st.lx.1491268.dir.10004
DaveCentral	http://linux.davecentral.com/

Freshmeat   http://freshmeat.net/

SourceForge   http://sourceforge.net/

I've given short shrift to the Debian packages used by Debian, Corel, and others in this chapter, but there are many such packages available at **http://www.debian.org/ distrib/packages**.

The other place to look is on the CD-ROM that came with your distribution. If you didn't install every available package when you did your initial Linux installation, there may be useful tools still available on the CD. Check out the manual or have a look at the discs that came with your distribution, looking especially for package files.

Making Your Own Packages

If you're developing software, you may decide that the advantages of a package manager are compelling enough that you'd like to distribute your programs in packages. I think that's a fine idea (especially if you make the package just one option for distributing your software).

I also like the idea of using package management toward the goal of system management, though not everyone will agree with this notion. There are a variety of other mechanisms people use to ensure consistency between systems and to provide a method for upgrading the operating system and tools on systems, but packages bring many useful features to the table. With a central repository for packages on your network, and some tasks scheduled weekly or monthly to ensure things are as they should be, you can ensure consistency that is difficult to attain in the relatively unregulated Windows world.

But while I think package creation is a good thing to learn, I don't have the space here to go through the process. Fortunately, the way has been blazed for you already. There's a fine RPM-HOWTO document that explains the RPM creation process; a copy should be available on your system; most distributions place it in /usr/doc/HOWTO/ RPM-HOWTO. You can also get it with additional documentation from **http:// www.rpm.org/**.

If you want to create the Debian packages also used by Corel Linux and others, the Debian New Maintainer's Guide is a good place to start. Find it at **http://www.debian.org/ ~elphick/ddp/manuals.html#newmaintguide**, and best of luck in your package creation.

CHAPTER
14

Step 11:
Share and
Schedule

In the last chapter, we investigated the process of adding more software to a Linux system using packages and source files. I think that's one of the most exciting parts of using Linux, because I'm always intrigued to see the great tools people are building and making available for others to use and improve.

In this chapter, we'll look at another kind of sharing; this one is between systems on your network. It's an important detail, so important that it is Step 11 on the route to recovery, which tells us to share files to improve conscious contact and schedule our jobs to carry them out.

FILE PERMISSIONS REVISITED

We've talked about file permissions before; if you recall, using the **ls -l** command to display a file listing also shows the permission bit settings in a directory's files and subdirectories. Knowing what those permissions are and knowing how to use them are two very different matters, however, so I'd like to return to both subjects.

Determining Permissions

Like any other multiuser system, Linux must keep track of who owns files and who is allowed to monkey with them. You don't want users idly stomping on each other's files, and you certainly don't want any tomfoolery going on with the system files. Naturally, Linux gives you the ability to restrict access to the system, or to share files as needed.

Just as NT and Windows 2000 have file and directory permissions, and NetWare systems have trustee rights at the file and directory level, Linux has permissions set for both files and directories. For the most part, dealing with the file and directory permissions separately will work fine, but there are plenty of circumstances in which the combination of permission settings is significant. Accordingly, we'll look first at the individual file and directory permissions, and then we'll examine ways in which the permissions interact.

Determining Ownership

The file-management tools that come with KDE and GNOME do a fine job of showing ownership, but you won't always have the luxury of access to an X Windows interface, so we'll consider the details of determining ownership using command-line tools. The concepts are easily applied to what you'll see using the widely used GUI file managers.

If I want to check out the ownership of Karen's Christmas card list, I can use the **ls** command with the **-l** option.

```
millerm@romans ~> ls -l ~karen/christmas_cards.txt
-rw-r----- 1 karen    karen       10345 May 23 20:05 christmas_cards.txt
```

From this listing, I see that the file is owned by the user karen and the group karen. Neither one is surprising. But what if the listing looked something like this instead?

```
-rw-r----- 1 501    501       10345 May 23 20:05 christmas_cards.txt
```

There are numbers where I'd ordinarily expect to find the username and group name. Those numbers are the user ID and the group ID that have ownership of the file, and when they're displayed instead of names, it's because the Linux system couldn't find user- and group names that matched the IDs associated with the file. That might happen if you delete a user account but don't change file ownership.

The user and the group with file ownership define two of the three levels of permissions that can apply to a file or directory. Thus, you can start the process of sharing files between users by putting the users in the same group, and then giving that group ownership of the files. The third permission level applies to every user on the system except the owning user and group. This set of accounts is often referred to as "world."

Reading Permissions

There are three levels of permission that apply to files and directories: read, write, and execute. Each permission's effect is shown in Table 14-1.

Each of these permissions may be separately and uniquely applied to the owning user account, the owning group, and the rest of the world. The way these permissions are applied is reflected in the output from the **ls-l** command. So to return to the Christmas card list, recall that the output looked like this:

```
-rw-r----- 1 karen    karen      10345 May 23 20:05 christmas_cards.txt
```

File Permissions   How do we read these permissions? It's clear that some read and write permissions have been granted, but to whom? We can figure this out by knowing that the permissions list consists of 10 digits, and that the second through fourth digits show the owner account's permissions, while the fifth through seventh digits show the owning group's permissions, and the eighth through tenth digits show the rest of the world's permissions. Table 14-2 can help us straighten out the meaning of this file's permissions.

Given the Christmas card file's permissions, we can determine from the contents of Table 14-2 that the user karen has read and write permissions to the file, so she can view or alter the file contents, and she may delete the file. The group karen has only read permissions for the file, and the rest of the world, including me, has no access.

Permission	Effect on File	Effect on Directory
Read	View file contents	View directory contents
Write	Modify file	Create, delete, and move files in directory
eXecute	Run a program or script file	Change into the directory

Table 14-1.   Permissions and Effects on Files and Directories

File Permission Listing	Permissions Granted
`-r--------`	Owner may read the file
`--w-------`	Owner may alter or delete the file
`---x------`	Owner may execute the program
`-r-x------`	Owner may execute the shell script
`---s------`	Program executes as the owner
`------s---`	Program executes as the owning group
`----r-----`	Owning group members may read the file
`-----w----`	Owning group members may alter or delete the file
`------x---`	Owning group members may execute the program
`----r-x---`	Owning group members may execute the shell script
`-------r-`	The world may read the file
`--------w-`	The world may alter or delete the file
`---------x`	The world may execute the file
`------r-x`	The world may execute the shell script

Table 14-2.   Reading File Permissions

But notice one more permission I snuck into Table 14-2, the "s" permission. When an "s" appears in the owning user's part of the permission list, it's referred to as the *setuid bit*, and when it appears in the owning group's part of the permission list, it's known as the *setgid bit*. If one of these bits is set, it means that when the file is executed, the effective ID of the process that is started will be set to the owner's user ID or group ID (depending on which bit is set). This is one way of allowing users to run programs without giving them impressive powers, but it can be as much a source of security problems as it is a solution to security problems.

Directory Permissions   The meanings of the permissions on a directory are slightly different from those on a file. While the permission flags are the same, their meanings may be somewhat different. Table 14-3 shows what the various permission flags mean for a directory.

Notice that I snuck in another new permission; this time it's the "T" value, which indicates that the "sticky bit" is set. When this permission value is set, someone who is not the owner (or the root user) cannot delete files in the directory, even if the whole world has "wx" permissions, which ordinarily allows deletion of files. When a directory's sticky bit

File Permission Listing	Permissions Granted
`dr--------`	Owner may list directory contents, but not attributes
`d--x------`	Owner may enter the directory
`dr-x------`	Owner may read the file attributes of the directory contents
`d-wx------`	Owner may add and delete files in the directory
`d--------T`	Sticky bit set: Files can't be deleted by non-owners
`d---r-----`	Owning group members may list directory contents
`d-----x---`	Owning group members may enter the directory
`d---r-x---`	Owning group members may read the file attributes of directory contents
`d----wx---`	Owning group members may add and delete files in the directory
`d------r--`	The world may enter the directory
`d--------x`	The world may read the file attributes of directory contents
`-------r-x`	The world may add and delete files in the directory
`d-------wx`	The world may execute the shell script

Table 14-3.   Reading Directory Permissions

is set, some people call it an "append-only" directory, meaning it's mostly protected from accidental deletion but can still receive new files.

Relating Permissions

File and directory permissions are not isolated from each other. On the contrary, a directory's permissions affect the effective permissions of the files it contains. The upshot of this situation is that if you're locked out of a directory, you're locked out of the files it contains. In fact, if you're locked out of any directories in the path of a file you're trying to access, you're out of luck.

Consider another example. Imagine Karen realizes I've been snooping around in her stuff, and wants to make sure that I don't see the invitations to the surprise birthday she's throwing for me. She could restrict the outside world's permissions on the invitation file itself. But she could also create a directory to which other users have no access:

```
drwx------ 5 karen   karen     4096 May 23 21:13 myob
```

Now I won't be able to access the files in this directory unless I'm searching through her files while logged in as root. Naturally, the presence of a sticky bit in a directory's permissions settings prohibits non-owners from deleting files in that directory, so that's another example of directory/file permission interaction.

Setting Permissions

The command-line utility used to set file and directory permissions is called **chmod**. This tool offers two different ways of specifying the permissions. One method designates the permissions using mnemonic codes, while the other uses a system of numbers.

The mnemonics often seem easier at first, so they're a good place to start. Suppose that Karen wants to change the access to her Christmas card file so that anyone on the system may read it. She could specify that all users get the read permission using the following command:

```
karen@romans ~> chmod a+r ~karen/christmas_cards.txt
```

This format simply says that all users (the **a** argument) should have read access (the **r** argument) added (the **+** argument) for the file. If Karen wants to check the results of this command using the **ls -l** option, she'll see this:

```
karen@romans ~> ls -l ~karen/christmas_cards.txt
-rw-r--r-- 1 karen    karen        10345 May 23 20:05 christmas_cards.txt
```

The user karen already had read and write access to the file, so her access hasn't changed. But now the group karen and the rest of the world have been granted read access to the file.

If Karen decides that she doesn't want every bozo we allow onto our Linux system to be able to see her Christmas list, she can use **chmod** to revoke the read permission for the rest of the world:

```
karen@romans ~> chmod o-r ~karen/christmas_cards.txt
karen@romans ~> ls -l ~karen/christmas_cards.txt
-rw-r----- 1 karen    karen        10345 May 23 20:05 christmas_cards.txt
```

She used **chmod** to revoke (the **-** argument) the read permission (the **r** argument) from the other users (the **o** argument). But what if, realizing that she has placed the file in a directory nobody could see anyway, she decides to create a new directory to keep files she wants to share? She can set the permissions explicitly:

```
karen@romans ~> chmod a=t,u=rwx,g=rwx,o= ~karen/share/
karen@romans ~> ls -l ~karen/share/
drwxrwx--T 5 karen    karen         4096 May 23 20:05 share
```

This time, instead of adding or subtracting permissions from the existing set, she has designated each and every permission. This is a convenient tool, and it's easier to remember the mnemonic codes than the numeric ones. But the numeric options are more efficiently set.

The numeric permission settings are based on an octal system in which four digits from 0 to 7 specify the owner permissions, group permissions, other permissions, and the special bits (sticky bit, setuid, or setgid).

For the standard permissions, a value of 1 sets the "x" permission, while a value of 2 sets the "w" permission, and a value of 4 sets the "r" permission. You can add values to set multiple permissions at once, or you can use 0 to turn all permissions off. The results are the digits shown in Table 14-4.

File and directory permissions are often set using three numeric digits. The first of the three digits sets the permissions for the owning user. The second digit sets the permissions for the owning group. And you won't be surprised to learn that the third digit sets the permissions for the rest of the world.

So if Karen wanted to give herself read and write access to a file, but only wanted to give the owning group read access and wanted to lock out the other users entirely, she could use this command:

```
karen@romans ~> chmod 640 ~karen/christmas_cards.txt
karen@romans ~> ls -l ~karen/christmas_cards.txt
-rw-r----- 1 karen    karen       10345 May 23 20:05 christmas_cards.txt
```

On the other hand, if she had less personal data and wanted to give full access to a directory to herself and the owning group, she could use the following syntax:

```
karen@romans ~> chmod 770 ~karen/share/
karen@romans ~> ls -l ~karen/share/
drwxrwx--- 5 karen    karen        4096 May 23 20:05 share
```

Value	Permissions Granted
0	No permissions
1	Execute only (x)
2	Write only (w)
3	Write and execute (wx)
4	Read only (r)
5	Read and execute (rx)
6	Read and write (rw)
7	Read, write, and execute (rwx)

Table 14-4.   Numeric Values for Setting File and Directory Permissions

These commands are efficient, and once you're familiar with the relationship between the numbers and the permissions they represent, they're easy to use. But I mentioned before that there are four digits possible. The fourth digit is for the special information that can be set for a file or directory. For files, you can enable setuid and setgid, and for directories, you can enable the sticky bit. The possible values for this additional bit, which is specified *first* when it's used, are shown in Table 14-5.

If Karen wanted to set the sticky bit on a directory to prevent other users from deleting in it, she could issue a command like this one:

```
karen@romans ~> chmod 1770 ~karen/myob
karen@romans ~> ls -l ~karen/myob
drwxrwx--t 5 karen    karen        4096 May 23 20:05 myob
```

Default Permissions

Perhaps you've wondered which permissions are assigned by default. That setting is configurable using the **umask** command, which is normally included in the /etc/profile and csh.login shell configuration files. The **umask** statement takes a numeric permission string that's similar to—but different from—the numeric permission strings used with **chmod**.

The three-digit umask string is the "complement" to the permissions you want to enable by default. In other words, while a value of 7 is as open as you get with a **chmod** command, it's as restrictive as you get with the **umask** command. Each digit of the default file permission setting is equal to 7 minus the corresponding umask digit. Thus, if the umask is 077, the default file permission setting is 700, which is a fine setting for the root user.

Value	Modes Designated
0	Set nothing
1	Set sticky bit
2	Set group ID (setgid) when executed
3	Set sticky bit and setgid
4	Set user ID (setuid) when executed
5	Set sticky bit and setuid
6	Set setuid and setgid when executed
7	Set sticky bit, and setuid and setgid when executed

Table 14-5. Numeric Values for Setting Special Permission Bits

The typical values used for normal account umasks are 022 if users normally share primary groups, or 002 if each user has a unique primary group. This option is what Red Hat and some other distributions default to; the resulting default file permission string of 775 is fine only if each user has a unique primary group.

USING LINKS

Links files are like Windows shortcuts, but they're more closely associated with their target than shortcuts are. When you use links under Linux, unless you do an **ls -l** and notice that the first file permission bit is an "l," you won't know that you're not directly manipulating the file. This makes links excellent tools to have in your belt, because they can be used for everything from simplifying upgrades to sharing files across a network.

Symbolic Links

The most common type of link is known as a *symbolic link*. These links aren't quite as intimately hooked to the target as *hard links*, which I'll describe momentarily. Let me put it this way: These are the links you'll be using.

You can create a symbolic link using the **ln** command, as shown here:

```
millerm@romans ~> ln -s ~albers/wassup.avi wu.avi
```

That command creates a link in my home directory, called wu.avi, which points to a file in another user's home directory. Notice that I gave the link a different name than the original filename; this is fine, and it can be quite useful.

For example, sometimes it can be useful to create links to files in the same directory. This is what happens in the /usr/src/ directory if you want to keep multiple versions of the linux kernel source files; the "linux" directory is often just a link to the version you're currently building.

Another example of the use of links to deal with versioning can be seen in the /usr/lib/ directory. If you do an **ls -l** there, you'll find that there are dozens of link files pointing from generic libraries to a specific version of that library. If a new version comes along, it can be plopped into the correct directory and linked to (but please don't do this yourself if you're not familiar with Linux library files).

Symbolic links are also useful for sharing files. You can create a shared directory on a server, NFS mount it on client stations, and then place a link in each user's directory to the shared directory. As far as the user knows, the files are local to their system. In fact, in some cases it's possible to move a file or a whole directory, create a link to make it look like it's where it always has been, and never let the user know anything's different. That's extremely useful.

One last use for symbolic links is for saving disk space. If you've got files that would ordinarily have to be duplicated in many different places on a system, you've got the option of just placing a single file and then creating links to that location.

No matter why you create a logical link, its permissions are always those of the target file. However, the link file will have its own list of permissions, which are a little misleading:

```
lrwxrwxrwx   1   karen   karen      4 May 30 13:52 new.sh -> old.sh
```

Although every permission bit appears to be enabled, this is just the way links are displayed. Notice that the symbolic link file even points to the target file in the listing, making tracing the link quite simple.

A symbolic link does not have to point to an existing file, so you can create the link before you place the target, or you can delete the target without worrying about links that point to it. Of course, anybody trying to follow the link will be flummoxed.

Hard Links

If you specify the **ln** command without the **-s** option, which makes a symbolic link, you get what's called a hard link.

```
millerm@romans ~> ln ~albers/wassup.avi ~/avi
```

A hard link is a little different in that it literally points to the same place on the filesystem as the real file does. In fact, as long as there are any hard links pointing to a file, deleting the file won't actually free up that space on the system. As far as the Linux system knows, the file still exists. That can make things a bit confusing, and because the **ls -l** command doesn't show hard links, it's even less likely that you'll want to use hard links.

SCHEDULING MAINTENANCE

While Windows 98, NT, and Windows 2000 have task scheduling features, they're somewhat limited compared to what you'll find on most any Linux system. While Windows attempts to insulate the user from the nitty-gritty tuning and tweaking by simply providing ways to launch a program on a schedule, Linux allows you to run existing programs, shell scripts of your own devising, or anything else your heart desires. This makes maintenance tasks very easy to schedule.

Tools for Scheduling

There are two primary tools Linux uses for scheduling jobs. The **at** commands allow delayed execution of jobs, while cron jobs execute jobs on an ongoing, scheduled basis. While both are useful for administrative and other tasks, you've got a better chance of never using an **at** command than a **cron** job.

at Commands

The **at** commands are used to schedule a task or a set of tasks for some point in the future. Details of your options for specifying the time of execution can be gotten from the man page, but I'd like to illustrate the flexibility of the tool with this example:

```
millerm@romans ~> at -f mysql_tidy.sh teatime
```

This statement causes the system to launch the mysql_tidy.sh script at 4:00 in the afternoon. Isn't that cute? You can specify the time in a variety of ways, including this one:

```
millerm@romans ~> at -f sync_time.sh now + 15 minutes
```

As an administrator, you can limit access to the **at** command using the /etc/at.allow and /etc/at.deny files; placing an account name in the at.allow file gives that user permission to use the **at** command, while placing the name in the at.deny file prevents the user from executing **at** commands.

It's also possible to manage the **at** command queue, using the **atq** and **atrm** commands. If you run **atq**, you can see the contents of the **at** command queue, which might look like this:

```
millerm@romans ~> atq
1    2000-05-30    14:25 a
2    2000-05-30    14:30 a
```

The first column indicates the job number. The second is the execution date, and the third is the execution time. The fourth column shows the queue being used; unless you specify a different queue, the **at** command defaults to the "a" queue.

To remove one of those jobs from the queue before it's executed, you can use the atrm command; just specify the job number you want to cancel, as shown here:

```
millerm@romans ~> atrm 2
```

A slight variation on the **at** command is the **batch** command. Instead of putting the job off until a specified time, this tool executes the job when the load on the system is low enough. While the default load value should work fine, you can designate your own threshold level. This is great for big processing or housecleaning tasks that need to be done but shouldn't slow down other tasks.

Cron Jobs

If you want to schedule a job to run more than once, the **at** command isn't much good. Fortunately, the cron daemon exists to perform these very tasks. The crond daemon (there are others in use, but this seems to be the most common cron tool) becomes active every minute, checking for scheduled jobs in various locations, launching any scheduled to be executed at the current time, and then dozing off again.

While different distributions have somewhat different implementations of the cron details, I like what Red Hat and others do using a master file called /etc/crontab. Rather than having you edit the file to add scripts as you need them, this approach makes the /etc/crontab contents run the scripts in several directories at different intervals.

The lines below are partial contents of the /etc/crontab on my system (which I've edited with the reminder of what each column means):

```
# Min Hr Day-of-month Month Day-of-wk run-by command
01 * * * * root run-parts /etc/cron.hourly
02 4 * * * root run-parts /etc/cron.daily
22 4 * * 0 root run-parts /etc/cron.weekly
42 4 1 * * root run-parts /etc/cron.monthly
```

The first non-comment line runs the **run-parts /etc/cron.hourly** command at one minute past each hour. The next line runs the **run-parts /etc/cron.daily** command at 4:02 each morning. The next line runs the **run-parts /etc/cron.weekly** command at 4:22 in the morning every Sunday. The last line runs the **run-parts /etc/cron.monthly** command at 4:42 in the morning on the first day of each month.

As you might guess, the **/usr/bin/run-parts** command runs the executables in a given directory, so if you want to run a particular program or script every day, you can just drop a copy in the /etc/cron.daily directory, and the cron daemon will faithfully execute it every day.

Root and other users can also create their own crontab files using the **crontab** command. Running **crontab -e** brings up the user's existing crontab file, if any, in a text editor. If there's not already a crontab file for the user, a new one is created. You can specify your own intervals in this file, which is saved to /var/spool/cron/crontabs; the filename is set to be the originating user's account name.

Jobs to Schedule

So what do you schedule with these options? The sky is the limit, really. If you want to reboot a server once a week, you can do that by running the **shutdown** command from a cron job. But because you're trying to get used to doing without excessive rebooting, here are some other suggestions for you:

▼ Schedule backups.

■ Synchronize time.

■ Send scheduled messages.

▲ Perform other maintenance tasks.

Backups

This is the core scheduled maintenance task anyway, isn't it? While you can use a full-blown commercial backup utility, a script that creates a dump or tars some essential directories to tape may be all you need. You can make the script you use as complicated as you want. Here's a simple sample script that creates a compressed archive from each user's home directory.

```
#!/bin/sh
# Called by crontab for root using this line:
# 0 19 * * 2-6 /usr/local/sbin/home_bak
D=`date +"%Y%m%d"`
tar cpvzf /bak/homebak/peter_kilner_$D.tgz /home/pkilner/*
tar cpvzf /bak/homebak/david_li_$D.tgz /home/dli/*
tar cpvzf /bak/homebak/deb_kilner_$D.tgz /home/dkilner/*
tar cpvzf /bak/homebak/omar_keblawi_$D.tgz /home/okeblawi/*
tar cpvzf /bak/homebak/eric_chamness_$D.tgz /home/echamness/*
```

In real life, I save files like these to a large hard disk partition, moving the files between directories as the backups age for a few days. A separate cron job writes the files to tape and rotates the files.

Synch Time

Whether you're on a big network or a little one, having your system's clocks synched up can make life lots easier, especially if you or some users will be building lots of software, as compilers can be quite fussy about time discrepancies between systems. One way to overcome this is to use the **ntpdate** program to synch your system's clock with that of a time server. You'll have to supply your own time server addresses, but a script like this one, dropped into the /etc/cron.daily directory, should do the trick:

```
#!/bin/sh
/usr/sbin/ntpdate  \
                   ntptime.msaddicts.com  \
                   time.prolificinc.com
```

Send Scheduled Messages

There are all kinds of tasks you can schedule that fit into this category, but you might consider sending yourself messages once a week or so that give you basic system information. The results of a **df** command, which tells you how much disk space is free on each of the system's partitions, might be a good start.

You can set the mail recipient a couple of different ways. Crontab files often include a MAILTO statement that specifies the user to whom output should be mailed; it can be specified like this:

```
MAILTO="millerm"
10 5 * * 0 /bin/df
```

You can also specify the output destination on the line with the command itself:

```
10 5 * * 0 /bin/df 1>david@romans 2>millerm@romans
```

This command will send standard output from the command to one user, and error messages (if any) to the other.

Other Maintenance Tasks

I hope you've got many exciting ideas about what jobs you want to schedule using **cron** or **at**. Here's one more suggestion that I recall reading some time ago in an early version of one of Matt Welsh's documents on getting started with Linux (for the latest versions of the documents he started, see the Linux Documentation Project at **http://www.linuxdoc.org/**).

You can schedule periodic checks of the filesystems on your Linux systems to make sure that they're in good health, especially if the system doesn't go down very often and therefore isn't getting checked very often at startup. If you're going to be checking filesystems, you should unmount them first; you don't want people touching the contents while the check is going on.

It would probably be best to write a full-blown script to accomplish this task in your environment, but the simple version might look like this:

```
/bin/umount /dev/sda2
/sbin/e2fsck -fpv /dev/sda2
/usr/bin/shutdown -r 5
```

This script would be dropped into the /etc/cron.monthly directory. It first unmounts the partition that will be checked (which excludes the root partition, which needs to be mounted while the system is running from it). Next, it runs the filesystem checking utility, forcing a check even if it doesn't look necessary, and repairing any damage it finds. Because there may have been corrected damage, we reboot when the check is done.

That's not a very elegant solution; a more sophisticated script could do other checks and might only restart the system if damage was detected. Or it might consider the current load on the system before blithely rebooting the server. If enhancements like that make sense to you, try your hand at writing a new script. Just test it on a non-production system, if you please.

CHAPTER 15

Step 12: Free Your Office

The steps we've taken so far have been focused on the process of making Linux a useful platform for a person who is accustomed to a Windows environment. But now the time has come to focus on the reason we tell ourselves we use computers: Productivity. If a Linux system can't run the tools you need as part of your daily work, its overall effectiveness will be greatly limited.

While plenty of people employ their Linux systems as web or file and print servers or as programming workstations and stop there, I hope you're ready to face Step 12: Having become Linux users as a result of these Steps, we continue by employing Linux-based office applications.

OPEN SOURCE OR FREEWARE OFFICE APPLICATIONS

You may recall from Chapter 1 that there has been some controversy over what is meant by "free software" and "open source" software. I don't intend to pick at that scab; I am primarily interested in solutions that are currently available without a charge, and these packages are. Whether you should be supporting their efforts is an entirely different matter, so I encourage you to go with your conscience. I'll try to point out the question marks I'm aware of as I discuss each package.

StarOffice

The StarOffice office suite is now part of the Sun Microsystems stable of software, which makes some people more interested in the product and makes others quite skittish about it. If you look past the politics of the situation, though, you'll find that StarOffice is a remarkably complete set of office productivity tools. Because StarOffice is widely available, relatively mature, and includes most of the features former Windows users want, I'll spend a little more time on it than on some of the other tools. Because Sun has released the source code to StarOffice, you can expect the product to improve.

What StarOffice Includes

The StarOffice tools include the essential document processing tool that can open Microsoft Word documents. A variety of HTML file templates are included for rapid creation of web pages. There's a spreadsheet, a web browser, a presentation tool with full graphing features, and a database builder/front end. Also included are a personal task list and scheduling application. A mail and Usenet news tool, vector drawing program, image editor, and formula builder round out the package. All in all, it contains enough functionality to meet most users' desktop application needs.

There is a downside to this massive conflagration of functionality, however. StarOffice has a monolithic look and feel, integrating the many tools into a single workspace, as shown in Figure 15-1.

While the design keeps all the different tool windows accessible, which can be a problem under X Windows, it also makes working with the tools cumbersome at times. The

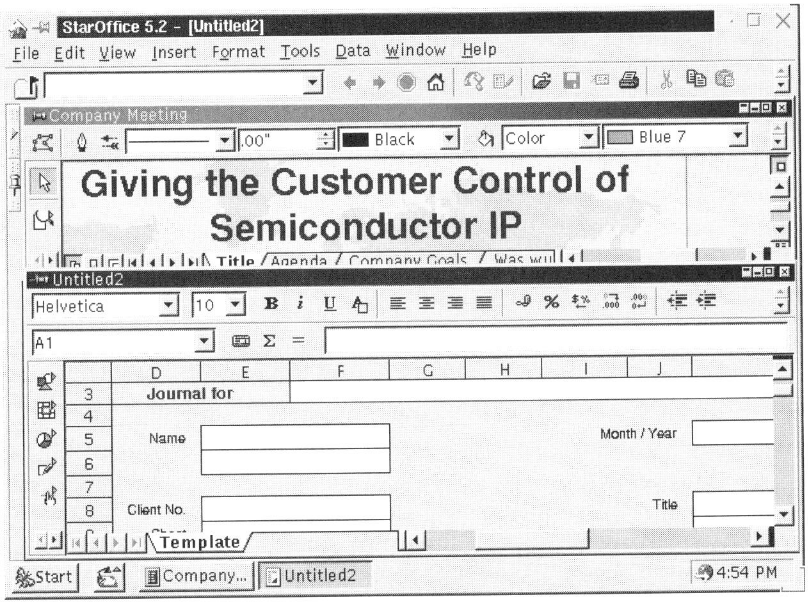

Figure 15-1.   StarOffice combines many desktop applications with a single user interface

idea of having to open an interface designed to help you access that whole list of tools, just to get at a spreadsheet, seems a little inefficient. Plans to modularize StarOffice are already afoot.

The StarOffice Installation Process

The installation process is similar to what you'll find on a Windows system; in fact, one of the great features of the StarOffice package is that it works across multiple platforms, including Windows and Unix. To get things started, you can load the CD-ROM that comes with several major Linux distributions and run the setup program appropriate to the operating system you're using.

If you're running Red Hat 7, StarOffice is included with the Deluxe Workstation package. The suite is included in RPM form on the CD-ROM impressively labeled "Third-party Workstation Server Applications Released with Red Hat Linux 7." To install the program from this CD-ROM, follow these steps:

1. After mounting the CD-ROM, become root, and then install the rpm:

```
root@romans /root > rpm -Uvh /mnt/cdrom/StarOffice/StarOffice*.rpm
StarOffice              ###########################################
```

2. Log in using your regular user account and run the setup file from the installation destination:

```
millerm@romans ~ > /opt/office52/program/setup
```

3. You'll be greeted by a window welcoming you to the installation program. Click Next to continue.

4. An informational file will appear next; read through it for information that may be relevant to your situation, and click Next when you're done.

5. The license agreement will appear; read through it, and if you agree to its terms, click Accept.

6. A user data form will appear, allowing you to enter customizing information such as your name, address, phone number, and job title. When you've filled out as much as you care to, click Next.

7. The next screen offers you either the Standard Workstation Installation or the Standard Local Installation. Because you installed the RPM onto the system already, you might as well take advantage of it by selecting the Workstation Installation. This will use much less space in the user area than the Local Installation option. Click Next to continue.

8. Select the installation directory, which defaults to ~/office52. This directory should be fine, so click Next.

9. Confirm creation of this directory, allowing it to be created by clicking Yes. Then click Complete to continue the installation.

10. The next screen shows your Java Runtime Environment; StarOffice will run without one, so you can click OK whether or not the installation process found one. Installation will begin, and files will be copied and components registered.

11. You will receive a message indicating that StarOffice has been added to the KDE Panel, but that you'll have to restart KDE to make the menu item available. If you use GNOME, you may still be able to get to the KDE menu if you haven't removed the KDE entry from the main panel menu. Click OK to continue and then click Complete to end the installation process.

To run StarOffice, restart KDE and use the icon, or run ~/office52/soffice from an xterm. When you first run StarOffice, it will ask if it can use Netscape to configure Internet-related information to help you connect through proxy servers or other tricky setups, which is a nice touch. Unfortunately, once you get everything installed, you may be disappointed by the overall performance of the tools. At times, loading files and switching between applications can be sluggish even on my 500MHz system with 512MB RAM. On the other hand, the functionality is quite good, and if you have used an office suite from Corel, Lotus, or Microsoft, you should be able to navigate this one easily.

StarOffice's greatest strengths are its comprehensive list of tools and features, Sun's promise to release a version as free software, its compatibility with Microsoft document files, and its multiplatform support. Its biggest limitation is its performance. Learn more about StarOffice at **http://www.sun.com/products/staroffice/**.

KOffice

The KOffice suite is still under development, but it is looking promising, especially if you like the look and feel of the KDE desktop. Like the other KDE applications, KOffice tools are reasonably well integrated into the desktop environment, so they take on the attributes of any special themes you're using.

Like the StarOffice suite, KOffice contains an ambitious array of tools; in fact, the only tools KOffice doesn't include are the mail tool and web browser, but these are already available for KDE without the KOffice package, so you're covered there, too. The KOffice packages include:

▼   KWord

■   KSpread

■   KPresenter

■   KIllustrator

■   KImageShop

■   Katabase

■   KFormula

■   KChart

▲   KImage (a viewer)

While KOffice looks good and is much more trim than the StarOffice programs, it still lacks many "must-have" features, and some of the pieces are not currently usable. Even for those that are, there are still problems. For example, the KWord application does not yet have an operational filter for importing or producing Microsoft Word documents. Such filters are a must in nearly every environment, so that's something to keep in mind as you consider your options.

KOffice is also not as platform-portable as StarOffice. It relies heavily on the KDE packages, and I'd be surprised if there are plans to move the application away from the desktop environment. At this time KOffice is really only an option for those who don't need to continue supporting Windows clients or Microsoft document files. Have a look at **http://koffice.kde.org/** to see if that's still the case as you read this.

Abiword

Unlike KOffice, Abiword is available on a wide variety of platforms, including Windows. Like KOffice, the current release of Abiword is pre-1.0. However, the overall functionality of the tool is more complete, and it's definitely a smaller piece of software than either KOffice or StarOffice.

One thing you give up with Abiword is the integration between tools that both KOffice and StarOffice offer. Abiword is a word-processing package with desktop publishing features, period. On the other hand, it's also usable and truly open source, so if you're looking mainly for document creation capability, it's not a bad choice.

For more information on Abiword's current functionality, check out the homepage at **http://www.abiword.org/**.

Siag Office

While the other packages in this category serve up typical office application functionality with some unique features, Siag Office is truly iconoclastic. For starters, you can run the Siag spreadsheet in text mode or under X Windows. The spreadsheet is written in and supports input from the Scheme dialect of the Lisp programming language. It offers one more fairly unique feature: It will serve as a "one shot" web server, allowing you to share a document across the Internet.

The Siag Office word processor, Pathetic Writer, sports integration with Siag, but it relies on external file-filtering programs to get you sharing files with colleagues who are still using Microsoft Office products. The Egon Animator tool rounds out this quirky office package with aplomb. Egon allows you to make simple animations (well, perhaps somebody with more skill than I have can make complex animation), giving you tight control over what each element is doing.

I don't see Siag Office getting a large following from the formerly Microsoft crowd; its sensibilities are a little too programmer-oriented for most Windows users. But for those of us who learned Scheme in U.C. Berkeley's undergraduate computer science program, and have never had cause to use it again, it's intriguing. For anyone who can take advantage of its unique features, it's a pretty cool suite. Learn more at **http://siag.nu/**.

COMMERCIAL OFFICE APPLICATIONS

The preceding tools were all either open source or available for free for end users. That's not the only type of application you can run on Linux systems, though, and some of the other products are worth investigating. In particular, the Applixware suite and the Linux port of Corel's WordPerfect may be suitable for your use.

Applixware

Applix Inc.'s Applixware is a full-featured office suite available on multiple platforms. The Applixware suite includes Words, a full-featured word processor; Graphics, a drawing and diagramming tool; Presents, a presentation graphics package; Email, a flexible mail client; and Data, which helps you build and access databases. Builder is an object-oriented programming tool that's useful for small-scale application design, not to mention integrating other applications with the Applix tools.

One strength of Applixware is their document filters, which are about on par with the StarOffice filters. Highly formatted Word documents won't look as nice in either product as they do in their native application, but simpler documents look and work just fine.

Whether you'd consider a rollout of Applixware to your Windows systems, or you'd only want to equip Linux users with the suite, it's worth consideration. It's not as ponderous as StarOffice, though it's not quite as elegantly designed, either. And while the price is greater than zero (it's $99 for the full suite as I write this), it's nowhere near the price of a Windows-based suite.

For more information on Applixware, see **http://www.vistasource.com/**. There's also information on Applix' open source offerings for application development at **http:// shelf.sourceforge.net/**.

WordPerfect

Corel has done a nice job with its entry into the Linux application suite arena, WordPerfect Office 2000 for Linux. The Standard edition includes the Linux versions of some desktop applications that have been around for quite some time: WordPerfect for word processing and page layout, and the Quattro Pro spreadsheet. Corel Presentations and CorelCentral, which includes an address book and calendaring/appointment reminder features, round out the package. The Deluxe version adds the user-friendly Paradox database program, which I found every bit as easy to use as Microsoft's Access. Figure 15-2 shows a desktop with WordPerfect Office 2000 in action.

Both versions of the suite come bundled with Corel Linux, so if you're interested in testing the packages, you can take advantage of the all-in-one packaging to make your evaluation process a little easier. Installation under other distributions was a snap using the graphical installation procedure.

The WordPerfect suite, which looked a little more trim than the StarOffice suite, was no speed demon; I was watching the disk activity on my desktop system and wondering whether it was time to take advantage of the dip in memory prices. The tools are mostly slow to open and close, though, and seemed to respond well as I used them. If you're not devoted to open source or zero price software, I'd recommend the WordPerfect package, which did an acceptable job opening Microsoft Office files and has Windows-based versions available. One downside is that WordPerfect's maker, Corel, has been in dire financial straits for some time, making its future a little questionable. And a recent influx of funds from Microsoft isn't likely to bolster Corel's Linux strategy.

OTHER BUSINESS APPLICATIONS

While I don't want to describe every major business product available for Linux, I would like to mention some highlights that you might want to investigate further. Linux users enjoy a wide range of no- or low-cost programming tools, database software, web tools, file utilities, graphics production programs, collaboration software, and "business entertainment" packages.

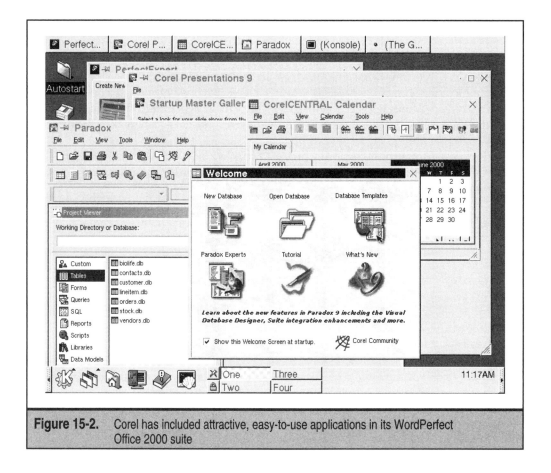

Figure 15-2. Corel has included attractive, easy-to-use applications in its WordPerfect Office 2000 suite

Programming Tools

Many Linux distributions include compilers or interpreters for a wide array of languages, including Assembly language, BASIC, C, C++, FORTRAN, Java, LISP, Pascal, Perl, Python, Scheme, and Tcl/Tk. Many development tools and aids are available for these resources, and one of the better places for information I've found is the Freshmeat application index at **http://freshmeat.net/appindex/development/**. Commercial development tools are available, but since I haven't used them, I don't have any recommendations for you.

Databases

The major database vendors all have products available for Linux, but some of the widely used packages are not from commercial companies; despite the reduced prices (often to $0), the big database companies are charging for their products. While MySQL lacks the transaction protection features of some of the other products here, it's readily available, and many ISPs install it for their web-hosting services, so if you just want to work with a database, it's probably a good choice. Table 15-1 shows some of the major options available to Linux users.

Web Tools

There is a mind-bogglingly large number of web tools available for Linux, both for clients and for Linux servers. On the client side, there's the Lynx text-based web browser (useful for pulling that new video driver off the Web when you can't get into X Windows and Netscape). There are many bookmarking utilities to make your surfing life easier. There are preprocessing programs and conversion programs to pump data from non-web sources into HTML pages for you. There are HTML editors.

Check Freshmeat's web tools archive (**http://freshmeat.net/appindex/web/tools.html**) for other useful programs, including ones that will convert your Microsoft Active Server Pages (ASP) to more Linux-friendly formats. Or you can look for the Apache server extension that allows ASP pages to run from an Apache server.

There are online shopping systems, including YAMS (Yet Another Merchant System), which is homepaged at **http://yams.sourceforge.net/**. Another transaction management tool is Akopia Interchange (**http://www.akopia.com/**). Both products are distributed under the GNU General Public License (GPL).

Company or Project	Product	Web Site
Sybase	Adaptive Server Enterprise	http://www.sybase.com/linux
IBM	DB2 Universal Database for Linux	http://www-4.ibm.com/software/data/db2/linux/
Informix	Several, including Informix Dynamic Server	http://www.informix.com/informix/products/linux/
Hughes Technologies	mSQL	http://www.hughes.com.au/
TCX DataKonsult AB	MySQL	http://www.mysql.org/
Oracle	Several offerings, including Oracle 8*i*	http://platforms.oracle.com/linux/
PostgreSQL Project	PostgreSQL	http://www.postgresql.org/

Table 15-1. Relational Databases Running on Linux

If you are building a large web site, you might consider looking into PHP and Zope. PHP is a scripting language designed to make creation of dynamic web content fast and easy. It is similar in functionality to Microsoft's Active Server Pages (ASP). It provides access to many database programs, including Access and SQL Server. PHP is used at many public web sites, and the administrators I know really like managing it. The PHP homepage is at **http://www.php.net/**.

Zope is another option for database-backed web site creation. It's an object-oriented application system for building web sites, and it comes with its own web server (or you can hook it into Apache if you prefer). Zope makes heavy use of the Python programming language, but you don't have to use much Python if you don't want to. You have control over the objects that you create for the web site, which allows you to be very precise about the security you impose on the site. The downside is that while Zope is attractive, it's not always intuitive, so the learning curve may be steep for a little while. See what you think with a visit to **http://www.zope.org/**.

There are many more web-related applications and tools available from the usual places: Freshmeat and Sourceforge would be good sites from which to start your search.

File Utilities

I've mentioned some of the utilities in previous chapters, including the compression and archiving options (gzip, bzip2, compress, zip, tar, and others). Linux distributions also tend to include image viewers that can display, and sometimes convert, AVI, GIF, JPEG, MPEG, Postscript, PDF, PNG, TIFF, MPEG, AVI, and QuickTime files.

There are also many different file managers available within distributions and on the Web. There are alternate filesystems, such as the Reiserfs, which is a journaling filesystem that works with Linux. You might also be interested in automatic distribution and file-mirroring utilities such as rdist and mirror.

Other file utilities include CD-ROM writers, MP3 rippers and burners, sound file players, command-line spell checkers, and heaven knows what else. If you need it, the chances are that someone else needed it, too. So check Freshmeat and other Internet web sites for utilities and procedures to do what you're looking for.

Graphics Production

The Gimp isn't just a bit character in Pulp Fiction, it's the GNU Image Manipulation Program, an extensible and profusely featured program that allows you to retouch photos, create images, convert graphic file formats, and even do screen captures. Imagine, all of that functionality, and it's free. What could be better? Well, it's also well documented and easy to use, even for an unskilled artist like me. Figure 15-3 shows The Gimp in action.

A distribution isn't really complete without a copy of The Gimp, but in case yours is missing, or you want more information, you can consult the project's web site at **http://www.gimp.org/**.

Don't forget that several of the free office software packages also include image-viewing, creation, and editing tools. These tend to be as powerful as most of the PC-based packages you've used; though if you're accustomed to a Mac, you'll undoubtedly be disappointed. But don't come whining to me.

Note that there are also several tools for converting files to and from the PDF format. For example, the ps2pdf program, which is included with Red Hat and many other distributions, converts a PostScript file to a .pdf file suitable for viewing in Adobe Acrobat. While this isn't as powerful as using Acrobat, it's cheaper. Acrobat Reader is freely available for Linux, just as it's available for other platforms. See **http://www.adobe.com/** for more information.

Collaboration

The collaborative process entails many different aspects, including revision control software such as CVS (Concurrent Versions System), which is a repository for maintaining source files, usually program code. CVS makes version control easy, and it's widely used in the Linux community and elsewhere. Check out the FAQ document at **http://www.cs.utah.edu/dept/old/texinfo/cvs/cvs_toc.html**.

I used to be a very enthusiastic Lotus Notes administrator; it's one of the few technologies that really excited me when I began using it. Notes was the first widely deployed groupware package in the PC world, and I've always liked its collaborative features and powerful application set. It's not a match for my current environment, but I still think it's

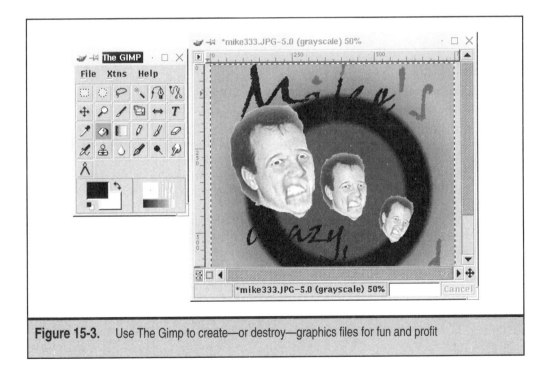

Figure 15-3. Use The Gimp to create—or destroy—graphics files for fun and profit

a fine product, and the server will run on Linux. If you're interested in Notes, you can find more information at **http://www.lotus.com/home.nsf/welcome/domino**. Follow the Linux link for Linux-specific information.

Bugzilla is the Mozilla Project's bug-tracking system, which uses a web interface and stores bug reports and resolution information in a MySQL database. It's not a trivial task to set up Bugzilla, but it's a pretty useful tool once you've configured it, and it's outstanding for the price you'll pay. More information is available at **http://www.mozilla.org/bugs/**.

The Apache Group's Jetspeed is a web-based information portal designed to handle data from many different sources, including XML files, SMTP data, and Web-specific formats and protocols. More information can be found at **http://java.apache.org/jetspeed/site/overview.html**.

Business Entertainment

Okay, they're games. But I enjoy them, and when I'm not pulling all-nighters trying to finish a manuscript, I like to spend a few minutes now and then playing games on my computer. Most of the mainstream Linux distributions include an assortment of games that makes the Windows options pale in comparison. Furthermore, there are many text-based games, including variations on my old favorite, Rogue, and many X Windows games available on the Web. I was recently embarrassed by my performance against three computer-controlled Scrabble players, and I've passed the time during a big compile playing a Breakout clone.

But what about the cool commercial games that line the shelves of Fry's Electronics and other computer retailers? Some of the older ones will run using the Wine Windows emulator—and we're talking about Starcraft, not just The Bard's Tale. Though, come to think of it, it would be fun to play Bard's Tale again. So that's one option; see **http://www.winehq.com/** for more information on Windows emulation via Wine.

Several popular games have been released on Linux, and you can certainly get versions of DOOM and Quake that run under Linux. For more information on the latest game news, try **http://www.linuxgames.com/** and **http://happypenguin.org/**. But for right now, the real player in making mainstream games available on Linux is Loki (**http://www.lokigames.com/**). They've worked with game makers to get Linux versions on the shelves. You can order everything from Civilization to Myth II, Heretic II, Heroes of Might and Magic III, Heavy Gear II, to Railroad Tycoon II Gold and Eric's Ultimate Solitaire from their web site, and these games are on the shelves at the computer stores I frequent.

Because all work and no play is no life for a penguin.

APPENDIX

Linux Resources

LINUX INFORMATION SOURCES

There are tons, heaps, and loads of information sources out there. Shucks, given how helpful Microsoft has been in explaining things about Linux, you might figure somebody else would have some information to share as well, right? There tends to be lots of inter-linking between Linux sites, so you should be able to gather lots of information by visiting just a few of these sites.

Publications and News

My favorite place for Linux news is the Linux Weekly News site's daily updates page, but there are many other good sites. Here are some of them:

Linux Weekly News	http://lwn.net
LWN Daily	http://lwn.net/daily
Linux Journal	http://www.linuxjournal.com/
Linux Magazine	http://www.linux-mag.com/
OSOpinion	http://www.osopinion.com/
LinuxWorld	http://www.linuxworld.com/
Linux Today	http://www.linuxtoday.com
Red Herring	http://www.redherring.com/
Linux Gazette	http://www.linuxgazette.com/
Slashdot	http://slashdot.org/
GeekNews	http://www.geeknews.org/

Linux Information

Linux users don't live by news alone, but also by documentation, position statements, and other sources of information.

Linux Documentation Project	http://www.linuxdoc.org/
Linux Software Map	http://www.execpc.com/lsm/
Free Patents	http://www.freepatents.org/
SecurityPortal	http://securityportal.com/linuxtopnews.html
Linuxpower	http://linuxpower.com/
Linux International	http://www.li.org/
LinuxSecurity.com	http://www.linuxsecurity.com/
Linux Security Audit Project	http://lsap.org/

Geek.com	http://www.geek.com/
Linux.com	http://www.linux.com/
RootPrompt	http://rootprompt.org/
Freedom Forum	http://www.freedomforum.org/technology/
Open Source Initiative	http://www.opensource.org
Temple of the Screaming Penguin	http://www.screaming-penguin.com/
Linux Center	http://www.portalux.com/
Linux Printing	http://www.linuxprinting.org/

Kernel News

It's not easy to keep up with the Linux kernel when development is flying fast and furious. While you could subscribe to the Linux-kernel mailing list, most people won't want that volume of detailed mail, so these sites are a way of getting highlighted information about what's going on.

Kernel Notes	http://www.kernelnotes.org
Kernel Traffic	http://kt.linuxcare.com
Kernel Journal	http://www.linuxcare.com/developers/kernel
Linux Kernel Archives	http://www.kernel.org

If you are interested in subscribing to the Linux-kernel mailing list, see the FAQ document at **http://www.tux.org/lkml/**. Or see if you can access the **muc.lists.linux-kernel** newsgroup, where the email from the list is posted.

Software

Half the fun of Linux is finding all the software people are working on, and helping out or putting it to use yourself. Here are some places to find software, and some software you might specifically look for.

Indexes, Etc.

These are searchable indexes of software that runs on Linux (and other operating systems). They're great if you're looking for a specific type of tool or if you're just browsing.

AppWatch	http://appwatch.com/Linux/
Freshmeat	http://www.freshmeat.net/
SourceForge	http://sourceforge.net/

Individual Tools, Products, and Projects

I've mentioned most of these pieces of software in the course of this book. If you were interested in one, but don't want to go leafing back to find it, you may find the reference here. Other links are contained in Chapter 15, in particular.

Apache	http://www.apache.org/
Beowulf clustering	http://www.beowulf.org
Gnome	http://www.gnome.org/
ht://Dig	http://www.htdig.org/
KDE	http://www.kde.org/
MagicPoint	http://www.mew.org/mgp/
Midgard	http://www.midgard-project.org/
Mozilla	http://www.mozilla.org/
MySQL	http://www.mysql.org/
Themes	http://themes.org/
Sudo	http://www.courtesan.com/sudo
WINE	http://www.winehq.com/
Zope	http://www.zope.org/

Personalities

This list is perhaps not as long as it should be, and Linus' page won't bowl you over. But these are the pages I thought were most important and/or interesting:

Linus Torvalds	http://www.cs.helsinki.fi/~torvalds/
Richard Stallman	http://www.stallman.org/
Alan Cox	http://www.linux.org.uk/diary/
Alan's wife Telsa	http://roadrunner.swansea.linux.org.uk/~hobbit/diary.html
Bruce Perens	http://perens.com/
Eric Raymond	http://www.tuxedo.org/~esr/

LINUX DISTRIBUTIONS

You can't swing a dead cat without hitting someone with a custom Linux distribution. But while many are built, it seems that few are chosen, and there's a certain rate at which the smaller distributions go defunct. These links are all active as I write this, and I suspect that most of these distributions will still exist as you read it. But I promise nothing. Nothing, I tell you!

The Big Boys

Unless you've got a reason to consider something else, I recommend that you stick with one of the major distributions. You've got enough on your mind without having to second-guess your distribution decision. If you're still uncertain about which one you want to use, I suggest you default to Red Hat.

Caldera OpenLinux	http://www.calderasystems.com/
Complete Linux	http://www.macmillansoftware.com/
Corel Linux	http://linux.corel.com/
Debian GNU/Linux	http://www.debian.org/
Mandrake	http://www.linux-mandrake.com/
Red Hat	http://www.redhat.com/
Slackware	http://www.slackware.com
SuSE	http://www.suse.com/
TurboLinux	http://www.turbolinux.com

Non-Intel, Non-PC Focus

While most of these distributions target Mac hardware, one is very much not like others; the Think Blue distribution runs on IBM System/390 computers.

Black Lab Linux	http://www.blacklablinux.com/
HA Linux	http://linux-ha.org/
LinuxPPC	http://www.linuxppc.com/
MkLinux	http://www.mklinux.org/
Think Blue Linux	http://linux.s390.org/
Yellow Dog Linux	http://www.yellowdoglinux.com/

Embedded Systems

Linux is making inroads into embedded systems; its price, stability, and potential for running lean make it a tempting choice. These distributions focus on embedded systems:

Blue Cat	http://www.lynuxworks.com/products/whatisbcl.html
Embedix	http://www.lineo.com/

Etlinux	http://www.prosa.it/etlinux/
Hard Hat Linux	http://www.mvista.com/products/
LEM	http://linux-embedded.com/
Royal Linux	http://www.isdcorp.com/company_info/RoyalLinux.shtml
White Dwarf Linux	http://www.emjembedded.com/linux/dimmpc.html

Security First

Consider these distributions the rad-hard (radiation-hardened) options. Actually, that sounds like a good name for a secure distribution, "Rad Hard Linux." Anyway, if you're a security freak, consider these distributions:

Bastille Linux	http://www.bastille-linux.org/
Immunix	http://www.immunix.org/
KRUD	http://www.tummy.com/krud/

Non-English

I've done my best to find distributions that aren't targeted to English speakers (actually, one listed here is targeted toward UK users, but this still seemed like the place to put it). Because I don't read most of these languages, I may be slightly off here and there.

Chinese

Blue Point Linux	http://www.bluepoint.com.cn/
Linpus	http://www.linpus.com.tw/
Xteam Linux	http://www.xteamlinux.com.cn/

Finnish

Best Linux	http://www.bestlinux.net/

French

eXecutive Linux	http://www.exelinux.com/
PingOO Linux	http://www.pingoo.org/

German

Halloween Linux	http://www.halloween-linux.de/
PX86 Linux	http://www.ix86linux.de/

| Red Linux | http://www.red-linux.de/ |

Italian

| Bad Penguin Linux | http://www.badpenguin.org/ |

Japanese

Kondara MNU/Linux	http://www.kondara.org/
LASER5 Linux	http://www.laser5.co.jp/
Linux MLD	http://www.mlb.co.jp/
Plamo Linux	http://www.linet.gr.jp/~kojima/Plamo/
Vine Linux	http://vinelinux.org/

Korean

| Alzza Linux | http://www.alzzalinux.com/ |
| RunOnCD | http://my.netian.com/~cgchoi/ |

Polish

| PLD | http://www.pld.org.pl/ |

Portuguese

| Conectiva Linux | http://www.conectiva.com/ |

Russian/Ukrainian

| Black Cat Linux | http://www.blackcatlinux.com/ |
| KSI-Linux | http://www.ksi-linux.com/ |

Spanish

ESware Linux	http://www.esware.com/
Eurielec Linux	http://www.eurielec.etsit.upm.es/linux/
HispaFuentes	http://www.hispafuentes.com/
LinuxPPP	http://www.os.com.mx/
One Disk Linux	http://linux.apostols.org/guru/wen/

Thai

Kaiwal Linux   http://www.kaiwal.com/

UK

Definite Linux   http://www.definitelinux.net/

Visually Impaired Users

I hope to see more distributions and applications focusing on the issue of access by physically challenged users. A list of frequently asked questions for visually impaired Linux users can be found at **http://leb.net/blinux/**.

ZipSpeak   http://www.linux-speakup.org/zipspeak.html

Others

These distributions have another hook, or what makes them unique is so elusive that I couldn't tell what it is. If anybody reading this is thinking about creating a new distribution, I suggest that you put a little more thought into what distinguishes you from the field than some of the distributions I've come across. Trying to be the "best distribution" isn't actually helpful to a user who's thinking about downloading your software, do you see?

Runs atop Windows

Armed Linux   http://www.armed.net/
Dragon Linux   http://www.c-cubedinc.com/dragon/
LoopLinux   http://www.tux.org/pub/people/kent-robotti/looplinux/index.html
Phat Linux   http://www.phatlinux.com/
WinLinux   http://www.winlinux.net/

Server/Router/Firewall Focus

Bifrost   http://www.data.slu.se/bifrost/index.en.html
Coyote Linux   http://www.coyotelinux.com/coyote.html
DLite   http://opensrc.org/dlite/dlite.html
floppyfw   http://www.zelow.no/floppyfw/
FREESCO   http://www.linuxsupportline.com/~router/
Linux Router Project http://www.linuxrouter.org/

ShareTheNet   http://www.sharethenet.com/
Trinux   http://www.trinux.org/
Whole Linux   http://www.wholelinux.com/

Old Hardware

TINY Linux   http://tiny.seul.org/
tomsrtbt   http://www.toms.net/rb/home.html

Other Distributions

Deep Linux   http://www.deeplinux.com/
Elfstone Linux   http://www.elflinux.com/
Gentus Linux (ABIT)   http://www.gentus.com/
Independence   http://independence.seul.org/
Libranet Linux Desktop   http://www.libranet.com/
Peanut Linux   http://metalab.unc.edu/peanut/
PeeWee Linux   http://embedded.adis.on.ca/
Rock Linux   http://www.rocklinux.org/
Stampede Linux   http://www.stampede.org/
Storm Linux   http://www.stormix.com/
Trustix   http://www.trustix.net/
Xdenu   http://xdenu.tcm.hut.fi/

Beginner Focus

easyLinux   http://www.easylinux.com/c/index.html
Floppix   http://floppix.ccai.com/index.html

Schools

OpenClassroom   http://www.openclassroom.org/

Glossary

bash The "Bourne Again Shell," a GNU Project creation that emulates the operation of the standard Bourne shell (sh) but offers more functionality. *See also* shell.

cat A feline, like my Siamese friend Magellan, who spent five years with me but had to go live with a friend when I married a person who's allergic to cats. Also a command that displays the contents of a file to a console, or concatenates two files to make one file. *See also* less, more.

clustering An arrangement of computers in which the systems are treated in certain ways as one unit. A cluster can be used to provide maximum processing power or to provide high availability of resources managed by the clustered servers. Administrators tend to want the cluster to do both things.

cron job While this sounds like something that would happen in a bad ninja movie, it's simply a job that's executed based on chronology. In other words, a cron job is one that's scheduled to be run periodically. You get to determine what the period is.

desktop environment More than a graphical user interface (GUI), a desktop environment is a set of tools that give the GUI desktop an integrated look and feel, providing consistency of interface across the applets commonly associated with the desktop. *See also* window manager, KDE, GNOME.

diff A command-line utility used to compare files and note the differences between them. This is particularly useful when you're attempting to determine differences between two different pieces of programming code or two different versions of a configuration file.

distributions In the Linux context, distributions are sets of programs and kernel code bundled together for distribution to users. While most distributions contain the same basic programs, many manage to distinguish themselves through use of innovative installation procedures, particularly focused program content, or specific approaches to system configuration. People tend to be passionately attached to or repulsed from different distributions. I tend to be passionately attached to a person and find that sort of commitment to a set of software a tad disturbing.

dot files On a Linux system, a file whose name begins with a period is not normally listed when a user views the contents of the directory it's in. Configuration files are often created as dot files to keep users from mistakenly trashing them and to keep them from cluttering up the directory listing. And we would have gotten away with it, too, if it weren't for those meddlesome kids.

environment variable A variable whose contents are shared by the whole environment—usually the shell—is an environment variable. Scripts and programs can use these variables to run correctly in any given environment.

free software This term means different things to different people. Some consider software given without a monetary cost to be free. Others believe that software is only free if its users are free to do with it what they want, including giving it to their neighbors. You make the call. *See also* Free Software Foundation.

Free Software Foundation The FSF (**http://www.fsf.org/**) is an organization committed to the proposition that software should give users the freedom to run the program for any purpose, the freedom to examine and alter the source code, the freedom to redistribute copies as you see fit, and the freedom to enhance the software and redistribute the improvements for mutual benefit. *See also* Richard Stallman.

FUD This acronym refers to "Fear, Uncertainty, and Doubt," which are three of the less honorable tools companies use to combat a rival's perceived advantages. For example, Microsoft attempted to spread FUD by releasing the Linux Myths document.

GNOME GNOME is an open source desktop environment in widespread use, and generally admired for its attractive appearance and extensive flexibility.

GNU This acronym stands for "GNU's Not Unix." It's not at all mandatory that you think that acronym is funny. The GNU Project is devoted to creating a complete Unix-like operating system based entirely on free software. *See also* Free Software Foundation.

grep Grep is a command-line utility used to find a string of characters, sometimes called a *regular expression*, in a file or set of files. It's commonly used for identifying a configuration file that contains a known parameter or for retrieving a text file based on part of its contents.

group ID   A group ID is the numeric value associated with a group name. Part of the file ownership and permissions system is based on knowledge of the group ID, and each file and directory in a Linux filesystem has a group ID assigned as an owner. *See also* user ID.

high availability   High availability refers to the practice of making systems accessible to additional users and jobs, even when under heavy load or when experiencing failure. High availability systems make use of redundant hardware and fault-tolerant software to continue operation despite component failures.

home directory   Each user on a Linux system has a directory designated as their home directory. These are the directories in which users are placed by default when they log in, and where users ordinarily keep their files. Some configuration files are found in the user's home directory. The shorthand notation for the current user's home directory is the tilde (~). You may also refer to another user's home directory using the tilde and their account name (~albers).

KDE   A desktop environment that looks and feels quite similar to the familiar Windows interfaces. The KDE project can be reached at **http://www.kde.org/**. *See also* desktop environment.

kernel   The kernel is the portion of the operating system that manages interactions with the computer hardware. The Linux kernel can be recompiled by users to maximize efficiency and include all desired features.

less   Less is a command-line utility that displays the contents of a file one screenful at a time. Less also allows the user to reverse the scrolling of the information, unlike cat, which doesn't allow you to scroll backwards or forwards. Less is also unlike more, which displays one screen at a time, but can't scroll backwards. *See also* more.

LILO   The Linux Loader is a program that boots the Linux kernel when the system starts up. It is capable of booting into other operating systems, such as Windows, so users can opt for a dual-boot system that allows a decision at startup time: Which OS should I use now?

Linus Torvalds   Linus is the father of Linux, the open-source operating system he started while still at university in Finland. He is currently an employee of Transmeta, a semiconductor firm, but still manages the development of the Linux kernel. *See also* Linux and *the rest of this book.*

Linux The open-source, Unix-like, collaboratively developed operating system created by Linus Torvalds and a world full of hackers. See Chapter 1 for more information, and then keep reading.

make A program that examines some program source files and compiles them as instructed to produce a working piece of software. Unless something goes wrong, of course.

man Hopefully someone has explained that definition to you. But man is also a command-line utility used to view the manual page for a program. Note that GNU tools in particular will often instruct you to use the info command instead of man.

Microsoft A wonderful, hardworking company that produces top-quality software and is primarily concerned with the wellbeing of its customers and the technical quality of its products. For other ideas about the company, see **http://dir.yahoo.com/Government/Law/Cases/ Microsoft_Antitrust_Case/**.

more A command-line program used to display a file's contents, one screen at a time. The SPACEBAR is typically used to bring up the next screen of contents. *See also* cat, less.

mount point The directory where a filesystem is mounted is called the mount point. The mount point can be anywhere within the file structure. For some reason, a horse breeder I know laughed uproariously when I told her about mount points.

open source Open source refers to software that is distributed in such a way that users can see, change, and share the source code. There are semantic differences between the definitions of open source software and free software. To see the Open Source Initiative's definition of open source, look at **http://www.opensource.org/osd.html**.

Open Source Initiative The Open Source Initiative (**http://www.opensource.org/**) is an organization created to define the meaning of the term "open source," and to evangelize its use and acceptance in the business world.

pipe A pipe is a type of process redirection, denoted by the "pipe" symbol (|), that takes the output from one program and feeds it to the input of another program. The pipe connects the standard output of the first command with the standard input of the second command.

processes   Processes are the jobs created when you run a program. Sometimes a program only creates one process, but in some cases, a single program can create dozens of processes...sometimes intentionally! Linux is truly multitasking and allows processes to be started, restarted, and killed without interfering with other processes.

redirection   Redirection is the practice of taking input or output from a process and putting it somewhere it wouldn't have gone otherwise. Common examples of redirection are piping a program's output to another program for input and writing output from a program to a file. *See also* pipe.

Richard Stallman   Famed programmer and free software advocate Richard Stallman started the GNU Project to build a complete Unix-like operating system. The Linux kernel is generally used along with many GNU tools, causing Stallman and others to refer to these operating systems as GNU/Linux. *See also* Free Software Foundation.

root (directory)   The top level of a Linux system's file structure is the root directory, denoted by a single forward slash (/). All other directories on a Linux system descend from this directory. This is different from the root user's home directory, which is usually /root, a subdirectory immediately under the root directory.

root (user)   The superuser of a Linux system is known as root. The root user has the power to change permissions on all files and can access all areas of the system. *See also* superuser.

shell   A text-level user interface to Unix or a Unix-like operating system. The shell provides basic functionality, including access to files and directories, the ability to run programs, and interaction with the operating system. There are several different shells in use on Linux systems. *See also* bash.

SMP   This acronym stands for "Symmetric Multi Processing," which refers to the ability of a system to run two or more CPUs in parallel, distributing processes or threads between the processors. Linux and Windows NT/2000 are SMP operating systems.

superuser The master of a Unix or Unix-like system, the superuser is usually the root account, which has unrestricted access to all the files and directories on the system. A regular user who wants to log in temporarily as root can use the su command to become the superuser. No phone booth is required for this transformation.

Unix-like An operating system that looks and feels like Unix isn't always Unix, especially back in the days when AT&T was vigorously enforcing its trademark on the name Unix. So a system that behaves more or less like Unix (a more certain standard would be POSIX compliance, but that's not absolutely necessary), but doesn't contain any of the original Unix code, is Unix-like.

user account On multiuser systems like Linux, users access the system and their individual files by means of a user account. Windows NT and Windows 2000 have similar account structures, though Windows 9x isn't quite as stringent about access.

user ID A user ID is the numeric value associated with a user name. Part of the file ownership and permissions system is based on knowledge of the user ID, and each file and directory in a Linux filesystem has a user ID assigned as an owner.

virtual console A virtual console refers to a series of full-screen text displays a user can access from a Linux system. Instead of having only a single command screen, like on a DOS system, Linux allows users to have several active sessions and be logged in on several different virtual consoles. These consoles all share the same physical console and are accessed by use of function keys.

Windows As a proper noun, this term refers to a large family of operating system products ranging from handheld and embedded applications to enterprise servers. A vast majority of the PCs in use today run one version or another of Microsoft's flagship operating system.

window manager A program responsible for controlling windows in a GUI, including placing, moving, resizing, iconifying, and destroying them. The window manager is also responsible for the appearance of the windows, including colors, fonts, and control widgets.

X Short for the X Windows system, which in the Linux environment is generally provided by XFree86 (**http://www.xfree86.org/**). This is the GUI system for Linux, which runs as just another application, not as part of the operating system like the GUI in Windows.

Index